Performing Remains

At last, the past has arrived! *Performing Remains* is Rebecca Schneider's authoritative statement on a major topic of interest to the field of theatre and performance studies. It extends and consolidates her pioneering contributions to the field through its interdisciplinary method, vivid writing, and stimulating polemic. *Performing Remains* has been eagerly awaited, and will be appreciated now and in the future for its rigorous investigations into the aesthetic and political potential of reenactments.
Tavia Nyong'o, *Tisch School of the Arts, New York University.*

I have often wondered where the big, important, paradigm-changing book about re-enactment is: Schneider's book seems to me to be that book. Her work is challenging, thoughtful and innovative and will set the agenda for study in a number of areas for the next decade.
Jerome de Groot, *University of Manchester.*

Performing Remains is a dazzling new study exploring the role of the fake, the false, and the faux in contemporary performance. Rebecca Schneider argues passionately that performance can be engaged as what remains, rather than what disappears.

Across seven essays, Schneider presents a forensic and unique examination of both contemporary and historical performance, drawing on a variety of elucidating sources including the "America" plays of Linda Mussmann and Suzan-Lori Parks, performances of Marina Abramović and Allison Smith, and the continued popular appeal of Civil War reenactments. *Performing Remains* questions the importance of representation throughout history and today, while boldly reassessing the ritual value of failure to recapture the past and recreate the "original."

Rebecca Schneider is Chair of the Department of the Theatre Arts and Performance Studies at Brown University. She is the author of *The Explicit Body in Performance* (Routledge, 1997) and co-editor of *Re:direction: A Theoretical and Practical Guide* (Routledge, 2001).

Performing Remains

Art and war in times of
theatrical reenactment

Rebecca Schneider

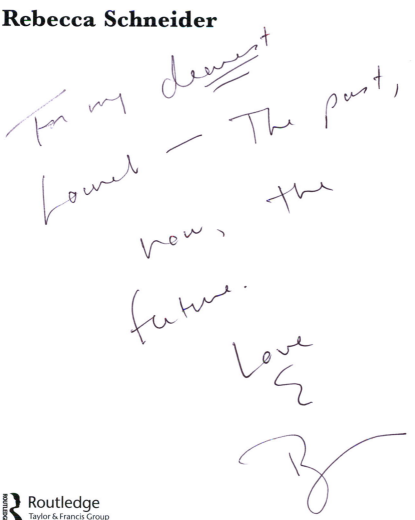

For my dearest Laurel — The past, the now, the future. Love B

Routledge
Taylor & Francis Group

LONDON AND NEW YORK

First published 2011
by Routledge
2 Park Square, Milton Park, Abingdon, Oxon OX14 4RN

Simultaneously published in the USA and Canada
by Routledge
270 Madison Avenue, New York, NY 10016

Routledge is an imprint of the Taylor & Francis Group, an informa business

Typeset in Baskerville MT by
Keystroke, Station Road, Codsall, Wolverhampton
Printed and bound in Great Britain by
TJ International Ltd, Padstow, Cornwall

British Library Cataloguing in Publication Data
A catalogue record for this book is available from the British Library

Library of Congress Cataloging in Publication Data
Schneider, Rebecca.
Performing remains : art and war in times of theatrical reenactment /
Rebecca Schneider.
p. cm.
Includes bibliographical references and index.
1. Performing arts. 2. Historical reenactments. 3. Historical reenactments--
United States. I. Title.
PN1584.S36 2011
792.02'8–dc22
2010032074

ISBN: 978–0–415–40441–9 (hbk)
ISBN: 978–0–415–40442–6 (pbk)
ISBN: 978–0–203–85287–3 (ebk)

For my father, Peter Schneider
In advance of memory
and always, again

Contents

List of illustrations   ix
Acknowledgements   xi

Foreword – By way of other directions   1

1   Reenactment and relative pain   32

2   Finding faux fathers   61

3   In the meantime: performance remains   87

4   Poor poor theatre   111

5   Still living   138

And back – Afterword   169

Notes   187
Bibliography   233
Index   251

Illustrations

0.1 Reperformance of Marina Abramović, *Nude with Skeleton*
(2002/05), 2010   5

0.2 Unnamed Civil War reenactor, lying "dead" after having been
carried off the battlefield to the surgeon's tent at a 2005 reenactment   8

0.3 "Allison Smith, Mustering Officer"   12

0.4 The Wooster Group's *Hamlet*   16

0.5 The statue *Return Visit* by J. Seward Johnson, Jr.   20

0.6 A wax effigy of Lincoln working on the Gettysburg Address at the
Wills house, Gettysburg, PA   21

1.1 Contemporary professional doctors reenacting surgical procedures
at the Civil War Reenactment Field Hospital at Hearthside
Homestead, Lincoln, RI   34

1.2 "Abes in the Grass." A gathering of the Association of Lincoln
Presenters   46

1.3 Faux finger   52

1.4 A renewal of vows at the Gettysburg, PA, Civil War Reenactments   56

2.1 Reggie Montgomery and Michael Potts in *The America Play* by
Suzan-Lori Parks   68

2.2 Claudia Bruce in *Cross Way Cross*, directed by Linda Mussmann   71

2.3 Eleanor Antin, "Myself 1854" from *The Angel of Mercy*   74

2.4 Claudia Bruce and other players in *Cross Way Cross*   85

4.1 The Wooster Group's *Poor Theater*   117

4.2 Rehearsal photograph, taken in advance of Grotowski's first version
of *Akropolis*   118

4.3 The Wooster Group's *Poor Theater*   120

5.1 Ghent altarpiece, *Adoration of the Mystic Lamb*   147

5.2 Félix Nadar's 1854 photograph, *Pierrot the Photographer, also called
The Mime Artist Deburau*   150

5.3 Cindy Sherman, *Untitled*, no. 96, 1981   151

5.4 Jane Fonda at a prisoner of war camp in North Vietnam, 1972   153

5.5 Cindy Sherman, *Untitled*, no. 210, 1989   155

5.6 Cindy Sherman, *Untitled*, no. 242, 1991   156

5.7 Yasumasa Morimura, *To My Little Sister: For Cindy Sherman*, 1998   157

5.8   Yasumasa Morimura, *Self-portrait (Actress)/after Jane Fonda* 4, 1996   158
5.9   Hippolyte Bayard, *Self-Portrait as a Drowned Man*, 1840   166
A.1   Allison Smith, *The Muster*, Governors Island, New York Harbor,
       New York, 2005   170
A.2   Actor Matthew Floyd Miller delivering Howard Zinn's 1971
       speech with Mark Tribe's *Port Huron Project*, 2007   179
A.3   Spectators at Mark Tribe's *Port Huron Project* reenactment of
       Howard Zinn's Boston Common Speech, 2007   181
A.4   Sharon Hayes, *In the Near Future, New York*, 2005   183

Acknowledgements

For a long time, this book was forthcoming. So long, in fact, that I considered titling it *Forthcoming*, as I had grown somewhat fond of knowing it in that way, and it even seemed appropriate to the subject matter. However, so many people have helped me finally bring the book through to completion, however vexed "completion" is as a category in this book, that it seemed appropriate to acknowledge them with a real title, and to put the project, unlike my gratitude, to rest. My colleagues at Brown University deserve my deep thanks for their conversation over the years on the topics that take shape here. I am particularly grateful for the way they never fully separate art practice and the practice of scholarship. My thanks to the students in the grad seminars in "Photography and Performance," both at Brown and as a Visiting Professor at New York University – it was with and through them that much of my thought took place. My participation in the Pembroke Center seminar on temporality, led by Rey Chow, was key in my thinking, and fellow participants were invaluable interlocutors.

I enjoyed a Fellowship as Visiting Distinguished Professor at Queen Mary University in London in 2006 while working on this book, and I thank colleagues there as well. My time in London generated important conversation with a wide range of artists and scholars at Queen Mary, at Roehampton, at Kings, and at Goldsmiths. To the Centre for Performance Research in Aberystwyth, and particularly Richard Gough, I am indebted.

Marten Spangberg is a hero for the incredibly smart encounters he organized in the late 1990s and early 2000s in Stockholm, Lisbon, Berlin, and elsewhere, bringing artists together with scholars to think/do performance based in dance. He introduced me to so much important work and conversation – Xavier Le Roy, Jérôme Bel, La Ribot, Tino Sehgal. Without his inspiration I might not have obsessed on the Michel de Certeau passage about the monument and the passer-by that appears at least twice in this book.

To those who read and responded to the manuscript (in part or in whole), I am most grateful. As the labor of some readers is meant to be anonymous, I can only signal my gratitude while blindfolded, but truly, the help was sincere and significant. From theatre/performance friends and colleagues too numerous to name, I lift out a few who directly discussed and helped me frame the issues presented here: Nicholas Ridout, Ann Pellegrini, Sally Charnow, Jennifer Brody, Richard

Schechner, Diana Taylor, Shannon Jackson, P. A. Skantze and Matthew Fink, Tavia Nyong'o, Patricia Ybarra, Michal Kobialka, Karen Shimakawa, Marvin Carlson, Paige McGinley, Harvey Young, Chris Salter, Nicole Ridgway, and Thalia Field among many others – thank you. Art historians who patiently put up with my rants, and who provided inspiration and support: Jane Blocker, Peter Chametzky, Amelia Jones, Julia Bryan-Wilson. My thanks to Carrie Lambert-Beatty for sharing her essay draft. And to Jennifer Blessing and Nancy Spector as well. I only wish that my editor, Talia Rodgers, lived next door – for reasons of friendship particularly. And to Niall Slater at Routledge as well, who helped with images and other particulars. To students who pitched in in various ways beyond the seminars: Michelle Carriger, James Dennen, Anna Fisher, Laura Green, Hollis Mickey, Christine Mok, Elise Morrison, Andrew Starner – my thanks.

Thanking family is like thanking your own skin. Bethany, Paul, and Pat Schneider all read the manuscript and provided invaluable comments. Peter and Laurel might as well have, because their support was equally significant. My friends not in academe, thank you for the kayak rolls and rescues over the years. Special thanks to Will Rogers, for heading me out of the shallows and into deeper water. Finally, to Sarah Schneider Kavanagh, my daughter and dearest one. During the course of this writing you grew up, got an education, and left home! But time flips and buckles, and you stand, laughing, right here beside me.

Foreword – By way of other directions

In order to go forward, one had to go back.
To go back, one had to turn around.
To turn around one had to pull over and look to see if anyone was coming.
——Linda Mussmann, *Civil War Chronicles*, 1988

It is our unparalleled glory that we have no reminiscences of battlefields [...]
Who, then, can doubt that our country is destined to be the great nation of futurity?
——John L. O'Sullivan, "The Great Nation of Futurity," 1839

So now then we begin again this history of us.
——Gertrude Stein, *The Making of Americans*, 1925

Whenever it all begins again,
I will be waiting.
——Sherman Alexie, *Crazy Horse Speaks*, 1993

I went to Civil War. I did not go to an archive, though that would have been the most legitimate path to set for myself as a scholar interested in history. Instead, I went to witness battles mounted in the *again* of a time out of joint, as a scholar interested in history's theatrical returns.

As such, the direction of my travel was never completely clear to me.

This book, too, weaves a crosshatched path in multiple directions between performance art, United States Civil War reenactment, performance theory, theatre events, photography, statuary, and all manner of "live art." The questions at its base concern the temporality of reenactment and the inter(in)animation – to borrow a word from Fred Moten and John Donne – of intermedia, of syncopated time, and of theatrical acts.

In some ways, this is a "Foreword" which is not one. That is, the opening to this book – more than any of the separate chapters – takes kaleidoscopic turns in intersecting directions, touching on multiple times, variant places, and overlapping fields of academic inquiry. If there can be an orienting point, heading in, it would be that the experience of reenactment (whether in replayed art or in replayed war) is an intense, embodied inquiry into temporal repetition, temporal recurrence. As such, an exploration of affect *as* inquiry (what in Chapter 4 I explore as the hard labor of the live) – and the promises and pitfalls of such investigation – is at the edges of every example of reenactment this book offers for analysis. The book begins, in Chapters 1 and 2, by exploring US Civil War reenactments, but it turns thereafter to theatre, performance, art, and photography, and returns, at the close, to questions of battle reenactment in the frame of art through Allison Smith's queer call to arms in her 2005 work *The Muster*. If the opening chapters suspend, though only partially, questions of the political stakes in reenactment, those political stakes – especially with regard to questions of the Confederacy – return at the end of the book, where the aim is to explore the sharp, double-edged politics (and perhaps even the hazards) of *affiliating* battle reenactment with decidedly Left-wing art practices, as well as to ask the question of what it means to *protest* then, now.

By way of other directions

"Reenactment" is a term that has entered into increased circulation in late twentieth- and early twenty-first-century art, theatre, and performance circles. The practice of re-playing or re-doing a precedent event, artwork, or act has exploded in performance-based art alongside the burgeoning of historical reenactment and "living history" in various history museums, theme parks, and preservation societies.[1] In many ways, reenactment has become the popular and practice-based wing of what has been called the twentieth-century academic "memory industry."[2]

In the syncopated time of reenactment, where *then* and *now* punctuate each other, reenactors in art and war romance and/or battle an "other" time and try to bring that time – that prior moment – to the very fingertips of the present. Read from front to back, the direction of my interest and inquiry in this book seems to lead away from "war" and into "art," but direction, here, is never a linear matter and my arguments do not rest on a linear logic of "from–to" nor do they rely on the parsing tool of "continuum." Across chapters in this book, my interests (at their impossibly broadest) concern the pulse and return across (in)discrete borders defining apparent beginnings and apparent endings of events, performances, and objects of representation in a variety of venues from battlegrounds to museums of modern art to theatre stages. I am interested in repetitions, doublings, and the call and response of cross- and inter-authorships. I am interested in the citational "get-up" of the before, during, and after of any action *taking place* in or as re-action: the affected effects and after-affects of art/events posed as relative to origin(al)s. I wonder here not only about the "as if" but also about the "what if": what if time (re)turns? What does it *drag* along with it? I am interested in the attempt to literally touch time through the residue of the gesture or the cross-temporality of the pose.

Ironically, the ultimate course of this book was influenced by a great deal of reenactment art I witnessed (or learned about) in countries other than the United States – from Xavier Le Roy's 1996 reenactment of Yvonne Rainer's 1970 Chair and Pillow Dance from her *Continuous Project – Altered Daily* which I saw performed in Stockholm, to Tania Bruguera's 1986 reenactment of Ana Mendieta's work in Cuba which she described to me at length in 2008 in Berlin as a means to "bring Ana back to Cuba" across her own body, to Jonathan Deller's 2001 reenactments of the Battle of Orgreave in South Yorkshire, England, which I viewed in documentation, to Lilibeth Cuenca's "Woman on Painting" and "Never Mind the Pollock" and "A Void," which I witnessed several times in several different versions in several European cities – to many other instances of art replaying precedent art. Such works are variously presented as reconstruction (a word preferred by Slovene theatre director Janez Janša), as reperformance (a word now common in art museums), as reenactment, or as re-do.[3] Nevertheless, and despite the global nature of the phenomenon of reenactment (as well as the phenomenon of "civil war"[4]), the focus of *this* book engages the tangled temporalities and crisscrossed geographies that interanimate a United States imaginary – though, clearly, the US imaginary is neither isolated to the US, nor uninformed by global cross-currents. In fact, contemporary scholarship on US performance has made it abundantly clear that thinking genealogically about US performance requires thinking in terms of circum-Atlantic, Pacific Rim, and hemispheric exchange.[5]

The US-specific slant of this book arose in part when I began research on US Civil War battle reenactments in the late 1990s, on the eve of the burgeoning of reenactment in art practice, and as such the force of my thought focused its energies early around what might be considered a particular US relationship to memory and futurity – as this Foreword will illustrate. During the long course of this writing, the popular pastime of US Civil War reenactment seemed at times to come very close and at other times to be leagues away from reenactments of performance art that recently have taken pride of place in such national treasures as the Guggenheim and the Museum of Modern Art (MoMA) in New York. What could these disparate reenactive energies – one the epitome of the "hobbyist" popular, the other the epitome of the "artist" elite – possibly have to say to each other?

Art and war: art

Helpfully, on March 10, 2010, just as I was completing this book, the *New York Times* ran an article titled "A Rebel Form Gains Favor. Fights Ensue."[6]

The article, by Carol Kino, concerned the recent upsurge of attempts on the part of art museums she termed temples of high modernism to collect and curate live performance. Kino reported specifically on a "workshop" about the preservation and exhibition of performance art held at MoMA in New York in advance of an exhibit of reenactments of Marina Abramović's performance art work. The exhibit, titled *The Artist Is Present*, was curated by Klaus Biesenbach and made possible in part by LVMH Moët Hennessy Louis Vuitton Inc. It ran from March 14 to May 31, 2010, and featured documents and artifacts of Abramović's historic performance work as well as reenactments by "other people" employed by the museum. The most widely discussed part of the exhibition was its inclusion of a new durational piece in which Abramović sat live, as still as a statue, for the entirety of the open hours of the museum during the exhibit.[7] The "fights" that ensued at the workshop in advance of the event were fights among the participant performance artists, but Kino's title "Fights Ensue" also gestures to a much longer history of battle between mainstream art establishments and rebel performance artists (sometimes feminist, other times influenced by feminism whether acknowledged or not).

> "Reperformance is the new concept, the new idea!" [Marina] Abramović proclaimed at the workshop. "Otherwise it will be dead as an art form." [Joan] Jonas grabbed a mike. "Well, maybe for you," she said heatedly. "But not for me."[8]

For the moment let us ignore the fact that reperformance is as old as . . . well, ancient Rome, to name one site of its frequent enunciation, or parlor games in Victorian England to name another.[9] Still, the battle of the "rebel art" to enter the esteemed galleries of high art museums should be approached with a great measure of irony, since so much performance-based artwork in the 1960s and 1970s (influenced by a lengthy heritage of "anti-art" avant-garde forms) was arguably more invested *at that time* in seceding from the exclusionary union of Great Masters than in joining it. Much of that work, *at that time*, was also invested in the impossibility of reperformance – what Amelia Jones has called the "heroic claims" that performance is "the only art form to guarantee the presence of the artist," a guarantee that Jones has long been articulate about debunking.[10]

Curators like Nancy Spector and Jennifer Blessing, who produced Abramović's *Seven Easy Pieces*, a series of reperformances in which Abramović collaborated with artists' estates to reenact precedent pieces of performance art at the Guggenheim in New York in 2005, deserve praise for bravely (and smartly) entering the fray of live performance to interrogate ways to re-present, in the twenty-first century, the strong current of live art in twentieth-century expression. But whatever the curators' interests, Marina Abramović herself is interested in the "correct" transmission of "seminal" works, including "extremely strict instructions," payment of copyright, and permissions to reperform[11] – and she sees the move into venerated art museums as ensuring her ability to control history from beyond the grave. Kino wrote about *Seven Easy Pieces* in her "Fights Ensue" *New York Times* article:

> Ms. Abramović saw [*Seven Easy Pieces*] as a way "to take charge of the history of performance." In the 1990s, as younger artists became interested in work of the '60s and '70s, she said she noticed that some were restaging historical works themselves, often without consulting or even crediting the originator. "I realized this is happening because performance is nobody's territory," she said. "It's never been mainstream art and there's no rules." Finding this unjust, she decided to set them herself, by recreating the works in consultation with the relevant artists and estates. Better she should do it now, she said, because "they will do it anyway when you're dead behind your back."

The tangle in Abramović's thinking in advance of herself as dead underscores that the *battle* of much reenactment, in art and in war, is a battle concerning the future of the past.

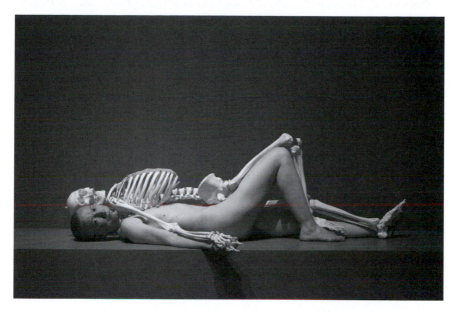

Figure 0.1 Reperformance of Marina Abramović, *Nude with Skeleton* (2002/05), 2010. Pictured in this image: Deborah Wing-Sproul. © 2010 The Museum of Modern Art, New York. Photo: Jonathan Muzikar.

Kino ends her article on the "rebel form" with a statement by Chrissie Iles, curator at the Whitney Museum of American Art and a scholar who has written a great deal on Abramović's work:

> "Performance challenges categorization, which was originally its point," Ms. Iles said. "But museums are about archiving, categorizing, and indexing." It's not always an easy fit, but "maybe what's interesting is the way in which the past is reframed in the present."[12]

One wonders when and what the "original point" Iles cites for performance might be taken to be – Aristotle had ideas on this, as have many others in a long history of thinkers and performance makers who grapple with art, mimesis, and repetition. But Iles is clearly referring to an "original point" of performance as concerns the modern visual art museum, and the challenge to categorization in that context is certainly correct – despite the fact that Abramović struggles to insist that performance is a discrete category, and seeks to categorize it according to a set of "moral rules" for conservation. Still, the fact remains that the visual arts have historically forgotten or overlooked other histories of performance – usually by handily dismissing them (as if nodding to Plato's doctrine of ideal forms) as stagey, fake, or *theatrical*.[13] The passion and fury in Michael Fried's 1967 diatribe against theatricality in minimalist art still rings loud and clear, and though performance artists such as Abramović storm the museum as a "rebel form" they are oddly armed with the long-tired tools of the antitheatricalist, arguing in the name of medial specificity that performance (unlike theatre) is "pure" and "raw"[14] (an issue we will return to in Chapter 4). Similarly, though Abramović speaks often of copyright, she shies away from any association with drama or theatre, preferring "music" and "literature" as her reference points:

> My idea was to establish certain moral rules. If someone wants to remake a performance, they must ask the artist for the rights and pay for it, just like it's done with music or literature. For me, this is the honest way to do it, even if you want to make your own version.[15]

Unlike Abramović's efforts to divorce reperformance from the taint of theatricality (she speaks of having to "de-act" and "de-dance" her students[16]), much of this book, in contrast, will be about the tangle of explicit theatricality and time. It can be argued that any time-based art encounters its most interesting aspect in the fold: the double, the second, the clone, the uncanny, the *againness* of (re)enactment. This book, then, troubles the prevalence of presentism, immediacy, and linear time in most thinking about live performance. As a result, in this project I am uninterested in Abramović's "moral rules" for a practice she refers to as the linear transmission of "seminal" works of performance art, charting a patrilineage of "masters." Instead, I am curious to ask here about a more porous approach to time and to art – time as full of holes or gaps and art as capable of falling or crossing in and out of the spaces between live iterations. I am invested, too, in the curious inadequacies of the copy, and *what inadequacy gets right* about our faulty steps backward, and forward, and to the side. Rather than a unidirectional art march toward an empiric future of preservation, time plays forward and backward and sideways across the imagined community of an otherwise spatialized national plot. This book explores the warp and draw of one time in another time – the *theatricality* of time – or what Gertrude Stein, thinking about *Hamlet*, referred to as the nervousness of "syncopated time."[17]

Here, the subject is the trouble between history proper and its many counter-constituents: the resilience of the seemingly forgotten (that nevertheless recurs); the domain of error and unreliability known as flesh memory in the embodied repertoires of live art practices; the irruptive experience of what Toni Morrison has termed involuntary and traumatic "rememory"[18] and, conversely but relatedly, the irruptive experience of what Adrienne Rich has termed voluntary and redressive acts of "re-vision":

> Re-vision – the act of looking back, of seeing with fresh eyes, of entering an old text from a new critical direction – is for women more than a chapter in cultural history; it is an act of survival.[19]

Rich was writing about *texts*, but the same sense of "re-vision" – if coupled with re-gesture, re-affect, re-sensation – might be applicable to performances or enactments of what Judith Butler has termed "sedimented acts."[20] Entering, or reenacting, an event or a set of acts (acts of art or acts of war) from a critical direction, a different temporal angle, may be, as Rich suggests, an act of survival, of keeping alive *as* passing on (in multiple senses of the phrase "to pass"). This keeping alive is not a liveness considered always in *advance of* death nor in some way *after* death, as Abramović might prefer in wanting to monumentalize her work to commemorate her as dead in advance, sealing her, in this way, into the archive. Rather, it is more a constant (re)turn of, to, from, and between states in animation – an inter-(in)animation (to quote Moten, to quote Donne again). For "survival," to use Rich's word, may be a critical mode of remaining, as well as a mode of remaining critical: passing on, staying alive, in order to pass on the past *as past*, not, indeed, as (only) present. Never (only) present.

If the above crosshatch of words seems more playfully poetic than cogently sensible, it is my hope that the book as a whole will elucidate my ideas. But perhaps we can close this opening section of this opening Foreword with Moten and Donne, again. John Donne used the word "interinanimates" in his 1633 love poem "The Exstasie" in which he tells of lovers lying still as stone statues while their souls intertwine, redouble, and multiply. Here, the live and the stone are inter(in)animate and the liveness of one or deadness of the other is ultimately neither decidable nor relevant. I. A. Richards, the architect of mid-twentieth century New Criticism, expropriated the term and applied it to poetic "attitudes" generally (interestingly, "attitudes" is also a nineteenth-century term for tableaux vivants). And, most interestingly for this project, Fred Moten has recently used the term "inter-inanimates" to suggest the ways live art and media of mechanical and technological reproduction, such as photography, cross-identify, and, more radically, cross-constitute and "improvise" each other.[21] Michel de Certeau, a philosopher of history and theorist of space, suggests something similar in a resonant sentence that has occupied my thought for years:

> The passing faces on the street seem [. . .] to multiply the indecipherable and nearby secret of the monument.[22]

In this sentence, to which we will return in Chapter 5, the monumental and the passing live co-constitute each other in a relationship that can be as much about forgetting (bypassing) as commemorating (monumentalizing). Rather than plotting for lineage, or privileging monument over passer-by, it is inter(in)animation that lies at the heart of my inquiry here.

Art and war: war

In 1998 I began to attend US Civil War battle reenactments to try and understand what reenactors were doing and why they were doing it. The crisis "oxymoronically known as the Civil War," as Shirley Samuels writes, or the War Between the States, or (as sometimes referred to by those sympathetic to the "rebel" Confederacy) the War of Northern Aggression, was fought in the US between 1861 and 1865, during

the Presidency of Abraham Lincoln.[23] Over 600,000 died. As textbooks will have
it, the defeat of the Southern Confederacy occasioned the Emancipation
Proclamation and the abolishment of slavery, but historians of various stripes
continue to debate in seemingly endless reverberation the relative importance of
slavery, territorial expansion, the rise of industrial capitalism, and other factors as
sources of the conflict. Lincoln was assassinated on April 14, 1865, five days after
the surrender of Robert E. Lee. Civil War reenactments began forty-eight years
later, in 1913, when elderly soldiers met again on their own battlegrounds. But
the "particular hobby" or "popular pastime" of Civil War reenactment by "history
buffs" or "enthusiasts" began to grow in the 1950s as the last people who could
remember the war were passing away.[24] Many of these "hobbyists" today fight to
keep the war "alive," and many would say, "it's not over."

In the course of attending Civil War reenactments, I repeatedly betrayed my
own biases in that I was continually surprised by the complexities involved in the
(re)actions I witnessed. Problems of ambivalence, simultaneous temporal registers,
anachronism, and the *everywhere* of error were not lost on any of the reenactors with
whom I spoke, despite their common depiction as, by and large, simple or naïve
"enthusiasts." In affective engagement, many of them find reenactment to be, if
not the thing itself (the past), somehow also *not not* the thing (the past), as it passes
across their bodies in again-time. In practice, reenactors draw a distinction between

Figure 0.2 Unnamed Civil War reenactor, lying "dead" after having been carried off the
battlefield to the surgeon's tent at a reenactment on June 4, 2005, at Chase Farm in
Lincoln, RI. Photo by Rebecca Schneider.

living history and reenactment, but the "liveness" of the matter is key across multiple styles, as is the ambivalence of the live, or its inter(in)animation with the no longer live.

When I began attending reenactments, I had only recently completed a book on feminist performance art of the explicit body and I was very confused as to why I was attending. I often asked myself what I was doing at such events. The politics of many of these players, some of whom truly fought so that "the South should win," were decidedly not the shared politics I had enjoyed with most of the performance artists I had written about in *The Explicit Body in Performance*. What kinship could these gritty war game players – chewing on salt pork and marching about battlefields in games where, often, "an unapologetic masculinity" was romanced and even legislated – share with my previous studies? What could supremely conservative notions of authenticity – wanting to control and correct events from beyond the grave to resemble a romantic notion of men as men and women as women – have to do with feminism?[25] And yet, the questions I brought to the battlefield concerned the pose, imposture, imposition, and the replay of evidence (photographs, documents, archival remains) back across the body in gestic negotiation – something I had argued that feminist artists of the explicit body had been engaging in. If in 1989 Barbara Kruger had imaged "Your Body is a Battleground" as a moment of feminist art and indicative of "the war at home,"[26] perhaps, I thought, "Your Battleground is a Body" might have an inverse, twisted kind of resonance in historical reenactment. I wanted to travel backward through Kruger's aphorism, to find out what that might mean. Crossing time sometimes meant crossing borders of comfortable political affiliation – as will be discussed in more depth in the Afterword – and such crossing often caused a distinct discomfort at the edge of very difficult questions.

I attended multiple Civil War reenactments between 1998 and 2006 where I observed participants putting themselves *in the place of* the past, reenacting that past by *posing as if* they were, indeed, soldiers and civilians of the 1860s. I did not participate, except as a witness to their actions. That is, I did not, myself, reenact – except insofar as witnessing any event is to participate to some degree – to *have been there*.[27] Still, when the event is a reenactment of a prior event the precision in "being, there, then" opens to question: Who? Where? When? To witness a reenactment is to be a bystander, a passer-by, possibly out of step, in the leak of another time, or in a syncopated temporal relationship to the event that (some) participants hope will *touch the actual past*, at least in a partial or incomplete or fragmented manner. My presence and the presence of others who did not cross-temporal-dress (and at most of the events I attended, those who did not cross-dress were fewer in number than those who did) always served as a reminder that it was not, or not *entirely*, 1861, 62, 63, 64, or 65.

What I witnessed attending reenactments was often surprisingly more than I had bargained for and this book is about the "more" of the bargain. Because I did not participate as a reenactor, this book is not about the experience of reenacting though it is about the experience of participating in reenactment. The book is a theoretical investigation into reenactment as an activity that nets us all (reenacted, reenactor, original, copy, event, re-event, bypassed, and passer-by) in a knotty and porous relationship to time. It is about the temporal tangle, about the temporal leak, and about the many questions that attend time's returns.

Though the project that became this book diverges significantly from my initial late 1990s research into Civil War reenactment, I became interested in the effort on the part of many battle reenactors to achieve a radically rigorous mimesis many of them feel can trip the transitivity of time. I am fascinated that for many reenactors there exists the lure: if they repeat an event *just so*, getting the details as close as possible to fidelity, they will have touched time and time will have recurred. Thus, "enthusiasts" play across their bodies particulars of "what really happened" gleaned from archival "evidence" such as testimony, lithographs, and photographs as a way, ironically, of "keeping the past alive." But they also engage in this activity as a way of accessing what they feel the documentary evidence upon which they rely misses – that is, live experience. Many fight not only to "get it right" as it *was* but to get it right as it *will be* in the future of the archive to which they see themselves contributing.

If Civil War reenactment provides a clear-cut case of the effort to play one time in another time – the effort to find "that was then" inside "this is now" – the tangle of then in now is far more widespread than the reenactment rendered explicit on American battlefields of wars past. Indeed, looking even cursorily at reenactment as a practice one is soon hounded by the paradoxes of performativity and the fecund question (one as long-beloved of feminist theory as it has been of sociology, linguistics, and performance studies) that all representational practice, and indeed all communicative behavior, is composed in reiteration, is engaged in citation, is *already* a practice of reenactment, or what Richard Schechner has termed "restored" or "twice-behaved" behavior.[28] That is, stepping back from the battlefield, we find solidly lodged in twentieth-century critical thought the notion that all bodily practice is, like language itself, always already composed in repetition and repetition is, paradoxically, both the vehicle for sameness and the vehicle for difference or change. Historical battle reenactors, heightening the level of their enterprise to extremes of the minutest possible detail, could be said to make restored behavior (always a basic ingredient in sociality) available for recognition – though, again, by the extremes of cross-temporal citation, they trip daily reenactment into *other daily*, or at least they move, using Eugenio Barba's terms, from "daily" to "extra-daily" behavior – a move Barba sees as a basic signature of theatricality in transcultural perspective.[29]

Citation, repetition, and "twice-behaved behavior," as the very material of daily behavior, provide the basis for why and how reenactors can reenact at all. Think of it this way: Battle reenactors can reenact the US Civil War because they can place their bodies in the gestic compositions – the sedimented sets of acts – that US Civil War soldiers composed when those soldiers were themselves behaving as they had been trained to behave, or as they emulated others to behave, behaviors likewise *and at the time* based on prior practices and precedent notions of what it means and what it might mean to fight. The physical act of fighting, as well as the affective mise en scene of the "theatre of war" in which the fighting took place, both followed precedent wars and left remains – both following footsteps and leaving footsteps to follow in directions not always, or only, *forward*.[30] The relationship of a "footprint" (to use a prime example of an indexical remain from C. S. Peirce) to bodily memory, or to what Teresa Brennan has called the "transmission of affect," is here a question provoked by historical reenactment, and one taken up in more depth in the chapters that follow. That the camera and the repeating rifle were both novel and privileged tools of the American Civil War is, certainly, one reason that this particular war is so rich a site for contemporary reenactors. It is a war engorged with indexical traces and the technological signatures of a culture increasingly aware of itself as repeating, re-composed, (and as a result of the war) "reconstructed."

Certainly, there is passionate investment in how any war is to be remembered, and the questions of what happened during the Civil War, why it was fought, who "won" the Civil War, or whether the war is actually over continue to see heated debate. Some argue, against common assumption, that the war was won by the South, and others that the war is ongoing.[31] Historian David Blight, for example, sees the war as ongoing in that it is continuing to be fought through commemoration. He reads the 1913 Gettysburg reunion as a battleground on which the fight for racial justice took a beating. Interestingly, Civil War reenactors often cite this reunion as the first reenactment – when veterans approached each other from the positions they had occupied during the "real" battle, this time marching across the field to shake hands. As Blight tells us, the 1913 Gettysburg reunion was attended by over 53,000 white veterans as a "festival of national reconciliation" –a reconciliation, it must be noted, of white America with white America.[32] The reunion was presided over by President Woodrow Wilson, a Southerner who had just fired a large number of black federal employees, imposed rigid policies of segregation on those that remained, and who would, in three years time, allow the showing of the racist film *Birth of a Nation* at the White House.

Blight's point is that segregation was *enacted* as policy in tandem with, if not by means of, *reenactment*. To remember the history of Civil War *reenactment* then (odd as that twist may seem), is not only to remember those remembering the Civil War, but to remember the part played by reenactment in the ongoing history of policy in the US in terms of negotiations of civil rights, veterans' rights, attitudes toward war, terrorism, and "war on terrorism" – a point to which we will return at various moments throughout this book.[33] One need think only of President George W. Bush selecting the USS *Abraham Lincoln* as the battleship on which to stand to declare, bogusly, the war in Iraq *over* in 2003. One need think only of the 2009 Lincolnalia in the inauguration of President Barack Obama to see the push-me-pull-you struggle over the signs and symbols of the Civil War by those who would redeploy those signs and symbols to enact policy stasis or policy change.

A range of approaches

At the brink of the US "War on Terror" in the late 1990s and early '00s, and from the seemingly safe vantage point of 140 years, I traveled "back" to the battlefields of the American Civil War: Gettysburg, Antietam, Vicksburg, and other sites that sought to pass as Gettysburg, Antietam, Vicksburg. I went to ghost the Civil War as if from its future, to peer both ahead and behind at the war's inexhaustible corpse as it twitched and jerked across the bodies of reenactors in the algebra of its own strange aftermath. I found that I wasn't entirely safe. And it wasn't entirely dead.

Who *are* these reenactors?

Artist Allison Smith asked much the same question when she called artists and activists together to create a reenactment of a Civil War battle encampment. Smith staged a reenactment titled *The Muster* as art in 2005 in New York City, asking: "Who are these people?" and "Why do they do this?" In the wake of this question, she calls for "intellectuals, activists, artists, and queers" to "engage for a moment, however audaciously, in a confederate fantasy, despite inevitable associations to the horrific institution of slavery and the perplexing persistence of Civil War battle reenactments."[34] Smith, whose art event and its questions are examined closely in

Figure 0.3 "Allison Smith, Mustering Officer." Allison Smith, 2004. *The Muster*, Mildred's Lane, Beach Lake, PA. Photo credit Bob Braine. Courtesy of the artist.

the Afterword, is indeed audacious in her call. *Despite* slavery? *Despite* horror? What can possibly be the critical status of this "despite"? Smith makes a radically uneasy affiliation between wars past and war present (the "War on Terror") in a form she calls "trench art" – wartime-art dug out of the spaces between times, between fields of inquiry, and between media – deeply discomforting sites of crossfire, where confusion between advance and retreat requires retrenchment and the critical analysis implied in *digging deeper*.

Smith staged battle camp explicitly as *camp* art, and the work's playful and carnivalesque war camp indirectly raises the question of what is *not* reenacted in popular history, a topic taken up productively in Lisa Woolfork's work on slave auction reenactments in *Embodying American Slavery in Contemporary Culture*.[35] Indeed, performance art and theatre reenactments in an art context can sometimes sit in an uneasy relationship, especially regarding the stakes of authenticity. Whether it should or not, the frame of "art" excuses errors and omissions – even expects them – in ways not excused as easily for "history." Most living history events and battle reenactments are neither framed (or re-framed) as art nor do they pretend to anything artistic – preferring instead the "authentic" and the "real." Rather, living history events and battle reenactments occur as "popular pastime" or "heritage activity" in some nether-space between theatre, history museum, religious ritual, sport, hobby, craft fair, archaeological dig, educational field trip, anthropological fieldwork, religion, and . . . yes, art installation.

Art reenactment practices contain a range of approaches. Some artists, like Allison Smith, borrow happily from some of the cross-disciplinary, cross-medial, cross-temporal, kinda-hobby/kinda-professional slipperiness of the category of reenactment as it exists more broadly in popular activities and invite "everyone" to participate. Other artists, like Abramović, disdain the popular "pastime" and reenact precedent art events in the interest of generating an elite, delimited aesthetic to be legitimated by art professionals invested in the purity of an "authentic" and "original" and (ironically) "timeless" act. Some artists try to repeat a precedent event, artifact, or act with as total exactness as possible (the Wooster Group's *Poor Theater* and *Hamlet* are composed of sections with extremely precise reenactment of precedent material, and Rod Dickinson's *Milgram Re-enactment* is invested in deliberate exactitude as well[36]). And still others feel that the true spirit of reenactment should be to "artistically" and "creatively" *interpret* a precedent act, event, or artwork to make it "original" again, not to replicate it or "slavishly" repeat it.[37]

This range of approaches is also evident in war reenactment societies and among individual hobbyists. Some battle reenactors are happy with a "come one, come all" approach to reenactment in which the past is tried on like a piece of clothing or a turn of phrase but not completely accessed. Here participants are encouraged to "get the feel" but not actually to *become*, or become overcome with, the past. However, those reenactors sometimes called "hardcore" are eager to touch an absolute and transcendent historical "authentic" through a repetition of acts as devoid of anachronism and temporal error as humanly possible. Chasing the effort at total immersion in the past, some history reenactment events take place as far away from spectators as possible as hardcore reenactors seek an experience completely unhampered by its own (future) reception. But most reenactments are staged with spectators invited and even encouraged to take part as active participants. In such cases, spectators are sometimes treated as sports fans, or as theatre audiences. Some reenactors even imagine that spectating "visitors from the future" are fieldworkers and that the reenactors themselves are "native informants."[38]

Amidst the hyper-weird mix of seriousness, frivolity, dress-up, fake blood, real salt pork, statistics on dysentery, mock amputation, and camp humor (both in the sense of tent life and in the sense of self-aware parody) there can arise at times a quasi and queasy sensation of cross-temporal slippage. At various and random moments, amidst the myriad strangeness of anachronism at play, it can occasionally feel "as if" the halfway dead came halfway to meet the halfway living, halfway. That is, despite or perhaps because of the error-ridden mayhem of trying to touch the past, something other than the discrete "now" of everyday life can be said to occasionally occur – or recur. This something other is well known in practices linked to theatre, art, and ritual, if more alien to practices such as historiography that profess to privilege "hard" facts or material remains over "softer," ephemeral traces such as the affective, bodily sensations or (re)actions of those living too far into the future for proper, evidentiary recall. The something other that can sometimes occur at battle reenactments might be Barba's "extra-daily," mentioned above, or we could borrow the word "liminality" from Victor Turner's writing on ritual and performance to discuss the common sense of betwixt and between that occurs during the "seriousness of play."[39] Though, as mentioned, Richard Schechner argues that all human activity – daily or otherwise – involves "restored" or "twice-behaved behavior," we might use his insights to explore how the very explicit *twiceness* of reenactment trips the otherwise daily condition of repetition into reflexive hyper-drive, expanding the experience into the uncanny.

The sense of the past *as past*, even though available to "re-do," or even as available to return to, is key. Elizabeth Freeman has written of queerness in temporal reenactment, reading temporal play as cross-generational negotiation, or what she terms "temporal drag."[40] David Romàn, writing in a similar vein, has coined the phrase "archival drag."[41] For Freeman, analyzing lesbian film and fashion, reenactment actively negotiates the temporal *labor* in subject formation and the social.[42] Freeman's notion of temporal drag can be read as implicitly building upon Homi Bhabha's engagement with temporal lag – or the theory of the "time-lag" he credits to Frantz Fanon's "The Fact of Blackness."[43] In her essay "Packing History, Count(er)ing Generations," Freeman refuses to dismiss temporal replay as "merely" citational, or a matter of simulacra for simulacra's sake, instead reading for the *force* of citation in the political present. She writes:

> To reduce all embodied performances to the status of copies without originals [the past as gone] is to ignore the interesting threat that the genuine *past*-ness of the past sometimes makes to the political present. [. . .] Might some bodies, in registering on their very surfaces the co-presence of several historically specific events, movements, and collective pleasures, complicate or displace the centrality of *gender*-transitive drag to queer performativity? Might they

articulate instead a kind of temporal transitivity that does not leave feminism, femininity, or other "anachronisms" behind?[44]

Here, the past can simultaneously be past – genuine pastness – *and on the move*, co-present, not "left behind."

Freeman is writing of the 1997 film *Shulie*, Elisabeth Subrin's shot-by-shot remake of an unreleased 1967 documentary of the same title about the then-unknown art student Shulamith Firestone (who went on to write the influential manifesto *The Dialectic of Sex: The Case for Feminist Revolution*, 1970). Subrin restaged the documentary and "meticulously duplicated its camerawork," though of course the impossibility of exact replication (the background is 1997, not 1967, etc.) makes for anachronistic touches that haunt the reenactment. Freeman is keen to explore how Subrin's film taps a kind of energy in passing, and she makes clear that this is a mode "fundamental to queer performance." "*Shulie*'s promise lies," she writes, "in what the language of feminist 'waves' and queer 'generations' sometimes effaces: The mutually disruptive energy of moments that are not yet past and yet are not entirely present either."[45]

This "mutually disruptive energy" is compelling, and it is, in Freeman's words, an energy of passing, an energy of affect's transmission.[46] It is one time passing on to and as another time, but also *not quite passing*. One time almost but not fully passing in and as another time. The past can disrupt the present (as when a Civil War reenactor claims that a war is not over), but so too can the present disrupt the past (as when a Civil War reenactor claims that a war is not over); neither are entirely "over" nor discrete, but partially and porously persist. Something is different here than simply remembering, or a simple negotiation with "a time gone by." Thinking through "mutually disruptive energy" implies that the bygone is not entirely gone by and the dead not completely disappeared nor lost, but also, and perhaps more complexly, the living are not entirely (or not only) live.

I am interested in live reenactment work that strives for literal precision rather than tries to avoid it with the rubric "interpretation." Much in the way that Sherrie Levine's appropriation of Walker Evan's photographs or Andy Warhol's appropriation of Campbell's soup or Brillo boxes, or, for that matter, Duchamp's readymades challenged the modernist myth of originality and the "solo" virility of the Great White Straight Male Visual Artist at the level of the object, so perhaps does the effort toward literality in touching the *performing* past trouble the prerogatives of ownership, authorship, authenticity, and "pure" art. For while theatre and its actors, scripts, sets, and emotional dramas have never been assumed to be pure, singular, or authentic, many performance artists and their modernist theatre ancestors – pioneers from Zola to Artaud to Grotowski who eschewed theatricality and conventions of imitation – have sought authenticity, and indeed pitched theatricality against authenticity, looking instead for what Richard Schechner termed "actuals" in 1970 and what Marina Abramović terms "pure and raw" today.[47] For antitheatrical modernist theatre and disappearance-invested or authenticity-driven (even copyright-seeking) performance art, the mantra has generally been: imitation is the opposite of creation; or, it takes a Great Solo Artist to make art or re-perform art acts; or, auratic art can't be copied because imitation destroys aura; or, true art vanishes in second hands.

The explicit replay of a time-based art troubles the prerogatives of singular artists, the assumptions of forward-marching time, and the frontier-driven development narratives of capital that – like a great perspective machine – invests in the linear geometry of vanishing points. Touching time against itself, by bringing time *again and again* out of joint into theatrical, even anamorphic, relief presents the real, the actual, the raw and the true as, precisely, the zigzagging, diagonal, and crookedly imprecise returns of time.

In Elizabeth Subrin's "meticulous duplication" in *Shulie*, Rod Dickinson's careful reenactment of the Milgram experiments, or the Wooster Group's painstaking reenactment of Grotowski's *Akropolis* as well as their hyper-reenactment of the Richard Burton *Hamlet*, what appears is very *hard work*. The labor of repetition is, in such work, rendered apparent as labor. In the Wooster Group's sardonically titled *Poor Theater*, explored at length in Chapter 4, actors deliver uncannily precise scenes together with the filmic document in a queasy reiteration in which the live actors appear ghost-like and the filmic actors appear oddly reenlivened *across* the undecidable interstices of their cross-temporal mimesis.

The effort to "redo" a performance-based piece *exactly* the same as a precedent piece – that is, not to interpret it anew, but (impossibly?) to stand again in its footprint, in its precise place – not only engages the uncanny (and theatrical) properties of the double, the clone, the second, or even simply "other" people, but

Figure 0.4 The Wooster Group's *Hamlet*, directed by Elizabeth LeCompte, 2007. Background, Richard Burton. Foreground, Scott Shepherd. Photo: © Paula Court.

also challenges the given *placedness* of an original through re-placedness, challenging the singular attributes of the auratic and "timelessness" of "master" arts through the mimetic problem-magic of the *live*. Such reenactment art traverses, performatively, Benjamin's worry over the auratic art object in "The Work of Art in the Age of its Technical Reproducibility."[48] Perhaps challenges to the auratic and singular artwork (re)encounter, as Fried already decried in 1967, less the seeming threat of technological or mechanical reproduction than a far more ancient Western anxiety, the revenant of Plato's worry over art in the age of *theatrical* reproducibility.[49]

In the interest of thinking through theatrical reproducibility, I have previously written about solo works in relation to precedent, to call and response, in order to ask whether solo is ever singular. I have written about doubling, about repetition, about cloning, and about patricidal patriarchy's simultaneous dependence upon and anxiety about mimesis.[50] In this project, which grows out of those essays, I ask after the possibility of temporal recurrence and explore the theatrical claim lodged in the logic of reenactment that the past is not (entirely) dead, that it can be accessed *live*, as in, for example, the simplicity of the slogan I encountered on a billboard heading into Gettysburg Pennsylvania in 1999: "Lincoln Lives."

US Civil War reenactors are cited here on the same pages as theatre and performance artists. A photograph here may be approached as "live," and a live act interrogated for its production of a "still." Throughout, the theatrical – most commonly a marker of the inauthentic, fake, overblown, error-ridden, or non-serious – is here taken very seriously. In *The Amalgamation Waltz: Race, Performance, and the Ruses of Memory*, an important work on performance, hybridity, and the "miscegenation of time," Tavia Nyong'o asks an important question:

> Most accounts of historical memory are preoccupied with truth: the possible deviation from the recorded truth that memory affords, the performative acts of reconciliation that truth-telling ostensibly effects, or else the higher truth that embodied, experiential memory somehow obtains over dry, written documents. By contrast, I am preoccupied not with the virtues of getting it right but with the ethical chance that may lie within getting it wrong. What does it mean to mistake a memory, to remember by mistake, or even to remember a mistake?[51]

Nyong'o's question recognizes the warp and woof of theatricality as always knit tightly in and through the so-called real. To ask what mistake gets right, or, what mistake corrects, is particularly pertinent to any study that takes seriously the theatricality of event in tandem with the theatricality of any historical interpretation of event. Michel Foucault, upon whom Nyong'o draws in depth, was trenchant on this point. As Foucault wrote in the essay "Nietzsche, Genealogy, History":

> [T]he development of humanity is a series of interpretations. The role of genealogy is to record its history: the history of morals, ideals, and metaphysical concepts, the history of the concept of liberty or of the ascetic life; as they stand

for the emergence of different interpretations, they must be made to appear as events on the *stage* of historical process.[52]

Anti-foundational approaches to history – approaches, like Foucault's, that submit that all epistemic categories of knowledge and modes of knowledge production are themselves historical and must be historicized – often rely on the metaphor of the stage. Making interpretations appear, as Foucault writes, "as events on the stage of historical process" is to underscore not only an interpretation's status *as* event, taking place in time and relative to conditions of possibility that lend it authority, but also to underscore that event as theatrical, which is to say, given to be an event by virtue of being a matter of (re)production: staged, enacted, reenacted. Here the tired mutual exclusivity knit into the binary distinction between the error-ridden theatrical on the one hand and the somehow actual or pure real on the other comes undone, and we can be done with nostalgic proclamations that the map has somehow replaced the "more real" category of the territory, producing everything as "mere" simulacra. There's nothing mere about the theatrical, and moreover, theatricality, like interpretation, is not a matter of the *loss* of some prior, purer *actual*. Rather, in line with Aristotle's rejoinder to Plato, mimesis is what we *do*. To ask how to do things with mimesis might be to ask how to engage with historical process – with history – with the antecedent and subsequent real at/on any given stage of time.

The objection may be raised that terms like mimesis, theatricality, imitation, simulation, the copy, the double, and the fake cross and confuse each other across these pages. One term (say, theatricality) cannot simply slide and morph into a related term (say, imitation). That objection, however, would miss the point: *slippage* is in fact part and parcel of the very words, all related in some way to the mimetic double, that I interweave. "Theatricality" – by which I mean to reference something theatrical, or something of (or reminiscent of) the theatre – is *relative* to mimesis, simulation, doubling, imitating, copying, even if not identical.[53] Identicality is already undone in all of these words, as they are all words for the side-step operation by which one thing stands in for another thing, either as the same or as almost the same but not quite.[54] There is something, too, of *queerness* in this slip and slide.

Queer time, the jump of affect, and temporal drag are all phrases employed in this book at regular intervals. So is "again and again." My reiterations of Adrienne Rich and Toni Morrison earlier in this Foreword are not incidental asides. The tracks that run through the book have been resolutely informed by feminist, queer, and critical race theory, particularly work on what Nyong'o (citing Darby English drawing on W. E. B. Dubois and Frantz Fanon) calls "black representational space" and work Carolyn Dinshaw (drawing on Roland Barthes) calls queer historiography or "the project of constructing queer histories."[55] So, for example, while my writing here on Civil War reenactments does not always, or even primarily, focus on the significant roles race or gender played in the Civil War (whether acknowledged by reenactors or not), the very means I use to *think through reenactment at all* is fundamentally indebted to the work of others who focus on the reverberant problems of dominant history's exclusions.

My attempt here is to piece a quilt using artworks and reenactment events that question temporal singularity in crosshatch with critical theories about time and performance. I use artworks and reenactment events in tandem with critical and cultural theory not only as needle and thread, but also as seam cutters and stitch rippers, working to loosen the *habit* of linear time.[56] Thinking through sewing in fact already borrows another notion from Allison Smith, whose work *The Muster* I discussed briefly above and will return to in the Afterword. For Smith's "Notion Nanny Project," begun in the UK in 2005, the US artist built collaborative relationships with other craftspeople seeking to exchange ideas, skills, objects, and experiences around the practices and politics of the handmade. "Notion Nannies" were popular Civil War-era dolls (called Peddler Dolls in Victorian England). They were miniature representations of itinerant female peddlers who, traveling the countryside, circulated household objects, sewing notions, and home remedies, as well as news and ideas between isolated locales (and certainly between women). In a series of exhibitions in the UK and the US, Smith attended as a contemporary "apprentice, trader, craftsmaker, and storyteller," exhibiting and trading hand-made items she collected along the way. Eventually, she was accompanied and replaced by a life-size doll, a clone she had made of herself in the garb of a Notion Nanny, carrying a basket filled with the objects she had collected in her cross-stitching, cross-continent, cross-century travels.

Crossing time in a "nation of futurity"

Notion Nanny Allison Smith, who was born in Manassas, Virginia, describes her investment in cross-temporality as influenced by her experiences growing up in the heartland of the US Civil War – if not exactly *during* the Civil War (she was born in 1972), still in some way enduring it. Growing up in the state of Virginia, Smith was instructed by war's performative remains in a cultural environment so tightly and intricately interwoven between then and now, that neither now nor then resolves to clearly discernable camps. Virginia is a state that prides itself not only on its history of battle, but also on its ongoing battle with history in a lively culture of reenactment. The "official" tourism website of the Commonwealth of Virginia baits the following hook for potential visitors:

> More major Civil War battles took place in Virginia than in any other state. Witness battles, ask questions and/or participate in the camp life of soldiers and their families.[57]

Note that the past tense of one sentence slips effortlessly into the present tense of another. In a sense, www.virginia.org is not peddling the history or even the memory of battlefields, but the *experience* of event, *participation* in the past, and, quite openly, camp "*life*." To "witness" and to "participate" are to attend a scene as it occurs, and thus the experience of Virginia's history is offered *in the future* when one visits or makes a "return visit" – attending again and again.

Virginia is not alone in the US roster of states inviting an experience of return. The Yankee state of Pennsylvania is home to a statue named "Return Visit" that stands in the town square in Gettysburg – a city also marked by the peddling of its past's future, its future past. The statue stands outside the David Wills House where Lincoln famously revised the Gettysburg Address on the night before delivering the speech in 1863. When I visited the house, a wax effigy of Lincoln sat at a writing desk in a second-story bedroom, his pen mid-sentence on a paper that was already fully inscribed.[58] Though it may seem complicated (if historically accurate) to present Lincoln in the process of revision, the "Return Visit" statue on the square just outside is also oddly engaged in the matter of rewriting – if to "speak the speech" (as Shakespeare put it) subjects writing to revision (as we will explore in Chapter 3). That is, amidst the bustle of passers-by, the bronze statue of a fatherly Lincoln appears to invite a bronze late twentieth-century man – a tourist Dad perhaps – to orate the Gettysburg Address himself. Bronze Dad, looking like a Duane Hanson sculpture knock-off and locally known as "Perry Como," holds a text of the Gettysburg Address as if about to speak. Meanwhile, the Bronze Lincoln gestures toward the second-floor bedroom of the Wills House where, for years, his waxen double simultaneously held the pose of perpetual revision. Passers-by often pause for snapshots, striking poses with the well known and the unknown father figures, making their own visit available for return.

Figure 0.5 Return Visit by J. Seward Johnson, Jr., placed on the Gettysburg Square in 1991. The Lincoln statue gestures to the Wills house where Lincoln completed writing the Gettysburg Address. Photo: Rebecca Schneider.

Figure 0.6 A wax effigy of Lincoln working on the Gettysburg Address at the Wills house, Gettysburg, PA, 1999. The pen is poised halfway down a page already fully filled with handwriting. He is rewriting. Photo: Rebecca Schneider.

But none of this is odd at all, considering the longstanding US investment in "the living" as proper site and substance of a past always explicitly unfinished. Recall, as quoted in the epigraph that opens this Foreword, that John O'Sullivan, the coiner of the phrase "Manifest Destiny," wrote in 1839:

> It is our unparalleled glory that we have no reminiscences of battlefields [. . .] Who, then, can doubt that our country is destined to be the great nation of futurity?[59]

While Lincoln's 1863 Gettysburg Address is a speech that begins with the securing of a past ("Four score and seven years ago our fathers [. . .]"), it is also a speech that remarks on memory's place less as record offered for history than as ongoing performative act – a *doing*:

> The world will little note nor long remember what we *say* here, but it cannot forget what they *did* here. It is for us the living, rather, to be dedicated here to the unfinished work which they who fought here have thus far so nobly

advanced. It is rather for us to be here dedicated to the great task remaining before us – that from these honored dead we take increased devotion to that cause for which they gave the last full measure of devotion – that we here highly resolve that these dead shall not have died in vain – that this nation, under God, shall have a new birth of freedom – and that government of the people, by the people, for the people, shall not perish from the earth.[60]

Lincoln was helping to dedicate a cemetery with this address, and so arguably "the great task remaining before us" was quite literal as well as symbolic. And yet the bronze statues and wax effigies and relentlessly ongoing mimetic activities of living historians and reenactors at such sites across the country suggest that Lincoln's emphasis on task – on a live doing "remaining before us"– continues to resound as a literal call to action. If "to remain" means to endure or even to stay behind, to "remain before" is to endure as both *ahead of* and *prior to* – a phrase that clearly tangles or crosses temporal registers. In this sense, before and behind cannot be plotted in a straight line, and so memory *remains* a future act: not yet recalled, if also never yet forgotten. In the gap between having "no reminiscences of battlefields" (O'Sullivan) and simultaneously belonging to a *world* that "cannot forget" (Lincoln) lies the projected US national imaginary as always pitched off of the word as record and onto the act as living, doing, *live*. The logic is contradictory: the past is elsewhere, a foreign country left behind. The future is America's geography of revision, and it's up ahead that America's past (the future's past) will be (re)encountered among the (so-called) living.

Indeed, the sense that the past is a future direction in which one can travel – that it can stretch out before us like an unfamiliar landscape waiting to be (re)discovered – is familiar.[61] It is also one of the basic logics of psychoanalytic trauma theory that events can lie both before us and behind us – in the past where an event may have been missed, forgotten, or not fully witnessed, and in the future where an event might (re)occur as it is (re)encountered, (re)discovered, (re)told and/or (re)enacted, experienced for the first time only as second time. The traumatized soldier, for instance, unwittingly prepares for and re-lives a battle in the future that, due to the shock of the event in the past, he or she could neither adequately experience nor account for at the time.[62] Whether reencountered via "acting out" or "working through," the past is given to lie ahead as well as behind – the stuff and substance limning a twisted and crosshatched footpath marked re-turn.

Going back over the seams, however, let us linger a little longer over O'Sullivan's claim that the US has no memory of battlefields. The orchestration of memory in close relationship with forgetting is certainly a landmark feature of any national self-fashioning. Well before 1873, when Nietzsche theorized that *any* national history is as much composed in forgetting as it is in remembering, O'Sullivan's 1839 boast attempted to position America as uniquely a "nation of futurity" precisely because its lack of memory was specific: it has no "reminiscences of battlefields."[63] Take careful note, however: O'Sullivan neither claimed that there were no battlefields, nor that they were exactly forgotten, but simply that there would be no memory of them.

Obviously, the United States in 1839, two decades before the Civil War, was hardly innocent of battle. Even if we discount wars that were acknowledged by the nation as wars – the American Revolution (which arguably was passing from living memory by 1839[64]), or the War of 1812 (which was not) – the land was rife with battlefields, and could even be said to be one vast battleground. By 1837, 46,000 Native Americans from southeastern nations had been removed from their homelands thereby opening 25 million acres for settlement by non-native Americans. Significant portions of native populations died in the process. And, of course, many "battles" (skirmishes, massacres, and other violent separations of people from land) preceded and surrounded removal. O'Sullivan wasn't denying that battles happened. Investing in collective denial, he simply refused to remember them. The vastness of the bloody battleground that was the New World was officially disremembered as part and parcel of the bid for "futurity" the nation was making not only with its white citizens, but ultimately, in Lincoln's words, with the "world." As Herman Melville put it in 1850, "The Past is dead, and has no resurrection; but the Future is endowed with such a life, that it lives to us even in anticipation. [. . .] The Past is the text-book of tyrants; the Future the Bible of the Free."[65] The New World was "free" of history and marching forward in a blind but living *now* whose past is "dead." Only the *living* matter here, and Americans *live* the future, Melville intones – living one time in another time. The future, alive in the present, makes of the present already its own past. If there is a past, by this way of thinking it would only be of consequence if it resides in anticipation. The past cannot be resurrected, because it cannot yet have occurred. History, like the burial of the dead for Lincoln, *remains before us.*

Time is decidedly folded and fraught. In the context of the "Post-Heroic" (or antebellum) generation, of which O'Sullivan was a member, the sense of "belonging to an age later than the beginning," as George B. Forgie puts it in *Patricide in the House Divided,* could be problematic.[66] If "beginning again" was the founding principal and certain mantra for the "Heroes" of the Republic, as Gertrude Stein intones in *The Making of Americans,*[67] coming after the beginning could be tough – a kind of structural fault line in the national enterprise. How to ensure that it was *always* the beginning? Perpetual forgetting might ensure that "beginning" could be forever (re)played as "a new birth of freedom" – and this might have been one way to cope with the belatedness of America's future fathers to America's founding fathers. Live recitation would always begin again, memory would never be achieved as complete, reenactment would insist upon re-beginning. In this sense (and in the sense of the statue "Return Visit"), Lincoln is already a founding father, standing beside a "son" given to reenact the founding for which Lincoln stands. In this complicated and convoluted sense, and as many have noted, keeping the (re)founders alive through ritualized fratricidal forgetting *in tandem with remembering* becomes a kind of foundational patricidic impulse to modern nationhood – inevitably a forward played backward that institutes forgetting as an error-filled "lest we forget." In this case the mantra goes as follows: Let us not forget that we have no memory of battlefields. Let us reenact our not knowing in advance.[68]

The notion of America as youthful and innocent is basic to its mythic placeholder as "new," "live," and "now" – and it's no mistake that the romantic ideas behind this came directly upon the heels of the genocide of the Indians. This mythic place was re-forged in the mid-twentieth century with the youth movements of the 1960s and the burgeoning of performance or action-based art.[69] American innocence, lack of memory, and naïveté are ideas that still carry weight today. Even as the heritage industry and practices of battle reenactment have become something of a national obsession – a fact that would seem to suggest an investment in the very reminiscences O'Sullivan claims we lack – the idea that America is innocent of battle and ignorant of loss still thrives. As recently as 2008, the widely respected historian Tony Judt could claim in the pages of the *New York Review of Books* in an essay titled "What Have We Learned, If Anything?" that "Americans" have no true experience of loss – at least not to equal European experience – because America "did not lose vast numbers of citizens, or huge swathes of territory, as a result of occupation or dismemberment." Unless Judt does not count Native Americans among those who might be remembered on the continent as having suffered loss (whether "citizens" or not, such losses might *count*, as they do in Europe, as the result of war between nations), his claim makes no sense. He goes on: "Although humiliated in distant neocolonial wars (in Vietnam and now in Iraq), the US has never suffered the full consequences of defeat." In a footnote, Judt makes the *only* exception to his claim about American naïveté to be the US Civil War, though he insists that this exception proves the rule because the South is "backward." He writes:

> The defeated South did indeed experience just such consequences following the Civil War, however. And its subsequent humiliation, resentment, and backwardness are the American exception that illustrates the rule.[70]

If Judt's memory is any indication of the answer to the question of what we have learned, we have learned (to acknowledge) very little concerning the history of violence and loss on the North American continent. If the US Civil War stands as exceptional for Judt (as for many others), its state of exception is perhaps better described as a scrim obscuring the magnitude of the (generational) suffering of the multitudes who died in battle or were otherwise "removed" from homelands to reservation camps, plantations, or other violent displacements.

But whether one agrees with Judt and O'Sullivan that "Americans have had no true experience of loss," or whether one believes that Americans perpetuate a less-than-innocent post-traumatic stress disorder of some kind, we certainly seem today to chase the past as if memory were the most precious vanishing commodity on earth. From reenactment societies, to heritage museums and theme parks, to historical reality TV shows offering time travel to contemporary contestants, to reenactment in the work of contemporary visual artists, photographers, and performance artists – the past is the stuff of the future, laid out like game show prizes for potential (re)encounter. To visit Boston is to "take a walk through

America's past"; to visit Asheville, North Carolina, is to "journey to a simpler time"; and, as already cited, to visit Virginia is to "witness battles, ask questions and/or participate in the camp life of soldiers and their families."[71] States offer literal time travel and the opportunity to "witness" as well as "participate" in a surfeit not of what *once* happened, but of what is given to happen again and again – this time for YOU.

A not-for-profit Colorado company named "You Can Live History" offers reenactment events for schools, corporations, foundations, and camps and makes explicit the bargain that is common in historical tourism: "You now have the opportunity to experience American history in a personal way!" They suggest:

> You provide the participants and location – we provide everything else to make a safe and realistic looking battle reenactment. In addition, we produce a video of the battle starring YOU![72]

Here, history begins again, taking place "as if" for the first time, now "starring YOU." The theatricality in the equation is as virulent as is the claim to authenticity – and oddly, theatricality and authenticity, sometime oxymorons, here go hand in hand. The explicit suggestion haunting much of the language of education that attends the heritage industry is that without YOU in a starring role, history might not take place – might not have taken place. History needs YOU *as futurity*. Here the historical investment is not as much about preservation as it is about regeneration.[73] History is not remembered (America has no reminiscence) as it was, but experienced as it will become. It must be acquired, purchased, begun again and again. A nation of futurity is here, still, a nation without reminiscences – unless reminiscence is relived as NOW, acquired (purchased even, copyrighted) as affective "present time" experience, beginning again.

Many have noted how America has become a kind of theme park of itself – "The Past as a Theme Park" writes David Lowenthal in a simple, catchy phrase.[74] And perhaps the present is a reality TV show taking place *as* the past. All of this might reflect the fact that in a daily world of screens and wireless proximities to everywhere, we are rarely exactly "in time" or "in place" but always also capable of multiple and simultaneous elsewheres, always a step or more behind or ahead or to the side, watching through open windows being watched, performing ourselves performing or being performed. We are passing the time by witnessing the passing time of doubling, redoubling, tripling, re-tripling, cross-, multi-, and hyper-citational events. What exactly we are witnessing, and how exactly we are witnessing, when we "take a walk through America's past" in Boston or "journey to a simpler time" in Asheville, make a "return visit" in Gettysburg, or sample "camp life" in Virginia is an open question. If events are not exactly happening (or not only happening) in a here that is *now* or a now that is *here* – where, then, is the here? And when, now, is the then?

The rapid growth of the time travel industry in the twenty-first century may seem like a "cannibalizing" of history – a condition of late capitalism disparaged by Fredric Jameson in *Postmodernism, or, the Cultural Logic of Late Capitalism*.[75] But

Jameson's bemoaned flip of Enlightenment linear time back upon itself, and the resulting wrinkles and folds and swerves in direction in an otherwise straight-shot to futurity, may not be as "post" as all that, as Jameson himself acknowledges. And anyway, as many have pointed out, when linear time was "over" (marking the predicted and widely debunked "end of history"), the appellation "post" became absurd, as did the "end" of anything – most especially history. In this case, a kind of thrall to ends and to death becomes an easily recognizable (if ironically eschatological) attempt of the modern to keep on keeping on: proclaiming death and disappearance a hyper-privileged condition of the real and celebrating, at and in its own wake, a self-proclaimed obsolescence that kept it *un*-obsolete.[76] It is strange that in all the death-centered thought in the arts and humanities of the late twentieth century, so many hyperactive ghosts would behave as if death were the *only* unchecked category on their "to-do" list, as they get up every day from their graves to "take a walk through America's past." Or maybe the two facts are linked. The result, in any case, is that the dead are living everywhere.

Of course this all rings with an alarming irony today, as there are no set of battlefields more given to obsessive American reminiscence than those of the US Civil War which lay in the very near future of O'Sullivan's declaration that America has no reminiscence of battlefields. And, perhaps even more importantly, there is still no theatre of war less acknowledged (or more "forgotten") by the nation as a whole for its scenes of violence than the vast stretches of land across which 300 years of Indian removal took place before the Civil War.

While this book is not about American settlement or Indian removal, or even about the Civil War, it *is* about practices of reminiscence in relation to disappearance, remains, memory, history, artifactual preserve, and live performance. The charged web-work of remembering and forgetting is tightly laced, corset-like, across the bodies of reenactors in Civil War battles, who sometimes fight as if forgetting *again* that the past is something that comes before and the future something in distinction to the past. Instead, for them, linear time is a ruse. As if having it both ways, or many ways at once, reenactors take the "past" in multiple directions. As they line up for war every weekend of every summer of every year across the States, repetition trips into something entirely outside of linear, narrative time, and practices of live forgetting recur as the very charge to remember.

And indeed, perhaps they are not *exactly* wrong.

As Rosemarie K. Banks suggests, in a book on theatre culture in antebellum America, the traditional Native American sense of history may be instructive: "What has happened in a place is always happening."[77]

Uneasily side by side: popular heritage and high art

A recent exhibit that took place between May 2006 and March 2007 at Massachusetts Museum of Contemporary Art (Mass MOCA) titled *Ahistoric Occasion: Artists Making History* included the following foreword by Joseph Thompson, Director of the Museum, in the publication accompanying the exhibition:

One of the strangest, most affecting and discomforting exhibits I've ever experienced is the Plimoth Plantation "live diorama" in which native Americans, dressed in historic clothing, recreate a 17th-century Wampanoag Homesite, all the while conversing with museum visitors in utterly twenty-first-century terms. Caught in a netherworld between role-playing and contemporary culture, the Native People speak of current events – Massachusetts politics, casino gambling, the socioeconomic challenges facing their kids – while patiently smoking venison, crafting dug-out canoes, and tanning animal hides. Instructive, accurate, decidedly restrained in tone – if not subtly disdainful – the Wampanoag Homesite is a peculiar form of museological theater. Inadvertent participation on stage can be deeply disquieting.

At Plimouth Plantation, the Native People are adept at exploiting the trappings of history in pursuit of an agenda that is much more about today than 1678. It is, in the end, a profoundly political exhibition, with an unequivocal point of view [. . .] all wrapped up in fur and smoke, and the Plantation didactics.

Ahistoric Occasion is a little like that, too, and the vibe is equally resonant and strange.[78]

Ahistoric Occasion, an art exhibition with work by such artists as Allison Smith and Lincoln impersonator Greta Pratt, was, for Thompson, "a little like" the Natives at Plimoth who were engaged as political performers in a ricocheting exploitation-arama that ultimately finds its closest art relative to be theatre – albeit, in Thompson's words, "a peculiar form of museological theater." The "deeply disquieting" aspects of the Plimoth exhibit seem clearly to be linked, for Thompson, to a temporal crosshatch. For him, people in the exhibit both pass as seventeenth-century ("instructive, accurate, and decidedly restrained") and do not pass ("utterly twenty-first-century"). They are "caught" between times. Thompson calls them "the Native People." But what else could he have called them: reenactors? actors? enthusiasts? models? activists? artists? museum employees? Wampanoag? Cherokee? Narragansett? Nipmuc? US citizens? For Thompson, the agenda appears to be "much more about today than 1678," but the question of how today is *not* about 1678 seems to me to clearly hang in the air of the Natives' conversation, making the question of agendas, like the question of "when," deeply vexed. The undoing of linear time is part of the nervousness or queasiness of theatricality, contributing to the uncertainty of where and how time *takes place*: today's agendas necessarily contain, recompose, recite, and *touch* 1678, *and vice versa*.

If Thompson was brave enough to call the artwork "a little like" popular history reenactment, other curators invested in reenactment are not as brave. Often, curators do what they can to completely distance themselves from that *other* history re-enactment happening outside the frame of art. Inke Arns, one of the curators of the 2007–8 exhibit *History Will Repeat Itself* at Hartware MedienKunstVerein in Dortmund and KW Institute for Contemporary Art in Berlin, has stated that popular cultural reenactments are "history for history's sake," and thus, to her mind, devoid of an interest in the present. Arns cited Nietzsche's call in *The Use and Abuse of History:* "[W]e need history. But we need it in a manner different from the way the spoilt idler in the garden of knowledge uses it." Clearly, the spoilt idlers are, for Arns, the "pop-cultural" reenactors. Despite the best efforts of Andy Warhol, artists are still, for Arns, completely distinct from the debasements of "pop culture." For her, reenactment artists make works that are "questionings of the present" and this she calls "exactly the opposite" of history reenactment outside of the art context.[79] It seems odd to assume that the art context is simply a perpetual present, especially when history reenactment framed or posed as art – and we can think of Jonathan Deller's *Battle at Orgreave* or Ron Dickinson's *Milgram Re-Enactment* and *Jonestown Re-Enactment* or Mark Tribe's *Port Huron Project* – clearly troubles boundaries between past and present and challenges any imagined dividing line between politics and aesthetics.

In some reenactment artwork, as discussed at the start of this Foreword, the historical event reenacted is a precedent performance art event. That is, art reenacting precedent art has become common alongside historical reenactment framed as art. Reenactments of Yoko Ono's *Cut Piece*, of Ana Mendieta's *Body Tracks*, of Kaprow's *18 Happenings in Six Parts*, of Vito Acconci's *Seedbed*, of Carolee Schneemann's *Meat Joy*, of Hermann Nitsch's *Orgien Mysterien Theater* and many more have recently undergone re-doing and in some cases multiple re-doings. Until recently, most '60s and '70s performance art work was considered non-reproduceable, existing only in time as one-time events, and in this way was arguably seen as "auratic."[80] Such work was considered completely contingent, lost to an irretrievable "then" that was only fleetingly "now" at the time of its singular articulation. As will be discussed in Chapter 5, photography had a great deal to do with that attitude. Performance art work of the 1960s and 1970s, captured in grainy black and whites or flickering film stock, could posit the event as having priority over its documentation. The document would stand as record that the event "that was there" was "no longer there." Photographs and film and, ultimately, video could therefore come to serve (ironically) as testimony to the event's disappearance, even positing the event as always essentially missed, fully dependent on the embodied in-time singularity of an auratic artist's embodied act.

The heatedness of contemporary debate – or, as Kino put it, "fights" of a "rebel form" in the archive of the museum – concerns the paradoxical battle to preserve the auratic live as *both* non-reproduceable (as was common to consider it mid-century) *and* recurrent (that is, like theatre, capable of being mounted *again*). The place of the documentation of the "original" event has, in this way, shifted – becoming score, script, or material for "instruction." Documents that had seemed to indicate *only* the past, are now pitched toward the possibility of a future reenactment as much as toward the event they apparently recorded. This double gesture forward and back (and to the side) was palpably evident in Abramović's exhibit *The Artist Is Present* at MoMA, where surrogates reenacted precedent Abramović performance pieces, but did so uneasily beside photographic and video documentation of Abramović's "original" actions that simultaneously adorned the gallery space. This besideness made the exhibit feel somewhat engorged with itself.

If "The Artist" was present, the question in each piece could become: which artist, where, when? Abramović in the documentation, or the "other people" in the live tableaux? Or, both? Was Abramović "present" in the documentation? And, as we will take up again in Chapter 4, was the live reenactment a document, standing as record of Abramović's acts?

As the liveness of in-time performance art work has recently become available for the re-liveness of reenactment, it is fascinating that photography, *not generally considered a medium of liveness*, has become a veritable hotbed for re-staging, re-playing, reenacting for the camera in work that mixes theatricality and documentality in tantalizing ways. Reenactment work in and for photography presses our questions quite fulsomely into the inter(in)animate tangle between liveness and documentation. Photo-performance "reenactment" is evident in the work of Sherrie Levine, Yasumasa Morimura, Gregory Crewdson, Eleanor Antin, Yinka Shonibare, Nikki S. Lee, Lorna Simpson, Jeff Wall, Bill Viola, Tina Barney, and many others (whether they accept the appellation "reenactment" or not) – in which work is staged, with *evident* theatricality, creating photographs that both document theatricality (the posing subject) and *are* theatrical (the photograph *is* the performance) – an issue we will return to in depth in Chapter 5.

In art contexts, the term "reenactment" is contested and in flux. The term "appropriation art" is arguably its most immediate precedent, even as, ironically, performance artists like Abramović are struggling *not* to be appropriated (at least not by reenactors they might not pre-approve). But if the term reenactment is fitting at all, it fits only because it is as yet porous, intermedial, and rather poorly defined. The *Oxford English Dictionary* gives us the verb form "reenact": to "reproduce, recreate, or perform again" but offers only the term "reenactment societies" and briefly describes "an association whose members re-enact events (often battles) from a particular historical period, in replica costume and using replica weapons." Princeton's database *Wordnet* offers reenactment as "performing a role in an event that occurred at an earlier time," replacing *Oxford*'s reference to "again" with the phrase "earlier time" – underscoring the temporal play at the base of reenactment. As the *OED* definition makes clear, we are still most familiar with the term reenactment as applied to historical societies. Certainly, much of the reenactment work in visual and performance art bears some relation to "historical" reenactments undertaken in these societies in that the term carries with it the sense of an act or event occurring *again*, recurring across participants' bodies in time. As such, reenactment art poses a certain challenge to our long-standing thrall, fueled by art-historical analyses of performance, to the notion that live performance disappears by insisting that, to the contrary, the live is a vehicle for recurrence – unruly or flawed or unfaithful to precedence as that recurrence may threaten to be.

Recurrence, of course, contests tightly stitched Enlightenment claims to the forward-driven linearity of temporality, the continuity of time, and challenges, as well, an attitude toward death as necessarily irrecoverable loss. There is, instead, a certain superabundance to reenactment, like a run-on sentence, as if an event in time, refusing to be fully or finally "over" or "gone" or "complete" pulses with a kind of living afterlife in an ecstasy of variables, a million insistent if recalcitrant possibilities for return (doubling as possibilities for error). The zillion details of the act of interpretation in an act of live repetition make the pastness of the past both palpable and a very *present* matter.

Reenactment troubles linear temporality by offering at least the suggestion of recurrence, or return, even if the practice is peppered with its own ongoing incompletion. There is a pointedly temporal aspect to the term unlike other terms for doubling that do not overtly accentuate time, such as mimesis, imitation, appropriation, citation, reiteration, performativity. Perhaps only the term "theatricality," through its nominal linkage to the widely varied practices of theatre – a famously time-based art of the live – carries within it a suggestion of the temporal. But theatricality's temporal register is cloaked or visored at best, and hounded by the term's inordinately vexed relationship to the imagined borderlands where war is waged between those who would police an "authentic" and those who find critical promise in the history and lineage of masquerade – critical promise, in fact, in error, and mistake.

To trouble linear temporality – to suggest that time may be touched, crossed, visited or revisited, that time is transitive and flexible, that time may recur in time, that time is not one – never only one – is to court the ancient (and tired) Western anxiety over ideality and originality. The threat of theatricality is still the threat of the imposter status of the copy, the double, the mimetic, the second, the surrogate, the feminine, or the queer. Detractors say: The then is *then*, the now is *now*, the dead are dead, lost: we cannot go back, we can only, in the spasms of our misguided traumatic remainders, lurch forward (backward and forward being the only imaginable directions). To some who ridicule the activities of reenactors as naïve, the faith that linear time is the one true time couples with an investment in the contingency offered by the linear temporal model to reassure that any *true* temporal return or overlap would be impossible because *different*. Of course, the question remains to be taken up in more depth in Chapter 3: why does difference necessarily cancel out authenticity? For those who invest in linear time as the only time, any event or act re-enacted can be dismissed as "just" or "merely" theatrical – spasmodic, hollow, and inconsequential to the long march of empiric time. The reenacted Civil War or the reenactment of precedent performance, such detractors would say, is not *the* Civil War or not *the* original art, because, to quote Richard Schechner, "it is not possible to get back to what was."[81] This impossibility seems intractable, despite the fact that one might easily suspect whether any war (or any art action) could ever have been discrete to itself, containable, occurring in singular time, or without reverberate echo, repetitive impact, or the syncopation of "twiceness" that marks behavior and, even, event.

For those suspicious of linearity and less willing to dismiss time's flexibility, mimesis and its close relative theatricality are not threats to authenticity, but, like language itself, vehicles for access to the transitive, performative, and cross-temporal real. Mimesis is always necessarily composed in what Homi Bhabha, after Frantz Fanon, has called temporal lag, and Elizabeth Freeman has spun to temporal drag. For such theorists, mimesis is not the antithesis of some discreet

authenticity or pure truth, but a powerful tool for cross- or intra-temporal negotiation, even (perhaps) interaction or inter(in)animation of one time with another
time. If, to quote Stein again more fully, the "endless trouble with theatre is its
syncopated time," that "trouble" is never "mere."[82] As this book will work to
explore, overt imitation (one descriptor of theatricality) may even be a kind of
syncopation machine for the touching of time beside or across itelf in the zigzagging lived experience of history's multi-directional ghost notes.

> If life is the path of a straight line, then theatricality is that *same path*, but traveling
> along a line that is wavy, zigzagged, or any kind of indirect line. [. . .] In the
> theatre, not a single path should be straight.[83]

> "'Everything straight lies,' murmured the dwarf disdainfully. 'All truth is
> crooked, time itself is a circle.'"[84]

1 Reenactment and relative pain

Reenactment

The Civil War isn't over, and that's why we fight. We fight to keep the past alive.
——Chuck Woodhead, Civil War reenactor

Now he belongs to the stages.
——Association of Lincoln Presenters' motto

I reenact things you've seen a million times before. Straight things, TV things, and medical things: These are the transactions that we all participate in and memorize accidentally. Then I wiggle my hand and wink and you know that everything I just said was in code, and the real truth is the sick or incredible way you feel.

——Miranda July, artist

The epigraphs above make evident a number of issues that attach to reenactment. The first, "The Civil War isn't over, and that's why we fight," suggests that historical events, like wars, are never discretely completed, but carry forth in embodied cycles of memory that do not delimit the remembered to the past. For many history reenactors, reenactments are more than "mere" remembering but are in fact the ongoing event itself, negotiated through sometimes radically shifting affiliation with the past *as* the present. The next quote, "Now he belongs to the stages," was the official motto of the Association of Lincoln Presenters (ALP) from 1990 to 1999.[1] The motto humorously underscores the theatricality of history and memory and suggests a "belonging" of history to a mobile or transient temporality of theatrical returns. And finally, filmmaker, digital artist, and performance-maker Miranda July's epigraph tells us that reenacting "straight things" – common things that at first pass as natural or accidental – becomes reenactment when *recognized* as composed in code, as always already a matter of reiteration. July reminds us that any enactment might be recognized as *re*-enactment – recognized as a matter of againness – through the manipulation of give-away signs of theatricality. Here a "wiggle" of a hand or a "wink" of an eye are theatrical gestures that give a scene away, prompting the recognition that seemingly discrete acts are never temporally singular nor straightforward but double, triple, or done "a million times before." If for ALP, history belongs to theatricality, for July, theatricality flips unconscious habit memory into "recognition."[2] Prompting recognition of the returns of history in recurrence, theatricality simultaneously prompts a kind of queasiness – or, in July's words, "the sick or incredible way you feel."[3]

Let's go through these three quotes again – in some cases more than once.

Civil war isn't over: one

"The Civil War isn't over, and that's why we fight" was reenactor Chuck Woodhead's answer to my interview question "Why fight?" Attending the 1999 reenactment of the 1863 Battle for Culps Hill at Gettysburg, I had been surprised to find that most of the action took place in the woods at such a distance from spectators that nothing but puffs of smoke and occasional muffled shouts could be witnessed by those of us in bleachers at the National Military Park. The past, replayed, was not necessarily given to be seen. Rather, it was given to be experienced, or "felt," by those who reenacted. Our witnessing was a kind of attention to the players' actions that could not, in this particular case, rely on images or on sight. When the reenactors rode and walked out of the woods again, everyone in the bleachers cheered. But what had we witnessed? Mostly we heard stories afterward of what it had been like to replay what it had been like . . . afterward. That is, our witnessing was laced with a belatedness that felt strangely true to the efforts. We were witness, in this instance, to belatedness and a lack of clear images made palpable as experience. In fact, even at reenactments I attended that were far more visible, the experience of "watching" was almost always a not-quite-seeing, as we were witnessing *others* attempt to do more than watch from the sidelines of the future.[4]

Woodhead's answer to "Why fight?" might at first seem to challenge the pastness of the past, if being "over" is one of the ways a secular, linear, or progress-oriented Enlightenment model of time disciplines our orientation to events that appear to precede the present. And yet, the quote might also suggest that it is the very pastness of the past that is never complete, never completely finished, but incomplete: cast into the future as a matter for ritual negotiation and as yet undecided interpretive acts of *reworking*. In this way, events are given to be past, or to become past, by virtue of both their ongoingness and their partialness, their incompleteness in the present.

If the past is never over, or never completed, "remains" might be understood not solely as object or document material, but also as the immaterial labor of bodies engaged in and with that incomplete past: bodies striking poses, making gestures, voicing calls, reading words, singing songs, or standing witness. Such acts of labor over and with the past might include a body sitting at a table in an archive, bent over an "original" manuscript or peering at a screen, interacting with history as material traces positioned as evidence.[5] Or, such bodily labor might be – though this a far more contested problematic – a twenty-first-century body interacting with traces of *acts* as history: carrying a replica nineteenth-century musket on a historic battlefield, uttering the "phonic materiality" of a cry to arms, or engaging in surgical

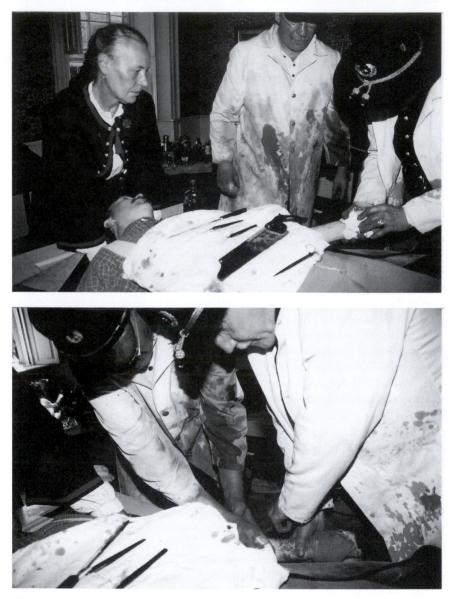

Figure 1.1 Contemporary professional doctors who are also reenactors, reenacting surgical procedures at the Civil War Reenactment Field Hospital at Hearthside Homestead, Lincoln, RI. Photos: Hearthside Homestead.

amputation practices of the 1860s.[6] In both cases – archive and battlefield – interaction with (and as) traces exercises a cross- or multi-temporal engagement with im/material understood to belong to the past in the present. Said more simply: inside the archive *or* out, times touch.

The status of touch is problematic, not least because it suggests *bodies* at least partially merged across difference – even, in this instance, temporal difference. To touch is not to become coextensive, to fully become that which is touched or which touches, but it is to (partially) collapse the distance marking one thing as fully distinct from another thing. "Even more than other perceptual systems," writes Eve Kosofsky Sedgwick, "the sense of touch makes nonsense out of any dualistic understanding of agency and passivity."[7] Reenactors who claim to experience a physical collapse, or at least a profound confusion of time, call the experience a "period rush," or a "wargasm," or say they are "seeing the elephant" or "*touching* time."

All of this is enough, of course, to cause some (though decidedly not all) university-based professional historians significant anxiety. In an essay noting the dangers of historical reenactment for scholarship, Vanessa Agnew argues that reenactment can be accused of "eclipsing the past with its own theatricality." In her formulation, as in others', history can be overrun by the error-ridden embarrassment of the live body (here indicated as "theatricality") reenacting the past in the present.[8] Alexander Cook agrees, erecting, as if unproblematic, the classic mind/body split to suggest reenactment's "persistent tendency to privilege a visceral, emotional engagement with the past at the expense of a more analytical treatment."[9] By this account, touch ("visceral"), and affective engagement ("emotional"), are in distinction to the "analytical."[10]

In marked contrast to this view, recent scholars in queer historiography, such as Carolyn Dinshaw, Chris Nealon, Louise Fradenberg, Carla Freccero, Elizabeth Freeman, Dana Luciano, Heather Love, and Judith Halberstam build on materialist, post-colonial, psychoanalytic, and post-structural theories to argue for an inquiry and analysis that challenges received modern Western conventions of temporal linearity (conventions Dipesh Chakrabarty calls "modern historical consciousness" and Ann Pellegrini and Janet Jakobsen call "secular time"). Such scholars argue for the value of crossing disparate and multiple historical moments to explore the ways that past, present, and future occur and recur *out of sequence* in a complex crosshatch not only of reference but of affective assemblage and investment.[11]

Indeed, there has been something of an "affective turn" in scholarship, coming close on the heels of the "performative turn" that arguably reached an apex in the 1990s. Patricia Clough is often cited for crafting the phrase "affective turn" and she links the turn to Gilles Deleuze and Brian Massumi, but the phrase appeared much earlier in feminist work by Kathleen Woodward, Lauren Berlant, and Linda Nicholson.[12] The affective turn is extremely interesting in regard to the fact that it seems to resist the binary still so virile in the linguistic ties of the performative turn – that is, the binary between writing or textuality on the one hand and embodied gestic repertoires of behavior on a seeming other. The affective turn resists replicating the body/text binary, but situates itself more interestingly in spaces between such binaries – including self/other – as much affect is situated, like atmosphere, between bodies. Thinking through affective engagement offers a radical shift in thinking about our mobilities in dealings with the binaried landscapes of social plots (such as gender, such as race), undoing the solidity of binaries in favor of mining the slip and slide of affect as negotiation. As such, affects – and feelings and emotions (though the differences in terminologies vary between scholars) – are often described via words that indicate viscosity, tactility, or a certain mobility in the way one is *moved*. Kathleen Stewart, following Alphonso Lingis, suggestively writes of the "jump" of affect – the way affect jumps between bodies – crosses borders of bodies, getting into and out of bodies as if there were no material border of consequence even "if only for a minute."[13] Teresa Brennan takes the jump as "transmission":

> Is there anyone who has not, at least once, walked into a room and "felt the atmosphere"? [. . .] The transmission of affect, whether it is grief, anxiety, or anger, is social or psychological in origin. But the transmission is also responsible for bodily changes; some are brief changes, as in a whiff of the room's atmosphere, some longer lasting. In other words, the transmission of affect, if only for an instant, alters the biochemistry and neurology of the subject. The "atmosphere" or the environment literally gets into the individual.[14]

This jump has also been shown to be cross-temporal as well as cross-spatial, cross-geographic, cross- and/or contra-national. Affect can circulate, bearing atmosphere-altering tendencies, in material remains or gestic/ritual remains, carried in a sentence or a song, shifting in and through bodies in encounter. Sara Ahmed, preferring the appellation emotion to affect, writes of emotion as *sticky*. A viscosity that does not sediment in a body as singular nor exist as completely contained, stickiness is a leaky, even fleshy descriptor suggestive of touch (and being "touched" or "moved" become monikers of affect that signify a between bodiness and between objectness or between materialities of emotion that can jump, or travel, in time as well as space).[15]

The jump and the touch of affect have been featured in queer theory's problematizing of identitarian politics, helping to unsettle approaches to the social that tend to sediment "identity" into solid-state positionalities. To be touched and to be moved indicates a level of libidinality in affective engagements in the social, suggestive of shift and slip. The Deleuzean notion of assemblage is also used in such work to unsettle the rootedness of identity, to gesture not only to mobility but also to the always already *crossingness*, or *betweeness*, or *relationality* of the sets of associations that make up something resembling identity. However, we can do away with arguments, such as Brian Massumi's, about affect's autonomy when we choose to invest in the betweenness or given relational aspects of affect.[16] The *stickiness* of emotion is evident in the residue of generational time, reminding us that histories of events and historical effects of identity fixing, *stick* to any mobility, *dragging* (in Elizabeth Freeman's sense) the temporal past into the sticky substance of any present. To be sticky with the past and the future is not to be autonomous, but to be engaged in a freighted, cross-temporal mobility. This is a mobility that drags the "past as past" (to quote Heather Love) – the "genuine *past*-ness of the past" (to quote Elizabeth Freeman) – into a negotiated future that is never simply *in front of us* (like a past that is never simply behind us) but in a kind of viscous, affective surround.[17] Indeed, jumpiness and stickiness are words that undo the step-by-step linearity of Enlightenment plots for autonomous, unfettered progress in an unimpeded forward march.

It is certainly possible to argue that any approach to history involving remains – material *or* immaterial remains – engages temporality at (and as) a chiasm, where times cross and, in crossing, in some way touch. For surely, to engage a temporal moment *as past and yet present in varied remains* is to engage across as well as in time – even to suggest, as Merleau-Ponty does, a certain logic of "reversibility."[18] To find the past resident in remains – material evidence, haunting trace, reiterative gesture – is to engage one time resident *in* another time – a logic rooted in the word "remain." Time, engaged *in* time, is always a matter of crossing, or passing, or touching, and perhaps always (at least) double. In the two examples above (the body accessing material in an archive and the body as an archive of material that might be accessed), the past is given to remain, but in each case that remaining is incomplete, fractured, partial – in the sense both of fragmentary and ongoing. Such remaining also presumes a threat, a site of contestation, a fight. In the archive, the fight is a battle to preserve the past in its material traces against the "archiviolithic" threat that it might disappear.[19] Such preservation is pitched toward a future in which the past might be engaged in a future present as a site of concern – recalling Benjamin's famous aphoristic claim that "every image of the past that is not recognized by the present as one of its own concerns threatens to disappear irretrievably."[20] At reenactments, participants fight to "keep the past *alive*," as Woodhead told me. The effort is to provoke an *in time* experience bearing some relation to "living." It is as if some history reenactors position their bodies to access, consciously and deliberately, a fleshy or pulsing kind of trace they deem accessible in a pose, or gesture, or set of acts.

If a pose or a gesture or a "move" recurs across time, what pulse of multiple time might a pose or a move or gesture contain? Can a trace take the form of a *living* foot – or only the form of a footprint? Can a gesture, such as a pointing index finger, itself be a remain in the form of an indexical action that haunts (or remains) via live repetition? This is to ask: what is the time of a live act when a live act is reiterative? To what degree is a live act *then* as well as *now*? Might a live act even "document" a precedent live act, rendering it, in some way, ongoing, even preserved? An action repeated again and again and again, however fractured or partial or incomplete, has a kind of staying power – persists through time – and even, in a sense, serves as a fleshy kind of "document" of its own recurrence.[21]

A live reiterative act, such as a pointing finger indicating "look at that" or "it happened there" or "it will happen there," casts itself both backward (as a matter of repetition) and forward (it can be enacted again) in time. We understand the gesture of the point, like the gesture of the waving hand, or any number of basic actions because others have pointed and waved before us (whether hard-wired genetically or mimetically learned, the gesture or the action is *passed on*). Given this, can the time of any gesture or live act be (only) singular? What is the evidentiary status of the trace carried forward and backward in the form and force of affective, incorporated, "live" actions?

Of course, these are not new questions, but reiterative riffs on a theme that has long obsessed the academy. In the past forty years we have seen the development of memory studies, collective memory studies, and trauma studies – to name three obvious academic interdisciplinary scions of the concern that Fredric Jameson placed under the moniker "postmodern": that we have collectively suffered a "disappearance of a sense of history."[22] If, for trauma studies generally, the crisis of a "sense of history" is most deeply and dearly articulated post World War II, it can hardly be said to have been born there. We can recall Emile Durkheim's 1897 study *Suicide,* in which he found the alienated modern subject in industrial capitalism to suffer a loss of connective tissue, a severed sense of social continuity. To search for ways to redress this loss, in his 1912 *The Elementary Forms of Religious Life* Durkheim turned "back in time" to "elementary" man to see what civilization had possibly forgotten about connectivity – though the "back in time" implied by the word "primitive" was in fact contemporaneous time – across colonial space to the living practices of indigenous peoples in North America and Australia. Such geopolitics played out as chronopolitics complicates the socially constructed site of "the past" as ever *only* temporal, as Johannes Fabian has argued. It is always also a matter of taking, as well as having taken, *place.*[23]

Forty-odd years of postmodernity, or 500 years of modernity, is still too narrow a channel in which to chart consistently irruptive Euro-Western anxieties about history, memory, and loss. Further back (if that is the correct direction) in the Western imaginary, in the *Phaedrus* of 370 BCE we find Plato ventriloquizing Socrates with the sense of a "memory crisis" (to use Richard Terdiman's phrase). The reader will object: Jameson's postmodern concern over the "disappearance of a sense of *history*" is not the same as Plato's riff on Socrates' worry over the disappearance of a sense of *memory*. But, from either end of the long Western corridor binarizing history (composed in document) and memory (composed in body), the space between is layered with anxiety about verity, authenticity, falsity, theatrically, truth, and claim.

To gesture in such broad strokes to the (sticky) weight of tradition that inevitably freights my own inquiry here, is to assure the reader that I make no claims to comprehensive overview. In fact, the anxious tune has been so often played, and the slippery corridor between history and memory so often worried that Paul Ricoeur has recently asked whether memory and history are not now "condemned to a forced cohabitation." He asks: "Has history finally melted into memory? And has memory broadened itself to the scale of historical memory?"[24]

Certainly if any space between history and memory ever really existed, it has, if not fully "melted," become porous and transient. The resiliently irruptive rub and call of live bodies (like biological machines of affective transmission) insist that physical acts are a means for knowing, bodies are sites for transmission even if, simultaneously, they are also manipulants of error and forgetting. Bodies engaged in repetition are boisterous aticulants of a liveness that just won't quit. Indeed, watching reenactment events it sometimes seems that participants do not suffer, as Jameson fretted, simply over a "disappearance of a sense of history," but rather that they suffer from a disappearance of a sense that history is that which disappears. Either way, at the crux, their live bodies are the means by which the past and the present negotiate disappearance (again).

If we have become somewhat comfortable with the notion of bodily memory (if not bodily history), and comfortable reading bodies engaged in ritual or repeated actions as carriers of collective memory, we are not entirely comfortable considering gestic acts (re)enacted live to be material trace, despite the material substance that is the body articulating the act. We do not say, in other words, that a gesture is a *record*, like a photograph or a written document or a tape-recorded testimony or a footprint – capable of registering in the annals of history. But neither do we say (though perhaps we could) that a photograph or a written testimony or a footprint is a live gesture, encountered between bodies in a cross-temporal space of the syncopated live (see Chapter 5). In any case, as the anxieties of Agnew and Cook make clear, a reenactment of the Civil War is not considered a *record* of the war, an artifact of the war, a document of the war despite claims that might be made for the war's affective *imprint* (not just its impression) on the social imaginary. This is perhaps because the words "document" and "evidence" and "record" are, by the repetitively assumed force of convention in cultures privileging literature over orature[25] (or archive over repertoire, to use Diana Taylor's words), habitually understood in distinction to the bodily, the messily, the "disappearing" live. That chronopolitics of race and gender haunt the privileging of document over embodied act should go without saying – but of course, cannot.[26]

Civil war isn't over: two

"The Civil War isn't over," reenactor Chuck Woodhead told me, "and that's why we fight." Another reenactor standing near him added: "The history books don't get it right, so we have to." Still others fight to counter the "forgotten pages" – a fascinating phrase – of history books.[27]

Woodhead, a Desert Storm veteran, had made the trip in 1999 from Georgia to Gettysburg for the annual reenactment of the Battle at Gettysburg, and he told me that he reenacts the Civil War to keep it alive – fighting the battles again as Union or Confederate, variously.[28] "Because if we don't," he said, "it will disappear." I applied what I'd learned in graduate school to what he had said, and concluded that Woodhead lives by a rule opposite to the one accepted by so many art and performance theorists: that live performance disappears.[29] For Woodhead, live performance is the best mode of refusing to disappear; when an event is left to artifact and document alone, it vanishes. "Artifacts are dead objects," he said. "You don't get that *feel*." He began to recite for me a phrase he said he repeats to himself. He paused a bit, admitting that he was paraphrasing, and wouldn't quite get the original verbatim: "Those who fail to learn from the history of the past are doomed to repeat the same mistakes."

"Mistakes" aside, I recognized Woodhead's reference: he was citing George Santayana. Santayana's aphorism was first published in 1905 in his *The Life of Reason*, where we find the text: "Those who cannot remember the past are condemned to repeat it."[30] Wikipedia ("the free encyclopedia that anyone can edit") records this aphorism as one of the most often misquoted "remarks" of all time, and Wikiquote respectfully lists a variety of errors that constitutes the afterlife of the written word, such as:

- Those who cannot learn from history are doomed to repeat it.
- Those who do not remember their past are condemned to repeat their mistakes.
- Those who do not read history are doomed to repeat it.
- Those who fail to learn from the mistakes of their predecessors are destined to repeat them.

Of course, the irony in Woodhead's oral recitation fascinated me because it came from a reenactor who repeats the past as exactly as possible. The standard trouble with orature is here illustrated: it "fails" to repeat exactly. But, is error necessarily failure? When is difference failure, and by what (geohistorical, chronopolitical) standard? And when, in the tracks of live acts, is a misquote or paraphrase a kind of revenant – getting it not so much wrong as getting it "live" in a complex crosshatch of cross-affiliation?

A conundrum presents itself: if repetition is what we're condemned to do if we do not remember adequately, repetition *is also*, at least for Woodhead and compatriots, a mode of remembering – a remembering that, somehow, might place history's mistakes at hand, as if through repeated enactment we could avoid . . . repetition. If Santayana distinguished "remember" from "repeat," and if (as in a game of telephone in which Aristotle is whispering down the line) the Wikiquote misquotes distinguish "learning" from "repeating," and if Woodhead distinguishes learning from *repeating the same mistakes*, might we say that repetition is what manipulates error in relation to an authenticity that invites, even demands, revision? Repetition with revision is a standard of oral history, and a standard that does not link difference always already to failure and loss. Thinking musically, we can remember that jazz "standards," for instance, are not all written by jazz musicians and not automatically registers of loss – a topic we will return to in subsequent chapters. Perhaps the stakes in history's mistakes are, as acknowledged in orature, as much a matter of the event as of the event re-membered, the event passed on. In this view, as in Aristotle's, learning is a *matter* of working through mimesis – always already a generative matter of mistake.

Woodhead himself is an accomplished bugler and on the faculty of the National Civil War Field Music School. Though we did not talk about his music, I wondered about using musicality versus documentary or object evidence as ways of thinking about reenactment. Let's consider the tune "Taps" – a tune that was played at the close of many of the reenactments I witnessed, including the 1863 Culps Hill Battle of 1999. The tune played is the same tune each time. That is: "Taps" *is* "Taps."

When a bugler plays "Taps," he or she plays *it* – the tune is not considered a "copy" of "Taps." Even if poorly played by a less than accomplished bugler, the tune, if recognizable at all, even through errors, *is* "Taps." That is, in playing music one does not (or does not only) *represent* playing it, which is not to say that music is never mimetic, but that the act of playing music is not, or not only, mimetic of music. Though one may be posing "as if" a Civil War bugler while playing, and arguably *representing* the Civil War, one is simultaneously *making* the music. The same goes for representing eating salt pork in a faux Civil War camp as well as, and simultaneously, engaging in the actual act of eating it. Both are true – real *and* faux – action *and* representation – and this both/and is the beloved and often discussed conundrum of theatricality in which the represented bumps uncomfortably (and ultimately undecideably) against the affective, bodily instrument of the real.

The question for theatre, as for reenactment, becomes: how do we ever confidently arbitrate the differences, especially when the frame is less than strictly delineated? The differences or the *lack* of differences between faux and real might not necessarily be failures or threats to the project of accessing, remembering, crossing the path of the past. With no proscenium arch, or theatrical black box, or even audience (at some reenactments) to provide the function of a frame reminding "this is only theatre," or "just pretend," or "merely play,"[31] the "period rush" reenactors' reference can function like a queasy portal in time where a momentary forgetting might take place, where time and space seem to come undone, or overlap and *touch* to the point of confluence. To the point, perhaps, of habit – where habit is an act or set of acts learned so well they become *body* knowledge, though acquired through sometimes quite arduous rigors of what Bergson calls "effort" or "search."[32] One learns to ride a bike, or learns to play the bugle, so that the skills acquired can become in-body habit. Forgetting is oddly a kind of prize at the end of the day – a skill, the hard-won step in the work of learning that enables becoming. When some things, like reading, *or even modes of critical thinking or patterns of analysis*, become habit-memory, they are skills, fully learned, available to call up as research tools or artistic craft. Sometimes skills or habits of knowing have to be unlearned, so that others can be acquired. For instance: a dancer deeply trained in classical ballet who wants to take up tae kwon do has to un-learn some habits of physical orientation. For instance: to approach time as potentially recurring, a scholar must suspend ingrained socio-cultural approaches to time as singularly linear and try to think outside of well-worn habits of thought. Or, for instance: to know something experiential about marching for days in snow or sleet, one has to at least momentarily suspend the habit of relying on plumbing, heating, dry clothing.

For battle reenactors, the act of putting their physical bodies into the (imaginative) picture, yields often unexpected results. In any case, according to Mike "Dusty" Chapman, of Virginia's Stonewall Brigade (and an accountant at the National Gallery of Art): "I'm not there to have a good time. I'm there to learn and be miserable."[33] Wargasm, apparently, is not necessarily blissful, even though it is full-on bodily engagement. As S. Chris Anders, a member of the Chesapeake Volunteer Guard, told Dan Zak of the *Washington Post:* "We've done picket post events where we've stood in the snow all night long in five-degree temperatures

[. . .] It's about having a deeper understanding. Today, everybody lives in climate-controlled environments with very little physical labor, for the most part, and you tend to *lose touch* with history in situations like that."[34] In an affective reverie, troubling the archive-driven tracks of a strictly linear approach to time, and manipulating the pitfalls and promises of anachronism like so many notes on a bugle, reenactors use their bodies to chase moments of forgetting where something learned (about time) becomes something played (in time), and where something played can touch or generate experience, even if "only for a minute."

If the Civil War played is not *the* Civil War again – or, not exactly – still, the war played may be recognizable, circling around the past event, or jumping and sticking like a misquote of Santayana reminds us of Santayana, or a riff on a tune that, as in jazz, brings a precedent melody into play through improvisation often *off* note. The travels of Santayana's 1905 aphorism showing up, as it did, at the 1999 re-event of the 1863 battle of Gettysburg, begs an account of the generative cross-temporal travels of error, and the generative cross-temporal errors of travel. We "remember" Santayana's quote as the tracks of the misquote circle the authentic, riff the original, and, perhaps more like orature than like literature (unless one approaches literature as embodied), illuminate its afterlife as live. To repeat: it's not so much gotten wrong, as gotten live, in an ambulatory againness. As Wikipedia offers, Santayana's aphorism is correctly remembered as often misremembered – or, in remembering the aphorism, we remember, as I did on the Civil War battlefield with Woodhead, the *error* that becomes the aphorism's history. The history of the quote, like history itself, must always already account for, and be an account of, error. Considering "mistakes of history," implied by Santayana's word "condemned," and continuing in the vein of conundrum: wouldn't remembering history's mistakes necessitate wrestling with mistakes in the remembering? And what does remembering mistake, like mistaken memory, get *right* about history in the replaying? What place should error have in the "faithful" account?

Civil war isn't over: three

Woodhead paraphrasing Santayana brought to mind Marx's famous and often discussed paraphrase in which Marx also can't quite recall an original. In *The Eighteenth Brumaire of Louis Bonaparte*, written in 1852, Marx wrote: "Hegel says somewhere that all great historic facts and personages recur twice. He forgot to add: 'Once as tragedy, and again as farce.'" Leaving aside the proto-Wikipedian editing, or the parodic ventriloquy Marx performs on Hegel, Marx makes explicit the theatricality in any venture we come to call (historical) event – such as revolution. I chose here the De Leon translation (though it arguably mistakes the source) for the conundrum in the phrase "recur twice":

> Hegel says somewhere that all great historic facts and personages *recur twice*. He forgot to add: "Once as tragedy, and again as farce." Caussidière for Danton, Louis Blanc for Robespierre, the "Mountain" of 1848–51 for the "Mountain" of 1793–05 [sic], the Nephew for the Uncle. And the identical

caricature marks also the conditions under which the second edition of the *Eighteenth Brumaire* is issued. Man makes his own history, but he does not make it out of whole cloth; he does not make it out of conditions chosen by himself, but of such as he finds at hand. The tradition of all past generations weighs like an alp upon the brain of the living. At the same time when men appear engaged in revolutionizing things and themselves, in bringing about what never was before, at such very epochs of revolutionary crisis do they anxiously conjure up into their service the spirits of the past, assume their names, their battle cries, their costumes to enact a new historic scene in such time-honored disguise and with such borrowed language.[35]

Lest we too quickly assume that Marx's correction to Hegel's "forgetting" is only, or entirely, dismissive of repetition, we can recall, as Connerton does in *How Societies Remember*, that all events, even the seemingly revolutionary, are composed in citational acts and embodied reperformance of precedent.[36] Reenactment, which Connerton links to incorporation, is a vital mode of collective social remembering, and it can be a critical mode as well as a reiterative mode. Indeed, to return to Marx via Connerton, Marx's use of "tragedy" and "farce" in *Eighteenth Brumaire* points quite explicitly to the always already theatrical in any "great historic fact," as even the "once" of tragedy is, as theatrical form, already a matter of recurrence.

Tracking the publication history of *Eighteenth Brumaire*, Peter Stallybrass argues that Marx is engaging the always already belatedness of events, dependent as they are on representation of the past to forge, as in revolution, something distinguishable as new. Marx's comments, writes Stallybrass, are not entirely pessimistic, nor antitheatrical, as they are often regarded. Tragedy and parody are here both figures for the tracks of reiteration, indeed the *theatricality* necessary to collective action, or, the "twice-behavedness" of any communicative behavior.[37] As Stallybrass notes, acknowledging Marx's profound interest in Shakespeare and in parodic forms generally, "caricature, parody, satire and farce were far from negative forms for Marx." Making of Marx a proto post-structuralist, Stallybrass reads Marx's interest in the double "recurrences" of tragedy and farce as linked to Marx's political engagement in play and replay, or the "settling and unsettling of origins."[38]

Theatricality plays in the sometimes infelicitous realms of the not exactly real. It can be distinguished from performativity where saying something (like "I do" at a wedding) is doing something – where the "real" in the reiterative saying is fully accomplished. Theatrical accomplishments, on the other hand, are always only partial (and for J. L. Austin, always "infelicitous"), riddled with the seeming problem of the false (the problem of *seeming*). And yet, the errors in theatricality (the way the saying is not exactly or not entirely or not completely the doing if we remember the above comments about the simultaneity of the "real" *and* "faux"), are generative of a relationship to history that partakes of the double negative: a reenactment *both* is *and* is not the acts of the Civil War. It is *not not* the Civil War. And, perhaps, through the cracks in the "not not," something cross-temporal, something affective, and something affirmative circulates. Something is touched.

In 1858, in a document unpublished until 1941, Marx wrote that:

> History does nothing; it does not possess immense riches, it does not fight
> battles. It is men, real, living men, who do all this, who possess things and fight
> battles. It is not 'history' which uses men as a means of achieving – as if it were
> an individual person – its own ends. History is nothing but the activity of men
> in pursuit of their ends.[39]

To pursue their ends, to return to Marx's paraphrastic reiteration of Hegel, "men"
submit history to recurrence – with the result that any event is composed in
repetition *for* revision: tragedy, farce, and the like. That is: "History" is itself one
of the things "used" by "real, living men" – and for many of the Civil War
reenactors I spoke with, history is, arguably, the battleground itself. History *is* the
fight. When "men, real, living men" fight *historical* battles again, conscious of
history's necessary composition in recurrence, do they touch something strangely
authentic, strangely real – which is the real of recurrence itself?

I lifted Marx out of the stream of writings on history, on repetition and revision,
because the handy happenstance of his famous paraphrase allows me to ask about
the "somewhere" ("Somewhere Hegel said") where an original takes place in
reiterative difference. But I might have lifted Freud on the reiterative returns of the
forgetful tracks that trauma makes of battlefields as soldiers struggle to experience
for the first time an event that already occurred. Or, for that matter, I could have
lifted the historic personage of Aristotle, for his investment in mimesis as the way
to improve upon history, to get it right next time in difference, after the fact of the
error-ridden first. But this book is less about origins, or which Famous Founding
Father had what great First insight First, than it is about the histories of our
reencounters, and the reencounters with our histories, and what we make of them.
A riff is a repetition of a familiar passage. Because Santayana, Marx, Freud, and
Aristotle have been long in circulation on these topics – all of them writing when
it was "men, real, living men" who published or otherwise archived the work of
men and rarely the work of women – to bring their *passages* into play, to repeat their
words in my words, might be to trouble them with the very theatricality and
repetition they generatively engage. If what we make of them, in making of them
again, is not only about the theatrical, but is theatrical – with all the effeminacies
of error theatricality has historically implied[40] – then it will not be too far afield for
a theatre historian and feminist, such as myself, to replay their questions *slant*. Emily
Dickinson wrote in 1866, three years after the Battle at Gettysburg: "Tell all the
Truth but tell it slant – Success in Circuit lies," suggesting that the roundabout way
such a thing as truth might best be accessed is through circulation – queer of straight
and off center of "fact." Infelicitous, perhaps. Theatrical. Poetic. And in any case,
attending the 1999 1863 battlefield, in the heat of the day and the heat of the battle,
it was precision that was both at stake and, constantly, undone by stray inadequacies: the sideways leaning inquiries of the nattering anachronistic detail. A detail
such as myself. That I was (not) there in 1863, notebook in hand, meant trouble
for any attempt at a fidelity that could not allow for significant slant.

I spoke to Woodhead for some time, and like many "Civil War buffs" (as the "enthusiasts" or "hobbyists" or "reenactors" are often called), he was very helpful, quite thoughtful and smart, and really interested in talking about what compelled him – and this was true of almost all the reenactors with whom I spoke. Yes, they strive to "get it right" and yes, they are after "that *feel* of authenticity." But, Woodhead said, he knew full well that total authenticity was impossible. "One third of us aren't barefoot. One third don't have dysentery." He didn't mention death and dismemberment. He didn't mention feminists from the future, notebooks in hand. Instead he said simply, "We're into keeping the war alive." And he added, "To keep telling the story history leaves out." This was an interesting oral historical argument, and one in line with a sentiment I'd heard more than once in my conversations with reenactors (though Woodhead himself did not say it): the South "really" won, and reenactment (troubled as it was) was the twitching, vibrant, and deeply strange revenant of what *might* have been, yet to come. Like the fictive fact that it is Hamlet's father's ghost who returns to tell a historical "truth" that the record had erased, and like the fictive fact that Hamlet requires players to, through the farce of a clown show, trip the King into account of that truth, the performance event that is battle reenactment is part ghost, part clown, part tragedy, part farce, part hailing, part parting, part reuniting, part coming apart. Always and already vexed, in a crease between times, the affective histories affectively encountered and affectively negotiated are often more than two.

Now he belongs to the stages: one

The second epigraph at the start of this chapter, "Now he belongs to the stages," takes us in a slightly different direction. The phrase makes a joke by way of a purposeful misquote – altering Edwin Stanton's oft-quoted famous words at Lincoln's deathbed: "Now he belongs to the ages." Here, the purposeful misquote underscores the past as given to play, to be played, upon "the stages." The epigraph suggests that the past "now" belongs to the future, perhaps in the way a dramatic script, such as *Hamlet*, is both a product of its author but also exists as a blueprint for future live production(s). Think of the way a footpath is both composed of footprints (traces of past event) and also an index *to the future* with the sedimented (or, perhaps more properly, eroded) suggestion: "walk this way." A footprint is thus a "scriptive thing."[41] Or think of twentieth-century instruction art – such as Yoko Ono's *Fly* – pitched to be taken up and tried. That is, the quote suggests that the past remains rather like a prompt, a script, an instruction, or a "training manual."[42] The past remains both as trace and as a matter for the deferred live of its (re)encounter.

Of course, the motto's very silliness, accompanied on the web by a photo of fifty Lincoln reenactors standing together in a field (with a single Frederick Douglas[43]) in their identical top-hatted, fake-bearded regalia, seems not only to render our inquiry farcical, but to underscore, flagrantly, its composition in *error*. The ribald, joking aspect of the scene seems the flipside of the melancholic structure of what Dana Luciano has termed "the time of Lincoln," referring not only to the historic

Figure 1.2 "Abes in the Grass." A gathering of the Association of Lincoln Presenters, 2006. Photo: Mary Armstrong.

period of Lincoln's presidency and assassination, but to a "transtemporal" mode of affective national belonging that thereupon took shape.[44] It seems the flipside until one recalls, however, the melancholic structure of camp performance that, in a significant way and as a mode of survival and belonging, sincerely eulogizes even as it ironically spoofs.[45]

For the moment, however, let us focus simply on the motto. "Now he belongs to the stages" might remind us not only that all evidence is theatrical (if we take "the stages" as a metonymic reference to theatre), but also that all evidence is deferred in time – encountered at *later stages*. Stages and ages are linked through a shared reference to temporality, with "age" meaning both a "distinct period of history" and "a very long time," and "stage" meaning "a point, period, or step in a process" as well as "a raised floor or platform, typically in a theater, on which actors, entertainers, or speakers perform" (*Oxford American Dictionary*). Why stages? Why not canvases, or pedestals, or *pages*? Clearly, there is more to the error "stages" than the felicity of the rhyme.

Though a close reading of the Lincoln Presenters' motto may seem to fall far afield the realm of historical authenticity in any shape or form, the matter of clowning, as of mimicry, is at the heart of the contest over whether historical reenactment touches anything viable or legitimate in the matter of historical record. And though the Association of Lincoln Presenters purposefully claim the appellation "presenters" rather than "impersonators" or "reenactors,"[46] the humor in their appearances together as multiples points to some of the problems that attend history reenactment generally. Recall, as mentioned above, Vanessa Agnew's disparaging argument that reenactment "eclipses the past with its own theatricality." Such phrasing causes one to wonder if the theatricality that "eclipses" is actually a kind of revenant, part of history returned – a kind of immaterial artifact, even. After all, Agnew writes that it is the past's "own" theatricality that threatens, somehow, through reenactment. Is she referring to the past's own composition in recurrence, and a recurrence not only performative in nature but engaged in the infelicities and strident errors of farce, parody, and caricature? This kind of conundrum might suggest that to render the past in and through "theatricality" would be to get something right, touch something actual, something even authentic about it. If it was theatrical *then*, should it not be remembered theatrically *now?* And yet, of course, it is theatricality that Agnew disparages as always already excessive, whether that theatricality belongs to the past as the past's own, or belongs to the reenactors who try to touch it – or, much more complicatedly, belongs *between* the two as a vehicle for syncopated time. In all cases, and sticky with Platonic affect or sentiment, theatricality appears to threaten the Ideality of the authentic – *even if the authentic had always already been theatrical.*

In fact, living history professionals, such as those who work at sites like Colonial Williamsburg, labor hard to segregate reenactment from "theatre," because theatre, almost invariably being associated with debased sentiment and, therefore, fantasy, appears to negate any claim to authenticity.[47] As Scott Magelssen records a Colonial Williamsburg staff member to say: "Theatre makes [living history] play. Pretend. Not real."[48] The Williamsburg staff member Magelssen cites is likely not a member of the ALP. The Lincoln Presenters are well aware, as their motto suggests, of the sometimes creepy crawlspace between the so-called theatrical and the so-called real. After all, they "present" Abraham Lincoln, a man who read and reread Shakespeare and attended the theatre consistently – literally to the very end. In 1863, a month after 50,000 died at Gettysburg, Lincoln wrote in a letter to actor James Hackett: "Unlike you gentlemen of the profession, I think the soliloquy in *Hamlet* commencing 'O, my offense is rank' surpasses that commencing 'To be or not to be.'"[49] Lincoln's preference for the imposter-father Claudius's speech, though probably not born of identification, might surprise those who would prefer to keep their Lincoln for Hamlet, or for whom a confederate Hamlet might "rub." At the very least we here see Lincoln navigating the touch between "fiction and friction," to borrow Stephen Greenblatt's words, looking for the swerve or slant of act in relation to event.[50] As Stephen Dickey of the Folger Shakespeare Library has written on a site intended for high school teachers:

> The analogies with Lincoln's own situation – presiding in this case over a national fratricide, agonizing daily over the death toll, and notoriously (perhaps even suicidally) heedless of his own personal safety despite being stalked by

various likely assassins [Hamlet hovers behind Claudius in the scene] – are too obvious to miss. Indeed, we would do well, I think, not to congratulate ourselves over discovering something secret here, but rather to assume that Lincoln himself perceived such analogies as clearly as anyone.[51]

Or perhaps the issue is not that Lincoln liked Shakespeare but that America – in history and literature classrooms — has liked its Lincoln Shakespearean, a sentiment spurred by Lincoln's own writing style as well as by the "tragedy" of the Civil War. Either way the tangle of theatricality and history makes a hard knot to untie, and a union too bound to simplistically dismiss.[52] As Adam Gopnik has written:

> Shakespeare suits liberal violence, with its corrupted currents, admirable ambition, and casual slaughters – and what makes Lincoln [. . .] admirable, if not heroic, is that [he] knew it.[53]

Now he belongs to the stages: two

To return to the clownish motto of the ALP, serving over 100 members who claim to be "the busiest dead guys on the planet"[54]: it is the rhyming word "stages" rather than a choice for the rhyme of "pages" that makes the motto a joke.[55] "Pages" would simply reference history as we conventionally accept it, whereas theatre is (not surprisingly nor even incorrectly) debased for all the bodily (and bawdy) error it potentially includes.[56] And yet, what is it we accept when accepting history in the pages? Stanton's statement "Now he belongs to the ages," reprinted as fact in many a high school textbook, may be the "most famous epitaph in American biography," and one "engraved in every American mind" – and yet, as Gopnik tracks the phrase for its history, he finds instead a tangled web of quote and re-quote and re-re-quote with nothing definitive at the core – nothing definitive *except* that "something like" these words were said.[57] The quote, that is, has *always* belonged to the stages.

Let us rehearse the scene. The words "Now he belongs to the ages" were the words Edwin Stanton, Lincoln's Secretary of War, said at Lincoln's deathbed. Or, were they? Some historians claim that Stanton's words were actually: "Now he belongs to the angels." The ideological stakes, of course, between belonging to History ("ages") or to Heaven ("angels") spells out a consistent American fault line that, perhaps, adds another kind of poignancy to the ALP motto. There is no absolute proof that Stanton said "ages," nor absolute proof that Stanton said "angels." In an age before mechanical recording, what was said and what was not said was a matter of oral account and belated reiteration – often contesting reiterations. Exploring the tracks of this quote, Gopnik, who takes us deeply into Lincoln's love for Shakespeare, searches for clues as to which – "angels" or "ages" – might have been what Stanton *really* said. But after looking in the Bible and in the Bard, as well as in the voluble stack of history books on all aspects of Lincolnalia, Gopnik decides to visit the very small room in which Lincoln died and try to account, as a reenactor might, for the *physical experience* of being there. His account is worth reprinting, as it illustrates, I think, something about what the error (or the "befoggedness") in reenactment perhaps gets right:

> As the queue inches forward and I can see, at last, into the room that I have been reading about [. . .] I want to laugh. This place isn't small; it's tiny. They brought him here, to this back room, I had learned, because all the other rooms in the house were too messy for a President to die in, and yet: four people would make it crowded; six would overwhelm it; the forty or so who passed in and out, and the ten or twenty who crowded inside at the end would have turned it into the stateroom scene in "A Night at the Opera."
>
> In the brief moment given to each visitor to look inside, I wished for a machine that would be able to re-create every breath of air, every vibration that ever took place in a room. And then I knew that we probably would not have understood any better had we been standing there than we do now. Stanton was weeping, Lincoln had just died, the room was overwhelmed, whatever he said was broken by a sob – the sob, in a sense, is the story. History is not an agreed-on fiction but what gets made in a crowded room; what is said isn't what's heard, and what is heard isn't what gets repeated. Civilization is an agreement to keep people from shouting "Fire!" in a crowded theatre, but the moments we call historical occur when there is a fire in a crowded theatre; and then we all try to remember afterward when we heard it, and if we ever really smelled smoke, and who went first, and what they said. The indeterminacy is built into the emotion of the moment. The past is so often unknowable not because it is befogged now but because it was befogged then, too, back when it was still the present. If we had been there listening, we still might not have been able to determine exactly what Stanton said. All we know for sure is that everyone was weeping, and the room was full.[58]

The sick or incredible way you feel: one

In the third epigraph at the start of this chapter, Miranda July tells us that "straight things" – common things that at first pass as natural or accidental – become reenactment when recognized as composed in code, as always already a matter of reiteration.

> I reenact things you've seen a million times before. Straight things, TV things, and medical things: These are the transactions that we all participate in and memorize accidentally. Then I wiggle my hand and wink and you know that everything I just said was in code, and the real truth is the sick or incredible way you feel.[59]

This July quote, lifted from the Lesbian magazine *Curve*, is perhaps most applicable to July's early performance work such as *Love Diamond* (1998–2000) and *Swan Tool* (2000–2). These were pieces July called "live movies" (as opposed to performance art) and they included a great deal of mimetic interaction with screened images.

The quote suggests that enactment becomes recognized as reenactment, recognized as a matter of againness, through explicit theatricality. Something in the everyday, taken for present and authentic, assumed as a singular and "true" occurrence, can slip out of synch with itself by virtue of even the most minor acknowledgement of its composition in repetition. Here a "wiggle" of a hand or a "wink" of an eye are stray details, theatrical gestures that give the scene away, prompting the recognition that seemingly discrete acts are never temporally singular nor straightforward but double, triple, or done "a million times before." As such, theatricality, prompting recognition of againness, oddly prompts the returns of history in that it prompts recognition of recurrence.

We might say that July is performing the opposite action of Civil War reenactors. If Civil War reenactors try to trip the historical tale into a "now time" experience, July attempts to flip the real of "straight things" that we participate in everyday into a sense of historicity – underscoring their composition in precedent, their status as "living history." Of course, this "flip" of temporalities, occasioned in both directions by a manipulation of theatricality, prompts a kind of "ontological queasiness"[60] – or, in July's words, "the sick or incredible way you feel."

The "sick or incredible way you feel" can move in multiple directions. As discussed, July accesses the queasiness of the moment when that which passes for original, natural, and real is exposed as (also) a matter of repetition. But in another register, history reenactors similarly refer to the queasiness they get on the flipside of the fake. That is, battle reenactors chase the overtly citational until it hits a point they speak of as "magic" and appears to cross from the theatrical (the pose *as if* back in time) to the actual (back in time). Many reenactors describe "special times" when "it seems really real" or when "you feel you have gone back in time and you are reliving a brief moment of history when it becomes real for an instant."[61] Either way – into the real via theatricality with battle camp reenactors, or out of the real via theatricality with campy performance art – the double at the limen provokes the quease.

In the course of attending Civil War reenactments I interviewed many different types of people, from reenactors who hoped to literally and actually travel in time, to those who came to observe the trip, to those who hoped to interact with history without leaving the present.[62] Interviews revealed that a relationship between striking the pose and being the thing so posed (or acting the part and being the part so acted), held for many (participants and observers alike) a fluid or at least indeterminate capacity – a being in uncertainty, a being toward becoming, or unbecoming. Most were curious, some were dogmatic, but everyone I spoke with was deeply excited by their collective investment in a possibility: the possibility of time redoubling, returning in fractured or fugitive moments of affective engagement. And though some I spoke with did fight for "Southern justice," many more fought simply for the *feel* of fighting, the *feel* of encampment, content that in the long run the Northern cause would (appear to) prevail (again).[63]

The *feel* – the affective engagement – is key. As stated earlier, reenactors who claim to experience a physical collapse of time, or at least a profound confusion of time – call their experience a "period rush," a "time warp," a "wargasm" (deeply troubling word), or they borrow a phrase from the Civil War itself to say they are "seeing the elephant."[64] It is important to note, however, that for most reenactors any experience of temporal return is, at best, partial and incomplete.[65] Most seemed deeply eager not to come off as ignorant of history, or as "bumbling idiot senti-mentalists," as one interviewee put it, or "nostalgia-heads" as another laughingly said. I encountered two equally prevalent modes for redressing the criticism reenactors feel is continually leveled at them (they are very aware and often concerned about the general perception that they are naïve): either they deny any claim to be historians, thereby hoping to escape the accusation that they produce bad history, or they defend the validity of their historio-mimesis by citing "extensive and rigorous research." Most claim that they aim for what "book history" misses – live experience – and some say their live experience informs their understanding of what they "also read" in books. When I have asked what "live" means, I've been generally offered a version of "here, now," meaning that reenactment is a form of "then, there" translated to "here, now." When I've asked whether time actually recurs for them, I've been told "yes" more than once, but "no" just as many if not more times. The status of experience varies across participants and the investment in the verity of time travel varies as well. With both yeas and nays to the question of time's actual (though always partial) return, I found a far more consistent sense across participants that whether or not time actually recurred, time did seem to bend, and almost all acknowledged a kind of touch or whisper or "shiver" of time seemingly gone ajar. Interestingly, this was an experience that most often occurred unexpectedly at a minor moment or in relation to a stray, unanticipated detail.

Beside the point

I myself stumbled over an unanticipated detail that tripped me into a kind of queasiness. At a Civil War reenactment on June 4, 2005, at Chase Farm in Lincoln, Rhode Island (a site too far north for any *real* historical precedent, meaning that reenactors were crossing time and space), I came across a severed forefinger lying alone in a field. Though not at all in the head-space of a reenactor, I was brought up short and had to gasp coming upon this severed index lying forgotten and left behind. I also had to laugh, but only after the initial moment of shock when faux finger passed for forefinger – or when the precise jointure between the two was not yet decided. Of course, such a gasp seems completely silly, utterly farcical, with any hindsight. Still, for a minor and brief moment, I was actually somewhat confused, not expecting this bit of digital detritus, and the confusion itself, over a stray bit of banality, captured for me, even as I thought about it later, something of the "more than I bargained for" nature of the entire event. A digital image of this encounter now graces the paperback cover of this book as if to *point*, troubled index, at the trace of the future of the past.

At this particular reenactment there were likely more witnesses than cross-dressing reenactors over the course of the weekend's entire event. But because reenactors often camped in the space, and spent entire days there, the witnesses who came and went more frequently seemed to pass though the space like ghosts

Figure 1.3 Faux finger. Chase Farm Civil War reenactment, Lincoln, RI. June 4, 2005. Photo: Rebecca Schneider.

from the future. Because of this passing by, there were often fewer witnesses than reenactors at any one time.[66] I came upon the finger lying on the ground at a lull in an afternoon, between battles, where fewer witnesses seemed to be about. I found the finger some distance to the side of a faux surgeon's faux tent where a faux soldier lay in faux pain as his faux leg was faux sawed off. This finger must have been from some operation earlier that day. It had missed the bucket of faux blood by the surgeon's side, to which it must have been tossed, and I barely saw it as others, milling around between battles, passed it by. To tell it like it happened, I ended up sitting on the ground beside the bloody point, contemplating its farcical detrital gesture for quite some time. I must have cut an odd figure hunched there, as others shuffled past between the parking lot, the surgeon's tent, and the Civil War to witness something they considered "the event." But for a moment this impasse seemed to me, sitting there as I was, a bit lost in the field, to be the point of the event. Not that I could translate what the point might "really" mean, nor what it pointed toward or away from – before or ahead, ahead or behind. Or to the side.

One of the reenactors I had spoken with earlier that morning was just back from Iraq where he has been in medical service. Hobbling about the surgeon's scene on crutches (with a wound whose "reality status" I could not ascertain), he told me that he felt that *this* war was "more real" to him. This war, I asked? Did he mean 1863? "It was a truer war, one worth keeping alive," he said – but the two wars, and the multiple times, were difficult to sever in our conversation.

In fact, most people I spoke with reflected on the horrific aspects of war – aspects which seemed to me to bind participants together in some way – and more than once, as if to head off condescension at the pass, I was delivered the following mantra in a tone of "We know, we know":

> Of course we know that *our pain is relative* – none of us really die, and no one is badly hurt, one third of us do not have dysentery, most of us are much older than the average soldier's age, etc., etc., etc.

But aside from the obligatory delivery of this mantra to outsiders, no one I spoke with seemed too deeply troubled by the persistence of inevitable error – the error of "relative" pain – of being *related*, but not *the thing itself*. And while the effort to erase as much anachronism as possible was enormous – and the lengths were often great to which reenactors went to shield the present from view, from sensation, from effect, from access – still, the persistent leaky drip of the present into their efforts to touch the past was not enough to thwart their enthusiasm. Indeed, though the persistent reminders of the twentieth (then, twenty-first) century were a problem, they were only as much of a problem as the mosquitoes in the evenings or the throngs of hovering no-see-ums in the heat of the mid-afternoons. To most, the present and the past were *both* possessed of leaky valves, the drip fed *both* ways (and probably more besides, as the Iraq War veteran testified), and so the effort to undo error was not overly troubled by error's inevitability. Error could be, in fact, *the way through* to success: the error of the past in the now was twin to the error of the now in the past. Error itself, that is, became "as if" when the double drip of time began to complicate, to render slippery, the solid-state habit of thinking or experiencing time as a singularly linear, progressive march. If, in any gathering of reenactors, the first few cross-(temporal)-dressers seem anachronistic, across the stretch of a long afternoon or multi-day reenactment the garb of the present could also come to seem in error. Which error, in such a setting, can be seen as more erroneous becomes a matter of parsing the errors – not parsing the truths. And this, in itself, beckons a kind of instruction about time and its inadequacies, authenticity and its promiscuities, that without question can boggle the mind of any true believer in the linearity of time. The trouble with reenactment, it seems, is its capacity to flummox those faith-keepers who hold that the present is fleeting and entirely self-identical, or who hold that the movement from the present to the future is never by way of the past, or who believe firmly in absolute disappearance and loss of the past as well as the impossibility of its recurrence.

Relative pain

Anachronism is at least a two-way street, with possibly more counter-directions than two. Because the manipulation of anachronism is the very stuff of the art or act of reenactment, it can never be entirely banished from the project at hand – a fact that reenactors know intimately. An example might suffice: I have been repeatedly surprised by the kind of exuberance I witnessed when, at the end of several of the battle reenactments I observed, the various cadavers strewn about the field would get up, dust off, and, quite simply, *return to camp.* They did this without the dismay of failure (that is, they did not seem dismayed that they had not achieved the status of "real" cadavers!). In fact, on the contrary, they rose up with a surprisingly exultant joy. Spectators often cheered as the tired corpses, clearly pleased with themselves, ambled off to everyday life (albeit everyday camp life on the front in the 1860s). The image of 50 or 100 or 200 or 500 dead getting up and dusting off was powerful, and the sensation surprised me, provoking me to ask myself: "What did I think I was seeing?" And "Why did I not expect or foresee this?" And "Why does this obvious failure feel instead like success?" It was not that I, for a single moment, had thought that the reenactors were "really" dead – I had never thought that – it was just that I did not expect the simplicity, the gentle awkwardness of the collective climb to knees, to feet, and back to upright. Nor the strange satisfaction in the slow progress of the troops of the dead, now tired, to camp.

Obviously, there is no curtain or jump-cut on the battlefield to shield participants from the moment between the completion of the feigned death and the actor's resurrection for the curtain call. Still, the "get up" caused a kind of surprise. Indeed, the resurrection – the moment of error when the dead (again) acknowledge that (again) they are not dead (again) – took on a valence hard to describe. It was a moment to imagine not just "as if" (as if dead) but "what if": what if the actual dead on the actual battlefields of the actual Civil War had actually gotten up from their dead bodies and also returned to camp, or continued to walk across the centuries to meet the future (again) in some ghostly way? It was this kind of question (admittedly creepy, and not the stuff of "solid" inquiry) that was the "more than I had bargained for" aspect of witnessing these re-events. Clearly, the reenactors wanted to touch something they deemed authentic, real, and actual in experience – something about fighting and falling on the field that would be other than what they could glean from textual accounts, photographic images, or watching film actors reenacting on screen. They wanted to *experience it for themselves* and add to their historical acumen by way of their own physical engagement. But, despite the force of their drive to authenticity, they wanted to return *live* from the battlefield. Of course they did. What did I expect? In any case, precisely what they brought with them upon their return-to-the-now was now, for me, an open question.

The determination of what are acceptable levels of error vary from reenactment regiment to regiment, as does the rigor of investment in authenticity. In his 1999 *Confederates in the Attic: Dispatches from the Unfinished Civil War*, Tony Horwitz wittily narrates the escapades of "hard core" reenactors – those who seek, with religious zeal, an "absolute fidelity to the 1860s: its homespun clothing, antique speech patterns, sparse diet and simple utensils." The hardcore have their own nickname for more mainstream reenactors. They call them "farbs," short for fabricators. In describing the intensity of attention to detail, and the force of mental and physical focus among the hardcore, Horwitz tells us that hardcore reenactors engage in "method acting," but he also relates that more mainstream reenactors (the farbs) generally fear that method acting, taken to the extreme, would become "performance art":

> [T]he hardcore faith, taken to its fundamentalist extreme, would turn the hobby into a *performance art* that no one would want to watch – much less participate in. "They're pushing the envelope in terms of authenticity," the *Camp Chase Gazette* editor, Bill Holschuh, told me [. . .]. "About the only thing left is live ammunition and Civil War diseases. I hope it doesn't come to that."[67]

In fact, like Horwitz, those who write on reenactment often find themselves navigating a spectrum of reference to theatre (method acting, performance art) on the one hand and religion (fundamentalist or mainstream) on the other, with "history" sitting somewhere, and often quite uncomfortably, in between.

The issue of authenticity in these battles is vexed. More than one reenactor, even those who claimed to be experts in period history, spoke of "simpler times." Many are apparently convinced that in the 1860s "women were women and men were men" – willfully ignoring the historical facts of gender crossing and the far from simple tangle of gender with racialization in the antebellum and wartime states. When I mentioned this in discussion with a number of interviewees at a reenactment in Connecticut in 2004 I sparked a heated argument and was kicked out of the sutler's tent where I was conducting the interview. The fight to get the times right – to *touch* the Civil War – was for many an effort to go back to an idealized time, and the drive to authenticity was a drive to an authenticity that *should have been*, according to reenactors' interpretations, not necessarily an authenticity that was. But any drive to "authenticity" will automatically be vexed, necessarily including strained and awkward attempts at mimesis – the *authenticity* of *mimesis* – such as blackface minstrel routines in the camp among white reenactors (attempting to authentically mime period acts of deliberate inauthenticity), or women cross-dressing as male soldiers and needing – even in the twenty-first century – to *pass*.[68] Elizabeth Young writes of the case of Lauren Cook Burgess who brought a law suit against the United States Department of Interior when she was banned from participating in reenactments after being discovered cross-dressing as male at an Antietam Reenactment in August 1989.[69] She won her case, but her case made it clear at the time that despite the fact that women had cross-dressed and passed as men during the war itself, and despite the record of cross-dressing women soldiers at Antietam, reenactment communities often want a history sanitized of troublesome "error," *even if those errors were fact*. So, too, writes Cathy Stanton and Stephen Belyea, potential trouble attends black reenactors:

> African American reenactors present no threat to the reenactment community's view of itself or of American history so long as they are depicting qualities such as gallantry, loyalty, martial decorum, and other "bedrock"

values. But when black reenactors' presence or discourse brings questions of race and morality to the fore, they inevitably disturb a community that prefers to avoid such issues and interpretations. [. . .] No matter how compatible they may be in many ways, they still represent moral and social dilemmas that most white reenactors have tried to expunge from their depictions of the Civil War.[70]

"Reenactment," then, is not *one* thing in relation to the past, but exists in a contested field of investment across sometimes wildly divergent affiliations to the question of what constitutes fact. Clearly, the inevitable errors in (contested) authenticity mean that even though a reenactive action might "touch" the past, as any "again" can be said to do, that touch is not entirely co-identical to the past nor itself unembattled. It is both/and – not *one* thing. Another way in which reenactment is not *one* thing, but always at least double, is illustrated in the multiplicity of descriptors that attempt to articulate the actions. Is it theatre? Is it art? Is it history? Is it religion? Sport? Hobby? Pastime? Education? Heritage? Commemoration? While such questions can arguably be asked of any art form or expressive activity (lines of medial or disciplinary distinction are never completely discrete), the intensity of the blur can be quite high in reenactment practices. For instance, just before the reenactment of the Culps Hill Battle at Gettysburg, Pennsylvania in 1999, I walked up to a large tent beside the battlefield and joined a gathered crowd for what I took to be a "living history" performance. It was open to the public, but most men and

Figure 1.4 A renewal of vows at the Gettysburg, PA, Civil War Reenactments, 1999.
Photo: Rebecca Schneider.

women in attendance were dressed in Civil War garb indicating that they were reenactors rather than spectators (or possibly spectators reenacting spectators). It took me a little while to figure out what was going on, but once I realized that it was a wedding, I was riveted. In fact, this was both a wedding *and* a reenactment of a historical wedding, and to complicate matters, the participants (Bob and Betty Fox) were already married but were ("for real") renewing their vows from their own wedding.

It was palpable that for the Foxes, cross-temporality added to the verity and the depth of their claims and underscored the security they felt in their commitment(s). The more "then," for them, then the more now. But I had to wonder what became of time: when the congregation reenacted prayer, were they also "really" praying? To be sure, when the vows were reenacted, they were also (according to Mr. and Mrs. Fox) really taken. Time was then *and* it was now as the minister said (again): "What God has joined together let no man tear asunder." There is something of temporal slippage and temporal fold here that trips us fully into the paradox that the actual – *to be actual* – is a negotiation of reactualization, the enacted a matter of negotiating reenactment. For these participants there was no temporal quandary: their re-wedding would be one and more: then and then and now and then now again. And while this is "Performativity 101," the blatancy of it at the Foxes *re-re-do* at the camp altar of "I do," sent my own head spinning – even as the reredo, in all its civic religiosity, seemed to offer a deep peace of mind to the Foxes and their family.

After the wedding – wherein happening upon a performance I mistook to be "only" performance I had, as witness, unwittingly taken responsibility for the health of the vows of Bob and Betty Fox[71] – I went to the bleachers on the edge of the very large field to await the (re)start of the Battle at Culps Hill. I was thinking, to be honest, that there might be something more comforting in battle than in marriage. But the battle I "saw" again also threw my role as witness into some question.

I sat in the bleachers with about 250 other spectators. It was a blisteringly hot day. The battle was set for 4 p.m., but many of us were there well in advance, and most had been there all day and many for several days. The 97th Regimental String Band played and sang as if to ease the heat, and their song underscored the difficulty of fully forgetting, or severing, present-day meaning from prior-day language – except that the crowd, singing along, all seemed more than content to let the double resonance ring:

> We'll all be gay when Johnny comes marching home [. . .]
> All the Ladies will turn out when Johnny comes marching home [. . .]

I offer a brief section of my field notes here, by way of accounting for my own queasiness at the event, my own engagement with the undecideabllity of *what was happening*, and the difficult question of what was being recalled and what forgotten, *when* and *where*:

Field Notes:

Hot – maybe 98 degrees Fahrenheit – and terrifically humid. Lots of folks seem to be giving up and going away. At 3:30 a pickup with a cannon on the back crosses the field – they must be getting it into position. An ambulance, too, drives to the edge of the field and waits. In this heat, apparently, "real" heart attacks can easily happen when overweight, middle-aged enthusiasts don wool and run with heavy weapons and other tack.

There is an announcement: "Ladies and Gentlemen, the battle has been delayed 1/2 hour. There's been an accident out in Emmetsville Road and some of the people who we need to be here aren't here yet." The family behind me on the bleachers switches their conversation to complain about the delay. "We've been here in the heat being 'real'– why can't they?" I think about the implications of this statement – for this family, the reenactors won't begin being real until they begin to reenact.

An overweight woman three rows down has brought a battery-operated fan/squirt gun. She's spritzing herself and her equally overweight companion. A young man behind her, under his mother's umbrella, reads *1000 Things You Should Know About the Civil War*. Time passes. The bandleader appeases the emptiness of time in advance of the "reality" about to take place. He asks over the loudspeaker: How many Yankees do we have here? A yay from the crowd. How many Rebels? Another yay.

The men behind me and to my left begin talking about ghosts. At first one tells about a woman in his church who claimed to have "experiences." They said that it was weird, odd, strange. But then, after ridiculing the woman, they began to tell their own "experiences." One tells of his Grandma – seeing her in his bedroom after she'd died. And then another story pours out – his wife's grandfather's legs . . . I can't catch it all.

At five minutes of four we begin to see troops advancing in the distance. Over the loudspeaker the announcer offers a history lesson of the war leading up to Gettysburg. Numbers drop like beads of sweat. 75,000 Confederates; 95,000 Union; 80,000 animals. He tells us about the logistics of the campaign: 80,000 gallons of water a day. This lesson is long – people fade in and out. Folks in the audience exchange tidbits of fact – what they know about what the announcer says. The army continues to advance — but it is very hard to see. I think it's the Union – but I can't be sure. They are about a quarter-mile away, and they are not marching toward us, but toward a large wood at the other end of the field: Culp's Hill. They're marching *further* away. It takes them a long time. I look at the audience as much as at the field. The bleachers fall below me in a sea of T-shirt slogans: San Diego Zoo; Lone Lake Lodge; a back with "All the Flags of the World"; Barefoot Bobs; and a slew of Football teams.

The announcer tells us that Dr. Somebody, whose doctoral dissertation was on this very battle at Culp's Hill, will take us through the reenactment itself. Facts begin to roll over the loudspeaker again, like the footprints we might have heard had we been closer. "20,000 casualties in three hours at Culp's Hill." We're asked to imagine the soldiers. The Professor says: If we think *we're* hot, imagine these soldiers. And the weather today is almost exactly what it was." Almost.

Then suddenly the guns begin and the Professor falls silent.

I am amazed to note that the soldiers are entirely in the woods and we cannot see them at all. Some on the bleachers have binoculars, but most do not. Given that there is nothing to spectate, everyone is surprisingly attentive.

Maybe twenty minutes in, a horse without a rider gallops out the woods and heads toward the ambulance. We can hear gunshot and muffled yelling.[72] We see puffs of smoke.

I don't know quite what I'm seeing, I think. That's not true, I tell myself: I'm seeing puffs of smoke. Again I don't feel like a spectator (there's nothing to see), but am I a witness to the nothing I see? What I'm witnessing is a mystery to me. Whatever it is, I can't see it. This event, it's very clear, is not given for me or to me, nor does it concern my ability to see. It is taking place elsewhere. I am a witness *to* the elsewhere of the event, and is that, in part, the reality that is touched here?? Elsewhere goes on, here and now?

I begin to stare at a woman in front of me. I could reach out and touch her but I do not. I am riveted by her large handbag. The bag has the words, over and over again in faux Louis Vuitton style: Cherokee Cherokee Cherokee Cherokee Cherokee Cherokee Cherokee.

Nowhere, at any Civil War reenactment I have attended so far, has the issue of "Indian Removal" or "Trail of Tears" – a veritable entr'acte for the Civil War itself – been anywhere recounted. Except here, on this faux European knock-off, among the detrital ghosts from the future. Who more properly owns the twitching inconsolable after-affects? The actors or the onlookers? And who is on which side of what? Where are the secessionists? Where the union? Which are the terrorists? Which the terrorized?

I begin to feel dizzy, and literally sick.

As the chant of the Cherokee Cherokee Cherokee branded handbag reminded me, the phrase "of course we know our pain is relative" can buckle and multiply.[73] The problem of transgenerational memory becomes a matter of account: with whom do we affiliate? To whom do we attribute event? Who do we count among associates? Among ancestors? Who among generations? Who within history? Who without? Of course, we know, our pain is *relatives*.

The hauntingness of history, its literal in-bodied articulation, the boisterous and rattling ghosts of ancestors, and the queasy "something living" of the pastness of the past, return us to the transmission of affect in the jumping and sticky viscosity of time.[74] I remark again on the oddness of traveling to a site to sit in bleachers to *see* the Civil War in all its theatrically blooded againness only to find that what I had traveled to see was not to be seen – happening "authentically" in the woods. What I saw instead was literal *distance*. And distance was not wrong. But what I also saw with a kind of shock of proximity was not what I'd expected to find, nor where I'd expected to find it. Like the finger in the field and the "wound" of the war veteran returned from Iraq, the minor detail of the commodity handbag – a container for personal belongings – recalled the resilient strayness, the wanderingness, of events *not* given to account, be they "minor," be they "forgotten," be they too recent, or be they erased from official record. As an intense if unintentional marker of what had been removed from the American South, now seemingly accidental and even seemingly farcical at a re-scene of Southern secession, the Louis Vuitton Cherokee commodity was both anachronistic and not anachronistic at all. It sat still in/as a witness's hands, undecideable, but resolute in its (re)cursive repetition. If the South might win . . . whose South, when?

Afterword

An unattributed notice, published roughly two months into the new millennium in the *Cleveland Plain Dealer* on March 8, 2000, illustrates perfectly the ongoing relation between reenactment, theatre, and the "work in progress" of War. The notice suggests something of the deeply political stakes that haunt "belongings" as our temporal affiliations play out in/on stages. The hazards of temporal return take a certain shape here, despite the promises that "doing it differently" might otherwise appear to afford in seemingly simple or simply straightforward humorous contexts (if humor is ever simple, ever straight, or ever forward). The queasiness of the following might caution us always to recall the masked force of seeming farce:

> Anyone in Cleveland's theatre district around lunchtime yesterday got a taste of the old days as a group of Civil War enthusiasts staged a mock battle to promote the opening of a play about the war. Yesterday, members of the 7th Ohio volunteer Infantry "battled" in the streets for about a half-hour from the Hanna Theatre building to the Palace Theatre, where *The Civil War – The Broadway Musical* opened yesterday and runs through March 19. Judges declared the winner: This time it was the Confederacy.

2 Finding faux fathers

[. . .] and so the figure, Booth, the murderer [. . .] turns fully toward the audience his face of statuesque beauty, lit by those basilisk eyes, [. . .] launches out in a firm and steady voice the words *sic semper tyrannis* – and then walks with neither slow nor very rapid pace diagonally across to the back of the stage, and disappears.

——Walt Whitman, "Death of Abraham Lincoln," 1879

Booth appears in the room.

——Suzan-Lori Parks, *Topdog/Underdog*, 2002

The task of historical materialism is to set in motion an experience with history original to every new present. It has recourse to a consciousness of the present that shatters the continuum of history. Historical materialism conceives historical understanding as an after-life of what is understood, whose *pulses can still be felt in the present.*

——Walter Benjamin, *One Way Street*, 1928 (emphasis added)

If this chapter begins in the theatre, it does not end in the theatre. But it never leaves the theatre either, though the theatre ceases to be "just pretend" when explored as a vehicle for collective reconstitution of the so-called real. That is, in the undecideable slip and slide between the multiple meanings of "act": to act as to feign, and to act as to do – between "acting" as merely citing and citation as an act – the theatre can turn inside out and all the way around.[1] Traversing the stage at a diagonal, this chapter sets out to think about patricidic culture at the pass.

To begin: in the theatre. When John Wilkes Booth famously uttered the words *sic semper tyrannis* either just before or just after killing Abraham Lincoln, he might have recalled a long line of precedent scenes, including Renaissance actors who, upon Shakespeare's stage, would have played Brutus murdering Julius Caesar, recalling that far more ancient murder, itself already citing precedent.[2] He was, thus, playing empiric patricide backward in the echo-chamber of an auditorium – refinding event in performance where, as Benjamin remarks (though of materialist history), "pulses can still be felt in the present." However, the astute reader will note that in his *Julius Caesar* Shakespeare does not have his character speak what would be recognized later, and surely apocryphally, as Brutus's most famous utterance. Still, as if building anaphors out of gesture, voice, and weapon as well as words, the actor John Wilkes Booth on stage at the Ford would complexly recall multiple precedents: the Roman historical patricide Brutus, Shakespeare's Renaissance character Brutus, his own renowned playing of Brutus, his brother Edwin's playing of Caesar, and the motto of Wilkes' home state of Virginia.[3] And though Shakespeare may not have scripted his Brutus to speak *sic semper tyrannis*, the phrase is now listened for by contemporary audiences. Heard but not sounded, the note that Wilkes hit in the midst of his own theatrical/patricidal act on April 14, 1865, has become a ghost note from the future.

Booth was an actor who would become far more famous for his patricide than for his role play – remembered more for his performative act than for his theatrical performance – and yet the clarity of the pass between "act" and act comes undone, or befogged, in Booth's case, just as it comes undone, as we will explore, between act and "act" in plays that replay his example.[4] Booth's act would become patricide in the future of Lincoln's afterlife as Father, indeed his afterlife as, oddly, "Founding Father." Though President Abraham Lincoln is included in the pantheon of US Founding Fathers in the popular imaginary, famously and repeatedly depicted in painting and in stone beside George Washington, he is perhaps more accurately (if such nominations can bear accuracy) a Re-Founder.[5] Through his role in the War Between the States, a war that required the foundation's "reconstuction," Lincoln (re)founded a "unified nation" poised to continue its empiric grab across Indian lands. But the lesson of history is nevertheless clear: re-founder *becomes* founder as national history casts its backward glance toward its truer stakes: the future of the imagined community. After Lincoln, that collective was (re)composed to begin again as the modernizing industrial nation.

Joseph Roach uses the word "surrogation" to argue, in *Cities of the Dead*, that performative acts of substitution (through the always already citational aspects of language as well as embodied acts) recompose and negotiate anew the fabric of the social, the crosshatch of collective memory: "The King is Dead, Long Live the King."[6] Surrogation happens both on stage and off, wherever the means of (theatrical) substitution can be manipulated toward the social and political "ends" of the real. On theatre stages, however, the contract of "just pretend" seems generally relatively stable. On a day when "Lincoln" is not actually being shot, the theatrical stage makes acts of surrogation both safe (we trust that stage acts are "only" acting), and explicit (given to explication and instruction). On stage, or in arenas marked for performance or display, we show ourselves to ourselves, telling ourselves about ourselves, through (ironically) performing as "others."[7] Laudatory or derogatory, and riddled with the errors of "as if," we negotiate identity and history at the pass. From the most naturalistic acting to the most alienated acting, the most improvised to the most codified, we play out our responses to the echo and call of and for the real. The actor as surrogate, standing in for a prior figure, or standing in for "whatever being" and bringing that "whatever" forward to a limen of representation, is the performer making explicit the (re)enactment-based warp and woof of everyday life in the social.[8] For if the theatre (and related media that rely on acting) makes the double its art, the everyday life of the social is already an everyday matter doubling and redoubling: of flexible negotiations of indentities, of surrogation, of interpellation, of performativity, of re-finding and re-founding collective architectures of enactment and assemblages of affect that traverse between home and street.[9] Of course, if John Wilkes Booth broke the play frame of "just pretend" (by actually shooting Lincoln), he also, and simultaneously, re-constituted the actual (the event) *as a matter of citation*, of re-finding patricide forward and backward at once – crossing on the diagonal.

Booth's citation of himself playing Brutus, sounding a line Shakespeare did not write in his play but that is nevertheless associated with the Brutus who killed Julius Caesar at Pompey's theatre in Rome (not in the Senate where Shakespeare placed the scene), casts the re-founding of the Roman Republic (an assassination that failed to stem the tide of empire) backward *through the theatre* and forward *through the theatre* across the bleeding body of Lincoln, shot in his theatre box.[10] Making this re-declamation, (not) citing Shakespeare (not) citing Brutus, Booth would, leaping from Lincoln's loge, have crossed into the frame of the proscenium arch (and in so doing he would literally "break a leg"[11]). Certainly a great deal has been made of the hyper-theatricality of this event that cannot be dismissed as "merely" theatre, even as we must account for a certain inextricable theatricality from "the scene." Any proscenium arch is a frame for display that bears its own conditions of possibility, citing, as the architecture does, the ancient Roman *scenae frons*. That is, it would not only have been Brutus's dramatic *words* that cited (however error-ridden or incomplete) empire's patricidic afterlife,[12] but the entire architecture of the frame and event might be read as already indexical, a (partial and incomplete) echo of patricidic culture's empiric paradigms.[13] Theatre auteur Robert Wilson arguably invoked the long arm of this same history in his 1983–6 international (but never fully realized) five-part series *CIVIL warS*, inspired in part by the Civil War photographs of Matthew Brady's employees. As if crawling back through the aperture toward the *scenae frons*, in the production designed for Rome Wilson has Lincoln appear as an enormous puppet crossing the stage, importantly as tall as the proscenium itself. The puppet then, as Marc Robinson describes it, "slowly falls backward until he's prone, hovering several feet off the ground, almost the width of the stage." For Robinson, who might view Wilson through Gertrude Stein, this fall choreographs time as geography: Lincoln, an "emblem of his time [. . .] becomes a second horizon line, border of his space."[14] The body of the dead Re-Father thus is given to re-fill the entire possibility of perspectival space, to be its ground, its basic scenario, in this formal literalization of what we might stretch to name a patricidic sedimentalism played within the vestiges of an ancient Roman architecture of a *house divided*.

If the above paragraph seems to play fast and loose and far afield – from Rome to Ford Theatre to Rome again – it does. For the purposes of this chapter we need only retain the echo of one patricide within another patricide (within another and another Freud might say, thinking as he did in terms of the surrogate in *Moses and Monotheism*), and that suggestion should be enough to set our scene. Crossing the limen of the perspective machine of the proscenium arch, this chapter aims to cross the stage by crossing two plays, plays that are themselves about crossing: plays that restage Lincoln's assassination at a cross between the so-called present and the so-called past. Like any play, these works are cast into the future of their enactment – plays being scripts for future bodies to (re)perform. As such, their temporalities are already vexed by virtue of their status as works *for the theatre*, which is, after all, an affect-assemblage machine of syncopated time. One of the plays is lesser known (Linda Mussmann's *Cross Way Cross*), the other greater known (Suzan-Lori Parks's *The America Play*), but both engage with history through the body of a surrogate rendered explicit as faux, as double, as second, as copy. Both plays engage an actor passing and not quite passing as the Re-Founding Father, remaking the re-founder re-pass away.

Blonde Lincoln

> A wink to Mr. Lincolns pasteboard cutout. (*Winks at Lincoln's pasteboard cutout*)
> [. . .]
> A nod to the bust of Mr. Lincoln. (*Nods to the bust of Lincoln*)[15]

The late twentieth century saw a turn in theatre practice to situating history's returns. As many scholars have made abundantly clear, twentieth-century theatre, dance, and performance practices have resulted less in the much-prophesied "end" to history, than in a heightened investment in the telling of re-telling, the simultaneously spectral and live returns of the so-called past.[16] Despite the fact that it has been the fashion to herald performance as the medium of "disappearance," the irruptive quality of the past on stage has been an overwhelming source of inspiration in both drama and performance art as well as in the burgeoning of reenactment practices, even if said (re)appearances of the past are theatrical, faulty, and riddled with error.

If we turn to Suzan-Lori Parks's *Topdog/Underdog* for a moment before moving on to discuss her earlier work, *The America Play*, we will find an example. *Topdog/Underdog*, a play that opened off-Broadway in 2001, is not exactly a "history play" unless one is willing to find history in its ongoing error-ridden repetitions, its irruptive tics and winces that might be called echoes, or aftermath, and as such even indices of event. In *Topdog* a contemporary character named Booth is the brother of a character named Lincoln. Lincoln is a man who makes his living in whiteface as a Lincoln impersonator. Booth is a would-be card shark who takes the name 3-card. Clearly, Booth is *not* the historical Booth (just as the actor playing Parks's character Booth is not Parks's character Booth). Similarly, the actor playing the character Lincoln (an actor) is not the historical Lincoln (though he is playing a Lincoln playing Lincoln). Yet, despite the concatenation of nots in play, we catch the phonic materiality of reference in the brothers' names and the historical event enters through the ear. The medium of double citation (these two names, together) imbricates one time in another time so that the "tune" of the historical Booth and Lincoln at Ford Theatre in 1864 is always something of a ghost note to the contemporary riff Parks plays in *whatever* theatre on *whatever* date. Booth is *not not* the historical Booth, just as the actor is *not not* Parks's Booth, and the brother (of Booth) is *not not* Lincoln, and *not not* Booth's historical actor brother Edwin, famous for acting Hamlet, a character famous for his inability to act.[17] As in jazz, the historical event (John Wilkes Booth assassinating Lincoln) is put into play but not precisely played. Rather, the historical event is a set of ghost notes audible through the skew and scat of Parks's (not not) tune. In jazz, one cannot accurately say that a tune is *misplayed* by the riff. So too history is not *mistold* via the riff by which Parks retells it. In fact, playing in difference might be one way to *get those notes right*. That is, something of the history is sounded in not being sounded directly, or in being sounded stepwise, off note, via "negative capability"[18] or the double or triple or quadruple speak of homonyms that tell, always, more tales than one.

Sounding, here, is key. Parks's plays are jazz poetics, and, as Meta Du Ewa Jones has written after Nathaniel Mackey, "orality and texuality work in tandem in jazz-inflected verse."[19] As Jones plays it, Mackey used the word "Strick" to title the compact disc recording of his *Song of the Andoumboulou* poem. Explaining "strick" in the liner notes, Mackey writes:

> But I hear in the word more than that. I hear the word *stick*, I hear the word *strike*, I hear the word *struck*, and I hear the word *strict*. I hear those words which are not really pronounced in that word, but there are overtones or undertones of those words, harmonics of those words. The word *strick*, then, is like a musical chord in which those words which are otherwise not present are present.[20]

Like stuck and trick. Like shtick.

The point, here, is that historical *and* surrogate, fore *and* faux, Booths and Lincolns *sound*. Not only words, but bodies, times, and spaces cross and multiply like the other words Mackey hears in one. This sounding happens undecideably yet unmistakably, not only in the names "Booth" and "Lincoln" but also by virtue of a few minor theatrical details that cite and recite: whiteface, top hat, fratri-patricide, and – simply – (re)crossing the stage.

If the improvising off-note, or playing one thing as or in another thing, or playing things otherwise "which are otherwise not present" is a basic of jazz, the quease of the double/triple/multiple is also a staple of theatre.[21] The double/triple/nth is stitched into theatre as sycopated time – where one body plays another body, where one time sounds an other time. As we will explore again in Chapter 3, Gertrude Stein writes in her essay "Plays" in *Lectures in America*:

> The thing that is fundamental about plays is that the scene as depicted on the stage is more often than not one might say it is almost always in syncopated time in relation to the emotion of anybody in the audience.
>
> What this says is this.
>
> Your sensation as one in the audience in relation to the play played before you your sensation I say your emotion concerning that play is always either behind or ahead of the play at which you are looking and to which you are listening.[22]

Though certainly not a theorist of jazz, the relation of this syncopation to jazz strikes
Stein as obvious:

> The jazz bands made of this thing, the thing that makes you nervous at the
> theatre, they made of this thing an end in itself. They made of this different
> tempo a something that was nothing but a difference in tempo between
> anybody and everybody including all those doing it and all those hearing and
> seeing it. [. . .]
> One will always be behind or in front of the other one.[23]

Those who manipulate the citation-production and affect-assemblage machinery
of the stage have long been aware that the "nervous" (to quote Stein) or "sick or
incredible" way you feel (to cite Miranda July from Chapter 1), can trip the switch
between "act" and act, on stage and off. Think only of Shakespeare's Hamlet's
reverberant line, "The play's the thing / Wherein I'll catch the conscience of the
King." Indeed, when King Claudius recognizes the theatrical jointure – the
lamination of "act" on act – he is made very nervous, "frighted," as Hamlet says,
"with false fire." In the long-standing logic of Hamlet's mousetrap, theatre-makers
are aware that hitting one time in another time, one tempo in another tempo, and
getting the (historical) matter *almost but not quite* right can, much in the style of the
jazz riff, get something both wrong and right simultaneously, spiking affect in the
spaces between bodies, and slide from act to "act" to act and back.[24]

The America Play was written between 1990 and 1993 on commission for the
Theatre for a New Audience and co-produced in 1994 by Yale Repertory Theatre
and the New York Shakespeare Festival. It is arguably a more interesting (and less
mainstream) play than the Pulitzer Prize-winning *Topdog/Underdog*. Reminiscent of
Stein as well as Adrienne Kennedy, the play is a landscape play, in which the
landscape is:

> A great hole. In the middle of nowhere. The hole is an exact replica of the
> Great Hole of History.[25]

I would argue that unlike Stein, Parks does not want to *avoid* the time-out-of-time
that makes Stein nervous in the theatre (Stein was not necessarily fond of being
nervous in the theatre, though she was very fond of jazz). Written in the jazz-
inspired style of repetition and revision,[26] *The America Play* is devoted to the
conundrums of re-finding re-founding fathers – particularly, as in *Topdog/Underdog*,
re-finding founders across bodies at the pass, or in the "almost but not quite" of
(not) passing. In *The America Play*, a gravedigger by trade who is referred to as the
"Lesser Known" and as the "Foundling Father" is so "taken" with Lincoln and his
own physical resemblance to the "Great Man" that he sets out West to dig his own
"Hole of History," his own theme park. The Foundling Father heads out to catch
up with the past and to meet the Great Man who has, he says, summoned him. He
forges ahead, in other words, to meet what came behind.

The Lesser Known left his wife and child and went out West finally. [. . .] As it had been back East everywhere out West he went people remarked on his likeness to Lincoln. How, in a limited sort of way, taking into account the course of his natural God-given limitations, how he was identical to the Great Man in gait and manner how his legs were long and torso short. The Lesser Known had by this time taken to wearing a false wart on his cheek in remembrance of the Great Mans wart. When the Westerners noted his wart they pronounced the 2 men in virtual twinship.
(Rest)
Goatee. Huh. Goatee.
(Rest)
"He digged the Hole and the Whole held him."
(Rest)[27]

To make money for his project, and to give himself pleasure, the Lesser Known sets himself up in a sideshow in which the public is invited to pay a penny (a Lincoln Head), choose from a selection of pistols, and "Shoot Mr. Lincoln." This sideshow of shooting is repeated over and over again on stage as different actors playing different folks enter the Lesser Known's booth as Booth to replay the famous death "live."

Parks begins the play with examples of chiasmus – structural inversions of syntactical relations within sentences so that words, grammatical constructions, or concepts are repeated in reverse order: "He digged the hole and the whole held him" and "To stop too fearful and too faint to go" and "He went to the theatre but home went she."[28] Though her opening chiasmi are brief sentences, as the play unfolds it is clear that Parks's chiasmi extend beyond the sentence and apply to discourse more generally, specifically the discourse of history. Because the play is, as plays are, given to be played, the play also suggests the chiasmatic tangle of bodies with language and language with bodies. In Greek, "chiasma" means a cross-shaped mark. In contemporary use, the meaning of the word chiasmus bears the body or the bodily as well as discursive marks within its frame of reference (as Maurice Merleau-Ponty and Luce Irigaray have, respectively, made clear).[29] "Chiasma," from which the linguistic chiasmus derives, refers to anatomy: to quote *Webster's Ninth Dictionary*, chiasma is "a cross-shaped configuration of paired chromatids visible in the diplotene of meiotic prophase and considered the cytological equivalent of genetic crossing-over." Differently said, chiasma refers to bodily decussation, or an anatomical intersection such as the crossing of nerves that construct vision. Bodies and language found and sound each other crossways – winking and nodding like homonyms and metonyms, touching with sound in multiple registers.

Indeed, the play Parks writes writes time itself as chiasmatic, capable and even composed of inversion, crossed between its inclusions (the Greater Known, the fore) and its exclusions (the Lesser Known, the faux). The play seems to scat history in irruptive moments of recognition as misrecognition: Lincoln is not here – Look, there's Lincoln – That's not Lincoln – Lincoln is not here – Look, there's Lincoln there! Returns are multiple, ongoing, partial, and vexed. That which is given to reappear is never the "whole" without the hole in the whole. Which is to say that

Figure 2.1 Reggie Montgomery and Michael Potts in *The America Play* by Suzan-Lori Parks. Directed by Liz Diamond. Photo: T. Charles Erickson, 1993. Yale Repertory Theatre, World Premiere.

the stuff and details of history's exclusions are as chiastically and palpably present as its inclusions are palpably (re)presented as absent. Present and absent come undone at the pass.

Theatre's play in the matter of holes in wholes bears further probing. We commonly attach words like "only" or "mere" to actions or activities engaging play or composed of overt theatricality – as in, "merely" masquerade, or "just" show, or "only" pretend. We are deeply familiar with this common dismissal. Theatricality, like masquerade, is also commonly feminized – a matter of the debased copy, the woman or clown at the mirror making herself into an image, the vapid chicanery of the "second sex," the aping other, the off-kilter queer. And much has been made of the antitheatrical bias (as likely to be the sentiment of modern avant-gardists and contemporary performance artists as of ancient philosophers).[30] If, as J. L. Austin famously articulated, "things" can be done with words – such as vows, threats, curses, etc. – these "things," for Austin, can only be accomplished off stage, via the virility of "ordinary" usage.[31] In theatre, Austin opined, performative utterances are "hollow." Despite the very odd fact that he finds an example of a performative in the play *Hippolytus*, he labels theatre summarily as "parasitic" in the following oft-cited dismissal:

> A performative utterance will, for example, be *in a peculiar way* hollow or void if said by an actor on the stage. [. . .] Language is in such circumstances in

special ways – intelligibly – used not seriously, but in ways *parasitic* upon its normal use – ways which fall under the doctrine of the *etiolations* of language.[32]

Austin's words pile up in admonition here, and his choice of italicization – rendering his words *as if spoken with emphasis* – gives the words "peculiar," "parasitic," "etiolations" more than "ordinary" punch. He seems to care deeply about this dismissal – if italics register a kind of affect, a kind of performative (to italicize it is to "do" it with intensity).[33] His words seem quite carefully chosen, like the very odd word *etiolation* (a synonym for "feeble" that means "light-deprived"). The *Oxford American Dictionary* gives us the following as synonyms for parasite: "hanger-on, cadger, leech, passenger, bloodsucker, sponger, bottom feeder, scrounger, freeloader, mooch." We don't find the word "actor" here, nor impersonator, nor reenactor, but the notion of living through others, or living *off* others, or *as if* others, and passing or not passing, might resonate with the synonym "passenger" offered above. Without question, however, the valence in Austin's chosen words for the theatre is not laudatory. The *Oxford American Dictionary* gives us two definitions for "hollow" that point to a cultural mis-appreciation of holes:

1   having a hole or empty space inside.
2   without significance.

To be hollow is not a positive attribute for Austin, in distinction to the felicitous virility of the "ordinary circumstance." To dig a Hole of History, then, is to place history in the theatre.

Theatricality, apparently "special" as well as "hollow," has no access to things, acts, or events in themselves, but only to holes – hollow copies, void versions, ineffectual errors of acts. And yet, if the infelicity of theatrical citation is "parasitic" on the act referenced, then, like a parasite, or a "Lesser Known," it also strangely has a life of its own, the "doings" of which might be "things done." What might a parasitical performativity actually achieve?[34] What does it get done in the hollow, or echo, of its articulation? Let us explore, for a moment, how perhaps on Parks's stage it is the labor of the precisely iterated error, the purposeful hole, or the calculated "misfire" that *does things*.

Let's look at the error of the beard in *The America Play*. The Lesser Known, the Lincoln look-alike, tells us that while some of the errors in his costuming are unfortunate – yes, he knows, Lincoln's beard was not blond – he still astonishes his clients with his resemblance as they come in, one by one, to reenact the murder. Still, he admits, the beard is a performance that might always misfire:

> This is my fancy beard. Yellow. Mr. Lincoln's hair was dark so I don't wear it much. If you deviate too much they wont get their pleasure. That's my experience. Some inconsistencies are perpetuatable because theyre good for business. But not the yellow beard. Its just my fancy. Ev-ery once and a while. Of course, his hair was dark.
> (*Rest*)

[. . .]
(*Enter B Man, as Booth. He "stands in position"*)

THE FOUNDLING FATHER: HAW HAW HAW HAW
(*Rest*)
HAW HAW HAW HAW

(*Booth shoots. Lincoln "slumps in his chair." Booth jumps*)

B MAN: "Now he belongs to the ages."
(*Rest*)
Blonde?

THE FOUNDLING FATHER: (I only talk with the regulars.)

B MAN: He wasn't blonde. (*Exits*)[35]

Of course, what is not said is that Lincoln was not black. But this not saying is a kind of saying, and a saying that says that Lincoln "was dark." More black than blonde. Lincoln's beard, we recall *through the error*, was black, and so the logic runs at the level of detail that Lincoln *would be best played black*. Thus an erroneous detail (metonymic of the larger detail of the color of the skin) takes the stage as a major player, playing history backward and forward through an error in passing in an effort to *touch*, via the error, something that might actually get the historical matter right. This getting something right through error is the equivalent of the theatrical "wink" and "nod" (a nod as if to say "Yes, that's right, I'm aware of the error") that Parks has her Foundling Father repeatedly give to a pasteboard cut-out of Lincoln that stands on the stage like an 1860s Flat Daddy, index of the past held out for return.[36] The matter of the blonde beard merits both a wink and a nod as the surrogate struggles "somehow to follow in the Great Mans footsteps footsteps that were of course behind him."[37] Stepping for a moment to the side, and remembering how reference moves theatrically from act to "act" to act and back – how can we not recall here the Lincolnantics that accompanied the US 2008 Democratic Presidential campaign of the "Junior Senator from Illinois"? In the Democratic race between Barack Obama and Hillary Clinton, the question of what it means to *perform the Great Man*, found (or refound) yet another global platform for the stepwise reenactment of return.[38]

A great hole in (theatre) history

"He went to the theatre, but home went she."[39]

People have asked me why I don't put any sex in my plays. "The Great Hole of History" – like, duh.[40]

"A blonde" is usually a metonym for "a woman." If a playwright were to write: "Enter, a blonde," readers would interpret the phrase at first pass to mean: "Enter, a woman." If a novelist were to write: "He was chased by a blonde in a Lincoln Continental" a reader would place a young woman at the wheel. Indeed, "blonde" with an "e" refers specifically to women. Parks might have written "Lincoln was not a woman" when she had Man B say "He wasn't blonde." Though the "e" doesn't sound when spoken, the chiasmic play of the homonym reverberates as a theatrical sht(r)ick: he wasn't a *blonde* (woman), he was a *black* (man).

In a play with striking similarity to *The America Play*, if much lesser known, Lincoln is enacted by a character/performer referred to as "She." Linda Mussmann's *Cross Way Cross*, first performed at Marymount Manhattan College in 1987, predated Parks's *America Play* by three to six years (as Parks was writing between 1990 and 1993).[41] Interestingly, Mussmann's *Cross Way Cross* begins with a related chiasmic inversion: "One could not go forward without going back."[42]

In *Cross Way Cross*, the woman "She" is traveling south. The stage is the street – the road to Waycross, the "city of dreams." "She" drives down the stage in a Lincoln continental (a large table center stage behind which she sits), listening and singing "The Radddioooo is [. . .] ON!" While there is no mention of physical resemblance as the driving force behind her becoming Lincoln (she does not claim to be a look-alike as Parks's Foundling Father does), nevertheless she does become Lincoln himself in the course of the play, while simultaneously remaining "She." The "driving force" may in fact be the commodity object of the car she drives. Or it may simply be the drag and pull of historical events that stretch, like roads, behind and before us in all directions. In any case, driving toward the city of dreams She

Figure 2.2 Claudia Bruce in *Cross Way Cross*, directed by Linda Mussmann. Time and Space Limited Theatre Company, New York City, 1987. Photo: Time and Space Limited Archives.

keeps getting lost, her Lincoln turned around, and she finds herself trying to read
the road:

> The lines on the road that she and the Lincoln traveled
>   "was" tellin' and tellin' –
> the lines sending a message to the driver and the car
> explaining the history of the road.
> [. . .]
> In making the turn around
>   the scenery moved from right to left now.
> Things seen once were seen again,
>   what was front was now back,
>   what was only was now recall.
> As she saw the moments as objects,
>   she came to;
>   in coming to,
>   she realized she had gotten turned around somehow
>   and was heading north.
> She pulled over
>   and took a hard right turn to the right
>   and returned to the south.
>
> The circling made her dizzy
>   and in regaining her direction,
>   the aim was corrected.
> In correcting the aim,
>   she could go forward.
> In going forward,
>   she could re-see the seen
>   and re-view the view –
>   the familiar made discontent, as they say.
> And soon she and Lincoln were on and on
>   to making their way through the South
>   in a southerly direction.
>
> This getting lost is no way to get there, she thought,
>   as she held on to the wheel.
> This circling is without conclusion, she thought,
>   as she hung on.[43]

After this lengthy opening monologue in which "She" charts her travels and travails
in getting turned around there is a sudden interruption, a kind of accident on the
road, and the play is plunged into a strict chronology of the events leading to
Lincoln's murder and on to his burial. Unlike J. G. Ballard's novel *Crash* (1973) and
Cronenberg's film of Ballard's novel (1996), which features sexual fetishism with

a black Lincoln Continental (an exact replica of the 1963 model in which Kennedy was shot), the accident in the Continental at the heart of *Cross Way Cross* does not result in necro-sexual reverie. Rather than being flipped over a guard rail (where Ballard's character Vaughn meets his death), Mussmann's "She" is flipped across time itself. From this point on it is not the car that drives, but the narrative drive – the force of event in the strength of a story's return – that commandeers the play in a kind of traumatic repetition machine. The collision with time is punctuated by "her" continued attempts to navigate space – the map and the road – in syncopated place with the present. The point at which Lincoln, "on April 14th, Good Friday, [. . .] leaves the White House at 8:30 to attend a performance of a comedy," "She" finds herself fully doubled as Lincoln. As Mussmann writes in the stage directions: "She assumes Lincoln-like gestures, putting on and taking off her hat, etc. She shifts from the 'She' character and joins the historical scene."[44] She is Lincoln.

In the performance I attended in 1987, blonde and female Claudia Bruce, the performer playing "She," gave us a sequence of actions in which the live performer was clearly wrestling to pass, to fit herself into a historical tableau. She would strike a set of poses indexing the photo-legible nineteenth-century Presidential Man: hand in breast coat pocket, head tilted just so, shoulder angled such, hat tipped – and she would hold the pose still. Stillness would take time. Then she'd move a bit, dissatisfied with her accuracy, or in the inevitable way that living sculpture ultimately gives in to the pulse, breath, twitch, glitch that undoes any ruse of stasis. Again and again, however, she'd strike a pose, again hold still, again break the still, again readjust, again strike the pose. The attempt to arrest herself in the shape of the past, to fit herself into the frame of precedence, was carried out here in a performed negotiation between living stills (tableaux vivants) in a tangled articulation of what it means to be still living, living *after* (re)construction. Bruce's holding and releasing of the poses was now campy, now sincere, now poignant, now absurd. Each attempt underscored the lines on the road between her twinned failure and success. By twinned failure and success I mean that in Mussmann's theatre we simultaneously saw Lincoln through the general set of nineteenth-century gestic signifiers we'd come to recognize in photographs from the period, even as we saw "She" not quite passing in her attempt to fully re-find the founder through his gestures, through his body, through his always somewhat melancholic stance. That is, we both saw him and saw that he was not there. Lincoln was not blonde, after all. But in the stills Bruce could hold, he was not not blonde. Something leaked.

In her notes accompanying the play's publication in *Women and Performance*, Mussmann wrote:

> This production has to achieve a balance between a bad history-play and its parody, between a vaudevillian entertainment and a serious poetic lyricism, between being a contemplation on the passing of time and a reduction of historical chronology to simple, mechanical repetition. Although the structure is somewhat non-linear, the flow is based on formal juxtapositions and "crossovers" of separate lines (mainly of the travels of Lincoln with those of "She").[45]

This striking of a balance between "bad" and "parody of bad" is very interesting, and one of the many "crossovers" the play sets out to realize. The description suggests something of a camp aesthetic. Though "campy" would not really describe an evening at Mussmann's theatre, camp often balances precariously between derogatory spoof and sincerely felt homage. The "between" is in fact a good moniker for camp's essential ambivalence, and "balance" might be a good word for what is either attempted in camp performance or flagrantly (and often fabulously) thrown to the wind. In Mussmann's *Civil War Chronicles*, balance was quite sincerely attempted, for at no time, watching *Cross Way Cross* (and I attended multiple times), could I definitively decide whether I was watching homage, parody, bad-history (Lincoln was not a woman), or brilliantly theoretical theatricality of the particular. I wasn't clear whether it was funny or sad. Whether it was musical or "straight." Whether it was theatre or dance or performance art. The evening was as laced with loss as with joy, and accumulation seemed to occur on an empty stage.

Despite considerable cross-dressing, questions of gender and sexuality were not emphasized on Mussmann's stage as is often the tradition with camp. History, however, was definitely dragged between clown-show and eulogy, tragedy and farce. In fact, the cross-dressing was mainly temporal, and it occurred without regard to other markers such as gender and race (in a pattern not dissimilar to

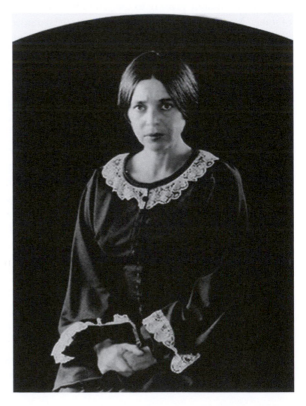

Figure 2.3 Eleanor Antin, "Myself 1854" from *The Angel of Mercy*, 1977. Tinted gelatin silver print mounted on paperboard, 18 × 13 inches. Courtesy Ronald Feldman Fine Arts, New York.

Parks). In fact, Mussmann writes that "'She,' played by Claudia Bruce, is used as the objective, third-person pronoun. 'She' refers to Claudia, the performer, as well as to everyone, regardless of sexual specification."[46]

A balance between poor and parody-of-poor is itself an aesthetic of the double negative: *not good* and *not not good*. Not right and not not right. At the tripping point of the "not not" is the chiasm, the crossroad. At the cross between Lincoln and "She" is the *something* of history's (re)turns. Remembering Mussmann and Bruce's 1987 piece of temporal drag, of archive drag, as Elizabeth Freeman and David Román have called such work respectively, one thinks of feminist precedents such as Elinor Antin's photo-performance "Myself 1854" from the 1977 series *The Angel of Mercy*, in which Antin simulated the pose and the look of sepia photographs using what curator Betti-Sue Hertz has called "a voice and hand appropriate to the character of Florence Nightingale and to the period."[47] Antin's use of archival photography to drag a historical scene into the live (and back to photography), was echoed chiasmically on Mussmann's stage: the historical performer enacting conventions was captured in an archival photo and dragged, then, to live re-performance – signifying the still, but also still living. The act to "act" to act and back aspect of this somewhat sticky pulse illustrates and becomes an affective (and temporal) jump between bodies. This dragging was, of course, nothing new – if newness should be a measure of anything – unless it was new *again*. Nineteenth-century tableaux vivants, dragging paintings, myths, statues, ethnographic photo-graphs, frozen scenes from drama, and historical events into the live and back into photos and again into stilled liveness, were a favorite "domestic entertainment" – and, laced as they were with theatricality and given to circulate in parlor albums and be reperformed at family gatherings, they were considered a "feminine" pastime.[48] Something, that is, to occupy the ladies.

Interestingly, feminism's turn to a critical practice of overt citation (a return that Elin Diamond articulated in 1987 as a return to Brechtian criticism and particularly *historicization* in performance) necessitated a return to narrative, history, and the convention of the pose even while exploring how narrative, historiography, and figuration has worked to delimit, fix, and still the figure of woman as *active participant* in its forms.[49] The delimiting forms and inhibiting architectures had to be entered, and rearranged through reenactment from the inside. With *Cross Way Cross*, Mussmann was returning to narrative – indeed, *Cross Way Cross* is redolent with the problem of the impossibility of escaping Great Man history and rife with the necessity of reenacting it from the parasitical and *minor* point of view of she who can not pass. Contra Audre Lorde, then, Mussmann turned to using the master's tools to interrogate the master's house.[50] As she wrote in *Cross Way Cross*, "Without the narrative line, they could not take the plunge, without the plunge there could be no end."

Of the six plays in Mussmann's *Civil War Chronicles*, developed across the 1980s, four were produced in New York City. The first to be presented was Part III, *Cross Way Cross*, in February 1987 at the Marymount Manhattan Theatre. *If Kansas Goes*, Part II, appeared at the Theatre of the Riverside Church in June 1987. *Blue Scene Grey*, Part I, was presented at the Marymount Manhattan Theatre in October of that year. *Mary Surratt*, Part IV, was mounted as a work in progress at the Village Community School in February 1988, appearing as a finished version at the Theatre of the Riverside Church in May 1988. Two other projected performances, *Go Between Gettysburg*, Part V, and *Lincoln Speak*, Part VI, were never mounted. Together, these plays make up the eight-year collaboration between playwright/director/designer Mussmann, performer/choreographer Claudia Bruce, and dramaturg/composer Semih Firincioglu.

The Civil War Chronicles marked Mussmann's return to narrative, though "throughline" never came out exactly straight and narrow in the "turns" she made to return. Across the ten years prior to Mussmann's *Chronicles*, her theatre in downtown Manhattan, Time and Space Limited Theatre (TSL), had experimented with either fully rejecting narrative line or rendering it so alienated that "story" evaporated into pure form. A look at the years prior to the *Civil War Chronicles* will help us situate Mussmann's turn. Because Mussmann is far less well-known than Suzan-Lori Parks (and she is probably better described as primarily a director and devisor), a bit of her own history bears recounting here. In fact, for a director as influential as Mussmann was in the experimental scene in New York in the '70s and '80s, there is a Great Hole of Theatre History where she is concerned. Though Mussmann was cited more than once as one of a triumverate of directors who would change the face of American theatre (the other two being Robert Wilson and Richard Foreman), indicating her influence in New York at the time, she has remained decidedly Lesser Known.[51]

When Mussmann arrived in New York in 1969, freshly graduated as a theatre studies major from Purdue University, she entered a New York experimental theatre and performance scene in which anti-narrative was almost an avant-garde dictate: artists who wanted to challenge traditional perspective in film and theatre did their best to subvert the mainstays of dramatic structure. Stepping outside the comfortable sense-making mechanisms of the well-made story allowed Mussmann and other avant-garde directors to highlight assumptions of plot, climax, closure, and the habits that usually determined the reception of theatrical work. Ironically, the same impulse to challenge structures of meaning and perspective that drove Mussmann, in her indebtedness to Gertrude Stein, away from narrative prompted her to carefully and "strategically" reincorporate narrative line into her plays when she returned to "the line" in the mid-1980s.[52] When Mussmann made the turn back to narrative line, she drove headlong into "the time of Lincoln," to quote Dana Luciano.[53] She did so via the older vehicle of "chronicle" – a formal procession of dates.[54] In *Cross Way Cross* dates were called out by a woman seated stage right in a rocking chair, almost chanting as she rocked back and forth as if stitching a road map with her voice. The sonorous long march of dates leading up to and beyond Lincoln's assassination became something like the whoosh and repeat of fields, farms, and national monuments whizzing past open car windows. "She," amazed by the landscape from the seat of her Lincoln center stage, seemed to be trying to keep up with her own drive. . . . But I get ahead of myself, and fall forward into the memories of a production that stays with me almost a quarter of a century later.

Mussmann came to the *Chronicles* after directing for Theatre East and the University of the Streets. She founded TSL in 1973 and Claudia Bruce joined as co-director in 1976. TSL's mission then was "to create theater that critiqued the status quo in art and politics and envisioned new ways of seeing and thinking."[55] (In 1991, TSL refused a grant from the National Endowment for the Arts that mandated an anti-obscenity pledge.[56] This, combined with rising costs in New York City led TSL to relocate to Hudson, New York, where Mussmann and Bruce converted an old bakery into their working space. They now run a vital and thriving arts program dedicated to efforts to "revitalize the community, inspire positive change, and encourage dialogue across divisions of class, color, gender, and ethnicity."[57])

In the early 1970s, TSL was the resident company at the Universalist Unitarian Church in Manhattan, where Mussmann mounted an incredibly ambitious set of seasons before moving her theatre into a Chelsea storefront and loft space in 1976. Between 1973 and 1976, Mussmann mounted the following hard working seasons:

1973/74
Sartre: *No Exit*
Ibsen: *Hedda Gabler*
Taylor: *The Portrait*
Ionesco: *Maid to Marry*
Genet: *The Maids*
Pinter: *Silence*
Mussmann: *Ko-Ko-Ro*
Beckett: *The Lost Ones* (adapted by Mussmann)
Ionesco: *The Bald Soprano*
Mussmann: *Imago*
Dürrenmatt: *Play Strindberg*
Mussmann: *White on White*

1974/75
Pinter: *The Birthday Party*
Ibsen: *The Ghosts*
Brecht: *Elephant Calf*
Brecht: *The Exception and the Rule*
Beckett: *Endgame*
Woolf, Olsen, Sexton, Stein, Toklas: *Everything is the Same And Everything is Different* (adapted by Mussmann)

1975/76
Shaw: *The Devil's Disciple*
Ibsen: *The Wild Duck*
Chekhov: *Uncle Vanya*
Stein: *The Making of Americans* (adapted by Mussmann)
    Also at St. Clements Church, NYC and at the Vorpal Gallery, NYC

The end of the 1970s saw a period in which Mussmann was influenced by Japanese arts through her association with playwright Kikue Tashiro. She studied various Japanese forms (Iado, Kabuki, Noh, Bunraku) but resisted imitation.

While producing Tashiro's *The Bandit Princess* she was simultaneously searching for "a language which was mine, outside of narrative structure," so she continued to tap the influence of Virginia Woolf and Gertrude Stein, adapting their writings in a theatrical form she referred to as nondramatic as well as nonnarrative.[58] Not entirely satisfied with a singular vision of purely formal concerns, Mussmann next turned her efforts toward "the Land of Content" – the work of nineteenth-century German playwright Georg Büchner. From 1979 to 1981 she worked on *Danton's Death*, but was attempting to make the content formal through "the formalism of the voice" in an operatic version of the play based on the music theories of Schoenberg and Berg. Always working in several directions at once, she directed Tashiro's *Katana* and produced her own triptych *Door/Window/Room* simultaneously with *Danton's Death*. Across the early 1980s, Mussmann and Bruce continued to develop nondramatic work, such as *The Nebraska of Questions* (1982), and often advertised their theatre as "intermedial."

Eventually, as strict denial of narrative line became downtown "chic" in what came to be called "The Theatre of Images," a phrase coined by Bonnie Marranca in 1976 that was running its course by the mid-1980s, Mussmann began to feel that the high formalism of antinarrative had lost its critical bite. She began to think about a turn, or a return, to narrative. The reasons were complex. Mussmann was sensing, as were other feminist artists such as dancer and filmmaker Yvonne Rainer, that working entirely outside of a narrative format could not fundamentally disturb or alter the internal mechanisms of that format, the cultural framework of under-standing to which we were so deeply habituated.[59] If the "familiar" was not in some way induced, it could not be essentially disturbed, which limited the influence or effectiveness of what she came to feel was formalism for formalism's sake. Mussmann said at the time of *Civil War Chronicles:* "I decided to have a relationship with [the audience] based on something they knew. Not knowing had simply become too easy."[60] The turn to narrative – to history – was in this sense a re-turn, a double-take of sorts, employing the profoundly Brechtian technique of historicization.

Mussmann's early formalism had grown out of a desire that her audiences see things in another way, and she had consistently been concerned with the problem of perspective. In narratology, and in feminist film theory of the late '70s and '80s, perspective haunts the particular way narrative is visually encoded, dictating the *line* of desire that Laura Mulvey had, in 1975, famously termed "the gaze."[61] When thinking about live performance, perspective might be said to be ordered not only by the frame of the proscenium arch and the division of house and stage – a formal and screenal division arguably sedimented as norm in Western drama and film – but also by the tenets of narrative structure that separate space from time, subject from object, past from present. Orientation to perspective dictates fundamental habits in time/space distinctions (such that time is given to be mobile and linear, moving from past to present to future; and space is given to be static and moved through).[62]

As feminists volubly argued in the 1980s, the problem of perspective in narrative – a problem outlined most famously by Teresa de Lauretis in an essay titled "Desire in Narrative" – is that the structure of narrative development fundamentally replays an essentialized heteronormative gender differentiation.[63] De Lauretis argued that narrative is a structure that both depends upon and essentially cloaks an "Oedipal" conception of sexual difference – a basis that both reflects and maintains deep-rooted patriarchal biases and belief systems. A system of meaning based on gender differentiation ascribes a conceptual male/female referent at the foundation of distinctions between opposites – active/passive, light/dark, conscious/unconscious, known/mysterious – such that qualities on the dark, passive, and mysterious side align themselves with the referent "female." A masculine hero, en route to the climax of his story, encounters obstacles (inevitably, like the Sphinx, feminized). The hero, or protagonist, must overcome the obstacles (or be overcome by them) for a story to contain an event (something that happens) and have, post-event, a close. Of course, as theorists have claimed for years, this bias has a profound effect on the representation of gendered subjects, as well as on women's and men's actual feelings about and perceptions of themselves.

In an attempt to prescribe alternative modes of representation, feminists in theatre in the 1980s recognized the need to go beyond the techniques that Sue-Ellen Case and Jeanie K. Forte labeled, at the time, the "New Formalism of the '80s." It was not enough, they argued, simply to ignore narrative, nor enough to stop at narrative's deconstruction. According to Case and Forte, "the problem is that in the closed system of deconstruction the only possible reference is to the dominant ideology it deconstructs. In effect, it reproduces things as they are." Calling for feminist theatre artists to forge an "alternative representation" outside of patriarchal reference systems, Case and Forte prescribed:

> When women on stage vocalize their experience as women rather than reflect the representation of them by men, the possibility for a new discourse arises, one never constituted within the patriarchal canon of plays. Yet what action could this subject play which would generate an alternative discourse, one constituted outside of the patriarchal codes? The action of the desiring subject, the drama of the woman who desires, is in contrast to the passive role tradi-tionally granted woman as the object of male desire. The desiring female subject frustrates the mystifications of morality, challenges the colonization of her body, and denies the use of her sexuality as a commodity in the markets of marriage and pornography.[64]

But Mussmann's theatre would not exactly fill this prescription, as Mussmann was more interested in getting beyond the inverse essentialism of a "desiring female subject" to questioning the foundation of humanist perspective that defined a mutually exclusive opposition between subject and object in the first place. Her *Civil War Chronicles* paradoxically fought to get beyond the delimiting snares of plotting for any essentialized "desiring female" identity by getting *into* history. But at base, Mussmann's various plays all wrestled with "what it means to know something" and thus with the problem of perspective, but the problem of perspective was rather complexly imbricated with problems of gender and problems of time. Problems Mussmann used her particular brand of Stein-meets-Brecht-meets-Stein to explore.

"Perspective" is not a word usually conflated with the "gaze." If the gaze is optical, perspective is an orientation that involves a particular spatial mapping and bears a genealogical link with Western theatre (Alberti constructed his models of perspective while working with Vitruvius's explications of the Roman theatre). Theories of "the gaze" were much debated at the time of Mussmann's *Chronicles*, and she wrestled with the arguments theatrically. For example, in *Blue Scene Grey*, actors exchanged multiple pairs of spectacles so subtly and nonchalantly that a less-than-vigilant spectator might have missed the shifts. I choose the word "perspective" rather than "gaze" to signify Mussmann's concerns because Mussmann's interests clearly exceeded gender categories, making her a somewhat unusual feminist at the time. I also choose the word because any gaze, after all, takes a perspective. Though perspective orients a geometric model of vision and carries within it a memory of its service to empiric expansion, it nevertheless, as Nietzsche observed, can be *changed* and thus it implies a potential multitude of positions rather than an essentially singular drive. For Nietzsche:

> Perspectival seeing is the only kind of seeing there is; perspectival "knowing" the only kind of "knowing"; and the more feelings about a matter which we allow to come to expression, the more eyes, different eyes through which we are able to view this same matter, the more complete our "conception" of it, our "objectivity" will be.[65]

Though we can surely disagree that all seeing and all knowing are necessarily perspectival, Nietzsche's point here is that perspective can shift (implying a shiftiness to perspectival knowledge as well). It is doubtful that Mussmann's aim was Nietzsche's lauded objectivity (enmeshed as "objectivity" is with the history that genders reason as masculine and emotion as feminine). Nevertheless her work invoked interest in the *shift* itself: the *move*, the *action*, the *turning around*, from one perspective to another. The space between the seer and the seen, traversed as if by an exchange of spectacles, generated an affective temporal fold in which "his"-"story" was clearly *repeated*. Thus, though the turn to narrative was necessarily also a re-turn to the empiric logic that haunts the geometry of perspective, the essential multiplicity of the venture's emphasis on *turn* rendered it queasy, slant, not quite straight. Of course, to take on a different or shifted perspective, as Nietzsche recommends, one has to look at something *again*. Gathering of perspective requires accumulation and a kind of re-view, a kind of standing beside or looking to the side. Mussmann's work emphasized the space between "different" points of perspective, different "affective interpretations," different times seen again in the same space.[66] For Mussmann, very interestingly, the spaces between perspective points could be temporal moments, crossed and passed, like objects, hand to hand, body to body.

Throughout the *Chronicles*, women on Mussmann's stage, such as "She"/Lincoln, crossed boundaries traditionally reserved for men – especially the one defining masculine Traveler and a feminine Destination or Traveled-Through. *Cross Way Cross* inverts normative plotting for gender, making "She" the traveler, and the historical figure of the founding father the traveled through, as "he" irrupts across her body as the narrative (vehicle) she herself drives. Consistently, Mussmann's women either travel the United States or are themselves a state on the move, such as the woman named "Kansas" in *If Kansas Goes*. The metaphor is persistent: What if a state ("Kansas," "Maryland," and, in another of her works, "Nebraska") was to refuse its boundaries? What if that which is traveled through gets up to go? What about *secession* from the (gender) union? If the landscape itself decides to secede from the union, can it still be mapped, plotted, and possessed?

The very first line of *If Kansas Goes* is "Action!" This is an obvious reflexive foregrounding of the theatricality of the event about to unfold (theatre played as if film becomes only more obviously theatre). But it also underscores the political imperative of "going" upon which Mussmann repeatedly insists. The next line emphasizes chronicle as the narrator announces: "If Kansas Goes: A Story in 14 sections and 23 episodes. Begin Prologue." Another performer then walks center stage and delivers the prologue:

> This is the story of Kansas
> This is the Kansas of stories.
> This is the story of storms.
> This is the storm of stories.
> This is how you see it
> And not how it sees you.
> This is how I see it
> And not how it sees me.
> This is how they see us
> And not how we see them.[67]

In the play that follows, the narrator gives effusive directions, sometimes calling out "Asides, please" or, again, "Action!" Throughout, the performers move with a matter-of-factness, attentive to their *labor*, performing women's tasks and chores without apparent concern for the audience (in terms of whether the audience knows why corn is poured from one bucket to another and back, for instance, or why there is detailed and less than grand talk of stoves or oats or chickens or eggs). In the middle of repetitive and mundane tasks, as if punctuating the tasks, a performer might suddenly and seemingly randomly cross downstage and speak to the audience about what she had been thinking just before she made her entrance. These "tasks" and "asides" appear to both interrupt the narrative line with the mundanity of women's labor, but also double the labor of the mundane with the labor of the actresses making their entrances and their exits: all an accumulation of mundanity in the face of an impending storm played in syncopated time (1861/1940/1987) as possible secession from the (theatrical, gendered, national) union.

As previously mentioned, in the 1980s Mussmann was less concerned with mapping a counter-gaze based upon some essentializing notion of female desire, than with foiling the fundamental assumptions of perception itself that pitted active against passive, subject against object, then against now. The disruption of conventional notions of time-as-linear and space-as-static was at the base of her aim. When, in *Cross Way Cross*, the traveling "She" triumphantly declares: "And she saw the moment as object!," Mussmann was proclaiming her journey *across* the "states" of time and space. As though claiming an aesthetic (and political) secession from the union conjoining but also demarcating one from the other, she crossed and blurred the elemental boundaries distinguishing temporal "moments" from spatial "objects" – boundaries that were disciplined (if not policed) by habits of perception fundamentally linked to ideologies of the social.

Each of the four produced plays of the *Civil War Chronicles* played the history it engaged in the spaces between normative distinctions marking time from space, female from male, words from objects from actions, comedy from tragedy, mundanity from profundity, and monumentality from detail. Danced and sung in a grand American musical style, *Blue Scene Grey* begins with the organization of the original thirteen states and proceeds to the start of the Civil War – going from 1781 to 1861 in, as a press release humorously intoned, "an hour and a half of fast-paced action."[68] The stage was set with platforms and lined with saloon-type swinging doors. In continual motion, performers enter and exit, as the states enter and secede on the eve of the war. Dressed as waiters wielding shiny silver trays, the performers fold accumulating piles of linens and stack increasing numbers of plates until their theatrical presentation of historical dates, events, and "characters" seems like history specials on a menu for the spectator's consumption. The "show" is interspersed with dialogue between two women who try on eye-glasses while discussing, in a series of vaudeville-meets-Stein asides, what it means to "know something."

If Kansas Goes, the most poetic and metaphoric of the Civil War plays, does not directly invoke the Civil War – at least not by name. A woman referred to as "Kansas" or, again, "She," sits at a table by a large and empty window frame. Outside, we are told, "storm's a comin'." As already mentioned, other women perform repetitive tasks such as sifting corn, anachronistically tuning in Caruso on an antique radio, bringing in a tea tray, moving a stool. Dressed in farm dresses circa 1940 (neither the "then" of the Civil war, nor the "now" of the 1980s, but possibly *still* on the eve of war), the performers talk of stoves and of storms, wonder about "Kansas," and wait.[69] Thinking of the "state" in which she finds herself – bounded on all sides – "Kansas" is in danger of choosing to go with the storm and crossing to the "other side." On the surface, the text and movement can be taken literally: "Kansas" is simply waiting to be swept away by a tornado. But as the performers begin to speak aloud their reasons for doing or saying things (such as saying "Linda [Mussmann] told me to"), multiple levels of meaning begin to take shape. In the midst of their repetitive tasks, the construction of the play becomes a topic, the mapping of states becomes a topic, the boundaries surrounding womanhood in a House Divided is a topic, and all collide at a crossroads with the oncoming storm of an unmentioned (and not quite locatable) war.

Similarly, as already suggested, in *Cross Way Cross*, a woman referred to as "She" drives a Lincoln Continental along the Lincoln/Dixie Highway to the town of Way Cross, Georgia. The woman tries to "go forward" – but, again, "in order to go forward, one had to go back, review the landscape." Behind the steering wheel of the Lincoln, her journey collides with the narrative of Lincoln's travels from Springfield to Washington and back (after death) to Springfield. Across the bodies of her cast, Mussmann sets a set of polished historic tableaux that glide past "her" Lincoln like natural landmarks.

Mary Surratt was in some ways the most disarming of the four produced plays, and the most difficult to understand. Here, Mussmann played with the distinction between life and death as well as distinctions between time and space, history and the present, subject and object. Mary Surratt, a Lesser Known or minor historical figure of the War Between the States, was convicted of conspiring to assassinate Lincoln, and thus she became the first woman to be hanged in the United States. But, in the play, she is also "all the Marys in the state of Maryland." As such, the play flips back and forth between public and private, factual and fictional ideas of "Mary." Played by Bruce in a loud nineteenth-century beet-red bathing suit, Mary takes a post-death boat ride "home" and speculates on the qualitative (private) sensations of her childhood home in Maryland, which, "once familiar, now seems strange."[70] At intervals she also stands before the audience as before an inquisition and recites quantitative (public) facts of her life and death for the historical record: date of birth, number of children, favorite food, color of eyes, precise time of death.

Together, the four plays examine how we determine to know something – and how we get there from here. After a musical meal of times and places, a woman's decision to ride the storm, and a journey backward in order to go forward, *Mary Surratt* presents a historical female subject alone on stage. At the close of *Surratt*, we peer at Mary, who has crawled inside a paper house of her past. Through the house we see only Mary's shadow, now larger than life, dancing and pressing against its walls. Is Mary of the land of Marys looking for the way out of her paper house, or is she trying to fit herself in?

Let us turn again to *Cross Way Cross* – to a woman traveling south to Way Cross and colliding with the historical narrative of Abraham Lincoln. *Cross Way Cross* presents an intersection of multiple perspectives – now a happy celebration of driving to the city of dreams in a radio-playing Lincoln, now a chanted textbook-rendition of historical events, now a dense metaphorical poem on "her" attempts to navigate an uncertain position in time and space. But *Cross Way Cross* has more intersections than appear in the text alone. Movement and music in Mussmann's theatre are in no way underprivileged in relation to play text. Though Firincioglu's music, Bruce's choreography, and Mussmann's text crossed precisely in performance, each medium also retained a kind of alienated, intermedial autonomy. The cross of media did not result in a hierarchy with text on top: on Mussmann and Bruce's stage, text, music, and movement engaged in a subtle process of translation and transformation from movement to word to movement to music to word, challenging conventional habits of reception of "the drama."[71] The interweave of mediums created a sensate heterogeneity that frustrated the authority of a monolithic, unified viewpoint – underlining (as well as undermining) the constructedness of narrative, of history, of perspective.

As *Cross Way Cross* opens, Claudia Bruce is seated center stage at the end of a long table. The table and the chair are the only objects on the wide proscenium stage. Wearing an immaculate white suit, a large black bow-tie, with her clipped-short blonde hair under a bowler hat, Bruce refers to herself only as "She," peppering her declarations with "she thought." The table becomes Bruce's car as she travels the Dixie Path south to Way Cross. Half-chanting, half-singing, gesturing widely and theatrically like a seasoned vaudevillian or a whistle-stop politician, she loudly extols her formula: "In order to go forward, one had to go back. To go back, one had to turn around. To turn around one had to pull over and look to see if anyone was coming."

Two women sit stage left and act as narrators. As they recite a list of states traveled through and weather encountered it seems clear that the travels of "She" are going forward in space. But the narrators also begin to chant chronicles of Abraham Lincoln's travels south. Other female actors, dressed in suspendered pants and bowler hats, strike daguerreotype-like tableaux and relate historical anecdotes making Bruce's "forward" and "backward" motion temporal as well as spatial. As the Lincoln narrative begins to unfold, Bruce, in her old-time britches and braces, swims in and out of focus between her journey in the Lincoln Continental and her collision with the legendary president himself. With a white line painted down its center, the stage floor looks like a huge road upon which the vehicle/chronicle of Lincoln is given to converge, intersecting like a crossroad in the traveling woman's path. Ultimately, she loses herself in Lincoln's tracks – or, he is lost in hers. History, re-cited, repeats itself in her journey. When Lincoln rests for a night, the narrator tells us, "There he sleeps, there he dreams." His sleeping and dreaming will be echoed by her story for when she stops driving we hear, "There she sleeps, there she dreams." Sleeping/dreaming history, she interacts with the familiar story line, driven, inexorably, to assassination and back. In a slow-motion dance repeated numerous times, the president is assassinated at the theatre. Much like Parks's *The America Play*, when Mussmann's "She" arrives at a cinema in Way Cross to go to a movie, the shooting of Lincoln recurs across the stage again and again. As "She" enters the cinema, Mussmann's actors repeatedly shout "CUT" and the assassination scene, with She *as* Lincoln, begins again. Again and again, She/Lincoln falls across the line on the road on the stage – the line tracking narrative, the line keeping time, the line marking the screenal threshold between stage and house (see Figure 2.4). A ritual reenactment of the murder of Lincoln is repeated again and again in slow motion across a body that cannot quite pass, can not quite get past.

As She *in* the Lincoln re-performs Lincoln *in* historical narrative, it becomes difficult for the spectator to precisely locate the Lesser Known unnamed woman – she becomes, rather, a kind of palimpsest with the re-Founding Father. As the third-person qualifier "she thought" constantly repeats, Mussmann's She is decidedly a gendered subject, but she is also and simultaneously crossed with the history she bears (or is borne by the history she crosses). Engaged as she is with the narrative she navigates, it is difficult to grant her a particularly or essentially "female"

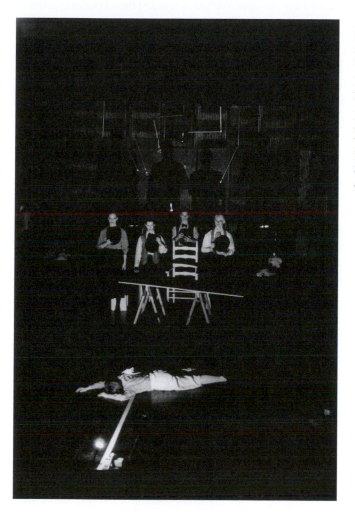

Figure 2.4
Claudia Bruce
and other players
in *Cross Way Cross*,
directed by Linda
Mussmann.
Time and Space
Limited Theatre
Company, New
York City, 1987.
Photo: Time and
Space Limited
Archives.

subjectivity that stands in any distinct opposition to His-story. Rather, towing the narrative line, "Lincoln" and "She" both become murder victims of the narrative throughline that tells one (the Great Man) and excludes the other (the Lesser Known). The much envied plot of the hero is both faithfully echoed and riddled with error as the parasitical copy both rides and carries the past it consumes.

Throughout Mussmann's *Chronicles*, simple narrative directives like "going forward" become a matter for reinterpretation. Yet, importantly, historical event in *Cross Way Cross* is not dissolved – it is not the "end" of history, nor is history rendered impossible across the body of a woman. Rather, the historical narrative of "what happened to whom" adds "when" and "where" as oscillating and malleable qualifiers. Mussmann's recited dates and facts are textbook clean and overtly familiar – what comes undone is the delimitation of their placement in a time considered linear and a space approached as fixed. The spectator is given to wonder: is it His past or Her present or an undecideable space between, outside, or beside? Is She in control of the narrative or does the narrative drive her? The curious relationship between the traveling woman and the sonorous ritual of history's recitation becomes increasingly confused. As She repeats her motto "in order to go forward one had to go back," we begin to re-view the familiar landscape of Lincoln's assassination from the perspective of the minor, affective engagements of the Lesser Known. We engage with a *history of the copy* – his/her history in the tracks of her attempt to stand in his place – her attempt to *take place* at all.

As if doubling Parks's play (in advance), a repeated ritualized reenactment of Lincoln's murder lies at the heart of Mussmann's *Cross Way Cross*. She/Lincoln is repeatedly killed on the stage, only to get up and fall again. And again. If Mussmann and Bruce's drive results (again) in Lincoln's death, and the death drive results, again, in repetition – we are, importantly, given repetition with a crucial and vital difference in the error of detail: Lincoln is not blonde. She can neither fully pass as the event she reenacts nor get past that event without accounting for the "sedimented acts" that precede and replay *her*. She gives a nod to history's affects and its affects become her – its inclusions, its exclusions, its syncopated times. In both Parks's and Mussmann's plays, the Lesser Known is (re)shot into the place of Founder, both passing and not passing at the pass. Again and again: the same difference, different. The changing same.

Crossing these plays is the question of the faulty reenactor as a vehicle for historicization. What does "getting it wrong" (as this white woman and this black man "do" the Fore Father Faux) get right about the returns of history? How does the off-note shtick bring the on-note to audibility? How does difference bring authenticity into being? What is accomplished through the refusals to disappear of the parasitical, failed performative *on the turn*?

> Failing to fetch me at first, keep encouraged;
> Missing me one place, search another;
> I stop somewhere, waiting for you.
> ——Walt Whitman, *Leaves of Grass*, 1855

3 In the meantime: performance remains

In this chapter, I turn to an essay I wrote in 2001, and, if the reader will allow a trip of the tongue, "reperform" it.[1] Here, I insert a precedent text into the heart of a new text, and use text within text to question several basic tenets of performance studies: first, that performance disappears and text remains; second, that live performance is not a recording; and third, that the live takes place in a "now" understood as singular, immediate, and vanishing. In the meantime, however, a preamble:

Meantime, syncopated time

> Hamlet: Speak the speech I pray you as I pronounced it to you, trippingly on the tongue; but if you mouth it as many of your players do, I had as lief the town crier spoke my lines. Nor do not saw the air too much with your hand thus, but use all gently [. . .] And let those that play your clowns speak no more than is set down for them, for there be of them that will themselves laugh, to set on some quantity of barren spectators to laugh too, though *in the meantime* some necessary *question of the play* be then to be considered. That's villainous, and shows a most pitiful ambition in the fool that uses it.
>
> ——*Hamlet* (3.2.1–47, emphasis added)

Hamlet has to work hard and in detail, as he begs – he prays – that his words, "set down," might find their way to a theatrical delivery he can approve. It's what happens to words "in the meantime" that makes Hamlet nervous. The meantime of the theatre is a volatile thing. An actor playing Hamlet, for instance, might speak the speech about speech "trippingly on the tongue," forming the text in his or her mouth "gently." And yet, no matter how gently delivered, the words "set down" are, when taken up, both the same words and not the same words. Still, we should be careful: Shakespeare sets no simple dichotomy here to suggest that text on the page is authentic and fixed while performance is shifty and mobile. The text/performance distinction, so beloved of twentieth- and twenty-first-century performance studies, doesn't work here as neatly as it might, at first, seem.

In Shakespeare's own example, and in line with theatrical practice in his day, text is hardly inviolable, hardly stable, but given to a certain ungovernability.

Hamlet has what W. B. Worthen describes as "no compunction" against rewriting.[2] He asks his actors to "study a speech of some dozen lines or sixteen lines which I would set down and insert" in *The Murder of Gonzago*, thus inserting a play within a play (within a play) (2.2.551–2). And so, here, the villainy that can occur between setting something down and taking it up again is not necessarily delimited to *performance*. The afterlife of the written word, set down and yet changing hands, jumping from body to body, eye to mouth, as text is interjected into text, is not entirely dissimilar to the promiscuous tracks of actorly acts.

In fact, the violability of words is not what bothers Hamlet here (it's a given in which Hamlet himself participates). His concern is for the adequate matching, or catching, of the theatrical condition he wants to *set in play in time*. The play, when set in play, holds not simply "the mirror up to nature," but, as Hamlet's speech to the actors suggests, contains the very "question of the play." And, most interestingly, the "question of the play" is given to occur in the "meantime" – in between possibly errant acts and possibly errant words – not only, that is, in some sacrosanct text, but in the temporal balancing acts of encounter with that text. The meantime could occur *any time* a text is taken up. The open space for villainy – the meantime – could occur in writing, in reading, in (re)writing, or in theatrical production. As Gertrude Stein would ask much later: "And there then comes the question which comes first and which is first, reading or seeing or hearing a play. I ask you."[3]

What can Hamlet's "meantime" mean? According to the Princeton *WordNet* it belongs to a semantic set that includes: "interim, meantime, meanwhile, lag (the time between one event, process, or period and another)."[4] But the *Oxford English Dictionary* gives us, as well, "at the same time."[5] The meaning is double – both between times and simultaneous. Two times, at the same time, between. The "question of the play" occurs "*meantime*" in encounter, and it is posed quite explicitly in *Hamlet* as *between* words set down and words taken up, between doing and re-doing as it were. The question of the play is a question of (villainous) "acts" re-encountered meantime, in double time, or across and in time – a matter of and for the *duration* of one time in (between) another time.[6]

The "meantime" makes Hamlet nervous. He is eager that it occurs as he wants it to occur, though other things (like laughter) may interrupt the meantime in the meantime. His nervousness might remind us (again) of Stein – specifically her nervousness over what she called theatre's "syncopated time":

> This that the thing seen and the thing felt about the thing seen not going on at the same tempo is what makes the being at the theatre something that makes anybody nervous.[7]

Of course, we can recall, Stein first caught this "fundamental thing about plays" while watching Edwin Booth play Hamlet when she was a child in San Francisco:

> Then I enormously remember Booth playing Hamlet but there again the only thing I noticed and it is rather a strange thing to have noticed is his lying at the Queen's feet during the play. One would suppose that a child would notice

other things in the play than that but that is what I remember and I noticed him there more than I did the play he saw, although I knew that there was a play going on there, that is the little play. It was in this way that I first felt two things going on at one time.[8]

The theatre, after all, is a temporal medium – but a temporal medium in the crease or fold of its own condition. Many have claimed temporality itself as theatre's primary medium, where any material, composed in if not contaminated by repetition, is spatially encountered both in time and of time.[9] However, this fundamental temporality is volatile, easily swerved. It is not straightforward. For Hamlet, the possibility of player error complicates an approach to time as linear, to time carried off without a hitch. For theatre, while composed of and in time, is also a medium of masquerade, of clowning, of passing and not passing, the faux, the posed, the inauthentic, the mimetic, the copy, the double, the gaffe – all given to interruption and remix.

Many in theatre and performance studies have recently approached the temporal condition of theatre (and performance art) through the rubric of the live. But with any careful look – even a look at *Hamlet* – the helpfulness of the handy rubric comes undone into the "trouble" of syncopation (not to mention the trouble of the ghost). Still the rubrics "live" and "liveness" have garnered considerable energy in the field. As Paul Allain and Jen Harvie put it in their *Routledge Companion to Theatre and Performance* in 2006:

> Liveness describes a quality of live performance – the sense that it is happening here and now. It is an important idea because it apparently distinguishes live performance from recorded performance-based media such as film and television, indicating that live performance has some intrinsic qualitative and even political difference from other forms of performance. [. . .] Performance's liveness is exciting because it cultivates a sense of *presence*, and because risk is unavoidable where accident cannot be edited out (as it can in recorded media). Performance's liveness is social because it produces meaning in a dynamic process, rather than in the fixed and passive form that recorded media seem to present.[10]

Here we hear the binaried distinction between the "live" and the "recorded" – a binary not unlike the faulty distinction between text and performance – though Allain and Harvie are well aware of the debates concerning this binary, which we will examine more closely in a moment. For now let us simply recall that *Hamlet* holds no such distinction. The character Hamlet is mounting a "live" performance to function as record – troubled as that record may be – for a prior event (his father's murder) otherwise recorded only by the testimony of a phantom, caught, as it were, *in the meantime* of the live. The problem of the record in relation to the live here slips away from tidy distinction. Add to this the vexed situation that in theatre (at least in theatre staging plays), the live act succeeds, surrogates, or comes after a precedent textual script. That is, in the dramatic theatre the live *is not first*, or not *only* first.

The live act does not necessarily, or does not only, precede that which has been set down, recorded. In the dramatic theatre, the live is a troubling trace of a precedent text and so (herein lies the double trouble) comes afterward, even arguably remains afterward, as a *record* of the text *set in play*.

To consider the live a record of precedent material flips on its head the supposition that the live is that which requires recording to remain. But drama is not the only example where the "live" is understood to take place in the future of that which has been "set down." The same could be said for liturgy, or any inscribed set of performatives written to require repetition where repetition is *both* reiteration of precedent *and* the performance of something occurring "again for the first time."[11]

Liveness, real time

"Live" and "liveness" are words that sometimes attend, like difficult cousins, to reenactment, for reenactment as a performance practice appears to "take place" in time, live, even as the times that take place are given to be multiple, layered, or crossed. Consider, simply, a pose. A pose is a posture, a stance, struck in reiterative gesture often signifying precedent. In this way, a pose can be said to be reenactive, citational. Even if the precise original of a pose is unclear, or nonexistent, there is still a citational quality to posing due to the fact that a pose is arrested, even if momentarily, in what is otherwise experienced as a flow in time. The pose articulates an interval, and so, in Henri Bergson's sense, is given to multiple and simultaneous time(s). The freeze or lag in time that is the moment of arrested stillness defines a pose as a pose and might grant the pose a kind of staginess, or theatricality, as if (paradoxically perhaps) theatricality were the very stuff of an inanimate stillness.[12] Liveness as an "in time" category is thus only apparently simple. At any second or third look the live shatters into complications. *The New Oxford American Dictionary* describes the adjective "live" negatively, giving us: "not dead or inanimate; living." And in terms of performance, we are given: "not a recording." Of a broadcast we read that "live" refers to an event transmitted at the time of occurrence, not from a recording. But a recording itself can be live: a recording made of a live musical event is a "live recording." "Live" also refers to unexploded, burning, glowing, unused, moving, or "of current interest." To "go live" is to "become operational." Thus we are given two antonyms of note: "dead" and "recorded."[13]

Clearly, a definition of "live" based on antonyms will prove problematic. "Live" Civil War reenactors, for example, consider themselves to be alive but do not think that everything that happens live is (only) live, or only "now." In this view, the archival records reenactors use to stage their reenactments are, like the events they reenact, *not complete* – not "over" in time. An ongoing tangle – a meantime – between live and dead, or live and recording, cannot usefully be approached only by way of strictly binarized antonyms.

As suggested above, the term "live" has been the subject of considerable attention and debate in performance studies because theatre, dance, orature, performance art, and other embodied, temporal art forms are generally considered to take place in the "immediacy" of "now," and while they can be recorded, the record of the event is often considered radically distinct from the experience of the "immediate" event.[14] Famously, Philip Auslander took up the term explicitly in his 1999 book, *Liveness: Performance in a Mediatized Culture*, where he resists what he terms the "reductive binary opposition of the live and the mediatized." Opposing the "reductive binary," Auslander reads the live (and liveness) as an *invention* of technological reproduction.[15] For him, the live (which he never fully articulates with regard to temporality, except in reference to the "im-mediate" and what he takes to be the "transitory present moment" of live performance) does not precede technologies of recording:

> Far from being encroached upon, contaminated, or threatened by mediation, live performance is always already inscribed with traces of the possibility of technical mediation (i.e., mediatization) that defines it as live. [. . .] The im-mediate is not prior to mediation but derives precisely from the mutually defining relationship between the im-mediate and the mediate. Similarly, live performance cannot be said to have ontological or historical priority over mediatization, since liveness was made visible only by the possibility of technical reproduction. [. . .] The live can exist only *within* an economy of reproduction.[16]

Here, Auslander takes issue with Peggy Phelan's investment in live performance as "representation without reproduction." Unlike Auslander, for Phelan the divide between the live and the mediated is fundamental and sacrosanct rather than co-constitutive. In her influential 1993 book, *Unmarked: The Politics of Performance*, she wrote: "performance's independence from mass reproduction, technologically, economically, and linguistically, is its greatest strength."[17]

The fundamental independence of performance from all reproduction (even "linguistic") is for Phelan a result of performance's temporal condition – which she reads as its disappearance from "visible" record in the vanishing "now" of the moment of performance's articulation in time.[18] In *Unmarked*, Phelan is invested in mining the *immaterial* conditions of live performance and though she problematically links the immaterial with disappearance, giving away a deeply Platonic investment in vision/blindness as *the* privileged way of knowing, she usefully asks: "what would it take to value the immaterial within a culture structured around the equation 'material equals value'?"[19]

That live performance has a different relationship to material remains, and indeed to recording, than objects easily housed in archives as remains, has been argued forcefully by Diana Taylor in her 2003 book, *The Archive and the Repertoire*. Taylor resists Phelan's equation of performance with disappearance. She also troubles Auslander's history of the "depreciated" live as relative only to modern technologies of recording. For Taylor, the history of the archive and the matter of the "record" is far older than Auslander would allow in his own thrall to the technology he prefers to read as determining, creating, the condition "live" at all.[20]

Phelan's *Unmarked* usefully complicated any approach to the live. Importantly, after Phelan we cannot comfortably counterpose death, or deadness, or stillness to life[21] – though she does, in distinction to Auslander, suggest that an antonym might be documentability, recordability, or mediatedness. As we have seen, in distinction to Phelan, Auslander does not allow mediatedness to stand as an antonym for liveness. And yet, both Phelan and Auslander share the notion that the temporality of liveness is the "im-mediate" (Auslander) or "maniacally charged present" (Phelan). If, for Phelan, performance "marks the body itself as loss," for Auslander liveness marks the body as always already referential, a kind of accumulation machine in relation to the mediatization it cites and incites. For Phelan, live performance "occurs over a time which will not be repeated." For Auslander, conversely, the live is in some senses always already reenactment (though not a record) in that: "live performance is now a recreation of itself at one remove, filtered through its own mediatized reproductions."[22]

For all their apparent disagreement, both Phelan and Auslander position the body performing live as not *already* a matter of record. Neither is it a means of recording.[23] And in this, the two are in closely aligned agreement: the live does not record. Indeed, for Auslander, after Baudrillard, the live is only "that which can be recorded,"[24] and for Phelan it is that which cannot be recorded. But either way, live performing bodies are not already recording machines. Here, Auslander and Phelan would be in disagreement not only with Taylor (and with Freud and Foucault as discussed below), but also with Woodhouse (discussed in Chapter 1), who fights the Civil War today, live, *for the record*. The record that is the live.

Is the live really only a matter of temporal immediacy, happening only in an uncomplicated now, a "transitory" present, an im-mediate moment? Is a "maniacally charged present" not punctuated by, syncopated with, indeed charged by other moments, other times? That is, is the present really so temporally straightforward or pure – devoid of a basic delay or deferral if not multiplicity and flexibility? Does it not take place or become composed in double, triple, or multiple time – especially if performance and the "sedimented acts" that comprise the social are already a matter of "twice-behaved behavior"?[25] Again: Stein's trouble with theatre's "syncopated time" (in a complex tangle of reading, hearing, and viewing without determination of priority) was her experience that the time *set in play* was not the time of her experience of that time, prompting us to ask whether a theatrical event can ever be live. That is, if liveness must imply an immediacy or a "real time" devoid of other times, as many might have it, then the delay, lag, doubling, duration, return, the betweenness of Hamlet's meantime could suggest that theatre can never be "live." Or, never *only* live.

To slip the words "real time" into congress with Gertrude Stein (as I did above) is perhaps to commit an error of anachronism – though anachronism is perhaps not off topic when time is allowed to be less (or more) than linear. In any case, "real time" is a phrase gaining currency in the computer age. A phrase used in some relation to duration and what is called "living time," "real time" neither requires live bodies nor antinomies of presence/absence to make its sense. The *Oxford English Dictionary* defines real time as "the actual time during which a process or event occurs, esp. one analyzed by a computer, in contrast to time subsequent to it when computer processing may be done, a recording replayed, or the like." In Mary Ann Doane's words:

> [R]eal time is the time of the now, of the "taking place" of events – it is specifically opposed to the subsequent, the "after." Ideally, in real time, there would be no gap between the phenomenon and its analysis. Current definitions of real time tend to emphasize speed of response or reaction time, suggesting that *interactivity, or the aspiration to interactivity*, is what distinguishes computer real time from film or television real time.[26]

Doane reminds us that the promise of real time is, ironically, a denial of mediation. But, as Doane notes, it is a denial of the very mediation involved in the production of that promise: "'Real time' suggests that represented time can be asymptotic to the instantaneous – with no delay, no distance, no deferral."[27] *The New Oxford American Dictionary* also defines real time as: "A two-way conversation, as opposed to the delay of written correspondence." Never mind, apparently, the force of Derrida's arguments (or Hamlet's) on the ways speech fundamentally partakes of the same delays and deferrals, cross-temporality and remixing, evident in writing – here "real time" promises to return us, through the newest of new media, to a fictive instantaneity nostalgically understood as prior not only to the mediatization that invents it, but to the "unreal time" of writing. "The very idea of a time that is real," writes Doane, "presupposes an unreal time, a technologically produced and mediated time."[28] She might have added: a *theatrical* time. Here, in distinction to "real time," live theatre *and* recorded media are both unreal time, syncopated against the grain of a manufactured instantaneity and immediacy.

Doane is keen to remind her readers that our contemporary investment in real time, and real time's investment in immediacy and interactivity, has a history. For historical precedence she cites film and television whereby continuity (the overlap of film time promised by the cinema) and instantaneity (the live broadcast promised by television) provide the lure of synchronicity – the promise of non-syncopated time. As such, real time mimics that which it constructs as nonmimetic: the notion of nonrepresentational time, and, simultaneously, the idea of an irreversible time without return. As Doane writes:

> When we watch [live broadcast] television, we have the impression that something is happening *only once*: this is not going to happen again, we think, it is "living," live, real time, whereas we also know, on the other hand, it is being produced by the strongest, the most sophisticated repetition machines.[29]

Not happy to let "new media" succumb to the fantasies of its own supposed new-ness, Doane is interested to ask: "[W]hat constitutes the historical specificity of this technologically mediated real time, what is the lure of its promise of instantaneity, of its disavowal of repetition, its insistence that events happen 'only once'?"[30] For her, the "historical specificity" is the invention of photography – specifically the instantaneous snapshots that inspired Walter Benjamin's notion of the optical unconscious. Following Doane, real time, then, in its link to "livingness," is (perhaps ironically) a product of the invention of the snapshot still.

Much more can be said (and will be said in Chapter 5) about the temporality of the still, and the paradoxical "liveness" instilled in and as photography. For Doane to situate, as Rosalind Krauss and others do, the invention of the still with the invention of the photograph, and to read in the (snapshot) still an equation of instantaneity with "only once," she must ignore the enormous history of the still in performance arts, and particularly, just before the invention of photography, in melodrama. At a curious moment in *Lectures on America*, Stein turns from the theatre – just as she is remarking upon her pleasure with Civil War melodramas – to photography: "[T]here is yet the trouble with the cinema that it is after all a photograph, and a photograph continues to be a photograph *and yet it can become something else.*"[31] Both one thing and another thing, simultaneously: a logic that undoes temporal singularity. Stein, having been raised on the tableaux vivants of Civil War melodrama – the "silence, stillness, and quick movement" that defined the genre – does not afford to photography the very fixity it appears to (im)pose.[32] Stein finds cracks in live theatre's seeming immediacy through which a syncopated doubleness – the same *and* something else – (re)occurs. And of course, syncopation (like Stein's writing) jumps. It jumps medial boundaries, from theatre to photography and back. It travels *and* returns. It passes *and* recurs. Syncopation troubles ephemerality. It troubles medial specificity. It "makes *one* endlessly troubled."[33]

A small history of ephemerality

The idea of the ephemeral has enjoyed a certain constitutive status in performance studies and has determined, to a great extent, how we think about "live" performance in the late twentieth and early twenty-first centuries. In 1965, Richard Schechner began to craft a definition of theatre as a tangle between permanence (drama) and ephemerality (performance), privileging ephemerality in the claim that theatre can have "no originals."[34] This would be an influential line of inquiry in the development of performance studies, particularly for the strand of thought that developed around Schechner and his colleagues at New York University in the 1980s and '90s. In 1968, Marcia B. Siegel, who would join the NYU faculty in the 1980s, wrote, "Dance exists at a perpetual vanishing point. [. . .] It is an event that disappears in the very act of materializing."[35] By 1974, Schechner wrote of theatre as "evanescent," saying that "it is an event characterized by ephemerality and immediacy."[36] Though Schechner and Siegel had begun writing about "theatre" and "dance," respectively, by the time the Department of Performance Studies was officially launched at NYU in 1980, the discourse about and investment in ephemerality had (promiscuously) moved from theatre and dance "proper" to the "broad spectrum" of performance where it effectively mingled with art history, anthropology, folklore studies, and literary studies.[37] In 1982, Herbert Blau, that year a visiting professor in performance studies at New York University, famously posited that performance is "always at the vanishing point," and Blau had significant influence on thinkers in drama studies and theatre studies, many of them in departments of literature.[38]

The fact that "vanishing" should be *the* prime budding attribute of performance, beating so insistently and so loudly within one of the progenital hearts of the emergent methodology of performance studies, is interesting. In the 1970s and early 1980s, French poststructural theory was widely circulated in English. Poststructural emphasis on the play of difference and *sous rature* in meaning-making had impact on literary and performance scholars alike. Heidegger read through Derrida was hot, and performance, seeming to literalize erasure in a temporal and visual vein as "vanishment," could capitalize on the academic moment. It was as if disappearance became a kind of intellectual kerosene fueling the flame through which more traditional theatre studies – studies focused on the dramatic script for example – seemed to struggle to signal (often, as in W. B. Worthen's important work, struggling to signal compatriotism while pleading for greater complexity of argument).[39]

By 1985, "disappearance" was a veritable mantra applied to all performance – from theatre, to ritual, to everyday life. In this year Schechner wrote:

> Performance originals disappear as fast as they are made. No notation, no reconstruction, no film or videotape recording can keep them. [. . .] One of the chief jobs challenging performance scholars is the making of a vocabulary and methodology that deal with performance in its immediacy and evanescence.[40]

In the late 1980s and early 1990s, Peggy Phelan, then an assistant professor in the department, took up Schechner's "chief job" and wedded performance studies to literary studies and art history, simultaneously extending Schechner's ephemerality and immediacy into a general association of performance with loss, disappearance, and death. Phelan declared famously in 1993 that:

> Performance cannot be saved, recorded, documented, or otherwise participate in the circulation of representations of representations: once it does so it becomes something other than performance. [. . .] Performance [. . .] becomes itself through disappearance.[41]

Similarly, Barbara Kirshenblatt-Gimblett, another foundational and influential thinker in the same department, employed the term "ephemeral" for *all* behavior that might be termed live: "The ephemeral encompasses all forms of behavior – everyday activities, story-telling, ritual, dance, speech, performance of all kinds."[42] When I was a student at New York University in the late 1980s and well into the 1990s, I recall anthropologist Michael Taussig, then a professor in the department, joking that the department should rename itself the Department of Ephemerality Studies.

Interestingly, Joseph Roach, who chaired the NYU Department of Performance Studies for one year in 1993, studiously avoided the word "ephemeral" and only used the word "disappearance" with utmost care in *Cities of the Dead*, published in

1996. Nevertheless, his influential theories of surrogacy were crafted in and influenced by the atmosphere of "ephemerality studies" as is evident in his rigorous investigations into how the *temporal* contingencies of enactment and reenactment operate and how, attentive to temporal operations as composed in repetition, we might chart genealogies of performance practice. Roach situates performance as a matter of surrogation and in turn explores surrogation as a matter of contingencies – even "desperate contingencies." But his reflection on performance's contingency, its fundamental in-timeness and in-placeness, is more readily invested in the politics and currents (or currencies) of "displacement" than it is in "disappearance" as manifested in Phelan's brand of pure and absolute loss.[43] Charting the displacements and replacements that make up operations of surrogation – as one thing or one person stands in for *and takes the place of* another thing or another person either on a stage or in a life event – is a charting that Roach terms performance genealogy. To be necessarily contingent, in Roach's way of thinking about performance, is *not* necessarily to disappear, though it is certainly to move, to step, to shift, to jump across bodies, objects, continents, and to be given to irruptive and even "desperate" repetition and revision.

José Esteban Muñoz articulated a similar resistance to disappearance-as-loss in an essay published in *Women and Performance* in 1996. Then an assistant professor in performance studies at NYU, Muñoz wrote "Ephemera as Evidence: Introductory Notes to Queer Acts," and turned the table on ephemerality to suggest that ephemera do not disappear but are distinctly material. In that essay, Muñoz relies on Raymond William's "structures of feeling" to argue that the ephemeral – "traces, glimmers, residues, and specks of things" – is a "mode" of "proofing" employed by necessity (and sometimes preference) by minoritarian culture and criticism makers.[44] Roach's and Muñoz's approaches to ephemera marked a significant shift, and it was a shift that would find further articulation when Diana Taylor joined the NYU department and continued the turn away from the assumption that performance disappears in her 2003 book, *The Archive and the Repertoire*. The question of the remains of performance, and the debate about whether and how performance disappears and/or remains, has arguably been one of the most fecund questions to result from the expansion of the study of performance into its broad spectrum, beyond the domain of textual primacy afforded previously by the study of drama, particularly in departments of literature.[45]

Of course, questions about ephemerality and performance have been addressed beyond theatre and dance studies, and well beyond those who passed through performance studies as faculty or students at NYU. Similarly, scholars and artists not associated with NYU have volubly influenced the NYU school of thought.[46] However, my own question in the late 1990s remained, like this "small history," considerably local – bred as I was in the air of the questions, and trained as I was in the shape of the footsteps I followed behind me.

The following re-do re-poses the questions.[47]

Re-do: performance remains (2001)

> The peculiar burden and problem of the theatre is that there is no *original artwork at all*. Unless one maintains that the text is the art work (which repudiates the entire history of the theatre), there seems no way of avoiding this difficult fact. Every other art has its original and its copies. Only music approximates the theatrical dilemma, but notation insures that each musical performance will at least come close to the composer's intention.
>
> ——Richard Schechner (1965)[48]

> Dance exists at a perpetual vanishing point. [. . .] It is an event that disappears in the very act of materializing.
>
> ——Marcia Siegel (1968)[49]

> In theatre, as in love, the subject is disappearance.
>
> ——Herbert Blau (1982)[50]

This essay is about performance and the archive, or the positioning of performance in archival culture. It takes up the long-standing invitations of many in performance studies to consider performance "always at the vanishing point."[51] Taking up these invitations, I've set myself the following question: If we consider performance as "of" disappearance, if we think of the ephemeral as that which "vanishes," and if we think of performance as the antithesis of preservation,[52] do we limit ourselves to an understanding of performance predetermined by a cultural habituation to the patrilineal, West-identified (arguably white-cultural) logic of the archive?

Troubling disappearance

The archive has long been habitual to Western culture. We understand ourselves relative to the remains we accumulate as indices of vanishment, the tracks we house, mark, and cite, the material traces we acknowledge as remaining. Jacques Le Goff stated the Western truism quite simply, noting that history, requiring remains, has been composed of documents because "the document is what remains." Even as the domain of the document has expanded to include "the spoken word, the image, and gesture," the fundamental relationship of remain to *document*-ability remains intact.[53] But the "we" of this mode of history as material remains is not necessarily universal. Rather, "archive culture" is appropriate to those who align historical knowledge with European traditions, or, even more precisely, those who chart a (mythic) descent from Greek antiquity.[54] As Derrida reminds in *Archive Fever*, the word archive stems from the Greek and is linked at the root to the prerogatives of the archon, the head of state. Tucked inside the word itself is the house of he who was "considered to possess the right to make or to represent the law," and to uphold, as Michel Foucault has written, the "system of its enunciability."[55]

In the theatre the issue of remains as material document, and the issue of performance as documentable, becomes complicated – necessarily imbricated, chiasmically, with the live body. The theatre, to the degree that it is composed in live performance, seems to resist remains. And yet, if live theatre in the West is approached as that which refuses to remain, as performance studies scholars have quite fulsomely insisted, it is precisely in live art and live theatre that scores of late twentieth-century and early twenty-first-century artists explore history – the recomposition of remains *in and as the live*.[56] If we consider performance as of disappearance, of an ephemerality read as vanishment and loss, are we perhaps limiting ourselves to an understanding of performance predetermined by our cultural habituation to the logic of the archive?

According to the logic of the archive, what is given to the archive is that which is recognized as constituting a remain, that which can have been documented or has *become* document. To the degree that performance is *not* its own document (as Schechner, Blau, and Phelan have argued), it is, constitutively, that which *does not remain*. As the logic goes, performance is so radically "in time" (with time considered linear) that it cannot reside in its material traces and therefore "disappears."

The definition of performance as that which disappears, which is continually lost in time, is a definition well suited to the concerns of art history and the curatorial pressure to understand performance in the museal context where performance appeared to challenge object status and seemed to refuse the archive its privileged "savable" original. Arguably even more than in the theatre, it is in the context of the museum, gallery, and art market that performance appears to *primarily* offer disappearance. Particularly in the context of visual art, performance suggests a challenge to the "ocular hegemony" that, to quote Kobena Mercer, "assumes that the visual world can be rendered knowable before the omnipotent gaze of the eye and the 'I' of the Western cogito."[57] Thus there is a political promise in this equation of performance with disappearance: if performance can be understood as disappearing, perhaps performance can rupture the ocular hegemony Mercer cites. And yet, in privileging an understanding of performance as a refusal to remain, do we ignore other ways of knowing, other modes of remembering, that might be situated precisely in the ways in which performance remains, but remains differently? The ways, that is, that performance resists a cultural habituation to the ocular – a thrall that would delimit performance as that which cannot remain to be seen.

The predominant performance-studies-meets-art-history attitude toward performance as disappearance might overlook different ways of accessing history offered by performance. Too often, the equation of performance with disappearance reiterates performance as necessarily a matter of loss, even annihilation. Curator Paul Schimmel made this perspective clear in his essay "Leap into the Void," writing that the orientation toward "the act," which he historicizes as a post-World War II preoccupation, is an orientation toward destruction. "Although there are instances of lighthearted irreverence, joy, and laughter in this work, there is always an underlying darkness, informed by the recognition of humanity's seemingly relentless drive toward self-annihilation."[58] In his analysis, performance becomes itself as void. It may be a medium of creation, but a creation subservient to a disappearance understood as loss, "destruction," and "darkness."

If we adopt the equation that performance does not save, does not remain, and apply it to performance generally, to what degree can performance interrogate archival thinking? *Is it not the case that it is precisely the logic of the archive that approaches performance as of disappearance?* Asked another way, does an equation of performance with impermanence, destruction, and loss follow rather than disrupt a cultural habituation to the imperialism inherent in archival logic? A simple example may serve us well: on a panel at a Columbia University conference in 1997 on documentation, archivists Mary Edsall and Catherine Johnson bemoaned the problems of preserving performance, declaring that the practices of "body-to-body transmission," such as dance and gesture, mean that "you lose a lot of history."[59] Such statements assume that memory cannot be housed in a body and remain, and thus that oral storytelling, live recitation, repeated gesture, and ritual enactment are not practices of telling or writing history. Such practices disappear. By this logic, being housed always in the live, "body-to-body transmission" disappears, is lost, and thus is no transmission at all. Obviously, the language of disappearance here is hugely culturally myopic. Here, performance is given to be as antithetical to memory as it is to the archive.

Should we not think of the ways in which the archive depends upon performance, indeed ways in which the archive *performs* the equation of performance with disappearance, even as it *performs* the service of "saving"? It is in accord with archival logic that performance is given to disappear, and mimesis (always in a tangled and complicated relationship to the performative) is, in line with a long history of antitheatricality, debased if not downright feared as destructive of the pristine ideality of all things marked "original."[60]

Performing the archive

It is thus in [. . .] *domiciliation*, in [. . .] house arrest, that archives take place.[61]

If the twentieth century was famous for, among other things, criticizing the concept of historical facticity, such criticism has not resulted in the end of our particular investments in the logic of the archive. Rather, we have broadened our range of documents to include that which we might have overlooked and included the stockpiling of recorded speech, image, gesture in the establishment of "oral archives" and the collection of "ethnotexts." The important recuperation of "lost histories" has gone on in the name of feminism, minoritarianism, and its compatriots. In light of this, what does it serve to remind ourselves that this privileging of site-able remains in the archive is linked, as is the root of the word archive, to the prerogatives of the archon, the head of state? In what way does the housing of memory in strictly material, quantifiable, domicilable remains lead both backward and forward to the principle of the archon, the patriarch? The Greek root of the word archive refers to the archon's *house* and, by extension, the architecture of a social memory linked to the law. The demand for a visible remain, at first a mnemonic mode of mapping for monument, would eventually become the architecture of a particular social power *over* memory.[62] Even if the earliest

Greek archive housed mnemonics for performance rather than material originals themselves, archive logic in modernity came to value the document over event. That is, if ancient archives housed back-ups *in case* of the failure of localized knowledge, colonial archives participated in the failure of localized knowledge – that failure had become a given. The document, as an arm of empire, could arrest and disable local knowledges while simultaneously scripting memory as necessarily failed, as Ann Laura Stoller has amply illustrated. The archive became a mode of governance *against* memory.[63] The question becomes: Does the logic of the archive, as that logic came to be central to modernity, in fact *demand that performance disappear* in favor of discrete remains – material presented as preserved, as non-theatrical, as "authentic," as "itself," as somehow non-mimetic?

In the archive, flesh is given to be that which slips away. According to archive logic, flesh can house no memory of bone. In the archive, only bone speaks memory of flesh. Flesh is blind spot.[64] Dissimulating and disappearing. Of course, this is a cultural equation, arguably foreign to those who claim orature, story-telling, visitation, improvisation, or embodied ritual practice *as history*. It is arguably foreign to practices in popular culture, such as the practices of US Civil War reenactors who consider performance as precisely a way of keeping memory alive, of making sure it does not disappear. In such practices – coded (like the body) primitive, popular, folk, naïve – performance does remain, does leave "residue."[65] Indeed the place of residue is arguably *flesh* in a network of body-to-body transmission of affect and enactment – evidence, across generations, of impact.

In scholarly treatments, the question of the performance remains of history, or more specifically history that remains in performance practice (versus written or object remains) generally falls under the rubric of memory versus history, and as such it is often labeled "mythic." Oral history also often falls under the rubric of ritual. In turn, "ritual" generally (or historically) has fallen under the rubric of "ethnic" – a term which generally means race- or class-marked people but which Le Goff cites as "primitive" or "peoples without writing."[66] Clearly, concatenations of primitivism and attendant racisms attach, in turn, to attempts to acknowledge performance as an appropriate means of remaining, of remembering. Is this perhaps because performance threatens the terms of captive or discrete remains dictated by the archive? Is this in part why the logic of the archive – that utopic "operational field of projected total knowledge" – scripts performance as disappearing?[67] Because oral history and its performance practices are always decidedly repeated, oral historical practices are always reconstructive, always incomplete, never in thrall to the singular or self-same origin that buttresses archontic lineage. In performance *as* memory, the pristine self-sameness of an "original," an artifact so valued by the archive, is rendered impossible – or, if you will, mythic.

Performance practice has been routinely disavowed as historical practice.[68] Though historiographers such as Pierre Nora claim that this attitude has shifted in favor of a "new" history that incorporates collective memory and performative practices, nevertheless that "new" history is manifested in the constitution of "radically new kinds of archives, of which the most characteristic are oral archives."[69] The oral is not here approached as *already* an archive, a performance-based archive.

Rather, oral histories are constituted anew, recorded and "saved" through technology in the name of identicality and materiality. Though this "new" archiving is supposedly against loss, doesn't it institute more profoundly than anything the loss of a *different approach to saving* that is not invested in identicality? Doesn't it further undo an understanding of performance as remaining? Do not such practices buttress the phallocentric insistence of the ocularcentric assumption that if it is not visible, or given to documentation or sonic recording, or otherwise "houseable" within an archive, it is lost, disappeared?

It is interesting to take the example of battle reenactment into account and look at the particular case of Robert Lee Hodge – an avid Civil War enthusiast who participates in reenactments. As Marvin Carlson described him in an essay on theatre and historical reenactment, Hodge has attained significant notoriety among reenactment communities for his "ability to fall to the ground and contort his body to simulate convincingly a bloated corpse."[70] The question is obvious: under what imaginable framework could we cite Hodge's actions as a viable mode of historical knowledge, or of remaining? Is Hodge's bloat not deeply problematic mimetic representation, and wildly bogus and indiscreet at that? Does Hodge, lying prone and fake-bloating in the sun, attempt to offer index of – as well as reference to – both the material photograph and the photographed material of Civil War corpses? Is the live bloater only offering a mimetic and perhaps even ludicrous copy of something only vaguely imagined as a bloated corpse? Yet, within the growing "living history" and reenactment movement, Hodge's bloating body is, for many enthusiasts, evidence of something that can *touch* the more distant historical record, if not evidence of something authentic itself.[71] In the often-ridiculed "popular" arena of reenactment, Hodge's bloat is a kind of affective remain – itself, in its performative repetition, a queer kind of evidence. If the living corpse is a remain of history, it is certainly revisited across a body that cannot pass as the corpse it re-calls. If it cannot pass, what kind of claim to authenticity can such a faulty corpse demand?

I am reminded of Charles Ludlam's queer Theatre of the Ridiculous in which the replaying of classics or the "camp" reenactment of the folk art of "vulgar" commercial entertainment (such as B-movies) offers a different though perhaps related kind of "living history." Ludlam's parodic evenings offered a fractured re-entry of remainders – a history of identifications, of role-playing and its discontents. In Ludlam's theatre, as Stefan Brecht described it in 1968, "Removal of cadavers, necessitated by the high onstage death-rate, is done with exaggerated clumsiness, the corpse does not cooperate – but mostly the dead just sit up after a while, walk off, reparticipate in the action."[72]

When we approach performance not as that which disappears (as the archive expects), but as both the *act* of remaining and a means of re-appearance and "reparticipation" (though not a metaphysic of presence) we are almost immediately forced to admit that remains do not have to be isolated to the document, to the object, to bone versus flesh. Here the body – Hodge's bloated one – becomes a kind of archive and host to a collective memory that we might situate with Freud as symptomatic, with Cathy Caruth with Freud as the compulsory repetitions of a collective trauma, with Foucault with Nietzsche as "counter-memory," or with Fred

Moten with Baraka, Minh-ha, and Derrida as transmutation.[73] The bodily, read through genealogies of impact and ricochet, is arguably always interactive. This body, given to performance, is here engaged with disappearance chiasmically – not only disappearing but resiliently eruptive, remaining through performance like so many ghosts at the door marked "disappeared." In this sense performance becomes itself through messy and eruptive re-appearance. It challenges, via the performative trace, any neat antimony between appearance and disappearance, or presence and absence through the basic repetitions that mark performance as indiscreet, non-original, relentlessly citational, and remaining.

Indeed, approached in this way, performance challenges loss. Still, we must be careful to avoid the habit of approaching performance remains as a metaphysic of presence that fetishizes a singular "present" moment. As theories of trauma and repetition might instruct us, it is not *presence* that appears in the syncopated time of citational performance but precisely (again) the missed encounter – the reverberations of the overlooked, the missed, the repressed, the seemingly forgotten. Performance does not disappear when approached from this perspective, though its remains are the immaterial of live, embodied acts. Rather, performance plays the "sedimented acts" and spectral meanings that haunt material in constant collective interaction, in constellation, in transmutation.

Death and living remains

Let us not too rapidly dispose of the issue of disappearance. If Schechner, Blau, Phelan, and others are correct and performance is given to become itself through disappearance – to resist document and record, to deny remains – we find ourselves in a bit of an awkward bind regarding the argument so far. In fact, Blau's work on this bind, particularly his *Take Up the Bodies: Theatre at the Vanishing Point*, has been particularly trenchant:

> Whatever the style, hieratic or realistic, texted or untexted – box it, mask it, deconstruct it as you will – the theatre disappears under any circumstances; but with all the ubiquity of the adhesive dead, from Antigone's brother to Strindberg's Mummy to the burgeoning corpse of Ionesco's *Amedée*, it's there when we look again.[74]

Upon any *second* look, disappearance is not antithetical to remains. And indeed, it is one of the primary insights of poststructuralism that disappearance is that which marks *all* documents, *all* records, and *all* material remains. Indeed, remains become themselves through disappearance as well.

We might think of it this way: death appears to result in the paradoxical production of both disappearance *and* remains. Disappearance, that citational practice, that after-the-factness, clings to remains – absent flesh *does* ghost bones. We have already noted that the habit of the West is to privilege bones as index of a flesh that was once, being "once" (as in both time and singularity) only after the fact. Flesh itself, in our ongoing cultural habituation to sight-able remains, supposedly cannot remain to signify "once" (upon a time). Even twice won't fit the constancy of cell replacing cell that is our everyday. Flesh, that slippery feminine subcutaneousness, is the tyrannical and oily, invisible-inked signature of the living. Flesh of my flesh of my flesh repeats, even as flesh is that which the archive presumes does not remain.

As Derrida notes, the archive is built on the domiciliation of this flesh with its feminine capacity to reproduce. The archive is built on "house arrest" – the solidification of value in ontology as retroactively secured in document, object, record. This retroaction is nevertheless a valorization of regular, necessary loss on (performative) display – with the document, the object, and the record being situated as survivor of time. Thus we have become increasingly comfortable in saying that the archivable object also becomes itself through disappearance – as it becomes the trace of that which remains when performance (the artist's action) disappears. This is trace-logic emphasizing loss – a loss that the archive can regulate, maintain, institutionalize – while forgetting that it is a loss that the archive *produces*. In the archive, bones are given not only to speak the disappearance of flesh, but to script that flesh as disappearing by disavowing recurrence or by marking the body always already "scandal."[75]

An instituted loss that spells the failure of the bodily to remain is rife with a "patriarchal principle." No one, Derrida notes, has shown more ably than Freud how the archival drive, which he labels as a "paternal and patriarchic principle," is both patriarchal and parricidic. The archival drive

> posited itself to repeat itself and returned to reposit itself only in parricide. It amounts to repressed or suppressed parricide, in the name of the father as dead father. The archontic is at best the takeover of the archive by the brothers. The equality and liberty of brothers. A certain, still vivacious idea of democracy.[76]

Ann Pellegrini has stated this Freudian schema succinctly: "son fathers parent(s); pre- is heir to post-; and 'proper' gender identification and 'appropriate' object choices are secured backward" – a "retroaction of objects lost and subjects founded."[77]

Elsewhere, I have discussed this parricidal impulse as productive of death in order to ensure remains.[78] I have suggested that the increasing domain of remains in the West, the increased technologies of archiving, may be why the late twentieth century was both so enamored of performance and so replete with deaths: death of author, death of science, death of history, death of literature, death of character, death of the avant-garde, death of modernism, and even, in Suzan-Lori Parks's brilliant and ironic rendition, *Death of the Last Black Man in the Whole Entire World*.[79] Within a culture that privileges object remains as indices of and survivors of death, to produce such a panoply of deaths may be the only way to insure remains in the wake of modernity's crises of authority, identity, and object. Killing the author, or sacrificing his station, may be, ironically, the means of ensuring that he remains.

For the moment let me simply suggest that when we read this "securing backward" Pellegrini discusses, this "retroaction" of objects, we are reading the archive as act – as an architecture housing rituals of "domiciliation" or "house arrest" – continually, as ritual, performed. The archive itself becomes a social performance space, a theatre of retroaction. The archive performs the institution of disappearance, with object remains as indices of disappearance and with performance as given to disappear. If, in Derrida's formation, it is in domiciliation, in "house arrest" that "archives take place" we are invited to think of this "taking place" as continual, of house arrest as performative – a performative, like a promise, that casts the retroaction of objects solidly into a future in which the patriarchic principle Derrida cites *will have* (retroactively) remained.

To read "history," then, as a set of sedimented acts that are not the historical acts themselves but the act of securing any incident backward – the repeated act of securing memory – is to rethink the site of history in ritual repetition. This is not to say that we have reached the "end of history," neither is it to say that past events didn't happen, nor that to access the past is impossible. It is rather to resituate the site of any knowing of history as body-to-body transmission. Whether that ritual repetition is the attendance to documents in the library (the physical acts of acquisition, the physical acts of reading, writing, educating), or the oral tales of family lineage (think of the African American descendents of Thomas Jefferson who didn't need the DNA test to tell them what they remembered through oral transmission), or the myriad traumatic reenactments engaged in both consciously and unconsciously, we refigure "history" onto bodies, the affective transmissions of showing and telling.[80] Architectures of access (the physical aspect of books, bookcases, glass display cases, or even the request desk at an archive) place us in particular experiential relations to knowledge. Those architectures also impact the knowledge imparted. Think of it this way: the same detail of information can *sound, feel, look, smell,* or *taste* radically different when accessed in radically different venues or via disparate media (or when *not* told in some venues but told in others). In line with this configuration performance is the mode of any architecture or environment of access (one *performs* a mode of access in the archive; one *performs* a mode of access at a theatre; one *performs* a mode of access on the dance floor; one *performs* a mode of access on a battlefield). In this sense, too, performance does not disappear. In the archive, the performance of access is a ritual act that, by occlusion and inclusion, scripts the depreciation of (and registers as disappeared) other modes of access.

Remaining on the stage

Artists such as Suzan-Lori Parks and Linda Mussmann (discussed in Chapter 2) attempt to unpack a way in which performance (or actions, or acts) remain – but remain *differently*. Such works are interested in the ways in which history is not limited to the imperial domain of the document, or in which history is not "lost" through body-to-body transmission. Is this less an investigation of disappearance than an interest in the politics of dislocation and relocation? The idea that flesh memory might remain challenges conventional notions of the archive. By this reading, the scandal of performance relative to the archive is not that it disappears (this is what the archive expects, this is the archive's requirement), but that it remains in ways that resist archontic "house arrest" and "domiciliation."

To the degree that it remains, but remains differently or *in difference*, the past performed and made explicit as (live) performance can function as the kind of bodily transmission conventional archivists dread, a counter-memory – almost in the sense of an echo (as Parks's character Lucy in *The America Play* might call it). If echoes, or in the performance troupe Spiderwoman's words "rever-ber-berations," resound off of lived experience produced in performance, then we are challenged to think beyond the ways in which performance seems, according to our habituation to the archive, to disappear.[81] We are also and simultaneously encouraged to articulate the ways in which performance, less bound to the ocular, "sounds" (or begins again and again, as Stein would have it), differently, via itself as repetition – like a copy or perhaps more like a ritual – like an echo in the ears of a confidence keeper, an audience member, a witness.

Arguably, this sense of performance is imbricated in Phelan's phrasing – that performance "*becomes itself through*" disappearance. This phrasing is arguably different from an ontological claim of being (despite Phelan's stated drive to ontology), even different from an ontology of being under erasure. This phrasing rather invites us to think of performance as a medium in which disappearance negotiates, perhaps becomes, materiality. That is, disappearance is passed *through*. As is materiality.

Works in which the political manipulations of "disappearance" demand a material criticism – works such as Diana Taylor's *Disappearing Acts* or José Esteban Muñoz's "Ephemera as Evidence" – thus create a productive tension within performance studies orientations to (and sometime celebrations of) ephemerality. It is in the midst of this tension (or this "pickle" as Parks might put it) that the notion of performance as disappearance crosses chiasmically with ritual – ritual, in which, through performance, we are asked, again, to (re)found ourselves – to find ourselves in repetition.

> Pickling
> [performance] iz trying to find an equation
> for time *saved*/saving time
> but theatre/experience/performing/
> being/living etc. is all about
> *spending* time. No equation or [. . .]?[82]

* * * * * * * *

Re: re-do and Derrida's *coup de théâtre*

In her important book *The Archive and the Repertoire*, Diana Taylor referred to the essay "Performance Remains" re-done above. She cited it as "Archive Performance Remains." This is, of course, a trivial error. A minor detail like a trip of the tongue. And yet the essay has been cited by this erroneous title in various other publications, whose authors either tracked the essay down through Taylor or made the same mistake on their own – some of them close affiliates of mine, others unknown. So, I have not been the only author making modifications in the afterlife of this essay.[83]

The nominal "error" is fully understandable because the word "Archives" is printed as a header in the journal *Performance Research*, announcing the section in which my essay appears, and thus, by virtue of an oddity in design, it truly seems to shadow and even become part of the title. In this way, "Performance Remains" *becomes* "Archives Performance Remains." (I would have made the same "error" had I been Taylor reading and writing). The slip of the word "Archive" into my title tells me that Taylor read the essay in the pages of *Performance Research*: so, how "wrong" can that really be, then, after all? In *The Archive and the Repertoire* Taylor writes:

> What is at risk politically in thinking about embodied knowledge and perfor-
> mance as ephemeral as that which disappears? Whose memories "disappear"
> if only archival knowledge is valorized and granted permanence? Should we
> simply expand our notion of the archive to house the mnemonic and gestural
> practices and specialized knowledge transmitted live? Or get beyond the
> confines of the archive? I echo Rebecca Schneider's question in "Archive
> Performance Remains": "If we consider performance as a process of disap-
> pearance [. . .] are we limiting ourselves to an understanding of performance
> predetermined by our cultural habituation to the logic of the archive?" On the
> contrary: as I have tried to establish here, there is an advantage to thinking
> about a repertoire performed through dance, theatre, song, ritual, witnessing,
> healing practices, memory paths, and the many other forms of repeatable
> behaviors as something that cannot be housed or contained in the archive.[84]

Clearly, the misnomer "Archive Performance Remains" might suggest that there is a performance-leaning palimpsestuousness to discourse and the tracks of its circulation that, despite the best promises of the archive, does not allow even text to settle *as fixed*. The tune twangs. It's an old poststructural saw: there can be no fixity, no complete arrest, even in the gentlest bed of the archive. There will always be the trip of the eye as it reads, the tongue as it mouths. Dwelling in the dust,[85] texts themselves necessarily meet bodies and engage in the repetition and revision, the citing and becoming that is *also* choreography, orature, song, and, *à la* Taylor, "other forms of repeatable behaviors."[86] Thus texts, too, take place in the deferred *live* space of their encounter – and the repertoire of our citations is a kind of discursive oratorio – where error in re-pronunciation is as much in play as ever. Books in hand give away the secret that an archive is *not*, cannot be, a house of arrest, despite its solid promise that preservation *will have been* the case. So the advantage gained by the promise of preservation in a house divided between writing on the one hand and repertoires of (given to disappear) embodied knowledge on the other is only the advantage of the social secret it props and the privilege of the patriarchic it protects: that the distinction is bogus.

But let's not be too hasty. I have just said, above, that archives too are houses of the theatrical slip and slide, the error-riddled tendencies of the live. But that is not what Taylor is saying. "On the contrary," Taylor insists, "there is an advantage" to keeping the archive separate from performance-based practices.[87] Despite the fact that both writing and performance are reiterative, and both take place live and in cross-temporal negotiation, Taylor nevertheless feels she must wrestle with "the centuries-old privileging of writing over embodied knowledge."[88] Given the historical tracks of this privilege, which her book charts through Spanish conquest, Taylor needs the archive's claim to stability to remain articulable as a claim. She needs this claim to remain stable in order that the underprivileged performance can continue to appear as *having been* underprivileged. Thus Taylor affirms performance as a means of remaining through bodily acts of repetition she labels "repertoire," but she maintains this remaining *in distinction to* the archive. This distinction is crucial to giving the repertoire its historical due:

> Even though the relationship between the archive and the repertoire is not by definition antagonistic or oppositional, written documents have repeatedly announced the disappearance of the performance practices involved in mnemonic transmission. Writing has served as a strategy for repudiating and foreclosing the very embodiedness it claims to describe.[89]

Although Taylor is careful to avoid resolidifying a binary opposition between the archive and the repertoire – writing that the relationship between the two "too readily falls into a binary with the written and the archival constituting hegemonic power and the repertoire providing the anti-hegemonic challenge" – nevertheless the pull of a binaried relationship proves very powerful as it seems to provide "an advantage."[90] Simply by virtue of the fact that the archive is posited as appearing to work across distance and over time while the repertoire is embodied and "requires presence," the binary is reinforced.[91] Taylor does not entirely succeed, in other words, in resisting the binary archive/performance. Simply by arguing that we "shift our focus *from* written *to* embodied culture, *from* the discursive *to* the performatic," Taylor realigns a distinction between the two and asserts a linear trajectory: as if writing were not an embodied act, nor an embodied encounter across time, and as if performance were not discursive (nor discourse performative or "performatic").[92] The parsing of discourse as belonging to the archive on the one hand and non-discourse as the realm of performance on the other replicates the very gnarled bind Taylor's book *simultaneously* works, so very productively, to trouble.[93]

It is important to recall that Derrida is careful to note, in *Archive Fever*, that that which is given to the archive is not so much a matter of discourse or the discursive nature of documents as it is a matter of "topology," by which he means placedness, givenness, *nomination* to remain. That which is *not* so nominated, not given to the archive to remain is – *whether discursive or not* – given to disappear by virtue of a social mandate. It is not discursivity on the one hand and performance on the other that constructs the privilege of the archive, but, for Derrida, "*patriarchic*" habits of nomination and consignation that police ways of knowing. Derrida writes:

> It is thus in this domiciliation, in house arrest, that archives take place. The dwelling, this place where they dwell permanently, marks the institutional

passage from the private to the public, which does not always mean from the secret to the nonsecret. [. . .] With such a status, the documents, *which are not always discursive writings*, are only kept and classified under the title of the archive by virtue of a *privileged topology*. They inhabit this uncommon place, this place of election where law and singularity intersect in privilege. At the intersection of the topological and the nomological, of the place and the law, of the substrate and the authority, a scene of domiciliation becomes at once visible and invisible.[94]

We may say that Taylor is less concerned with the inter(in)animation of the live and the archived (though she notes it) than she is in rescuing performance for archival account. That is, she works to situate the repertoire *as another kind of archive*, rather than emphasizing the twin effort of situating the archive as *another kind of performance*. To do this, she works to retain the distinguishing notion that posits repertoires as embodied acts of "presence" on the one hand and posits archives as houses for documents and objects that, in their very presence, record a qualitative absence on the other hand. In this way, Taylor does not situate the archive as *also* part of an embodied repertoire – a set of live practices of access, given to take place in a house (the literal archive) built for live encounter with privileged remains, remains that, ironically, *script* the encountering body as disappearing even as the return of the body is assumed by the very logic of preservation that assumes disappearance. That is, the split between archive and repertoire, a split that Taylor to some extent reiterates, is the archive's own division.

In *Archive Fever*, Derrida makes the case that archives "seem at first, admittedly, to point to the past, to refer to the signs of consigned memory, to recall faithfulness to tradition" but, on second glance, house "transgenerational memory" that, by virtue of a contract *across* time, "calls into question the coming of the future."[95] We might say, with Derrida, that archives call into question the coming of the future as future. He writes: "The question of the archive is not, we repeat, a question of the past. [. . .] It is a question of the future, the question of the future itself, the question of a response, or a promise and of a responsibility for tomorrow."[96] The slip in time between the nomination of the past as seemingly past and the archival consignment for a deferred future of that past – "what will have been" – is, Derrida repeatedly notes, a *coup de théâtre* at the heart of the archive's own self-contradictory logic of preservation of the past. Much as a dramatic script is given to remain for potential future production, or dance steps may be housed in bodily training for acts requiring dancers, materials in the archive are given, too, for the *future* of their (re)enactment. Here it becomes clear: the theatricality of this equation, even the performative bases of the archive, is that it is a house of and for performative repetition, not stasis. This, Derrida suggests, is the archive's biggest secret. Theatricality (linked to the "archiviolithic" of the death drive) is posited throughout *Archive Fever* as the archive's own performance. For even as a linear order of time appears to be kept intact by the archive, it is a continual *coup de théâtre* which "dislocates the linear order of presents" and folds the past into a deferred time of "much future work" – suggesting a future for pasts that have, much like a play-script in relation to production or dance steps sedimented in trained bodies, not *yet* taken place.[97] This is a dramatic turn at once essential to the archive but simultaneously destructive of its very tenet: that it preserves the past *as* past.

We might read Derrida to be making the point that archives are, first and foremost, *theatres* for repertoires of preservation, leaning toward and into a promise of the coming "liveness" of encounter. For, to make his argument about the archive's reliance on repetition and its promise for the future, he relies on words or phrases such as "drama," "performative," "staging," and "*coup de théâtre.*" In fact, he turns repeatedly, as he did in *Specters of Marx*, to *Hamlet* by way of example. Or, more specifically, to Hamlet's father's ghost:

> [T]he structure of the archive is *spectral*. It is spectral *a priori*: neither present nor absent "in the flesh," neither visible nor invisible, a trace always referring to another whose eyes can never be met, no more than those of Hamlet's father, thanks to the possibility of a visor. Also, the spectral motive *stages* [emphasis added] this disseminating fission from which the archontic principle, and the concept of the archive, and the concept in general suffer, from the principle on.[98]

Derrida uses the encounter between Marcellus, Horatio, and Hamlet's father's ghost to set the scene in which the scholar Yerulshami encounters the specter of Freud in and through Freud's archive.[99] And yet, despite this *staging*, Derrida simultaneously forgets that *Hamlet* is a play to be played *meantime* by live actors. That is, Derrida prefers to underscore the "*spectrality*" of Hamlet's ghost, rather than noting again that that spectrality is itself theatrical – a *coup de théâtre*. What do I mean that in privileging spectrality, Derrida forgets that the specter is staged, even as he employs the word "stages" to ensure it? It may seem like a simple error, or a minor choice of omission, but the question in play is: *does it matter* that Hamlet's father's ghost would be, in the futures of the script, played by *live* actors wearing visors? Derrida writes of the "visor effect" to suggest that "like the father of Hamlet behind his visor, and by virtue of a *visor effect*, the specter sees without being seen."[100] And he writes, as quoted above, that the archive preserves a "trace always referring to another whose eyes can never be met, no more than those of Hamlet's father, thanks to the possibility of a visor."[101] That is, for Derrida, the eyes of the dead can never be met – thanks to a visor.

But, what, here, does Derrida omit? What the visor effects in staging, from the point of few of mounting the play live, is that what is *not* seen is not the specter, but the live actor playing the revenant – the live body *enabling the specter to reappear across the surface of live encounter*. Recall, the visor hides the fact that rather than one "whose eyes can never be met," there is, indeed, another whose eyes can perhaps too easily be met – the live actor who, living surrogate for the apparently dead, reminds us that, indeed, we very well may be able to meet the eyes of an other. That is, we might well be able to encounter the other, but for a mask (masks and disguises being theatrical properties that seem to link theatre, for both Derrida and Roland Barthes, to death).[102] But, in the theatre as in the archive, it is not only the specter that can "see but not be seen": it is (also and already) the live body bearing the specter across the space, the place, of its consignation. The specter, by virtue of a *coup de théâtre*, can "see but not be seen" thanks to our embodied knowledge of how to attend to appearances: our collective and skillful forgetting of the actor – the fool or clown chasing trippingly the "question of the play" – who enables, *gently*, the manipulation of error (in the meantime between the dead and the live) that is an act of transmission, transmutation, transfer.

But perhaps it is even more complicated. Perhaps, our collective and skillful forgetting of the actor behind the visor concerns the troubling aspect that an actor, playing a specter, may not be *only* live. If we might indeed meet the eyes of an actor, between or meantime the visor and the face, might we "dislocate the linear order of presents," and find *not that we cannot meet the eyes of a nonlive or nonliving other, but that* (scandalous thought!) *we can?* That we might meet the eyes of an other – the eyes of the dead – in the very wink of the real in one another's eyes – now that would surely be syncopated time, not to mention "endless trouble."[103]

But, to return to my earlier question: *does it matter?* Does it matter that the actor playing the specter may be alive? Perhaps it does not. Or perhaps the question is simply undecidable. For Derrida, we might say, "undecidability is all."[104] For if behind the specter's visor may be a live actor, certainly behind (or to the side) of the actor may be a specter – of other actors, other specters, other faux fathers, other scripts. And before and after them all may be the persistent pressure of the re-do, and its indeterminate tangle between the done, the re-done, and the not yet done. Begin, begin again, begin again, said Stein, sounding Bergson beginning again. If the archive is a live performance space, and the performance space an archive for the revenant, perhaps Hamlet's famed inability to act (an inability played so ably by so many actors) is trumped by his own more famous line about undecidability: "readiness is all."

> If it be now, 'tis not to come; if it be not to come, it will be now; if it be not now, yet it will come: the readiness is all. Since no man has aught of what he leaves, what is't to leave betimes?
>
> ——*Hamlet* (5.2.221–5)

4 Poor poor theatre

I don't want it to be essentially the same – I want it to be *exactly* the same.
———Andy Warhol, 1980

I'm speaking to my ancestors. And of course I don't see eye-to-eye with my ancestors. But at the same time I cannot deny their existence.
———Jerzy Grotowski, 1987

I'm speaking to my ancestors. And of course I don't see eye-to-eye with my ancestors. But at the same time I cannot deny their existence.
———Elizabeth LeCompte, 2004

In her Spring 2004 program notes to *Poor Theater*, Elizabeth LeCompte, director of the Wooster Group, explained that the show was aimed at her "ancestors" and was "a personal question between me and them."[1] The statement points to the ways that practices of art (in her case theatre) can be conversations across time and can contain energies we might align with historical reenactments such that precedent art, no matter how "live" the event may be or may have been, is never so much "over" or "disappeared" as given to call and response – to (re)composition in transgenerational conversation. Yet LeCompte's words in this explanatory set of sentences from her own program, under the title "The Director," are stolen verbatim and unattributed. They are the words of director Jerzy Grotowski, from an essay he published in *TDR: The Drama Review* in 1987 titled "*Tu es le fils de quelqu'un* [You are someone's son]," with some minor alterations as the quote progresses.[2] In that essay, Grotowski speaks to "you," and directly genders all readers and legitimate future theatre directors as male. LeCompte, in a direct theatrical family tree with Grotowski and yet no one's son, talks back as if to someone's patriarch in this production. She argues in fact – they don't see eye-to-eye – using his own words, sometimes like reverence and sometimes like spit, in her own mouth. She's talking to her ancestor, all right, and handing his words right back to him. No one's son, she raises a pronounced "heritage" problem, making overly visible a "father" who would not have recognized her existence. Outside lineage by virtue of the long-echoing arm of Grotowski's sexism, she behaves like a foundling on the warpath of the copy.

LeCompte's *Poor Theater* contained, among other things, a reenactment – rendered as precisely as possible – of the last twenty minutes of Grotowski's theatre production of *Akropolis*. At the Performing Garage on Wooster Street in New York City in 2004, Wooster Group actors Kate Valk, Ari Fliakos, and Scott Shepherd intoned the voices and adopted the same gestures, stances, and positions the Polish Laboratory Theatre actors had struck in the 1968 London film version of Grotowski's Laboratorium Theatre's 1965 Wrocław production of Stanislaw Wyspianski's 1904 play *Akropolis*. The fervor of exactitude in their reenactment (that is, they don't attempt to reinterpret as much as to precisely repeat) seems like an attempt to clone the forebears, as precisely as possible: the tiniest or most specific of Grotowski's Lab actors' details are attended to – tilt of head, toss of hair, stamp of foot, furrow of brow, pitch of voice, direction of gaze, intake of breath. Exact particulars of affective, gestural, and aural bits (without, interestingly, attention to replica costume or make-up or other conventions of historical reconstruction) are attempted in replay across the bodies of the Wooster actors who play their efforts at exactness on a stage rendered as a "footprint" of the Wrocław stage.

The effort at gestic cloning both succeeds (the performances are technically stunning in their precision) and completely fails as the problem of unruly details (call it gender difference, bodily difference, language difference, anachronism, or any other number of inevitable errors) takes the stage with a palpable force in direct proportion to the technical accomplishment of reiterating the affects of the "master's piece" faithfully.[3] Indeed, watching the labor of *exact* replication from the audience, it seems as though the more they get the reenactment exactly right, the more uncannily *wrong* it begins to feel. Because the Wooster Group attempts to translate literally – in precise word-to-word, gesture-to-gesture exactitude – it is the force of literal precision itself that both upholds the entire enterprise of fidelity to event and, at the same time, challenges that enterprise. The logic of overt and hard-working replication seems to offer a kind of sincerity, but it is a sincerity that rings of drag, of camp aesthetic, and the essential threat of the double (that feared category of the mimetic), and therefore seems a queer interruption to modernity's thrall to the new, to the original, to the aim for the "pure" aesthetic act in which Grotowski's "sacred" theatre took a mid-century pride of place.

The potential aspect of camp at the undecidable edges of sincerity is deeply important here. For, as in camp performance generally, that which is gotten slightly wrong in the effort to get something right, is precisely the space where difference is unleashed as critical homage. There will be more to say on this point in the Afterword. Paradoxically, perhaps, it is the errors, the cracks in the effort, the almost but not quite, that give us some access to sincerity, to fidelity, to a kind of *touch* across time David Romàn has termed "archival drag."[4] When, in the twenty-minute reenactment, the actors simultaneously *can* and *cannot* hit the precise note or strike the exact pose, we feel a leak of affective engagement between the then and the now that brings time travel, as it were, into the fold of experience: shimmering on an edge, caught between the possible and the impossible, touching the interval itself.

The more precise or overt the replication *as replication* (without in this case the trappings of scenic or costume, gender or age visual verisimilitude), the greater the antitheatrical panic about the propriety of the pristine original. At the same time, the more precise the translation, the greater the challenge to comprehensibility, leaving the original both *touched* and distinct.[5] The more the same, the greater in respect to difference. Walter Benjamin pointed to this irony in "The Task of the Translator," writing:

> A literal rendering [is] a direct threat to comprehensibility. [. . .] It is self-evident how greatly fidelity in reproducing the form impedes the rendering of the sense.[6]

Benjamin was writing of translating text across languages. But we might ask: what comes undone, what escapes sense, what becomes uncanny (in Freud's definition, threatening comprehensibility through replicating the familiar) when a *temporal* event, approached as if a foreign language, is translated literally, with extreme and even painful precision, across bodies?

Poor Theater: the Wooster Group

What follows is a description of my evening at the theatre, though it might read something like Gertrude Stein's first play, *What Happened*, famous for seeming to offer no discrete event at all. What happened at the Performing Garage during *Poor Theater* was, precisely, nothing new. What happened was much like what has happened at the Performing Garage since the Wooster Group began to germinate its now famous style from within director Richard Schechner's Performance Group in the 1970s. *Poor Theater* contained all the hyper-identifiable marks of the Wooster Group's aesthetic – the performers in their own street clothes, the affect of a kind of studied boredom on their faces as they set up a punctuated set of scenes, the spare setting, the television as performer, the bursts of almost frenetic energy punctuated by uber-calm.

Entering the Performing Garage in March of 2004, in expectation of all of these signature markers, I was handed a program, containing the note from LeCompte, a diagram of the stage, and other information. This in itself was expected – and not on the surface part of the "Series of Simulacra" the subtitle of the evening promised. And yet, analysis of the ritual properties of theatre-going might invite one to claim that entering the theatre, purchasing the ticket, being handed the program are all part of a sedimented set of acts of repetition that are theatre's ongoing event – acts, we might recall, that led Søren Kierkegaard, like so many philosophers, to choose theatre as a privileged site for thinking about repetition *in situ*. So, if entering a theatre is agreeing to participate in a set of acts played out, most often, within clear boundaries of expectation, and part of that expectation is a givenness of repetition, then, already, attending the theatre at all is engaging in a repetitive event, the "footprint" of which precedes the specific enactment. That is, going to the theatre at all is engaging in reenactment.

Very well and good. But this playing fast and loose with the word "reenactment" (along the lines of "everything is performance") would not get us anywhere if it were not part and parcel of the simulacral soup the Wooster Group had in store. What was to be reenacted on the stage at the Performing Garage was a series of precedent moments in the theatre rendered as explicitly *again* as possible. Marvin Carlson has argued that theatre is always already haunted, composed in and through a ghosting that makes any theatre production an act of lamination upon precedent (whether precedent play text, precedent act, or simply precedent theatre-going), but the Wooster Group aimed to articulate that "always already" in extremis.[7] To that end, upon the Performing Garage stage floor was . . . a stage. As if laminated onto lamination, the Wooster Group had set the "footprint" of Grotowski's Theatre Lab onto its own floor.[8]

It was not immediately clear that there was a stage on the stage, since the stage simply looked like itself – a stage. We had already been handed the program – and walked to our seat – passing by the stage as if it were simply that – a stage – and not a stage upon a stage, or stage "as if" a stage. It looked like a stage – not the staging of a stage. Was the program, then, a program? Or was it a footprint of a program, or a blueprint for a program? Was my walk to the theatre *my* walk? Or had my walk fallen into the footprints of others' walks to this theatre, or to other theatres, or theirs into mine? To render simulacra of a theatre is, of course, to render simulacra of simulacra. The dizzying and even tiresome nature of such an enterprise, so beloved by the 1980s postmodernism in which the Wooster Group came of age, invites the dislocation of location such that one can't quite know, with hindsight, when the "simulacra" began, nor when (if ever) it might end.

The stage of Grotowski's Laboratorium footprinted upon the Performing Garage stage was only errantly reminiscent of the long-standing practice in dramatic writing of setting a stage *within* a stage, for there was nothing beyond the footprint to suggest the descriptor "within" except the walls of the Garage itself. There was no set within a set, in other words – the Lab footprint stage was built primarily by markings on the floor in tape with some thin pieces of metal added for visibility and gobos in lights made words that marked important labels on the floor plan like "door" and "window."[9]

On the issue of "speaking to [theatre] ancestors" and on generational revenge, the matter of the stage within the stage in theatre history is not inconsequential. Theatre history is rife with stages housing stages. Think of *Hamlet* and the "moustrap" or Treplev's symbolist stage within the drama of generational struggle that is Anton Chekhov's *The Seagull*. However, arguably unlike Shakespeare's and Chekhov's plays within plays, the stage on the stage at the Performing Garage for *Poor Theater* was not set up in order to have actors act *as if* they were actors acting. Recall that the actors who speak the speech "trippingly on the tongue" in Shakespeare's *Hamlet* are actors playing actors, whereas the Wooster Group company reenacting *Akropolis* resist the "as if." Far more alienated, rather like workers, the Wooster Group are actors *being* actors working, for there is no wider story within which their reenactment is nested, except for the story of their attempt to reenact (which they do not present as "acting" – though of course, the blurring of those lines is part and parcel of the point). Similarly, the reenactment of *Akropolis* does not offer itself "as if" for the first time. Rather, it is a "work in progress," and offered as a rehearsal – toward a first time that will never fully or finally arrive. If it is offered in advance of a first time, it is also explicitly offered as already a second time – after Grotowski.

The generational revenge drama, mounted by a director who is no one's son, is played out between directors here, *across* their temporal stages. We can recall that the conceit in *Hamlet* is that the king is caught unaware at a performance he is seeing "for the first time." Ironically, of course, the performance Hamlet sets before the king is a *reenactment* of the king's murder of Hamlet's *legitimate* father, disguised by Hamlet as a play. Shakespeare asks us to watch King Claudius slowly realize that in spectating a theatrical he is in fact witnessing a reenactment of an actual event. But Shakespeare does not ask the general theatre audience (at least not explicitly) to realize the same "trap" for themselves. LeCompte, on the other hand, is nothing but trap. Hamlet-like in that she is also not the "son" of her "father," she puts *her* spectator next to the Ghost of Grotowski, the ancestor to whom she is speaking, smack-dab in King Claudius's seat. Not surprisingly, the next production LeCompte mounted after *Poor Theater* was a precise reenactment of the 1964 film of John Gielgud's production of *Hamlet* starring Richard Burton (then) *and* Scott Shepherd (now) (see Figure 0.4).

In the opening of his 1968 *Towards a Poor Theatre*, Grotowski makes clear his own indebtedness to theatre ancestors such as Stanislavsky, Delsarte, Dullin, Meyerhold – rendering his own "origin" a matter of footprints on already well-worn tracks. So, one way to tell the story of the stage as footprint, then, would be to say that the Wooster Group had taken its baby steps through Grotowski's directives in *Towards a Poor Theatre*. Founding Wooster Group members had been members of Richard Schechner's Performance Group – LeCompte had joined the group in 1970, three years after its founding. Grotowski's conversations with Schechner, begun in the late 1960s, were important to both men, and Schechner used Grotowski's *plastiques* (physical exercises derived from the Russian ancestor Vsevlod Meyerhold) extensively when directing.[10] The Wooster Group broke off from the Performance Group in 1980, but continued to work in the Performing Garage on Wooster Street, and Schechner disbanded the Performance Group shortly thereafter, leaving the Wooster Group as inheritors of the Garage.

It's curious that the title for the Wooster Group work in progress should be *Poor Theater* – as if there could be "progress" in the direction of some kind of arrival at the theatre Grotowski was working "towards" in *Towards a Poor Theatre*. For here, it is the relational and future-oriented preposition *Towards* that has either been forgotten, or replaced by a suggestion of arrival. But of course, the "in progress" nature of all of the Wooster Group's work would mitigate any claim of arrival. And in any case, the work the Wooster Group has been presenting since its inception is arguably many steps removed from the impulses of the "total act" that Grotowski sought in his early "poor theatre" theatre.

What Grotowski meant by "poor theatre" was not, of course, "bad theatre." Bad theatre is a phrase more associated, variously, with battle reenactment, camp, kitsch, popular theatrical pastimes, amateur hours, or conventional commercial theatre in general. Bad theatre as commonly understood, and as Schechner himself claimed in a 1970 essay he titled "Actuals," is imitative theatre. Bad theatre postures and feigns and therefore cannot generate the original and uniquely primal act of a performer engaged in what Grotowski would call "sacrifice." Against imitation, Grotowski's "poor theatre" promoted the taking away of all things unnecessary to the primal and pure "offering" of an actor's bodily and "organic" sacrifice – and the way "towards" poor theatre Grotowski called "via negativa."[11] Indeed bad theatre was what Grotowski labeled "Rich Theatre," by which he referred to the tricks and trappings of any theatre more interested in the spectacle of an "as if" than in something that might be an experiential (or bodily) actuality. Grotowski had this to say about Rich Theatre (and note that Rich Theatre sounds a lot like the Wooster Group work):

> The Rich Theatre depends on artistic kleptomania, drawing from the other disciplines, creating hybrid-spectacles, conglomerates without backbone or integrity, yet presented as an organic artwork. By multiplying assimilated elements, the Rich Theatre tries to escape the impasse presented by movies and television. [. . .] The integration of borrowed mechanisms (movie screens onstage, for example) means a sophisticated technical plant, permitting great mobility and dynamism. [. . .] This is all nonsense. [. . .] Consequently, I propose poverty in the theatre.[12]

In the rabidly kleptomaniacal style for which they have long been known, the Wooster Group's *Poor Theater* begins with a pseudo-documentary of the company watching an actual documentary about the early days of the Polish Lab and trying to do the exercises demonstrated by Grotowski's company – Grotowski actors Ryszard Cieslak, Zigmunt Molik, Rena Mirecka, and others. To do this, members of the Wooster Group have gathered around a television set. Without costumes, make-up, or any of the trappings of Rich Theatre, they discuss how to realize their reenactment. Their acting style is strikingly disinterested, lacking pathos of any kind. They work, as Philip Auslander described in 1987, at all times against the tyranny of theatrical presence.[13] They seem to simply "do" whatever it is they do and this "doing" appears in distinction to "acting" – except when they are "doing" acting (which in this case takes the form of reenactment of Grotowski's actors on Grotowski's stage). The result is both radically alienated, and, being alienated, strangely real – at the same time.

While the tape of the pseudo-documentary is playing, the Wooster actors casually discuss what it was like to prepare the reenactment of the last segment of Grotowski's *Akropolis* and how they struggled to render the footprint of the stage as exactly as possible, translating materials across time and space. They then recreate a meeting the company had with Grotowski's secretary in the summer of 2003. They recorded the actual meeting with a mini-disk that they use to reenact it. Following this, they reenact the company's meeting with a Polish translator who watched *Akropolis* with them and simultaneously translated the Polish into English.

On a flat panel monitor behind this recreation is an image of designer Jennifer Tipton. As the production's dramaturg Sam Gold told me, "Jennifer is there as a video image because on the day we met with the translator she was there and we wanted to simulate her for the recreation."[14] After this, the Group begins reenacting *one of their own rehearsals* of the final minutes of *Akropolis*. This twenty minutes is, for me, the heart of the show as a whole. The group reenacts their rehearsal for the reenactment, in which they are, of course, reenacting. And quite impressively.

The actors carry out their reenactment of the film of the production while that film runs in video just behind them. They reenact as exactly as possible every intonation and gesture the film makes available for viewing. We hear film voices and live voices simultaneously – Grotowski's actors speaking Polish on the film, and LeCompte's actors speaking Polish with clone-like intonation live. On two other monitor "windows" at the back of the theatre we see the Wooster Group

Figure 4.1
The Wooster Group's *Poor Theater*, directed by Elizabeth LeCompte. Actors (l–r): Scott Shepherd, Kate Valk, Ari Fliakos. Photo: © Paula Court.

technicians (who are also visible running the show at the side of the stage). The technicians on the monitors have the video of the film of *Akropolis* superimposed on their faces.

The live reenactment is so precise as to be stunning, in the way that any feat of technical virtuosity is impressive. The *technical reproduction* of and in the live act (in the "technique" of the actors) is partially what is so striking. The Wooster Group actors technically reenact the Grotowski actors, who are technologically reproduced in film. They reenact the acting with precision, but it is a precision that cannot spark, or *enliven*, the very feelings it nevertheless appears to precisely cite. But the place of passion and affect here is extremely complicated, for as we will discuss in a moment, Grotowski's actors, too, are/were alienated and they present/presented their acts with a stark honesty, devoid of pathos while nevertheless full of affective stance.

At this juncture, before continuing with the Wooster Group description, it is worth considering a few things from Grotowski's production. The film of *Akropolis*,

Figure 4.2 Rehearsal photograph, taken in advance of Grotowski's first version of *Akropolis*. The 13 Rows Theatr, Opole April 1964. Actors (l–r): Zygmunt Milik, Ryszard Cieslak, Andrzej Bielski, Antoni Jahołkowski, Mieczysław Janowski, Gaston Kulig, Rena Mirecka. Unknown photographer. Image courtesy of Instytut im. Jerzego Grotowskiego/The Grotowski Institute, Wrocław, Poland.

on which the Wooster reenactment is based, is one well known to theatre history students, and when it was broadcast in New York in 1969 it would have been briefly known by a wider television audience. In fact, Grotowski began work on Wyspianski's *Akropolis* in 1962 and between 1962 and 1968 his adaptation was mounted in five different versions.

Screenings of the film *Akropolis*, directed by James Taggart, often make the error of calling it a recording of an "original performance" (for example, the Polish Cultural Institute in London screened it as such in 2002). But the 1967 version on which the 1968 filming was based, was already the fifth reiteration of the director's work. The recording took place between October 27 and November 2, 1968 at Twickenham studios in England. The film is prefaced by a twenty-five-minute introduction in English by theatre director Peter Brook, but the production itself is entirely in Polish with occasional voice-over in English providing key translations. It is this recreation of the fifth Wrocław production, mounted in England on (one can surmise) a "footprint" of the theatre in Wrocław, that the Wooster Group uses as its primary document for reenactment.

The film is a version of Grotowski's adaptation of the turn-of-the-century symbolist play by Stanislaw Wyspianski. Not insignificantly, Wyspianski's *Akropolis* is a play in which the statues in the Royal Cathedral in Cracow come to life and *reenact* scenes from the Bible, from Homer, and from historical events.[15] Grotowski's contribution was to set Wyspianski's play inside the concentration camp at Auschwitz, with the camp as a disturbing modern analogue for the cathedral.[16] Also in 1969, Grotowski brought his theatre to New York where *Akropolis* was performed in the Washington Square Methodist Church. "Here," wrote Elizabeth Hardwick in a lengthy review/commentary published in February of 1970 in the *New York Review of Books*, "between gestures of hard labor, the prisoners seem to fall into a day-dream of history." The fact that Grotowski's actors engaged in acting that Hardwick described as "gestures of hard labor" suggests that the actors made the labor of acting apparent. In fact, the hard labor of "total" acting was arguably what Grotowski meant, using religious rather than materialist language, by the actor's "sacrifice" in *Towards a Poor Theatre*.[17]

The "hard labor" of actorly sacrifice resulted in what Hardwick described as follows:

> In the Grotowski Theatre there are no pathos, no tears, no real laughter, no friendliness, no love, no personal history, no disappointment, no victory. There are, instead, constant activity and pain, suffering, death, torment, fear, mockery, persecution, submission, ecstasy – and a sense of history. [. . . There is] a lack of mere pathos – and this is the genius of the work – and a sense of the death of the world instead.[. . .] The prisoners go into a big box in the center of the square. They pull the top over their heads. A voice says, "They are gone and the coils of smoke hover in the air." The audience leaves.[18]

Note that very interestingly the passionate sacrifice of the actors – their hard labor – results in both a surplus of affect (pain, torment, fear, ecstasy) and a complete lack of what Hardwick terms "mere pathos." I take her to mean that they are engaged in the "constant *activity*" of "pain, suffering, death, torment, fear" and not the sentiment associated with those states. In fact, while full of affect, they appear devoid of sentiment – a fact clearly captured on the grainy Twickenham film. This, she wrote, is "the genius of the work."

During the reenactment of *Akropolis* at the Performing Garage, the Wooster Group actors were avidly concentrated on getting every gesture of Grotowski's cast and every intonation of their Polish letter-perfect. Thus, rather than being served the narrative arc of a drama, the audience at the Performing Garage was witness to the hard labor of replicating Laboratorium "activity." In the process of reenacting so explicitly, the sense of the actors' hard labor replaced any pretense to comprehensibility – to story, through-line, or narrative. In this production, as in Grotowski's Wyspianskian Auschwitz, a quality of horror begins to attend the inescapability of citation. A certain horror of history as composed in and through repetition became *sensible* – as in, available to physical experience. The absence of pathos in Grotowski strangely matched the absence of pathos in the Wooster

Figure 4.3 The Wooster Group's *Poor Theater*, directed by Elizabeth LeCompte. Actors (l–r): Scott Shepherd, Kate Valk. Photo: © Paula Court.

Group, resulting in a transmission of the hard labor of affect – detaining Grotowski through his own "Polish drag,"[19] in a work about *detention camp*.

The literalness and hard labor of the reenactment provoked something that flickered in the space between "original" and "copy," as if between stone statue and live passer-by,[20] – something not immediately accessible to account, and something of history's composition in mimesis and repetition that caused the skin to crawl with the stone-cold *presentness* of the absences that ghost. It was the space *between* Grotowski's overdetermined filmic document (seemingly the same every time it is played) and LeCompte's fervid living film that opened *something* out, much like a tear in the screen through which the "real" might return via negativa.[21] And most strangely, perhaps, it seemed to be LeCompte's live actors who flickered like shadows in their frenzied liveness – making room for the bygone, the stone-cold, to pass, again.

It was this attention to history's composition in repetition that reminded me of the Civil War reenactors I witnessed at the Battle for Culps Hill, discussed in Chapter 1. These "enthusiasts" were so concentrated on a kind of hard labor of authenticity (without being ignorant of its impossibility) that the "sense" of their actions did not result, for the spectator, in the scene as a comprehensible "show." It wasn't a "show" – it was *work* in progress. The case of the Culps Hill battle, where there was nothing for the audience in the stands to witness as happening, reminded me of the efforts of the Wooster Group actors to render their ancestors exactly. The sensibility of a scene entirely disappeared from view suggested, of course, that to do it again with precision is to miss it again. Reenactment, that is, especially when grounded in the attempt at exact replication, touches something that also attends to citation: the inevitability of citing and the simultaneous impossibility of fixing for a fully legislated comprehensibility.[22] In both the Gettysburg battle and the Wooster reenactment, the closer the reenactment came to a literal or clone-like precision, the more "other" it simultaneously grew, rendering both the first time and the second time out-of-time, unfinished, or ongoing – a work in progress that could never be complete, and never fully witnessed – even if available to analysis.

Returning to the description of the evening at *Poor Theater*, the reenactment stops a minute or so before the end of the film *Akropolis* and the company, dropping their hard work, simply watches the end of the film on a reflection of a monitor while the next section occurs. In this section, a theatre critic and long-time friend of Grotowski (unnamed by the Group for legal reasons) speaks with LeCompte (played by Sheena See) about why anyone would ever want to do *Akropolis* again. The critic says that the Wooster Group "must be joking." As the scene concludes, the volume comes back up on the end of the *Akropolis* film when the Laboratorium actors disappear into a "gas chamber" they have been hard at work, throughout the play, building out of junk and garbage. The British voice-over in the film translates the last line: "They went and only the smoke remains."

As the audience in the Performing Garage hears the filmed Twickenham/ Laboratorium audience leave the theatre, the Wooster Group wheels two video monitors to the front of the stage. On the video runs a banal street scene – snow falling on Canal Street, just beyond Wooster Street in New York. We then hear a recording of another piece of conversation with the critic. She says: "Don't try to improve on it. [. . .] Just leave it." The snow falls like the banal passing of everyday life, resiliently repetitive and cold. We hear the critic's voice again: "It was a great piece that was done. Don't try to improve on it or bring it up. Just leave it." This is the end of Part One.

The second half of the Wooster Group's *Poor Theater* is fascinating, if not concerned with Grotowski. The second part also contains reenactment, but this time of a documentary about choreographer William Forsythe. Forsythe created Ballett Frankfurt in 1984, choreographing many "cutting edge" works with his international company. The city of Frankfurt would disband the company permanently at midnight on August 31, 2004 – just months away from the Wooster Group reenactment (which I attended in March of 2004). Thus, the second half of *Poor Theater* was a "reenactment in advance" – a commemorative rite in advance of an end. The temporal dislocation in both halves of *Poor Theater* contributed to the overall sense that this was a theatre piece about the fold of time, where before and after, towards and against, were not clearly discernable. Intersecting the Forsythe material in *Poor Theater*'s second half are improvised bits seeming to reenact *High Noon*-style Westerns, as well as a section in which Scott Shepherd delivers a scathing performance of a Forsythe lecture with the same kind of literal exactitude that the company attempted for *Akropolis*. Most interesting is a section in which the actors reenact one of Forsythe's dances. Of course, they are actually dancing (not only acting dancing), yet because they are trained actors and not trained dancers there is an "almost but not quite" quality to their reenactment and their dancing looks, simply, untrained: Poor Dance. The absent dancers' bodies haunt the actors' dancing bodies. The actors *are* dancing, but their actorliness (as in-body training) is apparent, despite the *hard labor* that obviously attends this section. Thus, though they are *really* dancing, they do not fully pass as dancing. They are "poor theatre" artists.

The show closes with a return to the film *Akropolis* after at least one false ending in which the audience (in the Garage) thinks the show is over and claps – in error. In the last moments of *Poor Theater,* the Wooster technicians mix material from Western movies with the last moments of *Akropolis* as the Wooster actors improvise their way down a hole in the floor (actually under the bleachers on which the audience is sitting). Afterwards, we hear the British narrator from the film say again: "They went and only the smoke remains." We see the technicians on the video monitors, but their images are mixed with a cloudy sky (looking a lot like smoke). As we watch the technicians – both live and on the monitors – we listen to the audience file out at the end of the film until we hear a man in the film say: "Ladies and gentlemen, the performance is over." Bozkurt Karasu, the Wooster Group Production Manager, says the same words, simultaneously, into a microphone at the side of the stage. Much like the reenactment, when the Wooster actors synchronized their live voices to the Laboratorium voices on the film, we were again told in double-time that "the performance is over." Of course, we must choose which voice to believe, if any voice at all, since the "overness" of the work in progress was rendered both as restored behavior and as incomplete. The smoke that remains appears, in this instance, to be the shadowy fact of ongoing liveness itself.

Between Jerzy Grotowski and Elizabeth LeCompte

As I wrote in the Foreword, I am interested in live reenactment work that presses for literal precision, even that much maligned word "imitation," rather than trying to avoid it. There I cited Sherrie Levine's appropriation of Walker Evans's photographs and Andy Warhol's appropriation of Campbell's soup or Brillo's boxes and the longstanding challenge such works pose to the modernist myth of originality and the "solo" virility of the Great Artist and "pure" art acts. We do not need to be reminded that *theatre* artists have never been assumed to be pure, singular, or authentic, though many pioneers from Zola to Artaud to Grotowski eschewed conventions of imitation, instead seeking a theatre of authenticity and an arena for what Richard Schechner termed "actuals" in 1970 and what Marina Abramović terms "pure and raw" today.[23]

LeCompte's *Poor Theater* gives us cross-temporal conversation as a battle of sorts, arguably flipping into reverse the notion that ancestors speak austerely to the future from a pure, authentic, or pristine past through the echo of their archivable remains (in this case a grainy 1968 film). LeCompte suggests a theatrical switch, a *coup de théâtre*, by which "now" speaks or calls forward to (and through) "then" in gestures that are not only a reiterative response (as a copy appears to cite a so-called original) but also a call toward the past's future reply. LeCompte's appropriated Grotowski quote "I'm speaking to my ancestors" admits to a kind of fight or battle in that this speaking *to* is not a congenial speaking *with*, but rather, for LeCompte (using Grotowski's words), a mode of arguing ("we don't see eye to eye"), suggesting that transgenerational memory necessarily, in Derrida's words from *Archive Fever*, "dislocates the linear order of presents."[24] To speak *to* something is not necessarily to speak together, but to call out toward an auditor and demand an ear – to hail the object of the call (in this case the past) into the congress of future reply, bringing it forward into being beside itself, as it were, subject and subjected to response. In this way, repetition is not remembering the past as if the past were only behind, but pitching or stitching *forward* into the odd category Kierkegaard termed (somewhat farcically through his character Constantin) "time to live":

> Just as [the Greeks] taught that all knowing is a recollecting, modern philosophy will teach that all life is a repetition. [. . .] Repetition and recollection are the same movement except in opposite directions; for what is recollected has been, is repeated backwards, whereas genuine repetition is recollected forward. Repetition, therefore, if it is possible, makes a person happy, whereas recollection makes him unhappy – assuming, of course, that he gives himself time to live and does not promptly, at birth, find an excuse to sneak out of life again, for example, under the pretext that he has forgotten something.[25]

The pretext of forgetting may not be foreign to LeCompte's enterprise, for she both claims Grotowski as an ancestor in her program's director's notes by speaking to and through him (though "forgetting" to cite), but she also reports in the same notes, using her own words now, that she "never thought of him as a major influence." She may not have "thought of him," or may have tried not to think of him, but the tracks of her theatre traverse Grotowski's influence on Richard Schechner, out of whose theatre LeCompte's Wooster Group grew like a prosthetic limb, or like Athena, goddess of the Acropolis, who turned the head of Zeus into her own birth canal (causing him a monstrous headache). In any case, if forgetting is not entirely what occurs through LeCompte's overt reenactment of *Akropolis*, neither, exactly, is it remembering. Something between or to the side of remembering and forgetting – like the theatrical twitches of Charcot's hysterics or the anxious dreams of a trauma victim – lurches diagonally across the stage, making events available to forget or recall *again*. Indeed *againness* becomes the subject itself, both available to experience and to analysis.

Schechner himself can be considered an unspoken ancestor in *Poor Theater*, ambivalently falling between Grotowski and LeCompte. One of the inspirations of the disciplinary crossings of performance studies, which Schechner, as scholar (as well as theatre director), helped to found, is an emphasis on betweenness as generative not only of theatre but of thought. Performance studies sits academically between theatre and literary studies, between theatre and psychoanalysis, between theatre and folklore, between theatre and media studies, or, as the title of Schechner's influential 1985 book makes literal: *Between Theatre and Anthropology*. Indeed, much of the Wooster Group's work shows a deep investment in betweenness – between live theatre and mediated image, and, as in *Poor Theater*, between temporal instances of performance. Such "betweenness" – as between one stage and another – is linked to the notion of liminality at the core of performance studies itself.[26] It might serve us well, at this juncture, to look between Schechner's theatre-making and his scholarship, since his early scholarship must have influenced the nascent Wooster Group, even as it betrayed, as we will see, something of an antitheatrical bias.

Schechner's writings on theatre studies in the late 1960s and across the 1970s – at the same time as his work at the Performance Garage – were full of bravado and bravery. He was fast becoming famous not only for his brilliantly bold theatre-making, but for his scholarly work on theatre and his editorship of *The Drama Review*, the journal through which Grotowski was introduced to the US. By 1980, Schechner had helped found the Department of Performance Studies at New York University by, in part, changing the name of the department so that labor that formerly organized itself beneath the rubrics "theatre" and "drama" would in future take place under the rubric *performance*. His moves were often ahead of the curve – for example by 1981, well before it was fashionable, he had proclaimed, with simple manifesto clarity: *The End of Humanism*.[27] By 2000, he had long been using fighting words, decrying "the cult of playwriting" and the tyranny of text in the interest of shifting the field (a military term after all) toward performance.[28]

Schechner's work in the 1970s with anthropologist Victor Turner on the performance-based significance of ritual actions would have a great deal of impact on the future of the field. Schechner's aim to shift the site of theatre studies off of dramatic text and onto embodied actions carried with it an essential "liminality." Performance studies, that is, found various footholds in the academy by deploying an essential betweenness that could seem, in W. B. Worthen's words, like "interdisciplinary promiscuity":

> Performance studies' interdisciplinary promiscuity has enabled a rapprochement with more traditional areas of inquiry – psychoanalysis, art history, ethnography – in large part by distinguishing between its progressive agenda and the apparently retrograde traditions of theatre and drama studies. At the same time, though, this rapprochement has tended both to reiterate and reify conventional attitudes about drama and theatre, largely by reproducing the print-era formation of "text versus performance."[29]

Poor theatre! At the dawn of performance studies, it seemed that theatre would *again* have to take another hit for the team. Like the clown who gets slapped, the theatre would just have to be beaten back to get up again. Of course, as Martin Puchner has amply and ably explored, the ancestry here is hale and hearty: avant-garde modernist theatre provocateurs had long made a practice of antitheatricalism in mounting their various battles with progenitors and breaks with theatrical tradition.[30] In his 1970 essay "Actuals," republished in *Performance Theory* in 1977 and then again in 1988 and again in 2003, Schechner fell into line with the repetitive slap. He articulated the drive in performance as against a theatrical drive. Theatricality, for him then, smacked of imitation where performance engaged the "actual." Schechner wrote,

> The avant-garde from the Italian Futurists through the Dadaists, surrealists, and on to practitioners of earth art and other kinds of avant-gardists, introduces us to the idea that art is not a way of imitating reality or expressing states of mind. At the heart of what Kaprow calls a mystery is the simple but altogether upsetting idea of art as an event – an "actual."[31]

That this approach to the "actual" was articulated as in distinction to imitation (long considered the primary debauchery of theatricality) should be no surprise, and it has recently spurred accusations of antitheatricality leveled at Schechner himself.[32] At the time he was writing the essay, Schechner found this avant-garde drive toward the actual (or non-imitative) in Grotowski's theatre as well as in Allan Kaprow's performance art. Indeed he employed a long citation from a conversation he had with Grotowski actor Ryszard Cieslak in 1970 to aid his articulation of the way in which performance can deliver the past neither imitated nor reenacted but radically "here and now" – or, as he also put it, "living now."[33] Interestingly, and in keeping with the chronophobia and related drive for essentialism of the 1960s, Schechner followed Grotowski and attempted, in "Actuals," to dismiss the way in which repetition may be a vital part of bringing an event or an act or a sentence or a gesture indicated by a prior script or story or event to actuality (again) in the theatre.[34] He wrote:

> This special way of handling experience and jumping the gap between past and present, individual and group, inner and outer, I call "actualizing" (perhaps no better than Eliade's "reactualizing," but at least shorter).[35]

Paying close attention we can see that Schechner clowns here, making a joke at the level of a parenthetical – but it is a serious parenthetical that will have repercussions in his later work. Here, in 1970, Schechner effectively dismissed the extender "re-" as inconsequential or superfluous. And yet we might argue that dropping of the "re-" from reactualization makes a huge amount of difference. With "re-" intact, reactualization bears the sense of citation. Mircea Eliade, cited at length in Schechner's "Actuals," used the term *re*-actualization to signal the way in which ceremonial ritual, composed in repetition and imitation, could return participants to a prior moment – a prior moment that is, in a sense, ongoing or incomplete. In Eliade's sacred-time of reactualization, "then" could be both then *and* "here and now."[36] Time could *begin again* both as same and different (both then and now), like a work in progress – each time new and different as it had been new and different before – or in Eliade's words, "as it appeared *ab origine, in illo tempore*."[37]

Fabulously, and in line with his tendency to move in between – in one direction and back again – in his later work, notably *Between Theatre and Anthropology*, Schechner allows for double- and triple- and nth-time to resonate more fully in the "actual." In *Between*, he returns the "re-" to articulation. *Between Theatre and Anthropology* is, after all, where he offers the influential theory of performance as "*re*stored behavior." In 1985 he wrote:

> Restored behavior is living behavior treated as a film director treats a strip of film. [. . .] Restored behavior is the main characteristic of performance. [. . .] The performers get in touch with, recover, remember, or even invent these strips of behavior and then rebehave them according to these strips, either by being absorbed into them (playing the role, going into trance) or by existing side by side with them (Brecht's *Verfremdungseffekt*). [. . .] Symbolic and reflexive behavior is the hardening into theater of social, religious, aesthetic, medical, and educational process. Performance means: never for the first time. It means: for the second to the *n*th time. Performance is "twice-behaved behavior."[38]

In this text, the "actual" and its access in performance gains in complexity – grows haunted (and, surprisingly perhaps, filmic). For restored behavior is, also, actualization.[39]

Returning the "re-" to articulation, Schechner is nevertheless smart to the implications, and he works hard to unpack what this return of the "re-" might mean for "history." While he is careful to underscore that he considers exact replication of historical performances, and historical events, to be impossible (writing in *Between* that "contextual and historical circumstances make even the exact replication of a scored/notated original different than that original"), nevertheless he suggests that history can be accessed because "history is not what happened but what has been encoded and transmitted."[40] If this is the case, then, indeed, reenactments do touch history. And yet, Schechner insists that this touching of history is essentially bogus: "It is not possible to 'get back to' what was."[41]

However – here's the rub: the tension in the fact that "what was done" was already a matter of the enactment of codes and performatives (in J. L. Austin's sense) – that "what was" was itself *already* composed in conversation with ancestors, in restoration and "twice-behaved behavior" – should mean that to do restoration is to do what was because what was *was* already restored. What does this mean? If our everyday acts – our most common incidents as well as our most grand events – are, as Schechner argues in *Between Theatre and Anthropology*, always in some relation to performance and in some reiterative negotiation with what Judith Butler has termed "sedimented acts"[42] – then Schechner's dismissal of the potential to "get back to" what was bears troubling. If the past was already self-different by virtue of being composed in restoration, then in the dizzying toss and tumble that always attends mimesis the fact that restoration renders an event different really only renders it *the same as it originally was: different.*[43] So to touch historical events, even to "get back to" what was should be possible given that events themselves are already composed in strips of restored behavior. Clearly, however, the *actuality* of this touch – its property as an *actual* – is a dizzying proposition that Schechner chooses, with an assertive preference for linear and progressive time, to shunt to the "not possible" category. Here is where his earlier investment in the "actual" as the antithesis of imitation and repetition, and his circumcision of the "re-" as superfluous rather than constitutive, continues to reverberate.

Schechner spends a significant chunk of his chapter on "Restoration of Behavior" discussing living history reenactments at Plimoth Plantation and other similar "restored villages." He notes the rapid growth of the heritage industry in America, which has ballooned exponentially since his writing. At base, he has faith that heritage audiences "know it's all make-believe."[44] But what difference does "knowing it's all make-believe" ultimately make? The experience of attending such villages as well as engaging in reenactment is frequently promoted as "educational." Thus, the experience proffered at such villages is in important ways not only make-believe, but "make belief" – and this making belief is precisely where "make-believe" takes place as experience and flips, almost imperceptibly, into the actual. The *making* of knowledge, the *making* of ideological investment, very often finds its repetitive ground in the *making* of make-believe.[45]

As suggested above, Schechner's work, falling as it does between Grotowski's "restored behavior" of Wyspianski and LeCompte's "restored behavior" of Grotowski, in many ways offers a broad spectrum of thinking about betweenness. If we return to two books that had paradigmatic status for performance studies in the 1980s, Victor Turner's *From Ritual to Theatre* published in 1982, and Schechner's *Between Theatre and Anthropology* published in 1985, we can easily situate the then emergent performance studies as interdisciplinary. However, here again, the issue of the "re-" reemerges. The titles of these two works are extremely instructive. If the anthropologist Turner articulated (at the level of a title) a "from/to" model, Schechner, coming from theatre and his work as both a theatre director and a scholar, chose the word "between." Schechner's "between" befuddles any linear succession and invites a far more undecidable intersection connecting anthropology's arguable investment in the actual (how representational practices help peoples construct and maintain the real world of the social) and theatre studies' focus on practices of the representational. The subtitle of Turner's *From Ritual to Theatre* is "The Human Seriousness of Play"; it's entertaining to think that a subtitle written by Schechner might have been "From Playfulness to Seriousness and Back." Schechner had published an essay "From Ritual to Theatre and Back" in1974. Turner's 1982 title *From Ritual to Theatre* simply dropped Schechner's "and Back." Turner might have explained this by joking, as Schechner had of Eliade, "at least it is shorter." Indeed. But the drop of the "and Back" forgets the potential reversibility or irruptive alteration of sequence. It forgets, as well, the undecidable play of Eliade's eternal return (his sacralized alternative to Nietzsche's fundamental question) that *circles* any betweenness with difference and challenges legitimizing *lines* of authority.[46]

Betweenness is in fact a topic of debate among performance studies scholars. In *TDR: The Drama Review*, the journal edited by Richard Schechner, Fred Moten (an assistant professor at New York University's Performance Studies Department in the 1990s) published an essay taking betweenness to task. Drawing upon the black radical tradition, and particularly C. L. R. James, Moten discusses the "not in between" as a matter of syncopation. Moten's essay might remind us not to read Schechner's contributions as *simply* between LeCompte and Grotowski without remembering to read, as well, for that which is not in-between – such as LeCompte's clear indication that she irrupts from an inside that is outside of lineage, being illegitimate by being *not* "Someone's Son." Here's Moten:

> The not in between [. . .] would be some kind of syncopated but non-hesitational phrasing, the kind of phrasing James gets at when he puts this notion forward. It would be not in between enlightenment and darkness, narrative and lyric, all of that. [. . . A] disruptive but nonhesitational rhythm is the form and content of a dialectic of the not in between, of an identity and revolutionary political stance and movement not in between enlightenment and darkness (blackness), of a historiographical practice not in between narrative and lyric, disruptive of the rupture (between science and art, knowledge and mimesis) in historiography.[47]

The hard labor of the live

The in-betweenness (and the not in betweenness) that make for a certain irruptive undecidability (and hyphen trouble) in the study of performance is also a characteristic of intermediality, as Jennifer DeVere Brody has explored in *Punctuation: Art, Politics, and Play*.[48] Not only in between academic disciplines such as theatre and anthropology, scholars in performance studies are also between the study of theatre and dance, music and performance art, dance and visual art, theatre and every-day life, ritual and installation art, and all manner of what may somewhat simplistically be termed "live art." This is complicated by the fact that *all* art can be read as "live" when read as fundamentally relational.[49] When, that is, the viewer, spectator, or art patron is participant by being in physical relation to the work, or when a piece is approached as durational. As discussed in the previous chapter, "liveness" became the moniker of what constitutes performance for many who study in the field – though that term is laced with difficulties this book has aimed to illustrate.

Even as the live has been newly embraced as a category of *archival* presentation in visual arts contexts (that is, the somewhat recent museal interest in preserving a work through reperformance), there is a resilient medial panic that causes many performance artists working in museum contexts to go out of their way to say their work is *not* theatre and *not* dance and is unlike the other arts. Note that the "betweenness" at the base of investigations into performance at the heart of the scholarly enterprise of performance studies is met with concerns about medial specificity by artists looking to preserve their work within the archiving institution of the art museum. In the museal context, performance is *not in between* any number of arts and acts, but is often presented (as in the case of Abramović) as somehow essential and pure in and of itself. Debates about the critical and *social* work of "autonomous" art (in Theodor Adorno's sense) aside: in the plea for medial "purity" the long history of theatrical panic arguably recurs.[50]

Aligned with anti-commodity sentiment in late modernity, twentieth-century artists worked against the theatrical to seek the "pure" or the "raw" or the "actual" or the "natural" act *untainted* by theatricality, untainted by "imitation," untainted by reproducibility, untainted by the prostitution seemingly inherent in items "for sale." The so-called dematerialization of art (in Lucy Lippard's phrasing after Herbert Marcuse's "dematerialization of labor"[51]) resulted in explicitly time-based work often articulated as resistant to commodification. An artwork could resist commodification as long as it was assumed to have disappeared, to be gone in the vanishing of linear time, completely non-recouperable. With reperformance, what had been lost to time, returns – but so does a medial anxiety around the temporal gap in performance-based work. If another body performs a performance artist's "original," "pure," time-based act, then body-to-body transmission might threaten to unsettle the singularity of the original, and return that singular act again to the scandal of *unrestricted circulation and exchange* without regard to property and the authorizing arm of legitimizing institutions.

In an essay titled "Performance Police," Carrie Lambert-Beatty situates the move from performance to "reperformance" (and back) in the museum succinctly. In such contexts, questions raised about display become questions about institutions and rights: about, in short, policing. Policing questions, Lambert-Beatty writes,

> are about performances in the future: how they will be done, and by whom.
> In this mode what is owned are rights – the right to enact, stage, perform, or

reperform the work. On the one hand this seems fairly straightforward – the museum gets to hang up the painting it owns, and the museum gets to stage the performance it owns rights to. The difference is that the museum's right to stage the performance implies that no one else can. In this model each performance carries with it – we might say it is haunted by – the other possible performances, the ones it disallows. Policing [. . .] is built into performance's institutionalization by rights. [. . . The] rights model of performance's institutionalization belongs to and perhaps produces, a particular set of terms. The coordinates it gives for performance are not presence and trace, or embodiment and image, or immediacy and mediation – but circulation and restriction.[52]

Part of the policing of performance is a renewed investment in medial specificity. As discussed in the Foreword, Abramović (whose work has met with generous reperformance in major art museums) has argued that performance is "pure" and "raw" and – a truly odd claim – "different from other art forms."[53] But does the "difference" to "other arts" really include *all* other arts, or is this professed difference actually meant to be pitched most exhaustively against the messy, impure, and historically feminized performance-based arts of theatre and dance (both of which can be read as durational if one accepts, as I argued in the last chapter, that performance does not "disappear")? Note that curator Klaus Biesenbach happily offers the analogy that in MoMA's exhibit *The Artist Is Present*, the performers reenacting Abramović's pieces "will be present as if they were sculpture."[54] This *like* sculpture but *unlike* other arts is interesting, and not surprising, given the longstanding assumption in archive culture that objects, documents, and recordings are the only mode of remaining, and that monuments are the best mode of commemorating.[55] But the sometime resistance to theatricality as aesthetic tool in the re-presentation of live performance art is extremely curious, given the ways so much work across the twentieth century (in photography particularly, but also in appropriation art generally) has been mining the theatrical, or overtly stagey, unauthorized, or re-authorized copy for precisely its curious ability to pry open, tear open, the irruptive and always re-mediated real.

What I am interested in here, in the overt attempts to distance reperformance from theatre and to align performance art with sculpture in the museum, is a kind of reverse of Wyspianski's *Akropolis* in which cathedral statues come to life, and come to re-life in Grotowski's *Akropolis*, and again to re-life in LeCompte's *Poor Theater*. Arguably, the inter(in)animation of Wyspianski/Grotowski/LeCompte articulates a temporal syncopation that cannot render media, or artists, completely discrete. For curator Biesenbach and artist Abramović, in *The Artist Is Present* live art becomes sculpture. But the question of "and back again" in a chiasma of theatricality in which other artists (distinct from Abramović) are also present, is laced with medial panic about the singularity of the form, the isolable genius of the singular artist, and *legitimate* ownership of the rights to reperform.

The medial panic around reperformance is not necessarily about the lack of a material object (or the objectlessness "dematerialized" art) as much as it is about the singularity, the originality, of the artist and the restriction of rights to that artist's *work* – work that takes place as the labor of the live. At stake is also the status of timelessness and mastery that object-based art assumed and that performance art maintained as long as it was considered *not* reproduceable (except in documents, such as photographs, that appeared to underscore an event's singularity and disappearance). Now that museums are reperforming works live that were once deemed singular to the time and place of the event, the problem of theatre and the labor of performers recurs. Theatre and dance, those troublingly collaborative forms, might challenge lineage with the trouble of the feminized "second." In theatre and dance an "original" (if there ever can be such a thing) can be realized only in and through the jump of bodies from one artist (such as choreographer) to a second (such as dancer) and on from that artist (dancer) to yet another (dancer), and another and another.[56] As Richard Schechner articulated in 1965, despite the policing properties of copyright concerning *drama*, there can be no original in *theatre*.[57] Or, more troublingly for ideality, the "original" recurs, occurring always and only in and through difference.

The problem of the nature of the labor makes drawing comparisons to theatre extremely complicated when thinking about performance art reenactments. This is not only because of the wide variety of theatre styles one could use in comparison, but also because of the tradition of antitheatrical sentiment that disparages the labor of theatre actors as opposed to the valorized performance "works" of visual artists. Though most theatre productions are not imitative copies of original productions – rather they "mount" or "produce" or "realize" a prior document, usually (but not always) a dramatic script – nevertheless, it is not uncommon for artists, curators, and critics to align theatre with what curator Sven Lütticken has termed "slavish" imitation.[58]

The problem appears to concern the labor for hire – the immaterial labor – of the performing body. Listen to performance artist Guillermo Gómez-Peña explain why performance art cannot be reenacted by actors:

> It is simply impossible to replace the ineffable magic of a pulsating, sweaty body immersed in a live ritual in front of our eyes. It's both shamanic and communal. In my opinion, no actor, robot, or virtual avatar can replace the singular spectacle of the body-in-action of the performance artist. I simply cannot imagine a *hired* actor operating Chico McMurtrie's primitive robots, or reenacting Orlan's operations.[59]

Similarly, in Rotterdam in 2005, Sven Lütticken channeled Jackson Pollock when writing his description of the reenactment exhibition *Life, Once More: Forms of Reenactment in Contemporary Art*:

> Jackson Pollock already had the feeling that his existential "act" for the painting session filmed by Hans Namuth degenerated into "acting" in the sense of theatrical performance – something he found insufferable. Is it not the fate of reenactment to eventually become an image, a representation in the form of film, photo or video? And are such representations just part of a spectacle that breeds passivity, or can they in some sense be performative, active?[60]

Here, interestingly, acting is a mode of degeneracy – a passive corruption of a more virile original act. Like Gómez-Peña's disdain for the hired actor, for Pollock (and Lütticken) acting apparently does not instantiate the pure act, the "singular spectacle" of liveness, but rather it appears to be the very twin of documentation, "slavishly" "breeding" something Lütticken sees as passivity. That is (as discussed in Chapter 2 around J. L. Austin) there is an essential wedge driven between passive or degenerate, etiolated or "slavish" imitation in theatricality on the one hand, and active, virile (read masculine) performativity on the other. Lütticken seems to situate acting as a kind of proto-documentation, but because it is not documentation that Lütticken seeks (he seeks active and "artistic" reenactment), he disdains "phony" theatre as a mode. Poor, poor theatre, indeed! It has begun to be hard to parse the livenesses of the live. The mind boggles at the effort. Here, theatre acting, less live and more object-like, can be ushered, not-so-politely, out of the category of live art like an illegitimate interloper in the art museum (an institution that once privileged object over performance at all).

The conundrum seems irresolvable. Auslander has asked whether it is "worth considering whether performance recreations based on documentation actually recreate the underlying performances or perform the documentation." Curator Nancy Spector, taking issue with Auslander on this point, has written that Abramović rejects this dichotomy and imagines, instead, a "third term," namely "the idea of embodied documentation."[61] It's important to recall that Abramović's investment in "embodied documentation" is aimed to legislate which bodies, where, and when, can be commissioned to act or take place as embodied documentation. The promotional description of the project for the book *Seven Easy Pieces* describes Abramović's reenactments as "monumental." Is the effort toward an "embodied documentation" geared not simply to "keep the work alive," as Spector writes, but to keep its liveness in a *monumental* relationship to history, suitable to the conditions and terms of the archive?[62] But what, after all, is the "monumental live" if not the stalwartly slow-to-change conventional theatre?

The confusion here illustrates the panoply of anxiety that attends the tangle of liveness and documentation that "acting," and theatre, seem to incite so handily. In any case, distinctions no longer appear to revolve around the material object of the record versus the ephemerality of live event. Somehow the mode of distinction has shifted to something harder to pinpoint in the style and aim of the affective labor involved. The question of labor *for hire* not so subtly haunts and threatens the stakes in the idea of authentic and singular artists' virile "creativity."

Another example might be useful here. Jens Hoffmann curated *A Little Bit of History Repeated* at Kunst-Werke Berlin in 2001 in which eleven artists were invited to repeat but *not* to restage performance art "classics." Of this exhibit Hoffmann said, "I didn't ask the artists to reenact works from the '60s and '70s – I could have used actors – but to work with original pieces in a *creative* manner."[63] Apparently, a hired actor reenacting the piece might have been more prone to exactitude or imitation than something Hoffmann terms "creativity." In any case, the artist Tracey Rose reworked Vito Acconci's 1970 *Trademarks* and "gave herself soft hickeys instead of Acconci's virile bites."[64] Yoko Ono's *Cut Piece* was re-performed by Laura Lima who outsourced her own reperformance: Instead of doing it herself or instead of hiring an actor Lima borrowed a trained goat named Heidi from the Babelsberg film studios to take the place of the performer. Perhaps not surprisingly, Jennifer Allen concluded in an *Artforum* review that Hoffmann's efforts to "repeat history" in his exhibition failed. She wrote:

> If one hoped to get a glimpse into the past with "A Little Bit of History," the search was in vain. The evening seemed to confirm that the work of the period can be captured *only with methods that betray the medium:* grainy black-and-white photographs and poorly lit films.[65]

I am fascinated by Allen's claim that "capture" of an event occurs best through medial leaps. One medium recalls another medium by means, in fact, of *betrayal*. If photography (and poorly lit film) both preserves and betrays the medium (or preserves it *by* betraying it), apparently so too does the overt imitation of (hired) theatre actors. Here, the photographic still *and* the theatrical pose share a kind of betrayal that is, by virtue of its failure, successful (according to Allen). The photograph, like an actor for hire, is not the thing itself, but that very fact – the fact that it/he/she both passes and can not quite pass – is an ambivalence that seems, for Allen, to get something right by getting something wrong.

The problem of the reperformer's body standing in as surrogate for the 1960s or '70s *original* artist's body, and the seeming "betrayal" afforded by the surrogacy of a "for hire actor," is particularly interesting given the fact that, as Julia Bryan-Wilson has carefully explored, '60s and '70s work often overtly celebrated the artist as art "worker."[66] Warhol's factory was a case in point, as were organizations such as the Art Workers' Coalition. Grotowski's casting of Wyspianski's cathedral statuary-come-to-life as inmates in a work-camp also invites a complex of issues concerning art as labor (though Grotowski would say sacrifice) – issues that LeCompte used her own actors' overtly alienated labor to amplify.[67]

Let us try to take a turn, now, regarding the question of labor in (re)performance by considering, briefly, the work of Tino Sehgal. Sehgal makes live work that has been explicitly aligned with sculpture, though no object or document, aside from the transmission of live performance, is created. Sehgal has made "situations" in and out of museums for the past fifteen years, mostly exhibited in Europe but recently in New York as well. Sehgal's *Kiss* is a live artwork in which two performers enact a tightly choreographed sequence that repeats for the duration of a museum's open hours. This live work was "collected" by the Museum of Modern Art in New York in 2008 and exhibited at the Guggenheim in February 2010.

Kiss is exceedingly simple and excruciatingly beautiful. At the Guggenheim, the "dancers" (the issue of what to call the performers is taken up below) performed in the museum's large rotunda. When I attended, I noticed that art patrons often did not recognize the dancers at first, but cast about looking for object art. Time and again I observed the surprise on patrons' faces as they stopped to watch the dancers, who, dressed in street clothes, at first appeared as if two passers-by had become locked in a slow moving embrace. "Is this the artwork?" I heard one patron ask another. The question did not seem out of place.

As Dorothea von Hantelmann, an astute critic of Sehgal's work, describes *Kiss*:

> Sehgal's work *Kiss* is enacted by two dancers in a close embrace who move very slowly and continuously through different choreographic constellations that draw from images of kissing couples throughout the history of art: at times one may recognize the kiss of Rodin, or those of Brancusi and Klimt, or a Picasso, and at other times the sexual positions of Jeff Koons and Cicciolina, and then back to Rodin and so on. [. . .] In this reenactment of historical sculptural works as choreographed movements, we find again an understanding of continuity as the simultaneity of (art) history and the forms of history's *actualization*, which is precisely the modality of the performative – repetition and transformation.[68]

Von Hantelmann labels the performers "dancers" but does not term the piece dance. And Sehgal – an artist influenced by Xavier Le Roy, Jérôme Bel, and La Ribot among others who work in what André LePecki has termed "exhausting dance" – refuses documentation of any kind. For Sehgal there should be no material or technological "record" of the work (a refusal that has won him the term "eccentric").[69] He is also adamant that his work is neither theatre nor dance nor performance art.

What is it then?

It is *work*.

On Sehgal's *Kiss*, Arthur Lubow wrote for the *New York Times Magazine*:

> [Sehgal] is producing a work of art, not theater: unlike a performance, a Sehgal is on display for the entire time the institution is open, and the human actors are identified no more precisely than as if they were bronze or marble. (They are, however, paid.) But because the piece is formed of people, not of metal or stone, the viewer is aware that, regardless of how absorbed the models seem to be in their activity, at any moment they have the capability of turning their gaze on him.[70]

The work is art. But is not theatre or dance or even performance because of . . . museum hours? This is of course a rather ridiculous claim, given the numerous theatre, dance, and performances of lengthy duration that easily come to mind. Something else is clearly at stake in the disavowal of media other than sculpture, even if it's never clear exactly what that something else is.

Lubow cites Catherine Wood, curator of contemporary art and performance at London's Tate Modern, as saying: "There's a purity to [Sehgal's] approach." What sets Sehgal apart, she claims, is "his purist insistence on the immateriality – or ephemeral materiality – of the work [. . .] so there is no trace left at all." But what Lubow's citation of Wood completely ignores is the trace that might resonate in a viewer, who later might reperform the work, or talk about it – the trace that might be, indeed, composed in and as body-to-body transmission. In this way, Wood's analysis is in complete distinction to what von Hantelmann would call the trace that *is* performance, the trace that *is* body-to-body transmission, the affective stain that (as if anamorphic) *passes* between bodies and across time.

We can hear in Wood's remarks remarked by Lubow the trace of an anti-theatrical panic that links body-to-body transmission to impurity. For Wood, perhaps, performance can only be pure if it "leaves no trace." But Sehgal's approach is more complex. What of the trace that lodges in the live? What if live bodies trace precedence, trace sculpture for example, as much as the other way around? Performative acts are always reiterative, and as such are already a kind of document or record. Von Hantelmann suggests that all art is performative, in bodily transmission realized through ritualization (the context of any showing) and the performance-based properties of memorization and repetition. In this way of thinking artworks are *scriptive things*.[71] As scriptive things they are pitched, already, for the jump of affect, for reperformance across bodies, as a call is pitched for response. Indeed, Sehgal offers as much a response (to Rodin, to Brancusi) as he offers a call. The site of the work is always tilted off of itself and into the spaces and times it beckons into exchange – forward, backward, to the side, and all the way around.

While von Hantelmann is keen to point out a connective tissue between sculpture and *Kiss*, she does not require rigid medial distinction based on material support to do so. That is, unlike what Biesenbach and Abramović hope for *The Artist Is Present*, Sehgal's *Kiss* is arguably neither pure, nor singular, nor unlike other arts even as it is like sculpture. Rather, it is work. It is not dance, and not not dance. And as work in a citational, performative live, it is inter(in)animate, and always situated precariously between one of its own articulations and another, across the bodies of performers.

The connection between sculpture and *Kiss* lies in the immaterial labor of *passing* – arguably both the passing of the artwork (as it attempts to pass as that which it sites/cites), and the passing of the passers-by who encounter the work in the museum. Drawing on Adorno, von Hantelmann writes: "There is a connection between the art form of sculpture that attempts to transcend its own materiality and Adorno's postulate that art must strive to negate its own participation in society." The connection is "failure" (Hantelmann's word).[72] Sculpture will fail to fully transcend its own materiality, and "art" can strive to negate (but can never fully negate) its participation in society. But as I read von Hantelmann to say, these very failures are vital and secrete a kind of possibility. The point at which sculpture balances between achieving and failing to achieve the immaterial is a conditional theatrical *becoming*, based on a precarious performative negotiation (a social negotiation) between passing and not passing – passing as, passing on, passing through, passing over, and *passing by*.

A Sehgal work plays at the pass. It may work to *pass* as statuary, but the pass is rather like a ball-toss by a mime: the object thrown cannot be precisely located – and where does it land? It lands in the social, thrown right back upon the viewer, who has to figure out *where* and *what* to make of it. If a pass has been thrown from one medium to another, from dance to statuary or from statuary to dance, the emphasis should be placed on passing, and the spaces between our overly sedimented medial distinctions. The emphasis should be on passing, and not on authenticity, monumentality, or medial purity.

So what can we call Sehgal's hard laboring live statues? Frazer McIvor writes that: "We can only refer to Sehgal's actors as 'employees' due to the artist's insistence that his works are neither performances, nor theatrical set pieces."[73] I find this interesting for the emphasis on labor that the term "employees" brings to the fore. When we refer to Sehgal's performers as "employees" – what is the matter with that? Is this one way Sehgal makes Adorno's "participation in society" available for countenance? Does the resistance to medial specificity *underscore* labor, or it is an obfuscation of labor in the interest of a "timeless" art? To my mind, the term "employees" might be just right, as it underscores the means of production – the facts of production – that Sehgal includes in his work in general as a prompt for conversation.

Sehgal has made work with museum guards in which he incorporates museum employees directly into his art situations. Another of his pieces, *This Objective of That Object*, includes the phrase, repeated by his employed performers: "The objective of this work is to become an object of conversation." If we are discussing it now, as writer and reader, then we are realizing the artwork as a scriptive thing, in the deferred time of its hail. The work's object(ive) tilts off of itself to find itself in conversations among others. If that objective carries through all of Sehgal's work, is the *time* of his work deferred into the cracks where conversation takes place later (or does not)? This is certainly a jump not only across media, but also across time, and across performers – as you and I become the performers of his piece when we engage, if we engage, in conversation about it at another time and place.

More can be said about the term "employee," or terms such as interpreter and reperformer, especially as concerns the often careful problem of avoiding the word "actor" or "dancer." Note that "other people" is a descriptor on the MoMA website for *The Artist Is Present*: "In an endeavor to transmit the presence of the artist and make her historical performances accessible to a larger audience, the exhibition includes the first live reperformances of Abramović's works *by other people* ever to be undertaken in a museum setting."[74] "Other people" is not the same as saying "other artists"; almost but not quite.

In the interest of not being mistaken, I underscore here that I do not submit that we call these workers (or re-workers) actors or dancers, only that we mark our confusion surrounding their labor. The Wooster Group actors reenacting one of Forsythe's dances in the second act of *Poor Theater* marked much the same confusion, making their labor apparent as they labored to pass as dancers. In fact, descriptors for those who engage in reenactment activity rarely seem satisfying. Would "enthusiasts" or "hobbyists," appellations for battle reenactors (not paid to reenact), translate gracefully to employees reperforming at MoMA or the Guggenheim in New York? When battle reenactment enthusiasts are paid, as in major motion pictures such as *Gettysburg*, the word used to describe them is "extras." In any case, as the artist Allison Smith asked of Civil War reenactors for her 2005 piece *The Muster*, discussed in the Afterword: "Who are these people and why do they do this?"

Claire Bishop has written astutely about the widespread shift to delegated performances in contemporary art, smartly tying the increase in "outsourced authenticity" in live art practice since the 1990s to the rise in outsourcing as a mode of economic globalization in postindustrial capitalism.[75] In this case we can ask: Has the sometime "magic of the commodity" (a magic that secrets the laborer in Marx's analysis) become the "magic of the surrogate authentic"? If so, reenactment artwork may be an art precisely suited to a service economy. And we should not shy away from critique of such art, the economy it suits, and the accompanying neoliberal politics of privatization in which it thrives. If this is artwork well-suited to a service economy, we can then ask: In what ways might we use reperformance and the issues it raises about the labor of affect to help us think critically about our broader participation in neoliberal society, much as we have used object art and its discontents to help think through commodity capitalism.[76]

Sehgal's dancers are outsourced statuary, and Wooster actors become surrogates of other actors. Each render their surrogacy available to conversation, to question, to critique. Laborers in a service economy, they aim to give us what we came to see: art. And affect. But, as Lubow suggests, part of the bargain of the live is that we – the consumers of the art experience we purchase – might catch the laborer's eye – or she catch ours. Almost but not quite? Between monument and passer-by, the *possibility remains*. And that, after all, is the dangerous game of mimesis. The problem, and the promise, is that the surrogate *lives*, blinking and sweating beneath the ghost's visor. Citing precedents, almost but not quite, the performers employed in *The Kiss* and in *Poor Theater* seem to whisper an ancient game of gestic telephone played with artworks. Speaking to ancestors, body-to-body, we might not see eye-to-eye, *but we might*. Laboring at the pass between pasts and presents we might recognize our labor as collective. What questions would we ask each other then?

5 Still living

Photography is a kind of primitive theatre, a kind of *Tableau Vivant*, a figuration of the motionless and made-up face, beneath which we see the dead.

——Roland Barthes, *Camera Lucida*

We are prey to the ghostly power of the supplement; it is this unlocatable site which gives rise to the specter [. . .] "that rather terrible thing which is there in every photograph: the return of the dead."

——Jacques Derrida quoting Roland Barthes's *Camera Lucida* in "The Deaths of Roland Barthes"

Roland Barthes, the eloquent author of *Camera Lucida* and proponent of photography's indelible link to the dead, was also quite articulate on photography's link to theatre, as the epigraph above makes clear.[1] As discussed in Chapter 3 regarding the undecidable space of live performance, beneath Hamlet's father's visor hides the "made-up face" of the live performer – a liveness that, despite Barthes's proclivities of linking theatre, too, to death, may not resolve itself as death takes place again across the face of the live. The irruptive capacity of the live repetitively, continually, to take over the scene, is of course theatre's impurity, its "endless trouble" as Stein said, and its "danger," as Edward Gordon Craig bemoaned at the turn of the twentieth century.[2]

Consider that "death" may be, as it was for Derrida, foremost something that lives in others, or can at least be made available to the question: What death is lived?[3] The logics of commemoration, of mourning and melancholy, of trauma and repetition all are ample echo chambers for this question. The liveness of death – or, if preferred, the livingness of passing – becomes, then, another of the syncopated nerves of undecidability. It's not enough to say, with Jean Cocteau, that the camera films "death at work" if by that we assume that death does not do its work by, reiteratively and repetitively, engaging the hard labor of the live.[4] As explored in Chapter 4, when the Wooster Group actors in *Poor Theater* carefully reenact the grainy 1968 filmic images of Grotowski's actors playing Wyspianski's drama *Akropolis*, in which statues come to life, they render explicit an inter(in)animation at the temporal crossroads of representation (live *and* mediated) that is always *at work*.

In this chapter I weave a cross-temporal course between photography, medieval tableaux vivants, contemporary art reenactments, and, troublingly, the digital image of torture that circulated out of Abu Ghraib prison in 2004. I will let "photography" stand in and reference other modes of image capture, even though that very "standing in" might ultimately be troubled by my comments here. I have chosen photography in part because of the common claim that the invention of photography provoked a revolution in "visuality" – one "more profound," writes Jonathan Crary, "than the break that separates medieval imagery from Renaissance perspective."[5] I also let photography stand in for image capture generally because of recent work in media studies that situates the logic of the photograph as visual ground, fundamental to film and resilient in image culture. Arguing for the primary place of the "still" at the heart of moving images, such work struggles both to reassert the medium specificity of photography at a moment of its obsolescence and, at the same time, places photography as a kind of pro-genitor, and even template, of vital and subsistent visual cultural ways of knowing.[6] Such work also conflates the invention of the still with the invention of the camera, too often forgetting the long history of precedent living stills,[7] and continues the long-standing assumption that photography offers thanatical "evidence" of a time considered, in linear temporal logic, irretrievable.[8]

To begin, let us return to the efforts of reenactors to invest, however awkwardly, in *retrievable* time. Let us return to the digital snapshot on the cover of this book, discussed in Chapter 1. As the reader will recall, I snapped this image in the summer of 2004 at a Civil War reenactment in Lincoln, Rhode Island. This "finger" – severed index – was lying on the ground to the side of a reenacting surgeon's tent. Accoutrement of the faux, literal index of a past war replayed, the complications of this index finger astounded me. There in the field, it was of the present – in time – and therefore live in the "living history" mêlée of the faux surgeon's acts. And yet, this theatrical index of a live re-act was clearly a poor substitute for liveness, and a poor index of history: so, *what did this index index?* As I reported in Chapter 1, one of the reenactors who was milling about near the surgeon's tent was just back from the war in Iraq where he had been in medical service, and he told me that he felt that "this war" was more real to him. This war, I asked? It was a truer war, one worth keeping alive, he said. The fallen finger pointed, then, not only backward but to the side, overseas, as well as to the awkward actor behind the visor, attempting to replay the liveness of the dead (which dead, where?) that he struggled, poorly, to countenance.[9]

The "faux" Civil War in Rhode Island took place in June of 2004. In April of 2004, accounts of the torture and abuse of prisoners held in the detention camp of Abu Ghraib in Iraq had come to public attention through the leaky circulation of digital images snapped from the personal cameras of the personnel of the 372nd Military Police Company of the United States Army together with additional US governmental agencies. Grappling with the arresting Abu Ghraib images came to occupy a good deal of everyone's thoughts in those months and I had several conversations with reenactors about the scenes. The scenes in the photos were often clearly staged for the camera. That is, the photographs were digital images of *theatrical scenes* that were also and simultaneously scenes of war, of actual wartime torture and abuse.[10] They were snapped for circulation into a future of their display as souvenirs, or evidence, or some complicated intersection of the two. Of course, many Civil War reenactors use archival photographs, such as those taken by Alexander Gardner or Timothy O'Sullivan (who worked for Mathew Brady in the 1860s), as evidence on which to base their reenactments, though many of those scenes too were rearranged or staged for the camera – dead bodies moved and propped to enhance theatrical or formal effect of the image – to hail the viewer with the *scene* of the real.[11]

At the battle reenactment, in the midst of "The Civil War," I came to consider the images out of Abu Ghraib not only as record, but also as durational event – ongoing through the circulatory aspects of the hail, the reverberatory mechanics of interpellation in call and response.[12] For me, this thinking unsettled the site of "Abu Ghraib" or undid the prison scenes as discrete events for which the images stood *only* or even primarily as record, and placed the image and event instead in a cross-temporal and cross-geographic "between." Thinking of them in this way also rendered the event disturbingly ongoing, even "live," in the global space of the encountered photograph. If at first this seemed to me to disrespect the dead who died at a specific time in the past in the specific prison in Iraq, the more I thought about it, the more I felt that approaching the circulating document as durational – an ongoing live event – allowed for a dynamic of witness and a call for account that the scene so desperately required. Attempting to account for atrocity can never be complete, but must be ongoing. If I was hailed by the images, and the pointing fingers of the prison guards, to "Look! See!," I was intepellated into the images' theatre, and it was a theatre in which events unfolded live in the ongoing fact of encounter with those scenes and with the dead they disgraced.

In 1985 Craig Owens wrote about what he called "the power of images to arrest us, take us into custody."[13] Owens follows Jacques Lacan to suggest that it is the viewer of the object who, at a temporal remove, is arrested – "photo-graphed." The Abu Ghraib images lend a horrific literalness to this. The images of pointing fingers aimed at corpses, such as Charles Granier's grisly, grinning pose beside a dead Iraqi, only makes explicit the inherent gestic hail of the photo itself: "Hey, you there!" it calls forward in time to an anticipated viewer, "Look at this *here*." It seems to easily chime: "I'm talking to you. So turn around: You are in this scenario." When and where, then, does the event (of the scene) take place?

* * * * * * *

In this chapter, I struggle to ask whether some of our habitual assumptions – that the camera founds the still and that the still is (only) the stuff of death – might profitably be rethought by turning to aspects of the photographic scene other than the hyper-celebrated invention of the camera. Clearly there are other technologies of the still that are reconstituted (reenacted) in the scene of photography by which a viewer is arrested in the arrest of the image – technologies of the live, such as tableaux vivants or the ancient Western practice of placing live actors and stone statues together on stages, might serve for example. Are these not in some ways "technologies" of image capture? Reflecting on the legacy of living stills, and the relation of the pose to the scene and its frame, we might ask in what ways photography inherits (rather than invents) the still, and in that way ask in what ways photography can be considered another among a great many technologies of the live.

If we think of photography as a technology of the live in an inter(in)animate or syncopated relationship with other times and other places that it not only records but hails, what do we think? What theatre histories persist in the "still" of the photographic medium and how can those histories ask us to rethink visual culture *vis à vis* live performance and our complicities in the ongoingness, the forward- and backward-living gesture of the pose? Robin Bernstein has recently written of the pose as a "dense interaction between thing and human."[14] Bernstein writes of a light-skinned woman photographed circa 1930 with a larger-than-life caricature cut-out of a black boy eating watermelon. The woman appears to eat the wooden watermelon alongside the stereotype. Bernstein writes about way the cut-out "scripts" the woman's body in the pose in the photograph – and thus she calls this flat boy cut-out a "scriptive thing." But the camera is there as well, as a scriptive thing shaping the woman's pose and ensuring that the pose will, itself, become a thing to stand beside, look at, hold in the archive, or encounter reproduced in the pages of Bernstein's essay – thus, recurring in the future it casts forward as a hail.[15] If the pose, or even the accident captured as snapshot, is a kind of hail cast into a future moment of its invited recognition, then can that gestic call in its stilled articulation be considered, somehow, live? Or, at least, re-live? Can we think of the still not as an artifact of non-returning time, but as situated in a live moment of its encounter that it, through its articulation as gesture or hail, predicts? This is to ask: is the stilled image a call toward a future live moment when the image will be re-encountered, perhaps as an invitation to response? And if so, is it not live – taking place in time in the scene of its reception? Is it time deferred, finding its liveness in the time-lag, the temporal drag, "in your hands" at the moment of its encounter?[16]

It may be, as Sue-Ellen Case has productively argued, that there is an activism in reading against the grain of the life/death binary in our approach to supposedly distinct media of capture.[17] Case's important 1991 essay "Tracking the Vampire" reads for the heteronormative imperative that underscores and legislates the binarized borders marking living from dead, present from past, in images and apparatus of representation. Case makes very clear that the Platonic life/death binary opposition at the base of ontology is attended by a gender binary, thus explaining the ways in which a queer theory approach to thinking through representation might be invested more in passing (my word here, not Case's) than in ontology. It may be that our habit of reading the performed gesture as in-time and therefore "live" and reading the gesture caught by the camera as out-of-time, and thus somehow no longer live, misses a more complicated leakage of the live (and the remain) across seemingly discrete moments. It may be that reading the photograph as a record of time gone by, never to return, misses the point of our temporal cross-fashioning, our calls and responses across a time that is not (or not only) linear and nonrecurring. The question is actually simple: when we habitually read documents as evidence and evidence as indication of a past supposedly gone by, do we overlook the liveness of temporal deferral, the real time of our complicities?

Performance poses problems when thinking about photography. And photography poses problems to performance. We commonly parse the mediums (performance is not photography/photography is not performance) in line with notions of the "live." As discussed at length in Chapter 3, we are accustomed to thinking of performance as live, composed in a linear temporality that moves from a past through a present to a future in which it dissolves. We are led to think this because the live, as ephemeral, supposedly dissolves in time, and thus, it, too, whispers of its own constant disappearance and death. Performances supposedly disappear "as fast as they are made" and any record of a past performance supposedly indicates: no longer live.[18] According to this troubled logic, the live exists only in a binarized distinction to its record, while photography functions *as* record, recording "a time that passes without return."[19] Photography and cinema seem to function, writes Mary Ann Doane, "first and foremost as a record," as they primarily deal, she argues, with a compulsion particular to modernity: "the problematic and contradictory task of archiving the present."[20]

We generally assume that material objects such as photographs or texts or anything archivable remain and give evidence to the passing of acts and events in nonrecurring, linear time. Thus, we are encouraged to think of performance as that which eludes capture because it occurs in time and so we are comfortable saying that a film or a photograph is a record of the live, but not itself the live that it captures (or fails to capture, if one accepts Richard Schechner's and Peggy Phelan's terms, spelled out in Chapter 3). While something of performance is recorded in media of reproduction, that "something," Schechner and Phelan argue, cannot be performance itself. The live aspect – its in-timeness – appears to elude arrest. In line with this logic, we consider (perhaps shortsightedly) that a moment is past (i.e., no longer live) the moment an image appears to remain – appears, that is, to still.[21] We forget, in other words, the ways in which the live is not only vulnerable to suspension, but the very material of arrest.[22]

In her essay "The 'Eternal Return': Self-Portrait Photography as a Technology of Embodiment," Amelia Jones writes: "The photograph, after all, is a death-dealing apparatus in its capacity to fetishize and congeal time." And yet Jones is interested in wrestling further with the implications of such thanaticism. Her next sentence makes theatricality the "other" to photography's death machine, arguing that the theatricality in works by Cindy Sherman, Hannah Wilke, Lyle Ashton Harris, and Laura Aguilar invite a kind of "life" to the death space of the photo. She writes that through "their exaggerated theatricality, these works foreground the fact that the self-portrait photograph is eminently performative and so life-giving." Jones draws on Phelan to say that "this duality is not resolvable in either direction."[23] Yet, while I agree that this duality is not resolvable in either direction, I am interested in shifting the conversation off a "live" or "dead" duality; resolvable or not, such a duality re-sediments these registers as existing in photography on the one hand and theatre or performance on the other. Such a duality repeatedly, as Jones acknowledges, "casts us back into questions of lack and loss."[24] Instead, we might more productively begin to ask about situation and circulation *in return*.

André LePecki's important book *Exhausting Dance: Performance and the Politics of Movement* ruminates productively on stillness in dance. Building on the work of anthropologist Nadia Seremetakis, LePecki writes:

> [T]he 'still-act' is a concept [. . .] to describe moments when a subject interrupts historical flow and *practices* historical interrogation. Thus while the still-act does not entail rigidity or morbidity it requires a performance of suspension, a corporeally based interruption of modes of imposing flow. The still *acts* because it interrogates economies of time, because it reveals the possibility of one's agency within controlling regimes of capital, subjectivity, labor, and mobility.[25]

Rather than wholly distinct, both photography and live performance participate in the ambivalent gesture of the time-lag. The gesture of the time-lag is one that shows itself, by virtue of the still, *to be a gesture – to have posture, to enunciate*. That posture, that enunciation, does not solely happen in past time, nor singularly in present time, but steers a wobbly course through repetition and *reappearance* – a reappearance rife with all the tangled stuff of difference/sameness that anachronism, or syncopated time, or basic citationality affords.[26] Given this, it is not surprising that theatre consistently reappears in/as photography, just as photography reappears in/as theatre.[27]

A tiny history of living stills

Theatre's history winks in the wings of photography (and cinema). In many ways, photography reenacts basic tenets of Western theatre and works from within its logic to an extraordinary degree.[28] But for Roland Barthes in *Camera Lucida*, the "touch" between theatre and photography is not one that articulates the shared history of a foundational "screenal" divide – a house divided between stage and audience – but rather one that fetishizes a connection through loss and death. For Barthes it is neither the shared architecture of a screenal vision nor the history of the gestic still that conjoins theatre and photography, but Death the Leveller. In distinction to what I am hoping to suggest, Barthes sees both forms underscoring disappearance. For him, the theatre, like the photograph, is always more shadow than substance. This Platonic investment in mimesis as only or merely shadow-work is apparently a "given" that theatre enacts through the mask of the double, and that photography undergirds by turning the evidentiary claim that "X is here before the camera" into a winking clone of "X is dead." In this wink of ambivalence (Barthes's mother is both there and not there in his most cherished photograph) lies photography's essential theatricality – it both is, and is not. But Barthes's emphasis lies less in the undecidability of the chiasma is/is not, than in the equation he romances as an inevitable, pre-determined, linear-temporal synthesis: *is no longer*.

Of course it is interesting to question the degree to which the growth of photography fueled the habit of considering performance to be essentially ephemeral, essentially a medium of loss linked with death in an approach to time that is so stalwartly linear, without porous passage or fold.[29] It is surely the case that, contrary to this assumption, performance and live arts in general can be and have been at many times and places throughout history approached as a mode of remaining, in distinction to loss or disappearance – at least as persistent as any statue or canvas, script or celluloid print. Indeed, contemporary artists blur performance with photography (and photography with performance) so volubly that Barthes's ennobled place of disappearance and death arguably comes undone in an ebullient emphasis on reenactment, recurrence, and repetition. If this undoing rings of carnival – and "carnivalized time" – it should.[30] I will argue here, briefly, that what photography and performance share is not (or not only) the model of death-as-loss romanced by Barthes as the impossibility of return, but they also share the rowdier processional or street theatre legacy of theatrical irruption – instability, repetition, the ambulant freeze, the by-pass – that undoes archive-driven determinations of what disappears and what remains. This is the shared pre- and re-enactment of tableaux vivants, or living stills, that visual studies has sometimes overlooked in thrall to chemicals and the technological apparatus of reproduction.

Most accounts of photography offer a time-line of technological antecedents, citing Renaissance but ignoring ancient camera obscura and focusing the "invention" on nineteenth-century chemicals of capture. It is compelling, perhaps, to herald technological innovation ("new media") as radical, and to claim for photographic technology, with Crary as noted above, a transformation "more profound than the break that separates medieval imagery from Renaissance perspective." Yet the break between medieval imagery and Renaissance perspective might be narrated as far from clean. While I do not want to argue against rupture or thwart the privilege of marking historical discontinuity, I would advocate an increase in analysis less enamored of technology's supposed originalities.[31] I suspect that the "still" in theatrical reenactment – especially in the heritage of tableaux vivants – offers an invitation to constitute the historical tale differently. Troubling the habitual line of binary opposition between "the live" and the "archival remain" might provoke us, even if momentarily, to look differently at the photos we pass by everyday, whether hung in museums, plastered on billboards, scrunched in frames, glossed on the covers of magazines, packed away in drawers, embedded in archives, or lolling about like sirens waiting for surfers on the Web. This is an invitation, in other words, to go in search of "photographs" in the live space of temporal lag – in the processionals of the middle ages, for example.[32] Instead of looking for shrouds (the photography-equals-death school of thought), might we listen for photography's kin in rituals of reenactment?

It is common to refer, at least cursorily, to theatre's influence on photography. Barthes reminds his readers that when Daguerre took over from Niépce, he was running a panorama theatre at the Place du Château. But the echoes are far more substantial than Daguerre's day job. We hear, more often, that the camera obscura evolved from the arts of the Western stage, specifically the structure of the Greek theatre (as the orchestra was replaced by the *skene*, a nascent architectural screen). The screen and *theatron* was appropriated during the Roman Empire, and dutifully articulated by Vitruvius in 20 BCE. Vitruvius's writings were lost, rediscovered, and then "developed" by Alberti in the mid-fifteenth century to become perspective. This is the point at which "perspective" forgot one alignment to adopt another – painting – despite the fact that the (re)introduction of the architectural screen occurred in "imitation of the Greek theatre."[33]

If we cannot isolate a discrete moment of invention for the screen and for screenal aesthetics, the art of the still, too, is far from genealogically pure. Surely, histories of theatre and ritual are replete with stills. The stone remains of the theatres at Ostia, Palmyra, Ephesus, and Aspendos indicate that immediately above the central doorway of the stage was a niche for paying special honor to a statue.[34] Statuary also lines the sides of the theatre of Dionysus and placement of statues within niches in the Roman theatre background (*scenae frons*) was a citation of the Greek practice of placing statuary in the theatre. Again, I am not interested in mapping for patrimony or arguing "who did what first" in a linear line of descent. Rather, I am interested in troubling the distinction between live arts and the still arts to which we have been habituated. The niches for statuary and the statues themselves can remind us quite fulsomely that the "live" occurred and occurs not as distinct from but in direct relation to the place of the frozen or stilled or suspended – yet arguably observant – statues. The live, so often composed in the striking of stills, takes place in the place of the still; and the still takes place live. The same can be said of the monument. Consider the following observation from Michel de Certeau's *The Practice of Everyday Life*:

> The passing faces on the street seem [. . .] to multiply the indecipherable and nearby secret of the monument.[35]

In this resonant sentence, a monument is given to retain its secret, its monumentality, in and through passage, or the live act of passing by. Animate and inanimate, moving and stilled, are not in this sense diametrically opposed as much as part and parcel of an inter(in)animation.

George Kernodle argues that medieval tableaux vivants kept certain habits of ancient theatre in practice well before the resurfacing of drama and theatre in the Renaissance. He refers specifically to the flat screen against which one finds a framed scene, something of the *scenae frons* he wants to argue did not disappear in the Dark Ages but stayed alive in church mansions and other vestiges of the triumphal arch and statuary niche in medieval practice. These "still living" citations carried on in processional performance even where permanent theatres did not exist. Frozen scenes of living participants, tableaux vivants were often designed for the view of a sovereign, passing through a city on a temporary visit or upon return. But living tableaux had also appeared as biblical stills carried in Corpus Christi processions not primarily for the sovereign but for each parishioner or participant in view of the passage. As such, and this is what interests me most at present, many living stills were encountered *in passing*, in that either the performance remained still and the viewer passed by (such as a sovereign upon entrance to a city), or, conversely, the viewer remained still as live actors, standing as surrogate statues, passed by on wagons.

I am interested in the relationship of the "still" to circulation and to bypass. As mentioned, the art of the still is far from unique to photography. To try and unpack this, even if briefly, let us consider one example among many. At Ghent in 1458 a series of pageants and tableaux vivants were presented for Philip the Good of Burgundy's entrance to the city. The most elaborate attraction designed for Philip to pass by was an enormous live tableau of several of the painted panels of a van Eyck altarpiece, *The Adoration of the Mystic Lamb*, then in the Parish Church of St. John the Baptist (now called the Cathedral of St. Bavo). The reenactment in the form of a tableau occurred in the city about twenty years after the altar had been completed, on a stage 50 feet long and 38 feet tall, built in three stories and covered by a white curtain.[36] In George Kipling's description "God the Father" was posed at the center top, flanked by the Virgin Mary on the right, and John the Baptist on the left. The choirs of angels on the two side panels were also included on the top tier. On the middle tier "The Lamb" stood atop an altar, and "blood flowed from his chest into a chalice." Above the altar on this second tier, the Holy Ghost in the form of a dove would have been lowered into the scene. On the lowest tier would have been the multitude, and Kipling tells us that at least ninety "actors" would have participated in this staging. Standing on the ground in front of the scene would have been the enormous Fountain of Life, its central pillar 25 feet high. The fountain spouted wine from three spigots into a surrounding basin, from which Philip the Good "could drink as he pleases."[37]

As much as any photograph, these living stills blur distinctions we might like to find between the live and the passed away. Consider, for example, that an actor standing in a role in a medieval tableau might very well play that same part in everyday life. That is, the medieval actor cast to hammer the nails into Christ's hands might well have been an actual nailwright. So the tableau image of the biblical laborer would have been an image of the biblical laborer and the contemporary laborer simultaneously – and in this way, surrogacy was laminated atop simultaneous actuality.[38] My point here is that this is precisely the logic of the photograph, by which Barthes could say "This, here, is my mother" and, simultaneously, "My mother is not here."

What is interesting about considering the 1458 living tableau of the van Eyck altarpiece is the difficulty in claiming that the living tableau is any more reenactment than preenactment – or the painted altarpiece itself any more preenactment than reenactment.[39] And again, the question of "which came first" (painting or pre- or re-enactment) is not the most useful question, as becomes apparent when one considers the symbolism of the figure of the Lamb at the painting's center, and considers, as well, the painting's function as part of an altarpiece. The central figure of the Lamb stands not only for Christ on the cross in a temporal past, but the Lamb also symbolizes the reenactment of that sacrifice

Figure 5.1 Ghent altarpiece, *Adoration of the Mystic Lamb.* Mostly attributed to Jan van Eyck, 1432. Dimensions 3.75 m × 2.60 m when open.

in the Mass. The participant at the altarpiece is given to see the Lamb on an altar (actually, on an altar within an altar, given that the van Eyck is a folding altarpiece), its life-blood pouring into a chalice. At the center of the piece, then, is a figure for reenactment/preenactment/reenactment in the criss-cross temporality of ritual returns. To reenact the painting live – to stand *still* in the place of the painting – would have been to follow the painting as a script of sorts, but the script was a script that situated reenactment (of Christ's sacrifice as prefigured at the Last Supper) as its very topic. The question of live or not-live thus becomes a matter less of determination than of suspension and alternation between states in repetition. Repetition, or *ritual remains by means of performance,* takes on increased importance. In this case, live performance is the still that articulates not a distinction between remaining and disappearing, or life and death, but an inter(in)animation of registers that is ongoing by passing on. Here, the live and the painting come undone in each other – interanimate and inter(in)animate – as occasions for body-to-body transmission.

Hans Belting reminds us that it was common in the Middle Ages (an era of images he distinguishes from an era of art) for a religious statue or icon to have "a life of its own" or to be received at ceremonies "as if it were an actual person." Also, images could have what Belting has termed a "supratemporal presence" – saints could work miracles through their images after death "thus demonstrating that they were really still alive." Moreover, Belting writes, "the making of many replicas of icons in the Middle Ages reflects the belief that duplicating an original image would extend its power."[40] It would be hard to say that times have entirely changed, or that some of these orientations to image are not circulating (or recirculating or reenacted) in contemporary visual and performance arts. James Coleman's anamorphic doublings[41] or Cindy Sherman's duplications of movie stills in different ways both resist and underscore the live power of images as composed and *re*-composed in passage across bodies, across media, and across time.

Photography in theatre: liveness and the still

The delegation of live performance as vanishing in time and photography as capturing time has contributed to our inability to read the two media as intimately related, even co-constituted, in the gesture of the still. The common view has been that performance and photography are distinct – that a photo can offer a still record of a performance but is not itself a performance, and that a performance may contain a pose, but is not a record of a pose. Indeed, the relationship between performance and photography has sometimes been considered lethal. The appearance of photography was often narrated as the dawn of death for theatre and painting.[42]

We are well aware of, and have touched on in previous chapters, the long and complicated tradition of antitheatricality in the arts (including the performance arts). But the antiphotographic has also enjoyed a lively history of panic coming not only from painting but also from theatre. Theatre artists and historians have been wary of photography – as if the kindred medium were entirely threatening to liveness itself. In 2003, theatre historian Barbara Hodgdon wrote:

> [The theatrical still is] the visible remains of what is no longer visible, a fragment that steals theater, stills it – and dis-stills it. Considered as performance in pieces, the theater photograph undertakes a visual conversation with performance: silent, impoverished, partial, it seizes appearances, violently severs them from their original context; inseparable from and traversed by the lived experience of theater, it requires anecdote, narrative, to supplement it.[43]

Hodgdon here cites theatre in distinction to photography, claiming theatre as "lived experience" versus photography's violent stilling, a move that became endemic to performance arts and media criticism in the mid-twentieth century.[44] But we may well remind ourselves that this property of theatre – its liveness – was hotly contested at the very start of that century. Such a reminder will help us unsettle the habit of accepting the life/death distinction as necessarily *medial*, necessarily a function of the apparatus or material support.

Consider that Edward Gordon Craig, the famously misanthropic theatre director and designer, went to great lengths to curb the growing conventions of theatrical realism, which he linked to photography. Theatre, he argued passionately in 1905, would do well to resist the *liveness* of photography to attempt instead to evoke the properly theatrical realm of Death – a realm not indicated by ephemerality but rather by the inverse of accident.

My pleasure shall not be to compete with the strenuous photographer, and I shall ever aim to get something entirely opposed to life as we see it. This flesh-and-blood life, lovely as it is to us all, is for me not a thing made to search into, or to give out again to the world, even conventionalized. I think that my aim shall rather be to catch some far-off glimpse of that spirit which we call Death – to recall beautiful things from the imaginary world; they say they are cold, these dead things, I do not know – they often seem warmer and more living than that which parades as life.[45]

If Craig was antiphotographic and against categorical liveness or even "lived experience" for the theatre, other nineteenth- and early twentieth-century theatre makers *sought* life for the stage.[46] In doing so, many grappled with what W. B. Worthen has productively termed the basic "complicity of theater and photography" by, perhaps ironically, putting the camera itself on stage.[47] For those who, unlike Craig, were intent on bringing "living art" to the stage in even more basic ways than placing a camera on stage, the issue of the still took methodological pride of place as indicator of liveness, and an indicator, even, of live theatre.

Konstantin Stanislavsky (whose actor training method would deeply influence Hollywood) offered the foundational advice for the actor that a "living art" is, perhaps ironically, based on the performer's ability to articulate and hold a still – to hold the still live. The following, from *An Actor Prepares*, is a Platonic exchange between teacher and students in which "I" and "Grisha" are students and "the Director" is the teacher. The Director has just said that to sit immobile on stage "may not be of intrinsic interest in itself, *but it is life*, whereas showing yourself off takes you out of the realm of living art."

> "But," Grisha broke in, [. . .] "Why is it action to sit in a chair, as you did, *without moving a finger?* To me it looked like complete lack of action." I interrupted boldly: "I do not know whether it was action or inaction, but all of us are agreed that his so-called lack of action was of far more interest than your action." "You see," the Director said calmly, addressing Grisha, "the external immobility of a person sitting on the stage does not imply passiveness. You may sit without a motion and at the same time be in full action."[48]

Here, as it had been for Maurice Maeterlinck's "static" theatre, the still is not automatically or singularly the accent of death as it would become for later twentieth-century theorists of film and photography, but the very site where liveness, or "living art" (to use Stanislavsky's phrase) finds articulation. Worthen points to this through unpacking one of Stanislavsky's earliest moments as a director – the scene in Chekhov's *Three Sisters*, directed by Stanislavsky at the Moscow Art Theatre in 1901:

> Toward the end of the first act, the Prozorovs and their guests retire from the downstage drawing room to the partly concealed reception room upstage, to celebrate Irina's name-day. Natasha arrives, nervously checks herself in the

mirror, and rushes to join the party. The forestage is empty, when two of the omnipresent junior officers suddenly appear. Taking out a camera – still a novelty at the turn of the century – they pose and silence the party, taking one photograph and then another. It is a striking moment. Taking a picture syncopates the action and highlights the stylistic transparency of Chekhov's drama. As the characters withdraw upstage, the play becomes lifelike by becoming random, oblique, untheatrical; the photograph stops the action, fixing it as an image for a second or two in the blue halo of the flash.[49]

Citations of photography *in* theatre echo citations of theatre *in* photography, and trouble the assumption of a lethal or antagonistic relationship between the two. Consider Félix Nadar's 1854 photograph titled *Pierrot the Photographer, also called The Mime Artist Deburau.* The mime, standing in as the photographer, suggests that the product of the photographer – a photograph – is intimate kin to the theatrical product of the mime: mimetic and composed through an absence, live, of the objects presented.[50]

Figure 5.2 Félix Nadar's 1854 photograph titled *Pierrot the Photographer, also called The Mime Artist Deburau.* Tournochon Adrien (1825–1903), Tournachon Gaspard Félix (1820–1910), Nadar Félix (dit.) © RMN (Musée d'Orsay) Hervé Lewandowski.

Indeed, complementary scenarios in both mediums should cause us to rethink the ready anxiety about photography as a medium that, in some agonistic distinction to performance, "steals theatre, stills it." After all, Nadar shot Pierrot shooting Nadar as if to call out (as silence will): Hey, you there! Look here! Look into the lens of the mime.[51]

Performance *in* photography: like an astonishing actress

The anxiety can run both ways. Philosopher and art historian Arthur C. Danto's anxiety about the theatre/photography divide is just as palpable as Hodgdon's in his attempt to account for exactly what artists like Cindy Sherman were up to when posing so stagily in work they would dare to call photography. The following is from Danto's "Photography and Performance: Cindy Sherman's Stills" published in 1990 to accompany the publication of her 1977–80 series *Untitled Film Stills* in which Sherman photographed herself in a series of images that appeared to be stills from B-grade movies:

> While it is perfectly clear that [Cindy Sherman's] works are photographs [. . .] the question has often been raised as to whether she is a photographer. [. . .] The quality of a print is not something that concerns her, as if she would be glad if the print was on cheap paper and even blurred [. . .] So she is not a photographer [. . .][52]

Danto's difficulty locating what Sherman was doing in her *Untitled Film Stills* seems exceptionally odd, especially since so many so-called appropriation artists had been

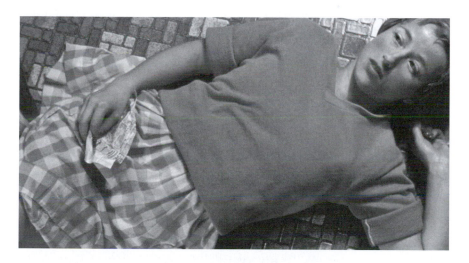

Figure 5.3 Cindy Sherman, *Untitled*, 1981 (#96). Color photograph, 24 × 48 inches. Courtesy of the artist and Metro Pictures.

developing such work, almost invariably gender-marked, across the century (think of early twentieth-century gender-queering photographs such as those by Claude Cahun or Man Ray's image of Rrose Sélavy).[53]

It may seem too easy a mark to pick on Danto here, but it is precisely the simple boldness of his inability regarding her work that is instructive. Though Danto cannot relate to Sherman as a photographer or a painter, he does find an identity that works for him, saying that she is "like an astonishing actress" – like a Jane Fonda perhaps, in North Vietnam? Interestingly, five years before Cindy Sherman's first *Untitled Film Still*, it was precisely the question of what it means to be an actress versus a person recognizable as other than an actress that prompted film directors Jean-Luc Godard and Jean-Pierre Gorin to reprimand Jane Fonda so soundly for "posing" in North Vietnam in 1972. Fonda had gone to North Vietnam as an activist, soon after shooting Godard and Gorin's film *Tout va bien*, to protest the US presence in Vietnam by visiting the Viet Cong and having her visit documented through photography. In a short film they titled *Letter to Jane: An Investigation About a Still*, Godard and Gorin claimed that Fonda (who had certainly appeared in her share of B-grade films) was so solidly influenced by what they suggest is Americanized Stanislavskian method that everything about her signified Hollywood's theatrical representation of the "natural."[54] That is, she could not be *recognizable* in a documentary photograph as anything other than The American Actress. And "The American Actress" was always already, they argued, a placeholder for capitalist imperialism, overfull of over-empty empathy – a product and habit of Hollywood's theatrical natural-affect machine. The significance of the Fonda documentary photo could only be found, they argued in 1972, in tracking its prior cinematic, photographic, and theatrical references, which (for them) impossibly complicated the wartime scenario the image pretended to document. Fonda, they argued, could only be "The Girl" or "The Face," and as such she could not be (and should not try to be) outside of the field of representation. They argue, instead, for using the Fonda image to read that field – and to read it critically.

Godard and Gorin may have been upset with Fonda because Fonda's appearance as a war protester appearing to listen to North Vietnamese interlocutors in an image first published in *Paris Match* in 1972 might have seemed, to them, to complicate their own use of the actress in *Tout va bien*. In that film, Fonda appears as both the female love interest "Her" and as Jane Fonda, American Actress. "Hanoi Jane" had *not* been part of Godard and Gorin's plans for their star, a film in which she appears to do only as she is instructed, if always somewhat awkwardly. It is a film that, intriguingly, includes a great many tableaux vivants, most of them concerned with labor.

Godard and Gorin's remarks on the Jane Fonda image sound like a plea to read the *Paris Match* shot *as if* it were (or would become) a Cindy Sherman – to read it for its theatricality, citationality, and temporal circulation. But what would reading Jane Fonda *as if* Cindy Sherman do to the photograph as documentary, and what would it do to the action it appears to document as anti-war protest? Relatedly, and in line with the questions feminists were asking with increasing force, what does a document of a *woman's pose* document? Can a *pose* stand as evidence of active agency if the

Figure 5.4 Jane Fonda
at a prisoner of war
camp in North
Vietnam, 1972.
Photo courtesy of Film
Reference Library.

essential action of a pose is theatrical, citational, or always in an anachronistic or
temporally syncopated relationship to action? Are problems of posing, personhood,
and protest *theatre* problems? Is the "trouble" with gender (by which all women could
be so often dismissed as actresses) one linked, historically, to mimesis, masquerade,
and the theatricality of the faux, the copy, the second sex?[55]

For Danto, in 1990, it was obvious the best he could do in thinking about
Sherman's photography was to gesture to Sherman's gender as somehow explanatory of the trouble he was having recognizing her as a visual artist, that is, as other
than The Actress (and we can note the derogatory tone in both Godard and Gorin
and in Danto on this point):

> I am uncertain that the idea of the stills of herself would have occurred to her
> had she not spent a fair amount of time before mirrors in the standard way of
> women making themselves up and trying for this look or that, the stills do not
> compose a sequential exploration of her own features, nor do they stand as a
> monument to feminine vanity. They do not have, for example the sequence of
> self-portraits by Rembrandt as an art historical precedent. Rembrandt's
> representations of his own features trace the inscriptions that life makes on the
> single human face across time, but Sherman's face is a neutral base on which
> she inscribes the countless faces of The Girl in her myriad embodiments. [. . .]
> *I cannot imagine anyone who could recognize Sherman from the stills.*[56]

That, for Danto, Sherman's face is not recognizable as *her* face points to a
heteronormative panic that spells *theatre* trouble in operations of faciality and

masquerade.[57] (That this same trouble – gender trouble – should irrupt in Japanese photographer Yasumasa Morimura's work, though *his* face will be considered recognizable, should not surprise us, as we will examine in a moment). Despite Danto's evident discomfort, the hyper-mimesis of gender trouble was clearly intended by Sherman in her *Untitled Film Stills*, and resonates in her later work including *History Portraits/Old Masters* (1988–90), *Civil War* (1991), and *Sex Pictures* (1992) in which the body is increasingly distorted. The *Civil War* photographs are details of faux corpses, mostly feet and fingers that one reads (because of her earlier work) as Sherman's own (whether they are or are not), intermingled with dirt either as if decomposing on the battlefield or trying to scratch up out of it.[58]

What I am curious about here is the slip and slide of (mis)recognition provoked by Sherman's arguably reenactive poses. Danto's claim to an inability to recognize Sherman in her *Untitled Film Stills* doubles as a problem not only of gender (with masquerade as the "standard way of women") but also of *mediality*. He can neither see *her* face (she is not recognizable to him) nor the face of a photographer (because he sees an actress). Not only do we find Danto stumbling over the simultaneity of media (acting, painting, photography, film) but his stumbling occurs relative to work that simultaneously crosses temporal registers (the temporal drag that affords both anachronism and theatricality). To be clear, temporal drag occurs in the following way in Sherman: in the late 1970s and early 1980s she poses in pseudo-film stills that appear to precede her (thus she steps back, fitting her own body into precedent, reenacting female bodies in clearly recognizable gestic configurations that suggest a "standard" B-grade movie narrative). Later she will step into oil paintings, sex pictures, and Civil War battlefields that mimic not-quite-precise precedents. In all cases, as in reenactment practices of "living history," there is no precise original but a reenactment of scenes that might have been, as the precise reference is intimated but not immediately apparent. That is, these are scenes that are recognizable both as bearing *some* relation to historical precedent (the viewer recognizes some low budget film or some Renaissance oil painting or some decomposing soldier) and as being in *some* future as if in response to *some* past. *Some* things are askew. The scenes appear to not quite or not yet have happened. Unlike the Wooster Group's extreme precision, Sherman works with precise details, but the details' errant faultiness cannot congeal to an exactly locatable original. Still, because of the overt imitation on the level of detail, they purposefully smack of replication, the copy, the second, the double: in short, the feminine and the theatrical.

Sherman shoots her photographs as portraits – she poses, that is, for her own camera. The record of Sherman's live pose is, of course, the photograph. But the photograph is also not *only* the record, since it is the reenactment itself, for it is through the material support of the photograph that the reenactment *takes place* as performance: the performance takes place *as* photograph, and in this sense might be considered redocumentation as much as reenactment, troubling a distinction between the two. This is to say that the photographs themselves (not just the actress/photographer) reenact film stills, reenact oil painting, and mimic other media as if standing in their footprint, tracing their form.[59]

Figure 5.5 Cindy Sherman, *Untitled*, 1989 (#210). *History Portraits/Old Masters*. Color photograph, 67 × 45 inches (image), 170.2 × 114.3 cm. Courtesy of the artist and Metro Pictures.

Figure 5.6 Cindy Sherman, *Untitled*, 1991 (#242). *Civil War Series.* Color photograph (framed) 49 × 72 inches. Courtesy of the artist and Metro Pictures.

But to return to Danto's trouble with recognition: perhaps he simply refuses to work very hard, for surely he misses the larger congress of Sherman's insights – insights about the hard work, the *labor*, both in mimesis and in recognition. As early as 1980 Craig Owens, drawing on Lacan, had precisely articulated Sherman's aim as the "unresolved margin of incongruity" in the labor of misrecognition that haunts relations between categories of selfhood and image.[60] Owens had spelled out the problematic doubleness, the "complicity," that attends work like Sherman's – work intent on (ex)posing processes of mimesis as requiring as much if not more of an awareness of the mechanisms of misrecognition (at the basis of subjecthood at all) as of recognition. To get it right, that is to *recognize* Sherman, necessarily requires that the viewer labor to recognize operations of misrecognition. And so again the question arises: what does the error, the missing, the not-quite-right get right about that which it strives to replay?

Photographs such as Sherman's operate not only in the cracks of time, but also in the cracks between theatre, film, painting, and photography. As such, this work courts a slippery or multiple set of (mis)recognitions requiring what Derrida after Bergson might call an "interval" that puts the still "in play." It is no accident that Owens cites Derrida's *Positions* at the close of his influential 1985 feminist essay "Posing" – an essay that troubles photography's claim to the still by articulating the live moment of arrest when the pose is struck and the shot taken.[61] And yet, despite Derrida's proposition in *Positions* (and elsewhere) that processes of signification in representation are "no longer conceivable on the basis of the opposition presence/absence," but rather engage the undecidable and "generative movement in the play of differences," we persist in parsing our mediums according to decidability: privileging remains-indicating-absence for photography *on the one hand* and presence-as-vanishing-liveness for performance *on the other*.[62] We forget, that is, as Toni Morrison reminds us, that the photograph or the text or the gesture is an event that takes place "in your hands, it's in your hands."[63]

Let us turn now briefly to photographer Yasumasa Morimura to press further the question of the gender panic that haunts the arguably always temporal intervals of intermediality. Recall, above, that in 1990 Danto was able to use Rembrandt as an example of how Sherman was *not* a photographer but was "like an astonishing actress." Morimura has taken "like an astonishing actress" very far in his own work, placing himself in his work not only as Rembrandt, but as Cindy Sherman (*To My Little Sister: For Cindy Sherman*, 1998), and, taking the matter quite literally, as a series of movie actresses – Marilyn Monroe, Sophia Loren, Elizabeth Taylor, Greta Garbo, Vivien Leigh, Liza Minnelli, and . . . Jane Fonda.[64]

The collection *Daughter of Art History: Photographs of Yasumasa Morimura* makes clear the gendered dynamic of masquerade and sutures it to a racialized dynamic of the feminized Asian male such that even when Morimura is standing in for the male masters Rembrandt, Goya, Ingres, and others, his surrogation renders him *female* progeny to the "masters."[65] Indeed, the feminization – *the actressization* – appears to ricochet back upon the artists and objects Morimura surrogates. For art historian Donald Kuspit, not only does the artist become, as Sherman does for Danto, "like an astonishing actress," but so too do the objects and subjects of art history.

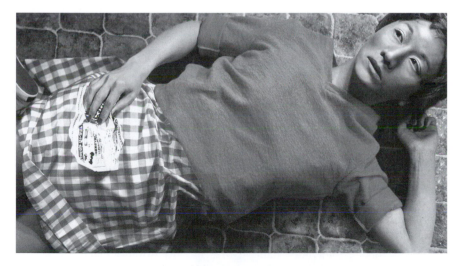

Figure 5.7 Yasumasa Morimura, *To My Little Sister: For Cindy Sherman*, 1998. Ilfochrome mounted on aluminum, 55 × 31 inches (139.7 × 78.7 cm). Photo: Luhring Augustine, New York.

Kuspit writes that Morimura:

> favors famous pictures by famous artists – Goya, Ingres, Rossetti, and
> Velazquez, among many others – as though in appropriating their works he
> could also appropriate their fame. It may be secondhand fame, but it's better
> than none. He has done some strange, funny things to their works, as though
> to show their own strange, funny character. By restaging them he shows their
> stagey character – their theatricality. He's operating in the theater of art
> history, reproducing some of its grandest productions, demonstrating that
> every masterpiece is a rhetorical performance, and that the people portrayed
> are actors – sometimes ham actors, like Rembrandt, sometimes self-
> dramatizing, like van Gogh. Indeed, the artists who star in their own works –
> the artists Morimura impersonates, confirming that he is a greater actor than
> any one of them because he can be all of them – may be the best actors of all.[66]

And where the feminine (the "daughter") is, there too, apparently, is theatre and intermediality. In accounting for the way Morimura stages his photographs – making a clay replica and painting it in greasepaint – Kuspit suggests that Morimura is offering "a kind of Wagnerian Gesamtkunstwerk." Earlier in the same essay Kuspit had said that Morimura is presenting "a kind of commedia dell'arte" as if those two modes of theatre history (*Gesamtkunstwerk* and *commedia*) were somehow interchangeable. The point is that Kuspit looks to theatre for his examples of *what is taking place*. But even as he references theatre, he occludes it again as that which disappears:

> There's no question that Morimura is a major master in his own right – certainly an important impresario – for what he offers, however ironically, is a kind of Wagnerian Gesamtkunstwerk, in which painting, sculpture, and photography combine for a seamless conceptual whole. His photographs may be mock masterpieces, but they are nonetheless masterpieces, for they show mastery of three mediums [painting, sculpture, photography] usually regarded as irreconcilable. Their paradoxical interplay and ironical integration, as well as the fact that Morimura produces, directs, and stars in his own art dramas, indicates that he is a consummate artist.[67]

What I am pointing to here is the way that theatre cannot be *one* of Kuspit's "three mediums" contributing to intermedial art, but rather that intermediality becomes an "art drama" with theatre as its strangely inter-articulated, feminized (actressized), and ultimately occluded referent.

For Danto, theatre is the reason why the female Sherman is not a consummate *artist*. For Kuspit, theatre is the reason Morimura is a consummate *female* artist. The question of the recognizability of a "consummate" artist trips here on three related problematics: theatre and gender and race. The most famous antitheatrical art historian remains Michael Fried of course, and though he's become too handy a whipping boy for too many, here we might do well to remember a phrase from his 1967 essay "Art and Objecthood" where he states, most succinctly, that the problem of theatre is its intermediality: "The concepts of quality and value – and to the extent that these are central to art, the concept of art itself – are meaningful, or wholly meaningful, only *within* the individual arts. What lies *between* the arts is theatre."[68] The problem of medial specificity is the problem of a boundaried sameness of material form – a problem of legitimation in clearly marked lines of patrilineal descent, parsing originals from copies, individual material from other material, and, clearly, daughters from sons, as well as almost-but-not-quite from white.

"Almost but not quite" is the phrase Homi Bhabha uses in his influential 1984 essay, "Of Mimicry and Man: The Ambivalence of Colonial Discourse," referring to the South Asian colonial subject conjoined to perform a colonized identity that is almost British but not quite – a performance *for* the white colonizer.[69] "Almost but not quite" points to an inherent ambivalence in mimicry through which the colonized subject must try to pass, but at the same time must not fully pass so as to preserve a racialized difference. If Morimura's "not quite" passing photographs are structured on differences of gender, race (he most often replays the Western canon), and temporal distance, Sherman's *Untitled Film Stills* posits a difference that is arguably less easy to locate. For a white woman re-posing as white women have been given to pose in minor popular films, the "difference" of the "not quite" becomes something not locatable as precisely bodily. That is, Sherman *is* a white woman posing *as* a white woman. She is not an Asian man posing as a white woman. Thus the question of recognition that Sherman poses is not exactly a gender difference, not exactly a race difference, and not much of a cross-temporal difference (though the films lack precise precedent, they are sort of 1960s, sort of 1970s). Rather, the "difference" that makes Sherman's scenario "almost but not quite" is something not necessarily given to be seen.[70] For Danto, it was something of the problem *between* being an actress and being a photographer – something between the act of the photographer and the "act" of the actress. This something is intermedial and cross-temporal (in the lag of time between the shoot and its circulation), and because Sherman passes as a white woman trying both to pass and not quite to pass, her work allows us to read the *labor* at the pass. The gender problematic (the problem of the second, the double, the masquerade, the theatrical) can, through her work, be acknowledged as a problem that haunts the intermedial: between theatre and photography/painting/sculpture and back.

Between "A Small History of Photography" and Abu Ghraib

There are many directions we could turn in exploring the inter(in)animation of theatre and photography. To turn to real torture after discussing the theatrical pose (and before moving on to art contexts again in the final sections of this chapter) may seem offensive to some readers, despite the fact that the torture perpetrated at Abu Ghraib was, itself, laced with the degradations of enforced scenes of feminization imaged by the torturers, and despite, as well, the overt theatricality of the scenarios staged for the camera. So far, we have briefly explored the unlikely site of "still living" through a medieval altarpiece. And we have considered the problem of gender, intermediality, and the pose in art photography. We return now to an unsettling site of inquiry – the "snapshot" digital images produced at Abu Ghraib prison and circulated beginning in 2004.

The Abu Ghraib images and the "scenarios"[71] that circulate *hand-to-hand* or *eye-to-eye* make evident that linking the photographic still always already with a death understood only as elsewhere (as there and then versus here and now) can disable deeper thinking on the ways in which, as we will explore Benjamin to suggest, the future subsists in the photograph. Does the future subsist in the photograph as a future performance subsists in play-script or instruction art – as hail or call, the posing of a question, the demanding of a response? That death and violence are literally countenanced in the Abu Ghraib images – in all their horror and outrage – should not stop us from questioning the possible cracks in the frames between image or art on one hand and violence, war, degradation, and torture on the other, as we will use Fred Moten's important study *In the Break* to inquire after below.

As we have been exploring: striking a pose partakes of reenactment, and reenactment defers its site in multiple directions. What is cited extends not only into the
past but also across complicated fields of possibility that undo any linearity that
would give us, securely, forward and backward. In his small piece "A Small History
of Photography," recall that Walter Benjamin gives us the paradoxical notion of a
"future that subsists" in the condition of the still – a "still" that is not relegated
(despite quite brilliant readings, like Eduardo Cadava's) to the condition of
"death."[72] Rather, I think Benjamin's famous essay can be read as engaged in the
tangle of the still living or the living still that reminds us as much of tableau vivant
or the ritual gest as of photography. Let us look briefly at a well-known passage
from this text. Benjamin writes:

> No matter how artful the photographer, no matter how carefully posed his
> subject, the beholder feels an irresistible urge to search such a picture for the
> tiny spark of contingency, of the Here and Now, with which reality has so to
> speak seared the subject, to find the inconspicuous spot where in the
> immediacy of that long-forgotten moment the future subsists so eloquently that
> we, looking back, may rediscover it.[73]

Here, Benjamin was writing about the image of Dauthendey with his fiancée, the
woman Dauthendey would later find dead of suicide after the birth of their sixth
child. Benjamin describes the happy engagement image and in the next breath
relates the later suicide. He then gives us the above citation on the urge to seek in
the photograph the spot of immediacy in which "the future subsists." At first read,
one might assume that the future Benjamin writes of is straightforward: the time
of the "immediacy" was the immediate moment of the shutter click – the "future"
contains the events that would progress from that moment but had not yet "stepped
out"[74] into the time in which the man and woman would marry, would procreate,
and would "live" until they died. The future as it existed in the instant the
photograph was taken seems, in the image, still possible, and thus it subsists in the
image as a future not yet unfolded. Thus, the future subsists as *still in* the future.
But it is not insignificant that Benjamin tells his reader of that future, and even hints
that it is already readable in the strange distance he finds in the woman's gaze, the
way in which she "passes him by." As readers, we are given to know – as a condition
of imagining the image – that that future contains the woman's suicide. This is an
event crucial to Benjamin's selection of *this* photograph for discussion, as Benjamin
has made apparent in the telling. And so, perhaps, the future that subsists is also
one of circulation – one that necessarily contains our moment of looking, of showing
and telling, when we seek to find the "immediacy" that Benjamin also refers to, on
the previous page, as "still real":

> [. . .] the woman who was alive there, who even now is still real [. . .][75]

As Benjamin makes clear, that future subsists not only *in* the photo but *through* the
"we" who look to "rediscover it" as "still" – "still" in the sense of that term that

signifies remaining, more than silence and motionlessness. The "still" for Benjamin, in this passage, is neither silent nor without motion, but generative of an unruliness:

> [In] Hill's Newhaven fishwife, her eyes cast down in such indolent, seductive modesty, there remains something that goes beyond testimony to the photographer's art, something that cannot be silenced, that fills you with an unruly desire to know what her name was, the woman who was alive there, who even now is still real and will never consent to be wholly absorbed in *art*.[76]

Figures in photographs (especially the earliest photographs, which Benjamin finds "innocent") are "still real" and exhibit a resistance to "absorption." The "tiny spark of contingency" of which Benjamin writes is "alive with contradiction" – already composed in multiple times, via a moment of immediacy of paradoxically long duration, given that it is "still real" and/or capable of *rediscovery* in (and only in) an encounter. Thus the future subsists not only in the photographic moment of the shot, but in our complicities in encounter with the *still*, or *ongoing*, or *live* mode of return. This is a twist on "still life" that asks for further analysis.

The Abu Ghraib torture images make terribly palpable a way in which the future in any moment of image-capture subsists, though the status of subsistence requires rigorous thought. Where most reception theory fetishizes the "death of the author," thereby relegating authorial presence to the irrecouperable contingencies of the past and positing the life, only, of the reader, thinking through Abu Ghraib suggests duration in an ongoing scene of inter-temporal enactment. Looking at the Abu Ghraib images we might ask whether the "long-forgotten moment" Benjamin cites is not only the moment of the click of the shutter, but also the shudder of contingency in the complicity of looking – that is, the moment in which we are *immediately caught looking*: the one in which *we are present misrecognizing the past as past*.

Let us consider that the Abu Ghraib images are digital images of torture in that the poses choreographed for the prisoners and often for the soldiers are reiterative positions of shame and degradation. But let us also consider that the shaming of the prisoners, taking place before the camera and through the camera, is, via the camera, cast into a future contained, already, as part of the scene. Thus these images and their clearly citational poses, their reenacted and horridly propped positions beside pointedly pointing guards, are cast into a future with the click of a shutter – the phonic materiality of photography.[77] The pointing fingers of the guards address a futured viewer. The moments arrested as images are cast, *as shame*, into a future that will encounter a "now" deferred.[78] The moment of shame is arguably one of considerable duration, intended to take place both now and later, when shame will occur (again and again) as a result of the image's circulation. The shame is meant to take place not only *in* the digital image but *as* the image, that is, as the image in a future of circulation. The snapshots thus take place and make their point in the future when they are seen . . . by you and by me. Moreover, the photographs as "scriptive things" assume that the hailed viewer, like Althusser's hailed passer-by, will *recognize* feminization and same-sex posturing as shameful. This is a future recognition pre-enacted in the moment of the shot and cast into its future production where it will stand before a viewer, much as a script is cast forward for future realization in a theatre. In this way, it can be said to take place again as event (a shaming) before "you" the live viewer, upon whom it depends, much like a play script, for (re)enactment. As previously mentioned, Toni Morrison writes of the future of any writing as being "in your hands." We might say the same for any image, whether your hands are on a book or magazine or newspaper where the image is printed, on your remote control as your television screens them, or on your keyboard as your computer streams them. What you *do* with your hands becomes the photograph.

To read the images this way is not to absolve them of their status as record, but to complicate the too-easy divide between record and script, or archive and repertoire. To read the images this way is to read one medium (photography) through another (theatre) in order to access the complicity of live encounter, and the itinerancy of the temporal scene that not only "took place" but "takes place" in the nervousness of syncopated time. Fred Moten has written that there is "a massive itinerancy here, a fugitivity" in the circulation of images into their future.[79] Moten writes of photography in general through the particular photograph of Emmet Till's broken face, taken as he lay in his coffin after his lynching. Writing both about and through the aesthetics of the black radical tradition, Moten takes the blues as a figure of thought when he writes that there is a political imperative in the display and circulation of such painful images and sounds, a political imperative that is "never disconnected from an aesthetic one."[80] The imperative is an encounter, not only across time but across medial forms, as a way of opening up, of negotiating and moving history into its alternatives.

It is vitally important that Moten reads one medium through another – in his case photography through music. To read media through each other is not the same as claiming the end of medial specificity or even suggesting that the twentieth-century is a post-medium age.[81] Rather, to read media through each other might be to situate the site of any medial or mixed-medial expression as already an inter(in)animate encounter, an encounter that requires syncopation or cross-temporality. I am reminded, again, of de Certeau's location of the monument not only in the stillness of the stone edifice but in the faces of those who pass by.[82] Perhaps like de Certeau, who reads a still monument through movement, Moten finds silent photographs cut through with sound. Moten writes: "In positing that this photo [of Till] and photographs in general bear a phonic substance, I want to challenge [. . .] the ocularcentrism that generally – perhaps necessarily – shapes theories of the nature of photography [. . .]." Moten wants to posit, instead, "something like a mimetic improvisation of and with materiality that moves in excess of meaning."[83] Moten engages medial specificity through mimesis, arguing that the meaning of one medial expression (one call) is located most compellingly in another medial expression (a response), so that the site of any expressing, like the torture/aestheticization of Emmett Till, is understood as *on the move*, or, like the title of his book, "in the break." This inter(in)animation of sensual modes always moves meaning *off* of the discrete site of material support and off of the discrete site of temporal event and onto not only the "spectator" or passer-by or reader (which would suggest only a one-way contingency in a linear temporal mode), but into chiasmatic reverberation across media and across time in a network of ongoing response-ability.

Intermedia, medial specificity, and photography

If I argued above for a movement *off* of discrete mediality in any work of art, some media scholars have been keen to resediment photography in medial specificity. In 1999 in an essay in *Critical Inquiry* titled "Reinventing the Medium," Rosalind Krauss charted the way in which photography historically afforded a means to thwart medial specificity. Indeed, photography enabled "an entire world of artistic technique and tradition" to "drop away."[84] Through photography, medium specificity was undone into reproduction or reproduceability. This, Krauss tells us, was Benjamin's point in "The Work of Art in the Age of Mechanical Reproduction" in which Benjamin charted "a historical path from the shock effects courted by futurism and dada collage, to the shocks delivered by the unconscious optics revealed by the photograph, to the shock specific to the montage procedures of film editing, a path that is now indifferent to the givens of a particular medium." Krauss notes the irony in the fact that "institutions of art – museums, collectors, historians, critics – turned their attention in the 1960s to the specificity of photographic medium at the very moment that photography entered artistic practice [. . .] as a tool for deconstructing that practice."[85] Krauss allows that photography's emergence as a "theoretical object" (that is, a deconstructive tool) had already occurred in the hands of Benjamin in 1931 in his "A Small History of Photography." It is in the 1960s, however, in the critical mix that included Barthes and Baudrillard and others, that photography fully exposed itself as a medium of undoing – undoing mediality, undoing verity, undoing art. As a multiple-without-an-original, and yet an object with a resilient link to the bodies and objects it cites (what Barthes terms photography's "that was there" aspect), the photograph as *copy* marked, in Krauss's words, "the site of so many ontological cave-ins."[86] Deeply inimical to the idea of autonomy, photography's "inherent hybridity," its "mimetic capacity," has been nowhere clearer than in its uses in the 1980s by the "whole cohort of appropriation artists" (such as Sherman).[87] Danto's 1990 medial confusion clearly exhibits the kind of anxiety that attends the *medium* of photography's resistance to medium specificity – its "post-medium condition."[88] As we have shown above, that such confusion should so often be laced with the problem of the non-specific "betweeness" of theatre and aligned with "acting" is no surprise at all. For in its "mimetic capacity," photography shares a good deal with performance, a mode that slips continually into indiscrete (and indiscreet) arenas of return via citation, repetition, theatricality, and the trouble of a "for hire" authenticity discussed in Chapter 4.

But we cannot leave Krauss merely remarking on Benjamin's point about photography's mimeticism, for Krauss is ultimately interested in something else. She charts the condition of photography's a-medial bias (or promise) lodged in Benjamin's "Small History" in order to point to a further irony; that just as photography becomes eclipsed by the digital it passes into a new relation to aesthetic production, "becoming, under precisely the guise of its own obsolescence, a means of what has to be called an act of reinventing the medium."[89] She sees, that is, photography rearticulating itself as a unique or separate medium precisely as it passes out of common use. This reinventing of medial specificity is photography's new (old) promise, a promise she sees nested in photography's first decade in the 1840s before its supposed cooptation by the commodity form. For Krauss, who combines Benjamin with Barthes at the midpoint of her essay, the medium specificity *reinvented* for photography in the "twilight zone of obsolescence" will be the "still."[90] Interestingly, she uses James Coleman's 1985 *Living and Presumed Dead* as exemplary of this reinvention, this second coming of the medium as medium. In *Living and Presumed Dead* Colman presents forty-five minutes of slides of actors lined up as if for a final curtain call, staged and restaged across photographs – stills, yes, but stills which process images from a theatre passing one after another through a slide projector: curtain call after curtain call after curtain call.[91] Of course, what I am arguing here is that the "still" – whether stagily posed or seemingly accidental as in a snapshot – is something photography shares with the medium of theatre, or with theatricality, in a forgotten interrelation that may now be newly available for analysis.

In the interest of reanimating photography's material support as specific, Krauss concludes her essay by suggesting that the first decade of photography's history can afford a "kind of promise folded within its medium of an openness and invention before the rigidification of the image as commodity." Now that photography is obsolete, she argues, we can be reminded of the promise it contained at its start: a promise she names as "the necessary *plurality* of the arts." If we lose the plurality of specific media, Krauss fears a "deadening" of the arts into an a-critical and commodified generality. Her effort to reclaim the plural specificity of media (for what in *A Voyage to the North Sea* she terms "differential specificity") is her way of stating "the need for the idea of the medium as such to reclaim the specific from the *deadening* embrace of the general."[92] If what lies between the individual arts is, as it was for Fried in 1967, always already theatre, it is theatre that is "deadening." Again, ironies abound. Theatre, a live form of the still, is ironically a signature of deadness for art historians such as Fried and Krauss. Is this perhaps because of theatre's always already anachronistic, always almost but not quite obsolescence? How can one "reinvent" a medium of reinvention?

Returning to the first decade of photography that Krauss finds so full of promise for the reinvented specificity of the medium, what do we find? Might we find something here to quell Danto's anxieties that Sherman is an actress and not a photographer, for instance? Nadar's Pierrot images come to mind as examples of early photographs in which theatre cannot be parsed from photography. But those photographs were taken in photography's second decade. What of the first decade – the late 1830s and early 1840s? The fact is that several founding fathers vied for title spot beside Daguerre (who may have stolen the position from Niépce). Also in the running, as "proto-photographers" at least, are William Henry Fox Talbot and Hippolyte Bayard. In fact, a series of three of Bayard's photographs from 1840, each titled *Self-Portrait as a Drowned Man*, are often read not only as linking the roots of photography to death but as Bayard's comical response to being eclipsed by

Daguerre in his bid for founder status. Each image shows a naked man propped against a wall, asleep or dead, eyes closed and lower body draped in cloth in what Geoffrey Batchen has called an overt reference "to classical tradition, specifically to the relief figures seen in sculptural friezes."[93] Also in the photograph is a straw hat, a ceramic vase, and a small plaster cast statuette.

The "joke" is evident on the back of one of the images, on which Bayard scribbled an attribution that begins: "The corpse which you see here is that of M. Bayard, inventor of the process that has just been shown to you, or the wonderful results of which you will soon see." Temporal indicators are interestingly here – "you have just seen, or you are going to see" render the present temporarily vacated. This is probably due to the fact that to read Bayard's note, the photo has to have been turned to its back – the viewing of the image will thus come before or after (or both) the event of reading. But the note goes on to suddenly include the present with the phrase "at this moment." The pointing finger here – hailing "you" into the scene – are words on the back of the image's material support:

Figure 5.9 Hippolyte Bayard, *Self-Portrait as a Drowned Man*. October, 1840, black and white reproduction of the original direct positif process, 18, 7 × 19, 3 cm. © Coll. Société Française de photographie. All rights reserved.

The corpse which you see here is that of M. Bayard, inventor of the process that has just been shown to you, or the wonderful results of which you will soon see. As far as I know, this inventive and indefatigable experimenter has been occupied for about three years with the perfection of his discovery.

The Academy, the King, and all those who have seen his pictures admired them as you do *at this very moment*, although he himself considers them still imperfect. This has brought him much honor but not a single *sou*. The Government, which has supported M. Daguerre more than is necessary, declared itself unable to do anything for M. Bayard, and the unhappy man threw himself into the water in despair. Oh, human fickleness! For a long time artists, scientists and the press took an interest in him, but now that he has been lying in the Morgue for days, no-one has recognized him or claimed him!

Ladies and gentlemen, let's talk of something else so that your sense of smell is not upset, for as you have probably noticed, the face and hands have already started to decompose.

H. B., 18 October, 1840[94]

The staged aspect of this photograph, and of the joke, is obvious. And more is going on here than meets the eye. For to understand the photograph, the photograph has to meet the hands – be turned around – looked at from all sides. A body is thus both imprinted *in* the photograph, and required *of* the photograph. Taking a closer look at the image, Bayard's face and hands were sunburned, as Bayard was an avid gardener and often photographed his garden and included his gardening hat in interior shots. This imprint of light on his skin points, as Batchen instructs us, to the human skin as "photographic surface," a "joke" remarked by the in-handedness required to turn the photograph around, to open it like a book or approach it from all sides – like sculpture. And like theatre. A "scriptive thing" it im-poses an action on the artist *and* on the viewer/participant.

Statuary is abundantly countenanced in the first decade of photography, not only in Bayard's photographs but in Talbot's and Daguerre's as well. I have alluded above to some ways in which thinking through this Western historical relationship between statuary and the live in theatre's history might invite us to complicate our habitual distinction between "live" art and "object" art. In "Recasting Ancestry: Statuettes as Imaged by Three Inventors of Photography," Julia Ballerini pushes beyond the easy answer – that early photographers used statuettes because they could hold still for the length of time necessary to shoot (which is no doubt true) – to ask what more the appearance of these plaster casts of Greek and Roman marbles and bronzes signifies at the inception of the medium.[95] To my mind, the in-handedness of Bayard's photographs in particular invites us to think, again, the tangled inter(in)animation of still with living, with still living, and the inter(in)animation of the theatrical live with the photographic still.

* * * * * * * *

If we can say that theatre or live performance exists as a prehistory to photography, we are not making an uncommon or bold claim. If we say that photography *is* performance or theatre, we encounter the trouble spot of temporal and medial blurring or simultaneity, the "deadening" generality that Krauss abjures. If we say that performance *is* photography, or suggest that we can locate ancient or medieval photographs – we undo a temporal logic that supports linear development and demarcates medial boundaries as matters of technological invention and/or material support. We also risk undoing a dividing line between the live and the dead. I like these risks, and admire those who take them. But while such risks may be worth taking as spurs to thought, we should be wary of ontological claims (photography *is* performance; performance *is* photography; medial specificity *is* dead; medial specificity *is not* dead) as such claims re-sediment our habits of distinction along new lines. Similarly, the performance studies lens that looks at everything "as" performance might limit cross-medial inquiry. Rather, let us ask the following: How can we account not only for the way differing media cite and incite each other but for the ways that the meaning of one form *takes place* in the response of another? Relatedly, how can we account for a temporal inter-(in)animation by which times touch, conversations take place inter-temporally, and the live lags or drags or *stills* ? Because the history of theatre is replete with stills, the seeming stillness of the photograph should not necessarily serve as evidence that the stilled is live no longer. To my mind, we would do well to trouble any distinction between live arts and still arts that relies on an (historically faulty) absolutist distinction between performance and remains.

* * * * * * * *

And the dead body of the Iraqi prisoner beside Charles Granier in the Abu Ghraib prison? If the photograph *takes place*, then in the logic of fugitivity articulated by Moten (and by Howard Zinn in the next chapter), the action we take in response is "in our hands." It's in our hands.

And back – Afterword

You know we're living in divided times,
When no one can define the battle lines.
To gain some ground, go find your feet,
Your stance a dance of advance and retreat.
And that's why I query,
What are you fighting for?

———Allison Smith, *The Muster*

If history is to be creative, to anticipate a possible future without denying the past,
it should, I believe, emphasize new possibilities by disclosing those hidden
episodes of the past when, even if in brief flashes, people showed their ability to
resist, to join together, and occasionally to win. I am supposing, or perhaps only
hoping, that our future may be found in the past's fugitive moments of compassion rather than in its solid centuries of warfare.

———Howard Zinn, *A Power Governments Cannot Suppress*

In 2005 the artist Allison Smith called "intellectuals, activists, artists, and queers"
as well as "Ladies and Gentlemen" to muster. In advance of a living history
reenactment she would mount in May 2005 on Governor's Island in New York
City as part of a Public Art Fund project, Smith delivered a speech that was a call
to arms – a call to pitch multicolored queer flags among the Confederate and Union
flags of the US Civil War.

Let every person come out! Emblazon your Cause on a self-fashioned uniform.
Enact your own costume drama. Wear your war on your sleeve. Show off your
revolutionary style. Assume a historical personage. Dress up in soldier drag.
Go into total role-playing. Take your shirt off. Form alliances. Form com-
panies. Raise a border regiment. Marshal a Middlesex infantry. Lead a bugle
brigade, drum corps, or dance troupe. Cause a Rebellion, provoke a skirmish,
or go AWOL. Use your art supplies to make new forms of trench art. For,
wherever you place yourself amidst the advances and retreats of art history,
we are making an arsenal, a record, a form of currency, and a conversation.
We want you![1]

Clearly, and in distinction to history reenactments not framed as performance art (such as the 1999 Gettysburg reenactment discussed in Chapter 1), the general aesthetic of Smith's reenactment could be marshaled by the word *camp* – a word not so very secretly folded within Smith's design of a "campsite-installation." And yet, as we have already explored Stallybrass and Nyong'o on carnival and farce to suggest, and as Ann Pellegrini has eloquently argued after Susan Sontag, the appellation "camp" applied to a performance or event should not dismiss the serious, the effective, even (contra Sontag) the political.[2] As an expressive form, camp is as deeply serious and sincere as it is unapologetically riddled with error and grounded in spoof. The sense of a *fight* is stitched into a camp "sensibility" that makes irony the height of sincerity (and sincerity the very matter of irony). The sense that camp is both a "mode of survival" (to use Pellegrini's words) and a mode expressing "a community, a subculture" (to use Smith's words) is an ingredient not only of the aesthetic form, but – in an entirely other sense – of battle encampment.[3] And it is in the ambivalent space between these senses of camp that Smith plays.

To camp is to set up impermanent residence. To camp is also to set up a space of exception marked by detention – a space suspended in time as well as space, where matters of survival, and citizenship, are both pronounced in the extreme, separated from the "norm" and, as such, rendered exceptional (and thus foundational by way of exclusion) to the norm.[4]

"What are you fighting for?" Smith asks her auditors and participants as she calls them to Civil War (re)encampment. This is a serious question, and the seriousness

Figure A.1 Allison Smith, 2005. *The Muster*, Governors Island, New York Harbor, New York. Pink Brigade (William Bryan Purcell): The Power of Pink. Photo credit Aaron Diskin. A project of the Public Art Fund. Courtesy of the artist. See image on the back cover for color.

of the question is palpable in the passion with which Smith approaches "trench art" in general – that is, art made in the trenches during wartime. When a war's on, Smith suggests, all art is trench art. Her call to art/arms is then just that: a serious call to *fight war*. But, and here the slope becomes muddy, the uniform torn, and the timepiece broken: which war? And are we fighting (in) war, or fighting (against) war? To muster to the Civil War seems, at first, a queer temporal displacement, an error of dates, a coming late to the scene, a matter of detention, a blatant disregard for the necessary linear flow of secular, Enlightenment time. How does camping (during) the Civil War (again) engage the war that's on when Smith musters: that is, the so-called War on Terror? How does Smith's camp detention (from the Latin *detinere*, "hold back"), touch the war *at hand*?

> It is to this ultimate end that I wish to address you, that this proclamation be heard by All who find themselves in the midst of War. This is a Call to Art! Whereas the issues before us, rapidly assuming a portentous magnitude, deserve formal acknowledgement, I hereby proclaim that the means which conduce to a desirable result are now in Your Hands.[5]

Smith was aware, of course, that in 2005, at the time of her art muster, the US was waging a war under the hubristic and ridiculous rubric: "War on Terror." She was aware that the Civil War had been declared over by Abraham Lincoln in 1864, and that the particulars of the nineteenth-century war for (and against) a unified capitalist nation fought in the crucible of debates around human rights were not the same as the twenty-first-century particulars of the war for (and against) a unified capitalist secular (read Protestant) empire propped by vexed neoliberal rhetorics about tolerance.[6] That is, Smith was aware of her anachronism. But getting linear time wrong, or rendering it out of joint, is not the prerogative only of theatre makers, performance artists, or clowns. For example, two years before Smith's muster for the Civil War, on May 1, 2003, George W. Bush had stood upon the USS *Abraham Lincoln* to declare his war in Iraq victorious and "over" (a war that had never officially been declared "on"). Of course, Bush's declaration, delivered as it may have been in all performative sincerity, got the time wrong – the war was and is far from over. Missing the date (and using strategies of theatre) seems to be a matter of due course when, as Smith declared, we find ourselves "in the midst of war." Running on a platform to end the war (again), Barack Obama would be inaugurated in 2009 in what could be called full-on Lincoln drag, dragging the "Founding Father" to *his* platform, standing beside his monument, laminating his body-in-time, chiasmically, upon the monumental time-in-body of a Founder who was, more properly, a Re-Founder, Father of Reconstruction.

Delivering her "call to arms" in 2005, Smith reminded her auditors of Bush's re-election three months before, and the Red and the Blue "patchwork" of the US map that had illustrated the electoral college votes in November of 2004 and replayed, almost exactly, the Blue and the Gray of the US Civil War. Dressed as a Civil War soldier (in drag), Smith declaimed:

> Do you remember the Red and Blue patchwork maps that appeared during the recent presidential elections? Is it not tempting to make a comparison to the Blue and the Gray, colors that came to signify the uniforms worn by Union and Confederate armies, respectively, during the American Civil War? Indeed, the national divide evidenced by these prolific illustrations recalls the unrest of the 1860s, suggesting the uncanny reenactment of an already unresolved battle.[7]

Whether the troops Smith would muster would be fighting the Civil War again or continuing to fight the Civil War is consistently unclear in her call, as is the phrase "already unresolved" in conjunction with reenactment. Across her speech, strange anachronisms of cadence and syntax trouble sensibility. Similarly, multiple battles bleed into each other as she refers to the Civil War, the Gulf War, the War in Iraq, the Stonewall riots, and the secessionism of Queer Nation protests in the 1990s. Indeed, in the mix and match of battles, of rubrics, of turns of phrase, Smith's speech unsettles not only the appellation "Civil War" but also the term "queer" as these terms fall from temporal specificity. In particular "queer" falls away from handy neoliberal hom(m)o-social[8] agendas cathected to the affective economies of empire (in this context, in the midst of her muster, Smith mentions the TV reality show *Queer Eye for the Straight Guy*). Instead, in Smith's call, "queer" comes to refer specifically to *secession*. The word "terrorist" is unspoken but, like ghost notes in jazz, perhaps, or the audibility of ellipses, the so-called terrorist haunts from the present:

> Friends, I draw your attention to the extraordinary coincidence that the Stonewall [Inn's] namesake is none other than Thomas J. Jackson, one of the most revered of all Confederate commanders, whose immovable presence at the Battle of Bull Run likened him to a stone wall. Ironically, the genesis of the gay liberation movement, The Stonewall Rebellion, began at the establishment named after a seceding confederate, fighting resolutely for his own cause in the so-called war of the Rebellion. And yet, it is difficult to imagine these mustering acts of queer succession today.[9]

Rather than leave the association with Stonewall as only an "extraordinary coincidence," Smith labels Stonewall's Confederacy queer. That is, the antecedent for "these acts of queer succession" crosses affiliation to include Stonewall and, again, Stonewall. Thus Smith's call to confederate arms is a re-call to Confederate arms as well as, simultaneously, to queer camp.

Here, any confident forward march or "progress narrative" of the clock falters, and queers the clarity of affiliation in "one nation, under God." In the present, Smith has made it clear that the "Red states," in uncanny resemblance to the Confederacy, had supported Bush's anti-LGBTQI (Lesbian, Gay, Bi, Trans, Queer, Intersex) agendas alongside his simultaneous Islamophobia and chronopolitics of "capitalist development." So, why call LGTBQI "transrevolutionaries" to reenact *with* the "wrong side" in disciplinary US history? Such a move undoes homosocial ease of association, and invites a more rigorous if discomforting account of queering (and the labeling of terrorist) in the neoliberal United States.

In an essay also published in 2005 (in advance of her 2007 book *Terrorist Assemblages*), Jasbir K. Puar remarked succinctly that "these are queer times indeed" – the plural "times" resonating clearly in a call to critical thinking that would not leave the word "terrorist" unsaid. Asking for a reexamination of "queer" that takes into account US neoliberal deployments of "terror" that sexualize the (racialized, Islamic) other as both homophobic and perverse, Puar unsettles the word queer from its identitarian lodging in US neoliberalism. She asks: "What about the war on terrorism, and its attendant assemblages of racism, nationalism, patriotism, and terrorism, is already profoundly queer?"[10] Puar is arguing for an approach to queerness that no longer relies solely on a binary opposition between homosexual and heterosexual practices, and no longer privileges the "first world" consumer-citizen unburdened by kinship and free to shop, but, instead, looks to queer as an assemblage that might not unquestioningly reproduce languages of tolerance in the "disciplinary interests of the US nation-state."[11]

Puar reminds her readers that proponents of gay marriage in the US have recently been called "domestic terrorists" engaged in "the worst form of terrorism," but she advises that we ask not, or not only ask, what is terrorist about the queer, but what is queer about the terrorist? The force of this chiasmic inversion is not to *identify* queer terrorists, but to see queerness as

> always already installed in the project of naming the terrorist; the terrorist does not appear as such without the concurrent entrance of perversion, deviance, deformity. The strategy of encouraging subjects of study to appear in all their queernesses, rather than primarily to queer the subjects of study, provides a subject-driven temporality in tandem with a method-driven temporality. Playing on this difference between the subject being queered versus queerness already existing within the subject [. . .] allows for both the temporality of being and the temporality of always becoming. [. . .] As opposed to an intersectional model of identity [. . . a Deleuzean model of] assemblage is more attuned to interwoven forces that merge and dissipate time, space, and body against linearity, coherency, and permanency.[12]

Asking trenchant questions, Puar aligns Palestinian suicide bombers in affective networks with other "queer" "terrorist" bodies (domestic and otherwise), drawing always shifting (or "already unresolved") maps of affiliation – a mapping that does not root, or place, but *shifts* time, space, and bodies according to contingencies and complicities of privilege, politics, and power. The nation's "perverse beings," she writes, cross a hetero/homo divide, having in common, in their perversity, the shared "tenor of queerness" that is "intrinsically anti-nationalist."[13]

The chronopolitics of multi-national capitalism makes of the global a *frontier*, and relies on forward-marching time as the engine of a broader project of denial: the denial, for example, as Jakobsen and Pellegrini have forcefully argued, of the religious basis of the so-called secular. The Protestantism foundational to secularism is twin, they suggest, to the denial stitched into a linear temporal model – that is, the denial of any other geometry for time than the work-ethic and "development" model serving modern capital. That time can be *porous, malleable, tactile, given to recurrence, given to cross-affiliate assemblage, given to buckling, given to rupture, given to return* is denied by the tick-tock of the time clock. Though the logic of "developing nations" suggests that some "backward" geopolitical sites do exist in a *prior time*, that time is an error and those peoples are anachronistic and simply "late" in coming to proper nationhood (or to proper participation in multi-national secular flows of capital). "Behind the times" on a linear plot, they are exceptions, *detainees*, rather than communities offering real and viable alternatives to the "real time" of progress.

In "Times Like These," their introduction to their 2008 anthology *Secularisms*, Pellegrini and Jakobsen write:

> The millennial time that conflates the Christian with the secular with the national with the global marks progress because of a conflation between time and value(s). These values prominently include what Raymond Williams has called the "structure of feelings" and what we will here dub "modernity's affect" so as to mark something of value's place, time, and feeling.[14]

In a 2000 version of the same essay, they had also written:

> We cannot change, then, without considering both secular-religious time and secular-religious values. We may still be implicated in Enlightenment problematics of time and values, but we need not remain completely within the Enlightenment frame.[15]

Explicitly crossing time – holding back, stepping back, calling back – might be a way of not remaining "completely within the Enlightenment frame." Rather, such dragging, lagging, syncopating, or detaining might simply make the Enlightenment frame apparent to itself *as* frame. Rather than fact, the habituation to linear time might become legible for its broader empiric (secular-religious) agendas. Ignoring the queerness of time – its nonlinearity, its refusal to run straight – is highly suspect in any case, given that queer time is everywhere (think of Bush dragging Lincoln, Obama dragging Lincoln, and the many tourist bureaus in various US states offering travel to a "simpler time," etc.). As explored previously in this book, Elizabeth Freeman, writing about queer transgenerational memory, offers the phrase "temporal drag" as a way to think of time's detention (Bergson) or lag (Fanon and Bhabha). Temporal drag is suggestive of time's theatricality as well as of the irruptive "counter memories" that theatrical parody can announce.[16] Rendering explicit the queerness of time gives the lie to the Enlightenment mandate that *we head into our futures undetained*, and so queer time is usually shrugged off as sentimental or theatrical, or a matter of playful, infelicitous farce. Undoing the denial of queer time, and recognizing the ways it is solidly sedimented in the everyday workings of the nation's capital(ism) – again Bush dragging Lincoln, Obama dragging Lincoln – makes matters of affective affiliation gain in complexity.

If Puar's cross-national, cross-spatial geographies of affiliation align the contemporary Palestinian suicide bomber with the contemporary US queer in an association that emphasizes a critical promise in discomfort, Allison Smith affiliates cross-temporal terrorists (the Civil War Confederacy, queer nation secessionists, and contemporary rainbow-flag fliers) with a similar flair for unease of association. Smith also aligns her project with the large body of US hobbyists who gather regularly to reenact the Civil War – some but by no means all of whom reenact battles so that the Old South might, this time, prove victorious. Needless to say, this imagined victory is an incredibly disturbing notion given the implications of white supremacy that attend to such fantasies. In any case, the affiliation is an uneasy one at best between Smith's call for "intellectuals, activists, artists, and queers," her call for "Ladies and Gentlemen," and her call for all to join with those who reenact the Civil War on a more regular basis as hobbyists. What can we make of such a contradictory call for shared filiation?

Referring to hobbyist Civil War reenactors, Smith has asked, "Who are these people and Why do they do this?":

> Despite their crushing defeat one hundred forty years ago, Confederates are still fighting with a passion. On any weekend in the calendar year, some battle, great or small, of the American Civil War is being reenacted with a theatrical flair and attention to detail that is impressive, to say the least. Who are these people and Why do they do this? I would like to call your attention to the fact, lest it be forgotten, that in the act of seceding from the Union, Confederate forces formed their own union, just as Civil War reenactors form a community, a subculture, of their own. Therefore, intellectuals, activists, artists, and queers, can we engage for a moment, however audaciously, in a confederate fantasy, despite inevitable associations to the horrific institution of slavery and the perplexing persistence of Civil War battle reenactments?[17]

"Despite slavery"? "Confederate fantasy"? There is discomfort here, to be sure, spiked deliberately into the general flavor of spoof that attends this call, but distress is surely part of any call to any arms. As Pellegrini's brilliant essay on Sontag's ambivalence about camp makes clear, ambivalence is always already part of camp's "sensibility" – that is, camp is always already between camps, as it were. Not only does an undeniable (and historical) horror haunt camp humor, but a "stinging" social commentary undergirds that humor's very investment in discomfort. Writing on Gilda Radner's and Sandra Bernhard's "Jewish camp," Pellegrini writes:

> In the wink of a camp eye, these acts of critical appropriation convert the sting of stereotype into the sharp wit of social commentary. These performances variously draw upon a genocidal history of anti-Semitic depictions of Jewishness, but do so by *refusing to refuse* the stereotype. Camp's refusal to refuse recalls Homi Bhabha's conception of colonial mimicry as "at once resemblance and menace." [. . .] It can also be profoundly uncomfortable.[18]

Pellegrini, like David Romàn and Elizabeth Freeman, also notes the aspect of temporal drag in the re-play that is camp. Camp "extends itself in time," she writes. And simultaneously collapses it (again) across performing and witnessing bodies. The parodic deployment of scare quotes – Smith's "confederates" – necessarily bears a fighting and sincere relationship to history as well as an ironic and playful one. For history, replayed, is not "merely" citational (as if citation were ever mere) in that history replayed is neither entirely removed nor significantly distanced from that which is cited, in the way, perhaps, that a slap is not removed from the face slapped, even as the hand and face do not become one and the same. There is, here, a "refusal to refuse" affiliation, even if the affiliation, like a stereotype, causes the sting of discomfort. Rather, camp history drags the past into the present and across its difference, asking for again-time witnesses to, in Freeman's words, "the mutually disruptive energy of moments that are not yet past and yet are not entirely present either."[19]

Might Smith's muster of cross-temporal secessionists, inviting offense, resonate with the "War on Terror" in ways intended by the (ana)chronopolitics of her engagement? Might we read her call to be asking what we are forgetting, or what we are overlooking, if we refuse to critically assess our complicities of association with "other" secessionists, or other "terrorists," especially as we assemble under rainbow flags that some neoliberal rhetorics of tolerance would *seem* to fly for everyone (everyone with a credit card in a Louis Vuitton Cherokee handbag, that is). Terrorist drag?[20] Which terrorists? Which secessionists? Which war? Which removal? Which relatives? Which return? Where? When? What are "we" fighting for? And what are the limits "we" institute on reversal, on return, in the fullness of syncopated time?

In this vein we can consider artists such as Mary Kelly and Sharon Hayes who have recently reenacted precedent feminist protest actions. Mary Kelly's *WLM Demo Remix* is a ninety-second film loop in which Kelly uses a slow dissolve to blend a photo of a reenactment of a 1970 Women's Liberation Movement political demonstration in New York City with the archival photo the first image reenacts. The loop begins with the later (reenacted) image and slowly dissolves to combine past and present – with the archival image either superimposed upon or shining through the photo of the reenactment. The present image never completely fades – the archival image is never completely clear. One can make out, however, that the protest placard the women carry changes. In 1970 it reads: "Unite for Women's Emancipation." In 2005 it reads "From Stone to Cloud" – an excerpt from a 1960 poem by Sylvia Plath titled "Love Letter."

On some levels, of course, *WLM Demo Remix* is stunningly simple. But it is only as simple as we're willing to let it be. As Rosalyn Deutsche reminds, the original image itself "does not picture an originary event" any more than the document of the reenactment pictures, wholly, a "copy," because "the 1970 demonstration, mounted by a second wave of feminists, was haunted by earlier street performances – late-nineteenth- and early-twentieth-century suffragist parades." The archival photo, then, "also depicts a restaging."[21] This, too, is simple enough. Of course, Deutsche might have said: the archival photo is also composed in theatricality (again, if the metonymic reference to "stage" allows for slippage into the broader category of theatricality). She might thus have said that the archival document, given as evidence of a singular event in time, already contains the palimpsestuous reality effect of faux upon faux that gives us, so promisingly, the transitivity of the real, which is to say its mutability, its availability for and as change. This is more complicated, but could go even further. She might also have said: the photos are the *durational live*.

To suppose the liveness of a photograph, as discussed in the previous chapter, undoes a line of faith that situates evidence of the past (to which photography has had a privileged relation in distinction to theatre) as evidence of time gone by. This is a credo to which we are habituated – a line that finds us commonly approaching archival material as index of the dead and gone, and conversely situating the live as somehow in unbridgeable distinction to its own bygone traces. In 1991 James Colman mounted his work *Line of Faith* using local Civil War reenactors to reconstruct, as precisely as he could, the Currier and Ives print of the Battle of Bull Run. Coleman took two photographs of the live reenactment of the print from slightly different angles and these were projected from two slide carousels stacked on top of each other in a presentation that mimicked the nineteenth-century stereopticon. As described by Lynne Cooke, "the backgrounds are aligned, but the foregrounds never come into precise registration: efforts to forge left and right into a single image are doomed, but nonetheless irresistible."[22] Cooke reads the result as a form of anamorphosis, by which Colman played not only with viewers' expectations of single-point perspective, but played as well with questions relating to historical objectivity and the returns of history across bodies constantly (re)-orienting to each other in time as well as in space. If efforts to forge a single image are impossible in this work, so are efforts to root our orientation to a singular, non-redoubling time.

To restage a Currier and Ives print with live Civil War reenactors and then to photograph the restaged lithograph to be mounted as a stereograph engages a viewer in a medial mêlée – a battle of media literally crossing eye-to-eye. Coleman's *Line of Faith* is a citationfest of technology in which Krauss's "differential specificities" (discussed in Chapter 5) become extremely hard to parse, particularly because they include the lamination of live upon dead upon live in circulation. Currier is, famously, the lithographer of the first image to be published in that once supreme mode of circulation, the newspaper.[23] Currier and Ives' "Bull Run" replayed for an art installation thus creates a queasy partnership: Civil War reenactors are committed to reenacting "history as it happened" for history as it will have been, and though they draw from lithographs and photographs and other documents as evidence, their mission is to bring history to life – not necessarily to bring lithography to tableau vivant then to photography and then to stereography – and yet Coleman's piece invites us to consider precisely the complicated interactions between bodies and documents in which reenactment engages technologies of iteration. If photography appears to arrest live bodies, seeming to seal those bodies into the equation "that has been and is no longer," reenactors strive to bring "dead" documents to "life," as if photography were better captured by the future anterior "that will have been," allowing for an indeterminate multi-directional durationality. Coleman's *Line of Faith* touches this tangle, this contest, this battle, in provocative ways, entering the dead, live, re-dead, re-live into something more akin to indeterminate circulation than to precise linear arbitration of what is past and what is present, what is finished and what is ongoing, what is dead and what is live.

Raymond Bellour has written that Coleman's work lies always: "Between the living and the dead. Between life and death." It also lies, he writes, "between film and photography, theater and painting: between all the forms of representation linked to these extremes of motion and stasis."[24] As previously mentioned, Coleman's 1983–5 installation *Living and Presumed Dead* is a piece that presents 160 slide images of twenty actors in costume in various arrangements of a straight line. In each case we see the very edge of a stage, the actors always seeming to be just before or just after a curtain call. The images process through the projector at irregular intervals, replacing each other one by one until it all repeats again from the beginning – or from the end. Bellour reads *Living and Presumed Dead* to both underscore and undo photography's presumed relationship to immobility and death, a relationship I take to be a matter of our habituation to the medium rather than something inherent in the medium itself. Because Coleman does not use the close-up so crucial to cinema, the work cites theatre in more ways than the theatrical costumes and stage make-up worn by the actors: it keeps the viewer in a consistent mnemonic relationship to theatricality. In effect, because we again and again encounter the line of the stage, we can never forget that "the line" in *Living and Presumed Dead* is, like a line between media, staged. Similarly, the obvious fact that the scenes are composed of poses, struck before the picture is taken – as tableaux vivants – submits the "live" as already a medium of capture, simply recaptured by the camera to enter into another mode of circulation. Because the freeze takes place live *and* afterlive the camera is neither the sole nor perhaps even the privileged means of capture and arrest. The camera arrests an arrest, reenacting a freeze – hardly in the nature of the shock of the shutter so romanced by modernity. Coleman's arrests (re)circulate, (re)live, displacing the priority or presumed totality of "death at work" in the scenario of encounter with his artwork.

If the processive nature of Coleman's repeating slide show seems to be reminiscent of cinema, as Bellour and others suggest, the reminiscence it performs is complicated. The images passing one into another might mimic cinema, but the speed and irregularity of passage mimic more as well. We can call to mind a much more ancient procession of stills: the live tableaux on medieval pageant wagons, for example, circulating through a town or city. We might call up, simultaneously, a complex of temporal referents that fold together the live and the still without fetishizing mechanical or technological reproduction or relegating "the still" to the stillness of death. Indeed, to return to Mary Kelly's use of an archival photograph of a 1970 protest march, we might think of the *circulation* of event, the procession of event in nonlinear time, as a durational scene of inter(in)animate enactment passed on as much by documents or objects operating as scriptive things as by persons passing them on, by, or around in the affective field of the ghost jump.

Protest "now" and again

I am supposing, or perhaps only hoping, that our future may be found in the past's fugitive moments of compassion rather than in its solid centuries of warfare.[25]

In 1971, historian and activist Howard Zinn delivered a speech on the Boston Common to protest the war in Vietnam. Thirty-six years later, in *A Power Governments Cannot Suppress,* he published a commentary on history as "creative." A creative history, he wrote, might disclose "hidden episodes of the past when, even if in brief flashes, people showed their ability to resist, to join together, and occasionally to win." The promise for the future, Zinn writes, is in the past's "fugitive moments."[26]

In the same year, 2007, artist and activist Mark Tribe staged a reenactment of Zinn's 1971 protest speech as part of his *Port Huron Project.* Tribe's *Project* takes the promise of fugitive time quite literally. Orchestrating the live reenactment of six protest speeches delivered between 1965 and 1971 by a variety of anti-war activists, Tribe disperses or circulates one time (1960s) across or within another time (2000s), and then further disperses or circulates that laminated time across multiple media at multiple and shifting sites.[27] The *Project* includes live reenactments of speeches, delivered by actors at original sites, which then become videos, DVDs, still photographs, billboard displays, and a book – all of which are the *Project,* none of

Figure A.2 Actor Matthew Floyd Miller delivering Howard Zinn's 1971 speech on location on the Boston Common, Boston, on July 14, 2007, as part of the *Port Huron Project.* Photo: Meghan Boudreau.

which is a privileged object nor singular event.[28] Thus the *Port Huron Project* itself takes place in multiple times, across multiple registers, in multiple media. Arguably, the sense of multiple sites gives a kind of material support to the aspect of multiple or fugitive time that is the politic of temporal play at the project's base.

What are fugitive moments? And *when* is fugitive time? Could such moments be, perhaps, past moments on the run in the present? Moments when the past flashes up *now* to present us with its own alternative futures – futures we might choose to realize differently? Might the past's "fugitive moments" be leaky, syncopated, and errant moments – moments stitched through with repetition and manipulated to recur in works of performance, works of ritual, works of art, works of reenactment that play with time as malleable material? As malleable *political* material? Might the past's fugitive moments not only remind us of yesterday's sense of tomorrow, but also compose the sense again and offer, without expiration date, a politic of possibility?

It is certainly true, and Tribe notes it as well: the question of how to effectively protest government and multinational corporate actions under neoliberal global capital has flummoxed the Left across the Bush era (and beyond). Tribe credits his students at Brown University for illustrating to him just how drastically basic questions of activism – such as, *What can we do now?* – get tongue-tied in neoliberal excuses or bummed out by what they see as old left-wing melancholies.[29] Any rhetoric of protest always already seems outdated, some students bemoan. Tribe, then, meets the issue of outdatedness head-on. In the *Port Huron Project*, he plays the outdate again as if to ask not only how to protest, but *when* to protest. His approach to "when" is not to say that now is not the right time, but to say that now is material, has duration, and, as if working in mixed media, to say that one time can be composed in another time. Think of it this way: must protest always only happen in a "now" considered distinct from prior nows or future nows? In another of his many spurs to action, Zinn wrote: "We are not starting from scratch."[30] That is, we are not starting now – or, our "now" is not *only now*.

Of course, when playing in the crossfire of time, letting anachronism do its creative work, things can feel a little uncanny, or dislocated, or unsettling, or queer. They can also feel like downright bad art. For surely, most would say: The speech was great *the first time*! The second time is farce, fake, theatre. The first time was on target. The second time is way off, late, minor, drag, DIY, any-clown-can-do-it. The first time was true. The second time is false, etiolated, hollow, or infelicitous. The second time, the third time, the nth times are *not actual*. Thus: the second time is lesser. But like Simone de Beauvoir's "second sex," or like Suzan-Lori Parks's character the "Lesser Known" in *The America Play* (himself a Lincoln reenactor), the minor, forgotten, overlooked, disavowed, unsung, second, double, and "lesser" gain a kind of agency in the re-do. Similarly, the idea that "anyone can do it" takes the nascent shape of hope in the odd arena of protest reenactment, troubling the prerogatives of linear time with the idea of the return not of the Great Man, but of anyone. In fact, questions of the returns of history that arise around such reenactments can be mind-boggling: What happens to linear history if nothing is ever fully completed nor discretely begun? When does a call to action, cast into the

Figure A.3 Spectators at Mark Tribe's *Port Huron Project* reenactment of Howard Zinn's Boston Common Speech, 2007. Photo: Michelle Liu Carriger.

future, fully take place? Only in the moment of the call? Or can a call to action be resonant in the varied and reverberant cross-temporal spaces where an echo might encounter response – even years and years later? Can we call *back* in time? Across time? What kind of response might we elicit? When does that which has sounded – deferred as an invocation or an appeal, a plea or a prod for "future" action "now" – ultimately occur? What are the limits of this future? What are the limits of this now?

Discussing the *Port Huron Project*, Tribe writes: "revolution seems impossible, at least for *now.*"[31] And so, the artist makes work that touches another temporal register, bringing an alternative now into play and using seeming anachronism, suggestive deferral, and explicit repetition as political and aesthetic spurs to thought. His work may be playing fast and loose with "now" – but Angela Davis studded her 1969 DeFremery Park speech with the word. "Now" resounds enough times that replaying it in the present might make anachronism less an error of happenstance and more a kind of tolling bell against the industry – war – that Davis so eloquently deplores. Now is still now if we are still, now, waging war.

Interestingly, the actress replaying Davis's speech (republished in *Mark Tribe: The Port Huron Project*) does not sound the "now" as often as the word occurs in the transcript of the speech – leaving it as a kind of ghost note in the present.[32] Of course, the minor "errors" inevitable in orature or live replaying invite extremely generative questions on theatrical error itself as a space for possibility, change, renewal, even activism as discussed in the Foreword and Chapters 1 and 2. However, and perhaps conservatively, Tribe's decision to cast his actors with a high degree of visual verisimilitude for gender, race, age, and ethnicity raises thorny questions. Why verisimilitude? Verisimilitude of race and gender is not the sense of *exactness* of gesture and affect (versus visual bodily markings) sought by the Wooster Group, discussed in Chapter 4. Tribe was casting for similarity; privileging visual realism in distinction to gestic precision. What are the bounds of replay and what are the wages of bodily recognition? Why not cross or trouble gender, race, or ethnicity in re-protest? Is re-protest really as open to alternative futures as we might imagine if an identity politics of bodily marking (re)determines the field?

Despite this critique, the site of "now" wobbles in the *Port Huron Project* enough to challenge thinking about performance as well as thinking about time. The site of "now" is, of course, the celebrated substance of live performance. Live performance is most often considered to be an ephemeral medium due to its composition in time. As discussed in Chapter 3, according to dominant art historical and performance studies logics, live performance takes place *only* now, or only in "im-mediacy," and otherwise disappears. But Tribe and many other artists currently engaging re-enactment complicate the singularity of "now" and approach performance by mixing and matching time, playing across temporal registers through explicit and literal re-play. The queering of time troubles our heritage of Enlightenment (and capitalist "development") investments in straightforward linearity as the *only* way to mark time, reminds us of a durational "now" for political action, and points to a politic in veering, revolving, turning around, and reappearing.

The sense of reappearance is stitched movingly into Sharon Hayes's ongoing project *In the Near Future* that, like Kelly and like Tribe, stages anachronistic actions of protest. Once a day, from 1 to 9 November 2005, Hayes stood on the street with a sign at nine different locations throughout New York City. The sign reads simply: "Ratify E.R.A. NOW!"[33]

So, to go back: even if "revolution seems impossible, at least for now," as Tribe writes, protest reenactment suggests that it may nevertheless be possible to revolve. This is the sense of revolution that the cultural materialist Raymond Williams, whose work was widely read by the New Left in the 1960s, brings out in his influential *Keywords* where he reminds his readers not to forget that the word revolution stems from simply turning around.[34] Perhaps this sense of revolution has gained a certain political viability – at least in art circles. The sheer numbers of twenty-first-century artists exploring reenactment as medial material, as a fertile mode of inquiry, as a means of making and as a mode of art practice, should be indicative of a *turn* toward or into temporality as malleable substance, capable of intervention and (re)articulation. In such a turn, in-time events themselves might be given, like an object, to (re)touch – causing one to question the promises as well as the limits in thinking through (and even acting in) cross-temporality. Does cross- or inter-temporality bear material weight or pull? Is there political efficacy in temporal drag? The act of revolving, or turning, or pivoting off a linear track, may not be "merely" nostalgic, if nostalgia implies a melancholic attachment to loss and an assumed

Figure A.4 Sharon Hayes, *In the Near Future, New York* (detail), 2005. Multiple-slide-projection installation. Courtesy of the artist.

impossibility of return.[35] Rather, the turn to the past as a gestic, affective journey through the past's possible alternative futures – the ghost jump if you will – bears a political purpose for a critical approach to futurity unhinged from capitalist development narratives of time and secular investments in Progress as strictly linear.

The Howard Zinn re-speech was the only one of Tribe's *Port Huron Project* reenactments I attended. Seeing the reenactment on the Boston Common, flush (if distinctly not packed) with photographers and videographers as well as passers-by, and listening to the againness of the actor re-intoning Zinn's speech, there was no hiding the fact that this re-event was *not* about singular moments, ephemerality, or the disappearance of some unitary performing subject. Rather, the "liveness" of the event was itself syncopated with other times. The time, then, was not (only) now. It was (multiple) past and present, present and deferred into the future when it would clearly be reencountered screenally (the presence of cameras, not unlike the presence of actors, being an indication of an again-time always capable of repeat forthcoming). The attendant technology and the explicit citationality of re-speech tilted time off the straight and narrow – even at moments when it seemed that "Zinn" might indeed be speaking about a "today" that was today, too. Perhaps particularly in the re-live event (more than in its technological afterlife), time was explicitly folded. There was simply no singular, discrete "nowness" to the action re-acted, nor was there any invitation to suspend disbelief and forget that it was, indeed, now – it was 2007 and not 1971. But then, even in 1971, Zinn was not "starting from scratch."

Listening to the Zinn reenactor, I looked across the way to other performers and activists simultaneously using some of the Common space nearby. There was a living sculpture mime standing rock still in whiteface as if timeless. Another man protested the Chinese government's treatment of the Falun Gong by displaying photographs of tortured practitioners. A Christian fundamentalist read aloud from the Bible beside a poster advertising salvation and Second Coming. I wondered exactly what was anachronistic in any of these scenes, including the faux Zinn, and what was not? How was there even such a thing as anachronism when the reiterative and ritual properties of passers-by waving hello, or stopping to listen to "Zinn" for a moment before tossing a dime to the "Statue of Liberty" mime, were as studded with cross-temporal possibilities, references, and memories as the Zinn reenactment itself? That the actor Matthew Floyd Miller was not Zinn himself, that the date was not May 1971, that references to "now" were also "then" – none of these things could fully dismiss the possibility of efficacy. That some attendees or passers-by might have shrugged and said "it's only an act," or that some YouTube viewers might sigh and think "too bad the time for action is over," or that some of us who are curious might wonder at the seeming ability of Tribe to arrive *so late* to the scene and accuse him of a romantic and apolitical left melancholy composed in nostalgia – these criticisms are, as in the ambivalence of camp remarked disparagingly by Susan Sontag and *re-marked* by Ann Pellegrini after Sontag, not inaccurate. Such criticisms are arguably actually provoked by the work and are a viable aspect of the event's time-warped theatricality.

In an insightful and searing critique, Paige Sarlin positions Tribe's *Port Huron Project* as not only nostalgic but fetishistic:

> More than simply an update, this new "left-wing melancholy" – or, as I term it, New Left-wing melancholy – fetishizes the history of the New Left as a way of avoiding addressing the present. [. . .] Tribe's reenactments are exemplary of how the reproduction of history can substitute for an analysis of specific histories. In the case of Tribe, the reproduction of a form of protest through the staging of speeches erases the politics and labor of organizing and movement building and in doing so points to a particular relation to history, one that is explained by Michel Foucault's concept of the archive. [. . .] As a result, the reference to the past functions to forestall an examination of the very real challenges to building a contemporary movement, some of which stem from the inheritances of the New Left and its rejection of previous modes of class-based analysis, but many of which derive from the varied developments in the world and on the left in the intervening years since 1968.[36]

Sarlin distinguishes what she sees as the apoliticalness of Tribe's reenactments from a weekend of testimony organized in March 2008 by Iraq Veterans Against the War, modeled on (if not precisely reenacted as) the series of Winter Soldier hearings that Vietnam Veterans Against the War had organized in 1971 and 1972. She argues:

Winter Soldier: Iraq and Afghanistan, while not calling itself a reenactment, demonstrates a mode through which history can be repeated so as to disturb the present. The "performance" of history can create a rupture in the safe contemporary evaluations of the past and conceptions of the future, and help build an antiwar movement and a movement that would transform the system in which wars are necessary.[37]

Sarlin's concern about "reenactment" regards the loss of the "specific" in the field of replay – the loss of "an analysis of *specific* histories." Iraq and Afghanistan are not Vietnam. But the space of tension and debate concern the "not not" in analysis: not Vietman, but not not Vietnam. How do we parse the "not" from the "not not" so as to, in Sarlin's words, "help build an antiwar movement and a movement that would transform the system"? To what degree is linear time and the specificities it legislates part of "the system"? And to what degree is linear time necessary for the "development" of a world without war?

Ironically, perhaps, Sarlin's concerns over the "specific" can be read as a parallel to Rosalind Krauss's worry over the loss of distinctions between "specific" media that Krauss sees as the apolitical heterogeneity of postmodern intermedia. Krauss argues for a "differential specific" – one that does not lose sight of its composition in citation so that citation is posed not to erase differences between media (like differences between times), but to question the afterlife of the so-called outmoded.[38] At base, however, is the legislation and policing of the tracks of citation: who gets to stand in the tracks, where, and how, and to what end.

* * * * * * * *

In order to go forward, one had to go back.
To go back, one had to turn around.
To turn around one had to pull over and look to see if anyone was coming.
———Linda Mussmann, *Cross Way Cross*

[. . .] trying somehow to follow in the Great Man's footsteps footsteps that were of course behind him.
———Suzan-Lori Parks, *The America Play*

If possible to imagine, Sarlin's arguments and my own regarding Smith, Kelly, Hayes, and Tribe (and Mussmann and Parks), should not be read in opposition, but as mutually articulating a field of inquiry in which reenactment poses its errors and takes its *turns*. After all, "errors" are never a matter of a discretely present or discreetly singular moment. What Julia Bryan-Wilson writes of historians' attempts to account for Vietnam era art may also be true for those who write on reenactment of that art:

Historians of [the Vietnam War] era must be wary of succumbing to a nostalgia that sentimentalizes the moment and glosses over its complicated risks, gains, and losses. *At the same time* dismissing the art workers as merely naïve threatens to diminish their lasting contributions to debates about institutional inclusion and the autonomy of art. It is therefore crucial to account for both the hopeful idealism and the ultimately untenable contradictions of art workers' desires to reconfigure the role of viewers, market values, commodity-objects, art institutions, and coalitional politics. This entails granting that their "successes" as well as their "failures" might be productive.[39]

In this vein, the flip side to Sarlin's important criticism is an equally important possibility that irrupts only sporadically in listening to Tribe's re-speeches or reviewing Kelly's re-photography or witnessing Hayes protest NOW. Moments of dis-temporality, of uncanniness, of error, or of a return to sense occur in pauses, or stray sentences, or tiny details of irruptive anachronisms as the "now" folds and multiplies – even if only for Zinn's "brief flash."

The promise in a flash of realization feels something like the open space of possibility – even if we only *begin again* with words that not only precede us but recirculate as scriptive things. To protest the limits of a "now" handily considered by left melancholists to be completely subjugated to the terms of linear time might risk nostalgia, certainly. Belatedness, certainly. Even fetishism. Such work certainly risks the problems, so clear in Smith's *The Muster*, of disquieting returns of cross-affiliation.

But the danger of falling, deliberately, into a supposedly bygone political action – how dangerous is that really? Does such cross-temporal articulation not also underscore the unfinished project of protest? Of vigilance? Of critical thinking about the vexed returns of affiliation, or "relative" pain? Certainly such anachronistic actions get it wrong – their time is out of joint. But the very wrongness of such acts might spark fugitive thinking against the grain of comfort.

The time to protest the war in Afghanistan is not over. The time to protest the war in Iraq is not over. The time to protest the war in Vietnam is not over. And as Zinn has made clear across his life's work, the time to protest World War II is not over. Clearly, if sadly, the time to protest the Crusades is not over. In fact, the time to protest war and its inevitable ties to industry, to capital, and to the drive to empire *is not, and is never, complete.* (My scholarship begins to sound like a protest speech – as if such speech might be infectious? As if scholarship might *muster?*):

The time to protest is Now. It is Again. It is the necessary vigilance, the hard labor, of reiterating *Nunca Màs*, Never Again.

Never, Again.

And, now, again.

Notes

Foreword – By way of other directions

1 Reenactment as a practice can be parsed from "living history," though the forms are related. In battle reenactment (though not in art reenactment), "reenactment" generally refers to replay of specific events with as much accuracy as possible. Living history, on the other hand, refers to the activity of enacting a past way of life where there may be no "event" of record. As such, "living history" is generally applied to reenactments of daily life or general practices from a historical era, though it can also be tied to a specific event. For a broad engagement of the terms and modes of combining historical investigation with performance practices in various arenas from history museums to heritage sites to archaeology digs to art galleries see Anderson (1984), Handler and Saxton (1988), Snow (1993), Bruner (1994), Roth (1998), Pearson and Shanks (2001), Tivers (2002), Lütticken (2005), Magelssen (2007), and Clarke and Warren (2009).

2 Kerwin Lee Klein, "On the Emergence of Memory in Historical Discourse," *Representations* 69, 2000: 127.

3 Janez Janša (formerly known as Emil Hvatin) reconstructed the 1960s Slovene theatre piece *Pupilija, papa Pupilo and the Pupilceks* in 2006 as well as the reenacted statuary/photography/performance "reconstruction action" of "Mt. Triglev on Mr. Triglev" (see http://www.aksioma.org/triglav/index.html). See Antonio Caronia, Janez Janša, and Domenico Quaranta, eds., *Re:Akt: Reconstruction, Re-Enactment, Re-porting* (Italy: FPeditions, 2009). The Janez Janša who edited *Re:Akt* is a conceptual artist, and artistic collaborator with Janez Janša the theatre director. Together, in 2007, with one other artist, they legally changed their names to the name of the then prime minister of the Republic of Slovenia, Janez Janša, with whose conservative policies they disagreed. From then on they made their art in his name, such as a piece appropriating a title from Derrida, "Signature, Event, Context" (see http://sec.arscenic.org/). The various works of the artists who changed their names to Janez Janša make clear the tangle of "appropriation art" with contemporary reenactment art and highlight the problem of the artist's signature – the singular name of the "great" artist – at the base of much work. What if those hired to reenact Marina Abramović's pieces at the Museum of Modern Art in *The Artist Is Present*, as discussed later in this Foreword, had legally changed their names to Marina Abramović?

4 The French collective Tiqqun theorizes "civil war" as an instrument of global neoliberal empire. Tiqqun, *Introduction to Civil War*, translated by Alexander R. Galloway and Jason E. Smith (New York: Semiotext(e), 2010).

5 Exemplary are Joseph Roach, *Cities of the Dead: Circum-Atlantic Performance* (New York: Columbia, 1996), Christopher Balme, *Pacific Performances: Theatricality and Cross-Cultural Encounter in the South Seas* (New York: Palgrave, 2007), and Diana Taylor, ed., *Negotiating Performance: Gender, Sexuality, and Theatricality in Latin/o America* (Durham, NC: Duke

University Press, 1994). Though this book does not investigate the cross-geographic as much as the cross-temporal, my hope is that readers will cross-read, and extend or complicate my returns to the US Civil War with the insights of such works.

6 Carol Kino, "A Rebel Form Gains Favor. Fights Ensue," *The New York Times*, March 10, 2010: AR25.

7 "Other people" is how the reenactors (whose names are also listed) are referred to on the website for the exhibition *The Artist Is Present*. The issue of delegated labor, or what Claire Bishops terms "outsourced authenticity" in performance reenactment will be taken up in Chapter 4. See http://www.moma.org/visit/calendar/exhibitions/965, last accessed May 22, 2010. Claire Bishop, "Outsourcing Authenticity: Delegated Performance in Contemporary Art," in *Double Agent*, Claire Bishop and Sylvia Tramontana, eds. (London: Institute of Contemporary Arts, 2008). See also Klaus Biesenbach, ed., *Marina Abramović: The Artist Is Present* (New York: Museum of Modern Art, 2010).

8 Carol Kino, op. cit.

9 See Marvin Carlson, "Performing the Past: Living History and Cultural Memory," *Paragrana* 9, no. 2, 2000. See also Lori Pauli, ed., *Acting the Part: Photography as Theatre* (New York: Merrell Publishers, 2006).

10 Amelia Jones, "'Presence' in Absentia: Experiencing Performance Art as Documentation," *Art Journal* 56, no. 4, 1997: 11–18; 13.

11 Marina Abramović, *Seven Easy Pieces* (New York: Charta, 2007): 11, 25.

12 Carol Kino, op. cit.

13 In distinction to this, Chrissie Iles's own essay in the collection accompanying the exhibition *The Artist Is Present* usefully explores the theatricality of Abramović's work, even extending her analysis briefly to the Theatro Olimpico, built 1580–5 in Vicenza as a reconstruction (with added perspective) of an ancient Roman theatre. See Iles, "Marina Abramović and the Public: A Theater of Exchange," in Klaus Biesenbach, ed., *Marina Abramović: The Artist Is Present*, 40–3 (New York: Museum of Modern Art, 2010).

14 Michael Fried, "Art and Objecthood" (1967), reprinted in Gregory Battock, ed., *Minimal Art* (Berkeley: University of California Press, 1995). Abramović cited in Chris Thompson and Katarina Weslien, "Pure Raw: Performance, Pedagogy, and (Re)Presentation, an interview with Marina Abramović," *PAJ: Performing Arts Journal* 82, 2006: 29–50.

15 Cited in Fabio Cypriano, "Performance and Reenactment: Analyzing Marina Abramović's *Seven Easy Pieces*," Idanca.net, (http://idanca.net/lang/en-us/2009/09/02/performance-e-reencenacao-uma-analise-de-seven-eeasy-pieces-de-marina-abramovic/12156/, written September 2009, accessed March 10, 2010.) Here, the rebel spirit of much performance-based work that had employed a politic of accessibility versus elitism (think of instruction art or feminist collective performance art), is simply ignored and replaced by a bid for high art canonization.

16 Marina Abramović and Tania Bruguera, "Conversation: Abramović and Bruguera," in Steven Maddoff, ed., *Art School (Propositions for the 21st Century)*, (Cambridge, MA: MIT Press, 2009): 181. Abramović usually situates "duration" as something that distinguishes theatre and dance from performance, despite the existence of theatre and dance forms that exhibit extremely lengthy duration in a variety of global forms, and despite performance art actions that are instantaneous. Rather, like so many European experimental theatre artists of the late nineteenth and early twentieth centuries, Abramović is actually writing against mainstream commercial and regional commercial theatre and film conventions rather than against theatre per se, and so her antitheatricality weds her intimately to modern European experimental theatre artists in general. See Martin Puchner, *Stage Fright: Modernism, Antitheatricality and Drama* (Baltimore, MD: Johns Hopkins University Press, 2002). See also Rebecca Schneider and Gabrielle Cody, "Introduction," in *Re:Direction* (New York: Routledge, 2001).

17 Gertrude Stein, *Lectures in America* (New York: Random House, 1935): 94.

18 In *Beloved*, a novel dealing with ghosts of the Civil War, Toni Morrison writes of "rememory" not only as the remembering of something forgotten, but the remembering of *someone else's* forgotten memory. Morrison, *Beloved* (New York: Everyman's Library, 2006): 47.

19 Adrienne Rich, "When We Dead Awaken: Writing as Re-vision," in *On Lies, Secrets, and Silence* (New York: W. W. Norton, 1979): 33–49.

20 "My suggestion is that the body becomes its gender through a series of acts which are renewed, revised, and consolidated through time. From a feminist point of view, one might try to reconceive the gendered body as the legacy of *sedimented acts* rather than a predetermined or foreclosed structure, essence or fact, whether natural, cultural, or linguistic." Judith Butler, "Performative Acts and Gender Constitution: An Essay in Phenomenology and Feminist Theory," in Sue-Ellen Case, ed. 270–82, *Performing Feminisms: Feminist Critical Theory and Theatre* (Baltimore, MD: Johns Hopkins University Press, 1990): 274. The temporal condition of sedimentation in Butler's thoughts on gender have recently been complicated and extended by Elizabeth Freeman to "displace gender-transitive drag" into a queer "temporal drag," a complication that will be useful throughout this book. See Freeman, "Packing History, Count(er)ing Generations," *New Literary History* 31, no. 4, 2000: 727–44.

21 It is through Moten, who does not mention Donne, that I returned to Donne's "The Exstasie," a poem I first read in college. There is nowhere here a sense, then, of citation as forward marching lineage. Moten, in my thinking here, came first, and Donne came as a matter of return, *after Moten*, though also, of course, before, as I had encountered the poem in advance of reading Moten. It felt rather like a sidestep, or a dance, to remember Donne through Moten who *reverberates* the word in several of his writings. The three – Moten, Richards, Donne – are syncopated, here, rather than derivative. I use the phrase with parentheticals as "inter(in)animate" to highlight the syncopation of interanimate and interinanimate. See Fred Moten, *In the Break: The Aesthetics of the Black Radical Tradition* (Minneapolis: University of Minnesota Press, 2003): 76, 192–210.

22 Michel de Certeau, *The Practice of Everyday Life* (Berkeley: University of California Press, 1984): 15.

23 Shirley Samuels, *Facing America: Iconography and the Civil War* (Oxford: Oxford University Press, 2004): 6.

24 See David Blight, *Race and Reunion: The Civil War in American Memory* (Cambridge: Harvard University Press, 2002); Rory Turner, "Bloodless Battles: The Civil War Reenacted," *TDR: The Drama Review* 34, no. 4, 1990: 123–36; Jay Anderson, *Time Machines: The World of Living History* (Nashville: American Association for State and Local History, 1984).

25 On authenticity and reenactment see Richard Handler and William Saxton, "Dyssimulation: Reflexivity, Narrative, and the Quest for Authenticity in 'Living History,'" *Cultural Anthropology* 3, no. 2, 1988: 242–60. On the "error" of gender crossing and its legislation in some reenactment societies see Elizabeth Young, *Disarming the Nation* (Chicago, IL: University of Chicago Press, 1999). Though rules on cross-gender participation vary widely by club, group, regiment, or society, Cathy Stanton and Stephen Belyea record that in their studies, "An unapologetic masculinity is central to Civil War reenactment." Stanton and Belyea, "'Their Time Will Yet Come': African American Presence in Civil War Reenactment," in *Hope and Glory: Essays on the Legacy of the 54th Massachusetts Regiment*, Martin Henry Blatt, Thomas J. Brown, and Donald Yakovone, eds. (Amherst, MA: University of Massachusetts Press, 2000): 268. On the trouble of gender "error" in both the Civil War and its reenactment see Tony Horwitz, *Confederates in the Attic: Dispatches from the Unfinished Civil War* (New York: Vintage): 196–7. When I interviewed reenactors in Lincoln, RI, in 2005 and asked whether I could enlist (a rhetorical

question), I was told that women were not allowed as members because "it would not be authentic." This was well after the court case of Lauren Cook Burgess who, in 1991, sued for sex discrimination and won her case based in part on ample evidence of women cross-dressers among the actual Civil War ranks (discussed briefly in Chapter 2).

26 See the Kruger image reproduced in Barbara Kruger, *Love for Sale: The Words and Pictures of Barbara Kruger* (New York: Harry N. Abrams, 1990): 58. See Rebecca Schneider, *Explicit Body in Performance* (New York: Routledge, 1997): 90–1.

27 On the politics of witnessing in contemporary art practices see Jane Blocker, *Seeing Witness: Visuality and the Ethics of Testimony* (Minneapolis: University of Minnesota Press, 2009).

28 Richard Schechner, *Between Theatre and Anthropology* (Chicago, IL: University of Chicago Press, 1985): 36.

29 Eugenio Barba, *Dictionary of Theatre Anthropology* (New York: Routledge, 2005): 32–5.

30 See Walt Whitman's poem "The Centenarian's Story" in which a Civil War volunteer of 1861 talks with a Revolutionary War veteran.

31 See, for example, popular historian Lerone Bennett's *Forced into Glory: Abraham Lincoln's White Dream* (Chicago, IL: Johnson Publishing Company, 2000).

32 David Blight, op. cit.: 9.

33 This is the broader point made by Paul Connerton in *How Societies Remember* (Chicago, IL: University of Chicago Press, 1989). Enactment – bringing something into being – is composed fundamentally in reenactment, either through citing identification or dis-identification with the past. See also Joseph Roach, *Cities of the Dead*, op. cit. Roach usefully employs the word "surrogation" to speak to the operations by which performance-based citation, often explicit reenactment, constructs a genealogy for the social.

34 Allison Smith, "Public Address," in *Ahistoric Occasion: Artists Making History*, Nato Thompson, ed. (North Adams, MA: Mass MOCA, 2007): 107.

35 Lisa Woolfork, *Embodying American Slavery in Contemporary Culture* (Bloomington: University of Indiana Press, 2008).

36 The Wooster Group work is examined in Chapter 4. Rod Dickinson's *The Milgram Re-enactment* was a reconstruction that aimed for precise replication of one part of Stanley Milgram's Obedience to Authority experiment conducted at Yale University in 1960. The reenactment took place in the Centre for Contemporary Art, Glasgow, on February 15th and 17th, 2002. See Steve Rushton, *The Milgram Re-Enactment* (Maastricht: Eyck Academie, 2004). As Dickinson told Alina Hoyne on his attempt at precision, "[. . .] everything whether it be the shock machine or the words spoken by the actors, or the details of the laboratory [. . .] all had to be absolutely spot-on." In Hoyne, "Doing it Again: Re-enactment in Contemporary British Art (1996–2007)," Ph.D. dissertation (University of Melbourne, 2009): 149.

37 For efforts at exact representation of original performance described as "slavish" versus "artistic," see Sven Lütticken, "Introduction," in *Life, Once More: Forms of Reenactment in Contemporary Art*, Sven Lütticken, ed. (Rotterdam: Witte de With, 2005): 5. The topic of "artistic" labor, especially as regards hired actors or delegated performers, returns in Chapter 4. See Marina Abramović in conversation with Nancy Spector on "interpretation" versus historical accuracy in *Seven Easy Pieces*, op. cit., 22–3.

38 Handler and Saxton, 1988, op. cit.: 245.

39 See Victor Turner, *From Ritual to Theatre: The Human Seriousness of Play*, (New York: PAJ Books, 1982).

40 Freeman, 2000, op. cit.: 728.

41 David Romàn, "Archival Drag: Or, The Afterlife of Performance" in *Performance in America: Contemporary US Culture and the Performing Arts*, David Romàn, ed. (Durham, NC: Duke University Press, 2005): 137–78.

42 On feminism and the problem of linear generationality see Robyn Wiegman, "Feminism's Apocalyptic Futures," *New Literary History* 31, no. 4, 2000: 805–25; Jennifer Purvis, "Grrrls and Women Together in the Third Wave: Embracing the Challenges of Intergenerational Feminism(s)," *NWSA Journal* 16, no. 3, 2004: 93–123; and Elizabeth Grosz, *Time Travels: Feminism, Nature, Power* (Durham, NC: Duke University Press, 2005). On women, othering, and linear time see also Rey Chow, *Women and Chinese Modernity: The Politics of Reading Between East and West* (Minneapolis: University of Minnesota Press, 1991).

43 In "'Race,' Time, and the Revision of Modernity," a 1991 essay reprinted as the conclusion of his 1994 *The Location of Culture*, Homi Bhabha writes: "Fanon uses the fact of blackness, of belatedness, to destroy the binary structure of power and identity: the imperative that 'the Black man must be Black; he must be Black in relation to the white man.' [. . .]" Fanon's discourse of the 'human' emerges from that temporal break or caesura effected in the continuist, progressivist myth of Man. He too speaks from the signifying time-lag of cultural difference that I have been attempting to develop as a structure for the representation of subaltern and postcolonial agency." Bhabha, *Location of Culture* (New York: Routledge, 1994): 237.

44 Freeman, 2000, op. cit.: 729.

45 Ibid.: 730, 735, 742.

46 If "mutually disruptive energy" quotes Freeman, in using the phrase "affect's transmission" I draw upon Teresa Brennan who writes on the ways in which affective states or stances cross or jump between bodies in the social. In *The Transmission of Affect* Brennan is eager to note that affects have "an energetic dimension." She writes that the transmission of affect means that "we are not self-contained in terms of our energies." Though Brennan is not writing of a cross-temporal "we" in the transmission of affect from one body to another and back, she underscores that in the transmission of affect there is "no secure distinction between the 'individual' and the 'environment.'" She is clear that this does not mean that there is *no* distinction, but that there is no secure distinction. "The idea of transmitted affects undermines the dichotomy between the individual and the environment and the related opposition between the biological and the social." The transmission of affect "breaches individual boundaries" and, as the word "transmit" suggests, travels across distance. *The Transmission of Affect* (Ithaca, NY: Cornell University Press, 2004): 6–7, 17. If Brennan is writing about a spatial difference between bodies, Laura U. Marks has written of "touch" and the transmission of affect across time in *The Skin of the Film: Intercultural Cinema, Embodiment and the Senses* (Durham, NC: Duke University Press, 2000). The issue of affect and cross-temporal touch will be taken up in more depth in Chapter 1.

47 Richard Schechner, "Actuals: A Look into Performance Theory," in *The Rarer Action: Essays in Honor of Frances Ferguson*, Alan Cheuse and Richard Koffler, eds. (New Brunswick, NJ: Routledge University Press, 1970): 97–135; Abramović cited in Thompson and Weslien, op. cit.

48 Walter Benjamin, *The Work of Art in the Age of its Technological Reproducibility* (Cambridge: Cambridge University Press, 2008).

49 Fried's 1967 essay "Art and Objecthood," op. cit., has been much discussed. Most useful for analyses of that essay for readers of this book will be Shannon Jackson, *Professing Performance: Theatre in the Academy from Philology to Performativity* (Cambridge: Cambridge University Press, 2004): 120–44; Nicholas Ridout, *Stage Fright, Animals, and Other Theatrical Problems* (Cambridge: Cambridge University Press, 2006): 5–15; and Philip Auslander, *From Acting to Performance: Essays in Modernism and Postmodernism* (New York: Routledge, 1997): 49–57.

50 For a more in-depth critique of this position, see Rebecca Schneider, "Solo Solo Solo," in *After Criticism: New Responses to Art and Performance*, Gavin Butt, ed. (London: Blackwell Press, 2004). See also Schneider, "Hello Dolly Well Hello Dolly: The

Double and its Theatre," in *Psychoanalysis and Performance*, Patrick Campbell and Adrian Kear, ed. (London: Routledge, 2001).

51 Tavia Nyong'o, *The Amalgamation Waltz: Race, Performance, and the Ruses of Memory* (Minneapolis: University of Minnesota Press, 2009): 136.

52 Michel Foucault, "Nietzsche, Genealogy, History," in *Language, Counter-Memory, Practice: Selected Essays and Interviews*, trans. Donald F. Bouchard and Sherry Simon (Ithaca, NY: Cornell University Press, 1977): 151–2, emphasis added.

53 On "theatricality" as a descriptor, see the essays in the special issue "Theatricality," ed. Josette Feral, *Sub-Stance* 31, nos. 2, 3, 2002; the collection edited by Tracy Davis and Thomas Postlewait, *Theatricality* (Cambridge University Press, 2004); Erika Fischer-Lichte, "Introduction" to "Theatricality: A Key Concept in Theatre and Cultural Studies," *Theatre Research International*, 20, no. 2, 1995: 97–105; And Samuel Weber, *Theatricality as Medium* (New York: Fordham University Press, 2004).

54 See Homi Bhabha, "Of Mimicry and Man: The Ambivalence of Colonial Discourse," first published in *October* in 1984 and republished in *The Location of Culture* (New York: Routledge, 1994).

55 Nyong'o, op. cit.: 135; Carolyn Dinshaw, *Getting Medieval: Sexual Communities Pre- and Post-Modern* (Durham, NC: Duke University Press, 1999): 2. Much of such work has contributed to what has been called the "affective turn" in scholarship – a turn discussed at some length in Chapter 1. I have been influenced, as well, by Avery Gordon's *Ghostly Matters: Haunting and the Sociological Imagination* (Minneapolis: University of Minnesota Press, 1997).

56 In this instance, and with the reader's indulgence, I use "critical theory" more broadly than in specific reference to the Frankfurt School in order to gesture toward the wide swath of theories influencing and influenced by materialist history. I use "cultural theory" similarly broadly, to reference the influence of anthropology and performance studies on analyses of the production of culture.

57 http://www.virginia.org/Site/features.asp?FeatureID=167 (visited January 26, 2010).

58 When I visited in 1999 and 2001, the Wills house was a private museum. The site of Lincoln's revision of the Gettysburg Address has since been architecturally revised. It was purchased by the National Park Service, completely renovated, and reopened in 2009. Interestingly, though the wax effigy no longer sits and writes in the room, the museum does employ "living historians" for special events, and a picture of a "living" Lincoln reenactor appears on their image masthead on the website: http://www.davidwillshouse.org, accessed November 25, 2009.

59 John L. O'Sullivan, "The Great Nation of Futurity," in *United States Magazine and Democratic Review* 6, no. 23, 1839: 426–30.

60 Abraham Lincoln cited in Gary Wills, *Lincoln at Gettysburg: The Words that Remade America* (New York: Simon and Schuster, 1993): 173, emphasis added. It bears noting that in alluding to "a new birth of freedom" Lincoln was explicitly labeling the Civil War a reenactment of the Revolutionary War. Southerners, in turn, tried to portray him as a "tyrant" – the word for King George.

61 See David Lowenthal, *The Past is a Foreign Country* (Cambridge University Press, 1999). Lowenthal's title cites the opening sentence of British novelist L. P. Hartley's *The Go-Between* which begins: "The past is a foreign country: they do things differently there." Lowenthal argues that the basic "otherness" of the past exemplifies an approach to time structured by modernity with a characteristically contradictory logic. An investment in linear time places the past clearly behind those who work for "progress" in the future. On the other hand, part of the world and its peoples are structurally "behind the times" and so the past is also a frontier, open for exploration and future development. On this sense see Johannes Fabian, *Time and the Other: How Anthropology Makes Its Object* (New York: Columbia University Press, 1983).

62 The vast literature on trauma theory and the psychoanalytic exploration of belatedness, repetition, and temporal return is far too voluminous to cite. Important

to note is Freud's "Repeating, Remembering, and Working Through" which, in 1914, marked the first appearance of the phrase "compulsion to repeat." In this essay Freud notes that hysterics (but not only hysterics) characteristically repeat in the place of remembering, such that affective states and bodily acts in the present keep past experience alive. "Remembering, Repeating and Working Through," in *The Standard Edition of the Complete Psychological Works of Sigmund Freud*, Volume 12, 147–56 (New York: Hogarth Press, 1958). On the soldier returned from war as the paradigmatic figure for repetition compulsion, see Sigmund Freud, *Beyond the Pleasure Principle*, James Strachey, trans. (New York: Norton, 1990). On trauma theory and the collective social see Cathy Caruth, *Unclaimed Experience: Trauma, Narrative and History* (Baltimore, MD: Johns Hopkins University Press, 1996).

63 Forty years after O'Sullivan, Ernst Renan famously observed in 1882: "forgetting, I would even go so far as to say historical error, is a crucial factor in the creation of a nation, which is why progress in historical studies often constitutes a danger for [the principle of] nationality." Renan, "What is a Nation?," in *Nation and Narration*, Homi Bhabha, ed. (New York: Routledge, 1990): 11. As the essays collected by Homi Bhabha in *Nation and Narration* collectively make clear, to explore a nation's history, its construction of itself *as* nation, it is necessary to engage in an analysis of the generative properties of error – of the mistelling in retelling. This, it seems to me, suggests that the history of any nation is a theatre history.

64 The limits of "living memory" pose difficult questions. Much work in performance studies has argued that "living" memories may exceed an immediate generation – that is, exceed those who lived the event – because memory can be "passed down" or "revisited" upon subsequent generations not only in the form of rituals, duties, habits, and inheritances, but by the experience of being raised by adults who construct their actions in relation to their own (inherited) pasts. See Connerton, 1989, op. cit., and Diana Taylor, *The Archive and the Repertoire: Performing Cultural Memory in the Americas* (Durham, NC: Duke University Press, 2003). The issue of "living memory" becomes more complicated, however, if we allow for "livingness" to extend to material objects or other remains, or what Susan E. Alcock has called (after Richard Bradley) the "lives and afterlives of monuments" in *Archaeologies of the Greek Past: Landscape, Monuments, and Memories* (Cambridge University Press, 2002): 31. This has been a recent fruitful topic at the intersections between theatre and archaeology. See Mike Pearson and Michael Shanks, op. cit. See also Victor Buchli and Gavin Lucas, "The Absent Present: Archaeologies of the Contemporary Present," in *Archaeologies of the Contemporary Past*, Buchli and Lucas, eds. (New York: Routledge, 2001): 3–18. Buchli and Lucas suggest the possibility of an "archaeology of now" that questions assumptions about and academic legislation of distance and proximity with regard to the past. Lucas has argued that all archaeology should be considered "cultural performance" in "Modern Disturbances: On the Ambiguities of Archaeology," in *Modernism/modernity* 11, no. 1, 2004: 109–20.

65 Herman Melville, *White-Jacket: Or, the World on a Man-of-War* (Chicago, IL: Northwestern University Press, 1970): 15. Anders Stephanson examines the influence of Manifest Destiny in US policy extending across the twentieth-century, particularly as articulated by Woodrow Wilson and Ronald Reagan. On the temporality in the notion of Manifest Destiny, Stephanson writes: "The nation, then, was bound by nothing but its founding principles, the eternal and universal principles. It existed, as the 'great nation of futurity,' only in a perpetual present centered on projects and expectations." Anders Stephanson, *Manifest Destiny: American Expansionism and the Empire of Right* (New York: Hill and Wang, 1995): 41. See also Stephanie LeMenager, *Manifest and Other Destinies: Territorial Fictions of the Nineteenth-Century United States* (Lincoln: University of Nebraska Press, 2008).

66 George B. Forgie, *Patricide in the House Divided* (New York: W. W. Norton, 1981): 7.

67 Gertrude Stein, *The Making of Americans* (New York: Dalkey Archive Press, 1995 [1925]): 67.

68 On reenactment as a foundation for forgetting, indeed as foundational, see Sigmund Freud's "historical novel" *Moses and Monotheism* (New York: Vintage, 1955). See Jacques Derrida, *Archive Fever* (Chicago, IL: University of Chicago Press, 1995).

69 I am not claiming that performance art was born in, nor singular to, the US, but that there is an irony that performance-based artwork should burgeon most profoundly in Europe, Japan, and the US concomitant with the post-World War II shift of the world art center to New York. For a fuller explication, see Schneider, 2004, op. cit.

70 Tony Judt, "What Have We Learned, If Anything?" in *The New York Review of Books*, 55, no. 7, May 1, 2008.

71 See http://www.virginia.org/Site/features.asp?FeatureID=167 (accessed January 26, 2010).

72 See http://www.youcanlivehistory.com/frames.html (accessed March 1, 2010).

73 See Jerome de Groot, *Consuming History: Historians and Heritage in Contemporary Popular Culture* (New York: Routledge, 2008) on rapidly changing attitudes to history and its consumption in popular culture, but also in historiographical practice as historians grapple with reenactment as a practice.

74 David Lowenthal, "The Past as a Theme Park," in *Theme Park Landscapes: Antecedents and Variations*, Terence Young and Robert Riley, eds., 11–23 (Washington, DC: Dumbarton Oaks Research Library and Collection, 2002).

75 Fredric Jameson, *Postmodernism, or, the Cultural Logic of Late Capitalism* (Durham, NC: Duke University Press, 1991): 26.

76 See Jacques Derrida, *Specters of Marx: State of the Debt, the Work of Mourning and the New International* (New York: Routledge, 1994).

77 Rosemarie K. Bank, *Theatre Culture in America, 1825–1860* (Cambridge: Cambridge University Press, 1997): 2.

78 Joseph Thompson, "Forward," in *Ahistoric Occasion: Artists Making History*, ed. Nato Thompson, (North Adams, MA: Mass MOCA, 2007): 8–9.

79 Inke Arns, "History Will Repeat Itself," in *History Will Repeat Itself: Strategies of Re-Enactment in Contemporary (Media) Art and Performance*, eds. Inke Arns and Gabriele Horn, 36–63 (Frankfurt: Revolver, 2007): 41, 43.

80 On the auratic in mid-century performance art, see Schneider, 2004, op. cit. See also Richard Schechner, "There's Something Happenin' Here . . ." in *TDR: The Drama Review* 54, no. 2, 2010: 12–17.

81 Richard Schechner, 1985, op. cit.: 50. This quote, and its context, will be more thoroughly unpacked in Chapter 4.

82 Gertrude Stein, 1935, op. cit.: 94.

83 This definition of theatricality was penned by Russian theatre director Vsevlod Meyerhold's colleague Samuel Vermel in his essay "Irony and Theatricality," published in 1914 in *Love for Three Oranges: The Journal of Doctor Dappertutto*. Cited in Dassia N. Posner, "A Theatrical Zigzag: Doctor Dappertutto, Columbine's Veil, and the Grotesque," in *Slavic and East European Performance* 29, no. 3, 2009: 43–53, emphasis added.

84 Friedrich Nietzsche, *Thus Spoke Zarathustra*, R. J. Hollingdale, trans. (New York: Penguin, 1961): 178.

1 Reenactment and relative pain

1 Email correspondence with Stanley Wernz, President of the Association of Lincoln Presenters, October 11, 2009.

2 On habit memory in relation to recognition see Henri Bergson, *Matter and Memory*, M. N. Paul and W. S. Palmer, trans. (New York: Zone Books, 1988): 77–132.

3 On the queasiness of theatricality see Nicholas Ridout citing Jonas Barish's *The Antitheatrical Prejudice* in *Stage Fright, Animals, and Other Theatrical Problems* (Cambridge: Cambridge University Press, 2006): 3. On the queasiness of the "real" that irrupts

through the hyperreal of the copy see Hal Foster, *Return of the Real* (Cambridge, MA: MIT Press, 1996). On the "nausea of the real" see Slavoj Žižek, "Grimaces of the Real, or When the Phallus Appears," in *October* 58, no. 1, 1991: 59.

4 At many reenactments that allow spectators (and not all do), some "spectators" reenact spectating – attending the battle in period dress and watching. When I asked one woman in period dress about whether she felt late to the scene – whether belatedness was part of her experience – she looked at me quizzically and said, but this is 1863, isn't it? See image http://www.shorpy.com/node/4662 for spectators watching the 1864 battle of Nashville.

5 On such labor as bodily, see Shannon Jackson, *Lines of Activity* (Ann Arbor: University of Michigan Press, 2000): 1–36.

6 On "phonic materiality" see Fred Moten, *In the Break: The Aesthetics of the Black Radical Tradition* (Minneapolis: University of Minnesota Press, 2003): 171–232. On the contested validity of reenactment as a mode of accessing history see Vanessa Agnew, "History's Affective Turn: Historical Reenactment and Its Work in the Present," in *Rethinking History* 11, no. 3, 2007: 299–312. On the body and collective memory see Maurice Halbwachs, *On Collective Memory* (Chicago, IL: University of Chicago Press, 1992); Paul Connerton, *How Societies Remember* (Cambridge: Cambridge University Press, 1989); Michel Foucault, *Language, Counter-Memory, Practice* (Ithaca, NY: Cornell University Press, 1977). On Bergson and the bodily "survival of images," see Paul Ricoeur's reading of *Matter and Memory* in *Memory, History, Forgetting* (Chicago, IL: University of Chicago Press, 2004): 427–43.

7 Eve Kosofsky Sedgwick, *Touching Feeling: Affect, Pedagogy, Performativity*, (Durham, NC: Duke University Press, 2003): 14.

8 Vanessa Agnew, "Introduction: What is Reenactment?" in *Criticism* 46, no. 3, 2004: 335. See also Agnew, "History's Affective Turn," op. cit.

9 Alexander Cook, "The Use and Abuse of Historical Reenactment: Thoughts on Recent Trends in Public History," *Criticism* 46, no. 3, 2004: 490. A binarization between "analysis" and "visceral engagement" is not the attitude of all historians. On the complex of issues and range of opinions – from R. G. Collingwood's opinion that historical understanding requires reenactment to those who voice concern over affective engagement – see Iain McCalman and Paul A. Pickering's anthology *Historical Reenactment: From Realism to the Affective Turn* (New York: Palgrave MacMillan, 2010), especially the essay by Kate Bowan, "R. G. Collingwood, Historical Reenactment, and the Early Music Revival," 134–58. See Peter Burke "Performing History: The Importance of Occasions," *Rethinking History* 9, no. 1, 2005: 35–52. Rich and varied approaches to history through and as literary fiction, performance, and such theatrical modes as melodrama have been usefully debated (including Agnew's and Cooke's contributions) in the journals *Rethinking History, Radical History Review, History and Theory*, and *Criticism*. A great deal has been done with documentary film and television in/as history as well, though that work is beyond the scope of this book. See Jerome de Groot, *Consuming History: Historians and Heritage in Contemporary Popular Culture* (New York: Routledge, 2008). Appropriately, live experiential practice as a potential mode of critical historical thinking is volatile territory. The question needs to be continually rearticulated: how can the category of lived and live experience be *critical* – both a mode of analysis *and* subject to analysis? Scholars such as Raymond Williams, Joan Wallach Scott, and Martin Jay have worked to situate and historicize the category of "experience" as a mode of historical knowledge. In her influential essay "The Evidence of Experience," Scott draws on Raymond Williams to make a call (one with which I agree): "Experience is at once always already an interpretation and something that needs to be interpreted. What counts as experience is neither self-evident nor straightforward; it is always contested, and always therefore political. The study of experience, therefore, must call into question its originary status in historical explanation. This will happen when historians take as their project not the

reproduction and transmission of knowledge said to be arrived at through experience, but the analysis of the production of that knowledge itself." Joan Scott, "The Evidence of Experience," *Critical Inquiry* 14, no. 4, 1991: 780, 797. See Martin Jay, *Songs of Experience: Modern American and European Variations on a Universal Theme* (Berkeley: University of California Press, 2006).

10 For some scholars, such as Brian Massumi after Gilles Deleuze, affect is autonomous versus relational and does not imply the emotional. But for others, such as Sara Ahmed, relationality and "emotion" are important to thinking through affect and affective histories. Massumi, *Parables for the Virtual* (Durham, NC: Duke University Press, 2002); Ahmed, *The Cultural Politics of Emotion* (New York: Routledge, 2004).

11 Carolyn Dinshaw, *Getting Medieval: Sexual Communities Pre- and Post-Modern* (Durham, NC: Duke University Press, 1999); Chris Nealon, *Foundlings: Lesbian and Gay Historical Emotion Before Stonewall* (Durham, NC: Duke University Press, 2001); Judith Halberstam, *In a Queer Time and Place* (New York: New York University Press 2005); Elizabeth Freeman "Packing History, Count(er)ing Generations," *New Literary History*, 31, 2000: 727–44; Elizabeth Freeman, "Time Binds, or Erotohistory," *Social Text* 23, nos. 3–4, 2005: 57–68; Louise Fradenberg and Carla Frecerro, "Caxton, Foucault, and the Pleasures of History," in *Premodern Sexualities*, Louise Fradenberg and Carla Frecerro, eds. (New York: Routledge, 1996); Carla Freccero, *Queer/Early/Modern* (Durham, NC: Duke University Press, 2006); and Heather Love, *Feeling Backward: Loss and the Politics of Queer History* (Cambridge, MA: Harvard University Press, 2009). See the special issue on "Queer Temporalities" edited by Elizabeth Freeman, *GLQ* 13, nos. 2–3, 2007. Dipesh Chakrabarty, "The Time of History and the Times of the Gods," in *The Politics of Culture in the Shadow of Capital* (Durham, NC: Duke University Press, 1997): 3–60. The "nation" can only be understood, and was indeed invented, in relationship to Enlightenment geometries of time, lending an irony to the time-bending replay of the US Civil War – a particular nineteenth-century threat to "one nation." The "turn" to affect in much queer historiography is informed by a broader analysis of Enlightenment value, including the Protestant "secular time" that sets up capitalism as if a non-religious branch of "Enlightened" nations. The affective turn in queer theory, and the turn to *dragging history* affectively, is fundamentally engaged in unthinking certain Enlightenment principles that are, many have argued, synonymous with nation. See Janet Jakobsen and Ann Pellegrini, "Times Like These," in *Secularisms*, Janet Jakobsen and Ann Pellegrini, eds. (Durham, NC: Duke University Press, 2008). See also Ann Cvetkovich, *An Archive of Feelings: Trauma, Sexuality, and Lesbian Public Cultures* (Durham, NC: Duke University Press, 2003); Prasenjit Duara, *Rescuing History from the Nation* (Chicago, IL: University of Chicago Press, 1995).

12 Patricia Clough, ed., *The Affective Turn: Theorizing the Social* (Durham, NC: Duke University Press, 2007). On the precedent feminist terrain for the turn see Kristyn Gorton, "Theorizing Emotion and Affect: Feminist Engagements," *Feminist Theory* 8, no. 3, 2007: 333–48. See also Eve Kosofsky Sedgwick, 2003, op. cit.

13 Kathleen Stewart, *Ordinary Affects* (Durham, NC: Duke University Press, 2007): 38–41. Alphonso Lingis, "The Society of Disremembered Body Parts," in *Deleuze and the Theatre of Philosophy*, Constantin Boundas and Dorothea Olkowski, eds. (New York: Routledge, 1994).

14 Teresa Brennan, *The Transmission of Affect* (Ithaca, NY: Cornell University Press, 2004): 1.

15 Sarah Ahmed, 2004, op. cit.: 11, 16, 82–100. On affect cross-temporally see Carolyn Dinshaw, 1999, op. cit.; Ann Cvetkovich, 2003, op. cit.; Heather Love, 2009, op. cit. On trauma as transmissible as theorized in the work of Shoshana Felman, Dori Laub, and Cathy Caruth see Amy Hungerford, "Memorizing Memory," *The Yale Journal of Criticism* 14, no.1, 2001: 67–92.

16 Brian Massumi, 2002, op. cit.

17 Love argues the importance of retaining the "past *as past*" and the simultaneous necessity to approach the past as "something living." Heather Love, 2009, op. cit.: 19, 9. Elizabeth Freeman, 2000, op. cit.: 728. Freeman also writes on Hilary Brougher's 1997 independent film *The Sticky Fingers of Time* in a related essay, "Time Binds, or Erotohistory," 2005, op. cit.: 57–68.

18 See Maurice Merleau-Ponty, *The Visible and the Invisible*, Alphonso Lingis, trans. (Chicago, IL: Northwestern University Press, 1969): 130–55.

19 Jacques Derrida, *Archive Fever: A Freudian Impression* (Chicago, IL: University of Chicago Press, 1995): 10.

20 Walter Benjamin, "Theses on the Philosophy of History," *Illuminations*, Harry Zohn, trans. (New York: Schocken Books, 1969): 257. Benjamin's distinction between historicism and historical materialism is one that challenges historicism's political investment in linear, non-recurring temporality. To articulate historical materialism, Benjamin repeatedly resorts to tropes of liveness-in-encounter. If historicism "presents the eternal image of the past," historical materialism offers "a specific and unique *experience with it* [. . .] Historical materialism conceives historical understanding as an after-life of what is understood, whose *pulses can still be felt in the present*." Benjamin, *One Way Street*, Edmund Jephcott and Kingsley Shorter, trans. (London: New Left Books, 1979): 352, emphasis added.

21 That live performance acts constitute a repertoire of behaviors (whether specialized as ritual, dance, theatre, or other modes of art performance, or less formalized repetitive gestures of everyday life), has been discussed at length by such scholars as Paul Connerton 1989, op. cit.; Joseph Roach, *Cities of the Dead* (New York: Columbia University Press, 1996); and Diana Taylor, *The Archive and the Repertoire* (Durham, NC: Duke University Press, 2003). To refer to live acts as "documents," however, goes against the distinction that Taylor, in particular, wants to retain between documents on the one side and performance acts on another – a matter I will address in depth in Chapter 3. Connerton is more flexible in crossing "inscription" with "incorporation," and yet he too is wary of the privilege "inscription" and document-based identification has wielded, historically, over embodied modes of remaining. Taylor and Connerton are correct, in my estimation, to be wary. And yet, crossing the wires of this long-sedimented binary is arguably a fertile way to interrogate the very privilege that document, inscription, and textuality have held over incorporation.

22 Fredric Jameson, "Postmodernism and Consumer Society," in *Postmodernism and Its Discontents*, E. Ann Kaplan, ed. (London: Verso, 1988): 28.

23 Emile Durkheim, *Suicide*, John A. Spaulding, trans. (New York: Free Press, 1987); Durkheim, *The Elementary Forms of Religious Life*, Carol Cosman, trans. (New York: Oxford University Press, 2008); Johannes Fabian, *Time and the Other: How Anthropology Makes Its Object* (New York: Columbia University Press, 1983).

24 Paul Ricoeur, 2004, op. cit.: 396–7.

25 A note on the word "orature." The word was coined by Ugandan scholar Pio Zirimu and brought into performance studies largely through the work of Ngũgĩ wa Thiong'o. For a sense of the deeper conversation the word invites, see his "Notes Toward a Performance Theory of Orature," *Performance Research* 12, no. 3, 2007: 4–7. A great deal of work on thinking through (or beyond or without) the sometimes false legislation of borders between orality and textuality as been generated in the journal *Callaloo*.

26 See Tavia Nyong'o, *The Amalgamation Waltz: Race, Performance, and the Ruses of Memory* (Minneapolis: University of Minnesota Press, 2009): 152–3. We will return to this topic in Chapter 3.

27 Some African-American reenactors fight to highlight the forgotten or overlooked sidebars in history. For example, the 38th regiment of the United States Colored Troops, Company D, gives the following reason for reenacting: "As members of the modern day 38th USCT, we are all historians seeking to preserve a much ignored part

of American history. Too often has the part of the gallant Colored Troops been shoved into the *forgotten pages* of the history books. We seek to bring the lives of these American heroes to the attention of the public, so that their legacy and sacrifices will never be forgotten by future generations" (emphasis added). Available online at http://community-1.webtv.net/yankeefred1/38THUNITEDSTATES/ (accessed August 2009). On battle reenactment in relationship to slavery reenactment, see Lisa Woolfork, *Embodying American Slavery in Contemporary Culture* (Bloomington: University of Indiana Press, 2008). Woolfork usefully writes of reenactment as "bodily epistemology" and terms it a form of "black vernacular trauma theory" (p. 9).

28 Chuck Woodhead is a retired Navy Lieutenant Commander and Desert Storm Veteran. As a reenactor, he is the chief bugler for the 1st Division of the Army of Northern VA, the Military District of Mississippi as well as the 125th Regiment OVI, a "Union only" reenacting unit covering Northern Georgia and East Tennessee.

29 See Chapter 3 for a full engagement with the basic performance studies proposition that performances "disappear as fast as they are made." Richard Schechner, *Between Theatre and Anthropology* (Chicago, IL: University of Chicago Press, 1985): 50.

30 The full Santayana quote: "Progress, far from consisting in change, depends on retentiveness. When change is absolute there remains no being to improve and no direction is set for possible improvement: and when experience is not retained, *as among savages*, infancy is perpetual. Those who cannot remember the past are condemned to repeat it." George Santayana, "Reason in Common Sense," volume 1 of *The Life of Reason*, 1905: 284, emphasis added. Not surprisingly, Sven Lütticken reports a very similar misquote at a reenactment at Gettysburg recorded by Christopher Hitchens in "An Arena in Which to Reenact," in *Life Once More: Forms of Re-enactment in Contemporary Art*, Sven Lütticken, ed. (Rotterdam: Witte de With Institute, 2005): 17–60.

31 The "frame" is the way the differentiation between theatre and reality, or faux and real, is often negotiated in performance studies, though countless examples from theatre history complicate any approach to the frame as non-porous. See Erving Goffman, *Frame Analysis* (Chicago, IL: Northwestern University Press, 1986); Gregory Bateson, "A Theory of Play and Fantasy," in *Steps to an Ecology of Mind* (New York: Ballantine, 1983): 177–93.

32 Henri Bergson, *Matter and Memory*, Nancy Margaret Paul and W. Scott Palmer, trans. (New York: Zone Books, 1988): 86–169.

33 Cited in Dan Zak, "Local Reenactment Groups Try to Keep It Real," *The Washington Post*, July 1, 2007: M06.

34 Ibid., emphasis added.

35 Karl Marx, *The Eighteenth Brumaire of Louis Bonaparte*, Daniel De Leon, trans. (Ann Arbor, MI: C. H. Kerr, 1913): 9–10.

36 Connerton, 1989, op. cit.

37 Schechner, 1985, op. cit.: 36.

38 Peter Stallybrass, "Well-Grubbed, Old Mole: Marx, *Hamlet*, and the Unfixing of Representation," in *Marxist Shakespeares*, Jean E. Howard and Scott Cutler Shershow, eds. (New York: Routledge, 2001): 19. For the antitheatrical reading of Marx that highlights the disparagement of farce, also grounded solidly in Marx's writing, see Slavoj Žižek, *First as Tragedy, Then as Farce* (New York: Verso, 2009). I do not contend here that Marx was entirely positive about returns of history as farce, but I do contend that he took "merely the clown" of world events (cited in Žižek: 2) very seriously, begging a reading of history's theatricality that is not entirely dismissive.

39 Karl Marx, *The Grundrisse*, David McLellan, trans. (New York: Harper and Row, 1972): 125.

40 On the femininity of mimesis and the related gender panic, see Rebecca Schneider, "Hello Dolly Well Hello Dolly," in *Psychoanalysis and Performance*, Patrick Campbell and Adrian Kear, eds. (New York: Routledge, 2001).

41 Robin Bernstein, "Dances With Things: Material Culture and the Performance of

Race," *Social Text* 27, no. 4, 67–94, 2009: 68. We will return to the "scriptive thing" in Chapter 5.

42 Some might object to my placement of dramatic texts (such as Shakespeare's *Hamlet*) in the same category as a footpath or as late twentieth-century instruction art such as Ono's *Fly*. I simply mean to point out that in all cases the site of the material given-to-remain (the stage direction "Hamlet dies," or Ono's instruction "Fly") is cast toward a future when it might be taken up and "produced" by whatever incomplete or inadequate, imperfect or inexact means fidelity (or infidelity) to the instruction or the stage direction will generate. Similarly, to put "footprint" beside "blueprint" might seem to pose problems. A footprint is an archetypal example of an "index" – something that remains to indicate the past by way of impression in C. S. Peirce's example. In most work on the index in visual studies, the indexicality of trace is not an example of a signpost for a future but generally read as a referent of irretrievable loss. Preferring by and large to make death antonymic to the live, media studies treatments of the "index" do not tend to treat the index as script, indicative of future acts. Laura Mulvey's *Death 24× a Second* (New York: Reaktion Books, 2006) can stand as a prime example. For Mulvey, it is only death before and death behind. "For human and all organic life, time marks the movement along a path to death, that is, to the stillness that represents the transformation of the animate to the inanimate" (p. 31). The inanimate, for Mulvey, does not *also* lead to the transformation of the animate. This can be read, as we will do in Chapter 5, in distinction to Walter Benjamin who refers suggestively to August Sander's photographs as "training manuals" in his 1931 essay "A Small History of Photography," in *One Way Street* (New York: New Left Books, 1979): 252.

43 To think about the irony of the single Frederick Douglas in this image, I refer readers to Dana Luciano's Chapter 5, "Representative Mournfulness: Nation and Race in the Time of Lincoln," in *Arranging Grief: Sacred Time and the Body in Nineteenth-Century America* (New York: New York University Press, 2007): 218.

44 Ibid.: 219.

45 See Ann Pellegrini, "After Sontag: Future Notes on Camp," in *The Blackwell Companion to Lesbian, Gay, Bisexual, Transgender, Queer Studies*, George E. Haggerty and Molly McGarry, eds. (London: Blackwell, 2007). See also Jennifer Brody, "'Queer' Quotation Marks," in *Punctuation: Art, Politics, and Play* (Durham, NC: Duke University Press, 2008). We will return to the question of camp in the Afterword.

46 Wes Smith, "Land of Lincolns," *Chicago Tribune*, "Tempo" section, January 27, 1995.

47 For the theatre historian, ironies abound in references to theatre as always already sentimental. The association of theatre with sentimentality not only exposes extreme ignorance of the varied history of the medium, but also betrays the assumption that "sentiment" can have no history, nor be, in itself, a kind of remain nor a kind of analytic. On the broad debasement of sentimentality, and its links to gender, race, and the Civil War, see the essays collected in Shirley Samuels, ed., *The Culture of Sentiment: Race, Gender and Sentimentality in 19th-Century America* (Oxford University Press, 1992). For a nuanced and less reductive approach to the intersections between theatre, live performance, and historical reenactment see Jacqueline Tivers, "Performing Heritage: The Use of Live 'Actors' in Heritage Presentations," *Leisure Studies* 21, 2002.

48 Scott Magelssen, *Living History Museums: Undoing History Through Performance* (Lanham, MD: Scarecrow Press, 2007): 18. At several stages I worked with graduate students on the topic of reenactment. Michelle Liu Carriger's work informed this section. See Carriger, "Historionics: Neither Here Nor There with Historical Reality TV," *Journal of Dramatic Theory and Criticism* 24, no. 2, 2010.

49 Abraham Lincoln to James H. Hackett, August 17, 1863, in *Lincoln, Speeches and Writings 1859–1865* (New York: Library of America, 1989): 493.

50 See Stephen Greenblatt, "Fiction and Friction" in *Shakespearean Negotiations* (Berkeley: University of California Press, 1988): 66–93.

51 Stephen Dickey, "Lincoln and Shakespeare," http://www.shakespeareinamericanlife. org/identity/politicians/presidents/pick/lincoln/lincoln_shakespeare_2.cfm (accessed August 3, 2009).

52 See Marjorie Garber on the liberal uses of Shakespeare by contemporary politicians, mimicking Lincoln, among others. This is a kind of misquoting which borrows the "weightiness" of drama to add impact to the real, an action Garber terms, para-doxically, "disembodied quotation." Garber, *Shakespeare After All* (New York: Anchor, 2005): 38.

53 Adam Gopnik, *Angels and Ages: A Short Book about Darwin, Lincoln, and Modern Life* (New York: Random House, 2009):141. See also Bethany Schneider, "Thus, Always: Julius Caesar and Abraham Lincoln," in *Shakesqueer*, Madhavi Menon, ed. (Durham, NC: Duke University Press, 2010).

54 Richard Miller in the March 2009 newsletter of ALP, p. 4. Available online at http://www.lincolnpresenters.net (last accessed November 2010).

55 Perhaps because of the overt humor in the motto and the invitation to, therefore, not take the presenters seriously, the organization's motto was recently changed to "Would I might rouse the Lincoln in you all" from the poem by Vashel Lindsay.

56 See Jonas Barish, *Antitheatricalism* (Berkeley: University of California Press, 1981).

57 Adam Gopnik, "Angels and Ages: Lincoln's Language and its Legacy," *The New Yorker*, May 28, 2007.

58 Ibid.

59 Twilight Greenaway, "Miranda July: Performance," *Curve Magazine*, n.d. Available online at http://backup.curvemag.com/Detailed/85.html (accessed October 11, 2002).

60 See Jonas Barish, 1981, op. cit., cited in Nicholas Ridout, 2006, op.cit.: 3, 14.

61 Richard Handler and William Saxton, "Dyssimulation: Reflexivity, Narrative, and the Quest for Authenticity in 'Living History,'" *Cultural Anthropology* 3, no. 2, 1988: 245–6. The "magic moment" of reliving is often a moment of multiple reference, where more than one past comes to pass. Handler and Saxton relate a story of a reenacting Confederate private, who, immediately after a battle, described the moment he had just experienced: "as he was lost in the smoke, all he could see was the enemy flag coming toward him, and this had created a double emotion in him, allegiance to the Confederacy as well as to the United States. (He explained the latter sentiment as natural for a Vietnam veteran.) He also told of another magic moment achieved at a previous reenactment. 'Killed' in front of a line of cannon, he had lain on the ground feeling their repercussions and thinking about what it must have been like to die in battle" (p. 246).

62 Unless directly cited by interviewee's name, citations from these collected interviews refer to Schneider 2006, a series of interviews I conducted at Civil War reenactments between 1999 and 2006, unpublished.

63 Southern reenactor George Moates told Rory Turner that he fought for "the South, for its ideals and its way of life." His attitude was, "We'll show them that we're still the South and we have a right to our beliefs." He framed his remarks relative to mid-twentieth-century civil rights efforts and policies of integration required of the South. Turner, "Bloodless Battles: The Civil War Reenacted," *TDR: The Drama Review* 34, no. 4, 1990: 129.

64 Turner op. cit.: 127; Tony Horwitz, *Confederates in the Attic: Dispatches from the Unfinished Civil War* (New York: Vintage, 1999): 209–81; Handler and Saxton, op. cit.: 245–7. Captain John Zdroj, Commander of CoE 2nd Missouri Cavalry CSA, described his first battle reenactment in the following way: "Both armies march past the spectators who cheer for their respective team (we lovingly call them "sports fans" the hobby needs them because after all we are only actors in a play). They encourage us defeated rebels by telling us we'll get those evil Yankees tomorrow and even the score and God save the South! Though defeated today, we proudly march back to camp. All this took

45 minutes! I'm in camp and finally have a steady hand. I've had my first taste of combat, my eyes are as big as silver dollars, I am happy and satisfied, hot and sweaty and dirty with black powder all over my face and arms. I have survived the War for Southern Independence! My 16-year-old veterans tell me that I just saw the elephant! I can't shut up. I keep talking about the battle. I am doomed! I am now an addicted civil war reenactor, forever I hope! My war is over until tomorrow, when those Yankees will pay dearly for their victory today. It's the Confederates turn to win tomorrow!" In "What's It Like Being a Reenactor?," available online at http://members.tripod.com/2ndmocavcsa/id17.htm (last accessed November 2010).

65 Handler and Saxton's research in late 1980s corroborates mine ten years later. They wrote: "Despite the dream of a definitively authentic history, practitioners are well aware that the past in *all* its detail can never be recovered." They cite Darwin Kelsey who admits that "As is any historical account, they are based on incomplete evidence." Handler and Saxton, 1988, op. cit.: 244.

66 This particular reenactment included "nearly 400 reenactors and six mounted cavalry." See http://www.hearthsidehouse.org/photos/civil.war.html.

67 Tony Horwitz, op. cit.: 7, 127, emphasis added.

68 On blackface minstrel shows in Civil War reenactment camps see Rory Turner, op. cit.: 11–12.

69 On gender crossing in the Civil War era and in Civil War reenactment, see Elizabeth Young, "Confederate Counterfeit: The Case of the Cross-Dressed Civil War Soldier," 149–94, and "Afterward" in *Disarming the Nation* (Chicago, IL: University of Chicago Press, 1999).

70 Cathy Stanton and Stephen Belyea, "'Their Time Will Yet Come': African American Presence in Civil War Reenactment," in *Hope and Glory: Essays on the Legacy of the 54th Massachusetts Regiment*, Martin Henry Blatt, Thomas J. Brown, and Donald Yakovone, eds. (Amherst, MA: University of Massachusetts Press, 2000): 265.

71 On the constellation of issues involved in witnessing weddings, see Jane Blocker, "Binding to Another's Wound: Of Weddings and Witness," in *After Criticism: New Responses to Art and Performance*, Gavin Butt, ed. (New York: Blackwell, 2005): 48–64.

72 On the soundscapes of the Civil War, and sound as a subject of historical knowledge (and historical residue) see Mark M. Smith, "Listening to the Heard Worlds of Antebellum America," *Journal of the Historical Society* 1, no. 1, 2000: 65–99.

73 This book does not take up the matter of Native American approaches to history and reenactment, nor the complicated ways in which whites have reenacted Native American identities in playing white history and Native Americans have "counter-mimicked" whites reenacting Natives. See the collection edited by Gerald Vizenor, *Survivance: Narratives of Native Presence* (Lincoln: Nebraska University Press, 2008). Though "literary" in exploration, for Vizenor writing is taken up as orature and the "storied" is a mode of embodiment. On mimicry and counter-mimicry see Philip J. Deloria, *Playing Indian* (New Haven, CT: Yale University Press, 1999). In citing the oversight of this book, I perhaps replay it here, even though attempting to note, as Joseph Roach writes in *Cities of the Dead*, that "forgetting, like miscegenation, is an opportunistic tactic of whiteness." Roach, 1996, op. cit.: 6. I would like to refer the reader to the work of Native American artist James Luna, whose work, as Jane Blocker writes, "seeks to explore the pure theatricality of the living history museum, the historical theme park, the waxworks diorama, and the brown highway markers that map the tourist experience of history. To accomplish this, he *overacts the part and runs history's shtick into the ground.*" In Jane Blocker, *Seeing Witness: Visuality and the Ethics of Testimony* (Minneapolis: University of Minnesota Press, 2009): 28, emphasis added. See also my own chapter on Spiderwoman Theatre in *The Explicit Body in Performance* (New York: Routledge, 1997).

74 See Avery Gordon, *Ghostly Matters: Haunting and the Sociological Imagination* (Minneapolis: University of Minnesota Press, 1997).

2 Finding faux fathers

1 See Alice Rayner, *To Act, To Do, To Perform: The Phenomenology of Action* (Ann Arbor: University of Michigan Press, 1994).

2 On what "Booth either did or did not say, just as, right before, or shortly after he murdered the President" see Adam Gopnik, *Angels and Ages* (New York: Knopf, 2009): 27–8. Interestingly, most eyewitnesses to the shooting "did not understand what Booth said on the stage, but agreed he had spoken twice." Michael W. Kauffman, *American Brutus: John Wilkes Booth and the Lincoln Conspiracies* (New York: Random House, 2004): 404, Fn29.

3 The phrase is attributed to Marcus Junius Brutus, the most famous figure in the assassination of Julius Caesar on March 15, 44 BCE. The phrase was likely a later embellishment, as Roman historians of the period do not record it. According to François Jost, a version of the phrase appears in Friedrich Schiller's *Die Rauber*, which contains a recitation of a dialogue between Brutus and Caesar. Jost in fact argues that Lincoln's actual murder was "re-enacted" by Booth who was playing both Shakespeare's Brutus and Schiller's Moor (assassins Wilkes had played to acclaim on American stages), though, Jost writes, "it cannot be my intention to impute to Schiller the assassination of a President of the United States." In "John Wilkes Booth and Abraham Lincoln: The Reenactment of a Murder," *MLN* 93, no. 3, 1978: 505. In American history, the phrase was recommended by George Mason to the Virginia Convention in 1776 as part of the state's seal. The phrase is also the motto of Allentown, Pennsylvania, and is referenced in the official state song of Maryland. Timothy McVeigh was wearing a T-shirt with this phrase and a picture of Lincoln on it when he was arrested on April 19, 1995, the day of the Oklahoma City bombing.

4 James L. Swanson suggests the tangle between "act" and act by calling on theatre history – though erroneously: "Booth had not only committed murder, he had performed it, fully staged before a packed house. At Ford's Theatre, Booth broke the fourth wall between artist and audience by creating a new, dark art – performance assassination." *Manhunt* (New York: William Morrow, 2006): 327. Such remarks illustrate how little many popular historians understand of theatre history. The play that night, *Our American Cousin*, was full of asides – and, as a farcical comedy, hardly a fourth-wall play. That is, the "wall" would never have been there to break. At the most, it would have been broken by the first aside, not thirty short lines into the play.

5 Gary Wills has described Lincoln's speech at Gettysburg as a "refounding act." He also argues that the speech changed the way Americans thought about "the nation's founding acts," essentially shifting the significance of those acts through citation and retroactively winning him a place on the progenitors' collective pedestal. *Lincoln at Gettysburg: The Words that Remade America* (New York: Simon and Schuster, 1993): 40, 174.

6 Joseph Roach, *Cities of the Dead: Circum-Atlantic Performance* (New York: Columbia University Press, 1996): 1–25, 38, 68–71.

7 See Clifford Geertz, *The Interpretation of Cultures* (New York: Basic Books, 1977): 448.

8 See Karen Shimakawa on Giorgio Agamben's notion of "whatever being" as potentially manifest in performance in "The Things We Share: Ethnic Performativity and 'Whatever Being,'" *The Journal of Speculative Philosophy* 18, no. 2, 2004: 149–60.

9 It has become something of a given in performance studies, that social life is a matter of negotiating rituals of convention based in the sedimented sets of acts that precede any subject's entry into collective life. The citational aspects of everyday life – the way that words, gestures, poses, bodily behaviors, and physical architectures "stand in" for their signifieds and the ways we communicate with each other through arranging and rearranging precedence – lend a broad pallette to words such as "surrogation." We use stand-ins to "do things." A conglomerate of words like surrogation have come to stand in for multiple operations by which acts achieved in the social are composed in

and through "acts" of citation, convention, habit, and ritual. If the word "surrogation" cites Joseph Roach on operations of the social, "interpellation" through ritual cites Louis Althusser, and "performativity" cites J. L. Austin. On the combination of Althusser and Austin see Judith Butler, "Performative Acts and Gender Constitution: An Essay in Phenomenology and Feminist Theory," in *Performing Feminisms: Feminist Critical Theory and Theatre*, Sue-Ellen Case, ed. (Baltimore: Johns Hopkins University Press, 1990).

10 When he killed Caesar at Pompey's theatre, Marcus Junius Brutus was himself knowingly reenacting his distant ancestral namesake, Lucius Junius Brutus, who killed the last king of Rome in 509 BCE and founded the Republic. The citational/theatrical *mise en abyme* of patricide resonates with Joseph Roach's thesis on surrogation as well as with Derrida's mediations on Freud in *Archive Fever* (Chicago, IL: University of Chicago Press, 1995), as discussed in Chapter 3.

11 This is contested. The status of the break's verity, like his spoken words, is impossible to adjudicate. Some argue Booth faked the break, and his staggering may have been caused by a "dizziness" incurred from leaping onto the stage. See Kauffman, 2004, op. cit.: 273.

12 See Bethany Schneider, "Thus, Always: Julius Caesar and Abraham Lincoln," in *Shakesqueer*, Madhavi Menon, ed. (Durham, NC: Duke University Press, 2010). See Rebecca Schneider, "Patricide and the Passerby," in *Performance and the City*, D. J. Hopkins, Shelley Orr, and Kim Solga, eds. (New York: Palgrave, 2009). See also John Borneman on the long history of Western conceptualizations of sovereignty as patriarchal, with the right of the father to kill sons shifting, in modernity, to the right and even obligation of "sons" to kill "fathers" in what Borneman calls the ritualization and institutionalization of the death of the father in the complex of the nation state. "Introduction: Theorizing Regime Ends," in *Death of the Father: An Anthropology of the End in Political Authority*, John Borneman, ed. (New York: Berghahn Books, 2004): 1–32.

13 The Romans built theatres across the empire. The *scenae frons* was a massive stone background to the Roman stage (itself a stone repetition and revision of the Greek *theatron*). An elaborate expansion of the Greek *skene*, the *scenae frons* was built to represent the street. Faux stone row houses lined the back of the narrow stage with multiple false portals, like mini, private triumphal arches, signifying faux doorways to patrician interiors. Porticoes and niches in the façade were studded with stonily still bodies and busts of city fathers. That the Roman stage described by Vitruvius should morph over time into the very machinery of perspective – an architecture that would re-find itself as the camera – is a dizzying matter taken up in Chapter 5.

14 Marc Robinson, "Robert Wilson, Nicolas Poussin, and Lohengrin," in *Land/Scape/Theater*, Elinor Fuchs and Una Chaudhuri, eds. (Ann Arbor: University of Michigan Press, 2002): 167.

15 Suzan-Lori Parks, "The America Play," in *The America Play: And Other Works* (New York: Theater Communications Group, 1995): 160–1.

16 See for example, Spencer Golub, *The Recurrence of Fate: Theatre and Memory in Twentieth-Century Russia* (Iowa City: University of Iowa Press, 1994); Susan Leigh Foster, *Choreographing History* (Bloomington: Indiana University Press, 1995); Jeanette Malkin, *Memory-Theater and Postmodern Drama* (Ann Arbor: University of Michigan Press, 1999); Freddie Rokem, *Performing History: Theatrical Representations of the Past*, (Iowa City: University of Iowa Press, 2000); Mark Franko and Annette Richards, *Acting on the Past: Historical Performance Across the Disciplines* (Middletown, CT: Wesleyan University Press, 2000); Marvin Carlson, *The Haunted Stage: The Theatre as Memory Machine* (Ann Arbor: University of Michigan Press, 2001).

17 That the characters are "brothers" in *Topdog* signifies among other things that they are black men. That they are "brothers" also carries resonance regarding the rivalries of the Booth brothers. Multiple temporal references, or anachronisms, function like

homonyms in Parks's plays. Race, in this play as well as in Parks's other plays, is often referenced indirectly. On the "complex participations of the dramatic event" in oscillation between fictions and nonfictions, and between actors, spectators, and "characters," see Stanton B. Garner, *Bodied Spaces: Phenomenology and Performance in Contemporary Drama* (Ithaca, NY: Cornell University Press, 1994): 7.

18 Looking to Shakespeare, the poet John Keats defined "negative capability" as "capable of being in uncertainties." "Letter from John Keats to Benjamin Bailey, 22 November, 1817," in *Romanticism: An Anthology*, Duncan Wu, ed. (London: Blackwell, 2006): 1351.

19 Meta Du Ewa Jones, "Jazz Prosodies: Orality and Textuality," *Callaloo* 25, no. 1, 2002: 66–91. See also Richard Quinn, "The Creak of Categories: Nathaniel Mackey's *Strick: Song of the Andoumboulou 16–25*," *Callaloo* 23, no. 2, 2000: 608–20.

20 Cited in Jones, 2002, op. cit.: 69.

21 Amiri Baraka, who writes and thinks between jazz and theatre, has written that jazz "remains" the "changing same" – an idea fertile in its implications for the ways performance, too, *preserves* by way of difference, again and again. The "changing same" might challenge mechanisms of preservation that can only validate identicality, as discussed in Chapter 3. See Amiri Baraka (LeRoi Jones), *Black Music* (New York: William Morrow, 1968): 232.

22 Gertrude Stein, *Lectures in America* (New York: Random House, 1935): 93.

23 Gertrude Stein, 1935, op. cit.: 95. I cite Stein here, one early influence on the playwright Parks, to underscore how Stein came to think about theatre as syncopated time, a notion of syncopation she took from jazz. However, if Stein can certainly be claimed as a theatre theorist, she cannot be productively listed among theorists of jazz and blues. Nevertheless she is a figure who, early on, attempted to think theatre time and jazz time *together*, especially as concerns the question of what is American about American theatre. Still, the fact is too often elided that it is African American (and Native American) practice and innovation that contributes so deeply to what is American in American art, an ongoing blind spot in historicizing the rise of performance art in the twentieth century. For my own attempt to situate this elision, especially regarding the habit of naming Jackson Pollock the "Founding Father" of performance art, see Schneider, "Solo Solo Solo" in *After Criticism: New Responses to Art and Performance*, Gavin Butt, ed. (London: Blackwell Press, 2004).

24 *Hamlet* citations are from 2.2.604–5 and 3.2.272. Writing on mimesis and the colonized subject, Homi Bhaba made the phrase "almost but not quite" famous, resounding as it does with "almost but not quite white" in his essay "Of Mimicry and Man: The Ambivalence of Colonial Discourse" republished in *The Location of Culture* (New York: Routledge, 1994). On "act" to act and back, in conjunction with Hamlet, ghost-notes, and Parks's *The America Play*, see Alice Rayner, *Ghosts: Death's Double and the Phenomena of Theatre* (Minneapolis: University of Minnesota Press, 2006).

25 Parks, *The America Play*, 1995, op. cit.: 159. See Elinor Fuchs on *The America Play* as a Steinian landscape play in "Reading for Landscape: The Case of American Drama" in *Land/Scape/Theater*, Una Chaudhuri and Elinor Fuchs, eds. (Ann Arbor: University of Michigan Press, 2002): 39–43.

26 Many have written on Parks and jazz. For an early interview see Steven Drukman, "Suzan-Lori Parks and Liz Diamond: Do-a-Diddly-Dit-Dit," *TDR: The Drama Review* 39, 3, 1995: 56–73.

27 Parks, *The America Play*, 1995, op. cit.: 163.

28 Ibid.: 159.

29 See Maurice Merleau-Ponty, *The Visible and the Invisible* (Chicago. IL: Northwestern University Press, 1969): 130–55; Luce Irigaray, *An Ethics of Sexual Difference* (Ithaca, NY: Cornell University Press, 1993): 151–85.

30 Jonas Barish, *Antitheatrical Prejudice* (Berkeley: University of California Press, 1981); Martin Puchner, *Stage Fright: Modernism, Antitheatricality and Drama* (Baltimore, MD:

Johns Hopkins University Press, 2002); Nicholas Ridout, *Stage Fright, Animals, and Other Theatrical Problems* (Cambridge: Cambridge University Press, 2006). For a discussion of antitheatricality in the Renaissance that situates several scholars on the topic, see Bryan Reynolds, *Becoming Criminal: Transversal Performance and Cultural Dissidence in Early Modern England* (Baltimore, MD: Johns Hopkins University Press, 2002).

31 J. L. Austin, *How to Do Things with Words* (Cambridge, MA: President and Fellows of Harvard College, 1955): 22.

32 Ibid.

33 See Jennifer Brody, *Punctuation: Art, Politics, and Play* (Durham, NC: Duke University Press, 2008): 64; on "holes" see pp. 27–84.

34 See Michel Serres, *The Parasite* (Minneapolis: University of Minnesota Press, 2007).

35 Parks, *The America Play*, 1995, op. cit.: 163–9.

36 Flat Daddies are life-sized cardboard cut-out replicas (from the waist up) of military personnel deployed in the "war on terror" available for military American families to set up in their homes. See Kate Zezima, "When Soldiers Go to War, Flat Daddies Hold Their Place at Home," *The New York Times*, September 30, 2006. From that article, the following bears citing: "Rachel Austin of Colorado Springs paid $50 for a flat version of her husband, Toby, in February after hearing about them through the Colorado National Guard. Ms. Austin said Toby was at the dinner table every night with their sons, Ayden, 20 months, and Ryan, 5. Flat Toby also has been to pre-kindergarten graduation, an uncle's 50th birthday party in Cheyenne, Wyo., and a Denver Broncos game, although he sat in the car because it was raining. Ms. Austin said Ayden, who was 13 months old when she brought Flat Toby home, recognized his father, often taking the image off its usual chair and kissing it. Flat Toby is a real person in their house, she said. 'It's nice to see him each day, just to remember that he's still with us,' Ms. Austin said. 'It's one of the best things I've done during this deployment. I really think it's helped us stay connected, to remember that he's still with us.'" See http://flatdaddies.com/. The issue of the future-citing liveness of photographic images is taken up in depth in Chapter 5.

37 Parks, *The America Play*, 1995, op. cit.: 171.

38 The matter of the beard is apparently a matter for confession beyond Parks's stage. At the 2009 gathering of the Lincoln Presenters Association in Washington, DC, *Washington Post* journalist Michael E. Ruane noted: "Among the presenters was J. P. Wammack, a life insurance salesman from La Canada, Calif. His beard was fake, he admitted. He said he was following in his father's footsteps. He used to think it was a 'dorky' pastime. But once he tried it, 'I was hooked,' he said." Michael E. Ruane, "Lots of Lincolns Bring Honest Abe's Ethics to Town," *The Washington Post*, April 19, 2009.

39 Parks, *The America Play*, 1995, op. cit.: 159.

40 Parks, "Elements of Style," in *The America Play and Other Works*, 1995, op. cit.: 16.

41 Linda Mussmann, "*Cross Way Cross: Civil War Chronicles*, Part III," *Women and Performance* 4, 1, 1988/89. For reviews of the 1987 production of *Cross Way Cross* see Ann Daly, "Cross Way Cross," *High Performance* 38, 1987: 74, and Jack Anderson, "Stage: 'Cross Way Cross,' A Journey," *The New York Times*, Sunday, March 1, 1987. See also Marianne Goldberg, "Turning History Around: Linda Mussmann's *Chronicles*," *Women and Performance* 4, no. 1, 1988/89: 150–6.

42 Mussmann, 1988/89, op. cit.: 94.

43 Ibid.

44 Ibid.: 111.

45 Ibid.: 85.

46 Ibid.

47 It is interesting to note that Betti-Sue Hertz labels Nightingale a "character" though Nightingale was Antin herself played *as if* Nightingale in such works as "Myself 1854." That is, Antin did not lift Nightingale from a dramatic play in order to play

Nightingale as a character, but lifted Nightingale from archival documents and photographs to place *herself*, like Mussmann's "She," in the scene. Perhaps Hertz means to signify Nightingale's "having" character, but the example illustrates how theatre plays back over history, even as history plays forward through theatrical reenactment. This interplay has itself been a focus of Antin's work from her *Recollections of My Live with Diaghilev* (1976–7) to her recent stagings of such works as "Roman Allegories" and "The Last Days of Pompeii" which curator Hertz recently collected under the rubric "Historical Takes." Betti-Sue Hertz, "Eleanor Antin's Transpositions: A Feminist View of Academic Painting in the Age of Digital Photography," in *Eleanor Antin: Historical Takes*, Betti-Sue Hertz, ed. (San Diego, CA: San Diego Museum of Art, 2008): 81–91.

48 See Marta Weiss, "Staged Photography in the Victorian Album," in *Acting the Part: Photography as Theatre*, edited by Lori Pauli (New York: Merrel, 2006): 82; 94.

49 Elin Diamond, "Brechtian Theory/Feminist Theory: Toward a Gestic Feminist Criticism," *TDR: The Drama Review* 32, no. 1, 1988: 82–94.

50 Audre Lorde, "The Master's Tools Will Never Dismantle the Master's House," in *Sister Outsider: Essays and Speeches* (Trumansburg, NY: The Crossing Press, 1984): 110–14.

51 See for example Richard Kostelanetz, "Robert Wilson, Richard Foreman, Linda Mussmann: A Symposium on Writing and Performance," *New York Arts Journal* 25–6, 1981: 4–9. In 1991, TSL moved to Hudson, New York, where it expanded its role as an experimental company to become, as well, a community arts organization.

52 The return to narrative, or to structures of convention, in order to explore them critically from the inside was a move employed at the time in materialist feminist art and criticism. See Jill Dolan, *The Feminist Spectator as Critic* (Ann Arbor: UMI Research Press, 1985): 99–118. Following on her important 1985 essay "Desire in Narrative," Teresa de Lauretis published *Technologies of Gender* in the same year that Mussmann produced *Cross Way Cross* (Bloomington: Indiana University Press, 1987). In that book, de Lauretis explored how "narrative and narrativity, because of their capacity to inscribe desire and to direct, sustain, or undercut identification (in all senses of the term), are mechanisms to be employed strategically and tactically in the effort to construct other forms of coherence, to shift the terms of representation, to produce the conditions of representability of another – and gendered – social subject" (p. 109). In a chapter titled "Strategies of Coherence" she called for feminist artists to grapple with narrative, but the call could just as well be applied to feminists who had begun to grapple with dramatic or filmic tableaux vivants in which a narrative is implied, as in the late 1970s and early 1980s photographic performance work of Cindy Sherman.

53 Dana Luciano, *Arranging Grief: Sacred Time and the Body in Nineteenth-Century America* (New York: New York University Press, 2007): 219.

54 On the difference between chronicle and narrative, see Hayden White, "The Value of Narrativity in the Representation of Reality," in *On Narrative*, W. J. T. Mitchell, ed. (Chicago: University of Chicago Press, 1980): 1–24.

55 See http://timeandspace.org/about.html (accessed May 23, 2010).

56 On the crisis in the NEA, see Peggy Phelan's commentaries: "Serrano, Mapplethorpe, the NEA, and You: Money Talks," *TDR: The Drama Review* 34, no. 1, 1990: 4–15 , and "Money Talks, Again," *TDR: The Drama Review* 35, no. 3, 1991: 131–41.

57 The quote is taken from the TSL website, http://timeandspace.org/about.html (accessed May 23, 2010).

58 I interviewed Linda Mussmann twice, in 1987 and 1988, for an article I published in *Women and Performance* in 1988. During the late 1970s Mussmann was grappling with three simultaneous concerns in her work: "First, I was tired of telling stories in theatre and found little hope in traveling down that corridor so I turned to Woolf and Stein for help. Second, I was tired of emotionalism and psychology as the primary motivators of theatrical expression (Stanislavskian acting). I wanted to look for some

other means of expression, using Brecht as a starting point rather than a finishing point. Third, I was moving away from content and toward form, developing the voice and gesture. I was experimenting with Kabuki which uses men in women's roles, resolving sex role-playing through form – if one could capture the form of a character it didn't matter who played the role." On Mussmann's work in this period see Harmony Hammond, "Hearing and Seeing: Linda Mussmann and Ann Wilson on Creating Nonnarrative Theater," *Heresies*, 17, 1984: 89–93, and Jim O'Quinn "Linda Mussman's Time and Space Limited Theatre," *TDR: The Drama Review* 24, no. 2, 1980: 17–84.

59 See Yvonne Rainer, "More Kicking and Screaming from the Narrative Front/Backwater," *Wide Angle* 7, nos. 1–2, 1985: 8–12.

60 From an interview with Linda Mussmann, 1987/88, unpublished.

61 Laura Mulvey's "Visual Pleasure and Narrative Cinema," *Screen* 16, no. 3, 1975: 6–18, was enormously influential on a generation of feminist film and theatre scholars and artists. The essay employs psychoanalytic theories of the gaze to read Hollywood cinema, suturing the gaze to gendered identity and narrative development.

62 In a paper presented after a performance of *Mary Surratt*, Peggy Phelan presented a provocative view of the particular time/space warp of Time and Space Limited (an insight which profoundly influenced my thinking at the time): "Time, for Mussmann, is an immobile and cumbersome steel column, and space is this wonderfully slippery thing that moves. [. . .] To predicate an entire theatrical enterprise on such angles produces the strange vertigo of Time and Space Limited; the theatre, in other words, investigates the moments at which time and space got turned around and time became misrepresented as a thing that moves, and space as that solid column." Unpublished paper presented February 12, 1988, Village Community School, New York, 1–2.

63 Teresa de Lauretis, "Desire in Narrative," in *Alice Doesn't* (Bloomington: Indiana University Press, 1954): 103–57.

64 Sue-Ellen Case and Jeanie K. Forte, "From Formalism to Feminism," *Theater* 16, no. 2, 1985: 63, 64–5.

65 Friedrich Nietzsche, *On the Genealogy of Morals*, Douglas Smith, trans. (Oxford: Oxford University Press, 2009): 98.

66 Ibid.

67 Linda Mussmann, "If Kansas Goes," unpublished play, 1987.

68 Time and Space Limited, *Civil War Chronicles*, press release, 1988.

69 Mussmann insists there is no intended resemblance to the 1939 *Wizard of Oz*. *If Kansas Goes* implies the Civil War motif: the "stormy" entrance of the state of Kansas into the Union, January 29, 1861, which precipitated the secession of the Southern states.

70 Citations of lines from *Mary Surratt* are taken from my notes written while watching the play in 1988. Thus, they are what I heard, not necessarily what was scripted. I did not check them with the unpublished manuscript, because the status of aural record is, itself, of interest in terms of what constitutes "performance remains."

71 See Marianne Goldberg, "Turning History Around: Linda Mussmann's *Chronicles*," *Women and Performance* 4, no. 1, 1988: 150–6.

3 In the meantime: performance remains

1 Rebecca Schneider, "Performance Remains," *Performance Research* 6, no. 2, 2001: 100–8.

2 W. B. Worthen, *Shakespeare and the Authority of Performance* (Cambridge: Cambridge University Press, 1997): 28. See also Alice Rayner on Hamlet's writing, *Ghosts: Death's Double and the Phenomena of Theatre* (Minneapolis: University of Minnesota Press, 2006): 49–52.

3 Gertrude Stein, *Lectures in America* (New York: Random House, 1935): 94.

4 http://wordnetweb.princeton.edu/perl/webwn?s=meantime (accessed October 26, 2009).

5 *The New Oxford Dictionary of English*, 2nd edition revised (Oxford University Press, 2005).

6 In *Matter and Memory*, first published in 1896, Henri Bergson articulated an approach to the non-linearity of time that would influence modernist artists, writers, and philosophers and spark "postmodern" thought, including that of Gilles Deleuze. For Bergson, time is not measurable by a linear series of instances and any perception involves an "interval" between times that cannot be considered discrete. Bergson's notion of "duration" is never, then, a straight line between measurable points, but a wavier set of porous simultaneities, traversed by intuition, memory, movement, and the rhythm of "always beginning again." *Matter and Memory*, trans. N. M. Paul and W. S. Palmer (New York: Zone Books, 1988): 279. See also "Time as Lived Duration" from *Duration and Simultaneity*, in *The Human Experience of Time*, Charles M. Sherover, ed. (Evanston, IL: Northwestern University Press, 2001): 218–38.

7 Gertrude Stein, *Lectures in America*, op. cit.: 94–5.

8 Ibid.: 114.

9 It is useful to cite Michael Fried in this context: "[T]he sense which, at bottom, theatre addresses is a sense of temporality, of time both passing and to come, *simultaneously approaching and receding*." The time, then, of theatre is never singular, and never transcendent (which is why Fried disparaged it), but always simultaneous and ambivalent, composed in the other feature Fried remarks as basic to theatre: distance, required for beholding, perceiving, or spectating. For Fried, distance is also essential to doubling, copying, repeating, or to rendering anything simultaneous – that is both the same and different. Fried, "Art and Objecthood," reprinted in *Minimal Art*, Gregory Battock, ed. (Berkeley: University of California Press, 1995): 145. Samuel Weber, too, remarks on theatre as "primarily a temporal medium," a temporality he finds articulate because it is always in tension with what he terms "spatial dislocation." Weber, *Theatricality as Medium* (New York: Fordham University Press, 2004): 300.

10 Paul Allain and Jen Harvie, *Routledge Companion to Theatre and Performance* (New York: Routlege, 2006): 168–9, emphasis in original.

11 I take the phrase "again for the first time" from Andrew Benjamin, *Present Hope: Philosophy, Architecture, Judaism* (New York: Routledge, 1997): x.

12 See Craig Owens, "Posing" in *Beyond Recognition* (Berkeley: University of California Press, 1994). Though he somewhat reductively distinguishes acting from modeling, see also David Campany, "Posing, Acting, Photography," in *Stillness and Time: Photography and the Moving Image*, David Green and Joanna Lowry, ed. (Brighton: Photoforum/Photoworks, 2006): 101–3.

13 *The New Oxford American Dictionary*, op. cit.

14 "Immediacy" often attends to definitions of "live art," a phrase for performance art employed widely in Britain. See Adrian Heathfield, ed., *Live: Art and Performance* (London: Tate Publishing, 2004). Heathfield defines the live as "immediate, immersive, interactive," (p. 8) though Henry Sayre, in the same collection, resists the limits of immediacy and prefers, usefully, to link the live, with Deleuze through Bergson, to duration. See Henry Sayre, "In the Space of Duration," in *Live: Art and Performance*, Adrian Heathfield, ed. (London: Tate Publishing, 2004): 39–44.

15 Philip Auslander, *Liveness* (New York: Routledge, 1999): 3. Auslander published a second edition in 2008. References to *Liveness* here are from the 1999 edition. Though page numbers changed, the quotes I have cited in this essay did not alter in the updated edition.

16 Auslander, *Liveness*, op. cit.: 53–4. Auslander also writes that "Live performance [. . .] exists only in the transitory present moment" (p. 132). Though the word transitory might suggest *some* duration – with the root transit meaning "to pass across or through"

– it is used here to signify too short a duration to result in what copyright law recognizes as a work "sufficiently permanent."

17 Peggy Phelan, *Unmarked: The Politics of Performance* (New York: Routledge, 1993): 3, 149.

18 It is important to note that Phelan does not romance the term "live," nor offer her terms for performance's resistance to reproduction relative to that term, and Auslander brazenly (and unapologetically) misses Phelan's larger point by twisting her claims to suit his aims. In fact, Phelan is far more interested in (live) performance's "death" – or inanimation if you will. The word "death" garners twenty-three entries in her index; there is not a single one for "live." Phelan's argument is far more complicated than Auslander's reduction will allow. While we can certainly accept Auslander's assertion about the impossibility of parsing liveness and mediatedness, we might remark that Auslander, like Hamlet, has inserted a trap into Phelan's play that Phelan herself did not pen. It could be argued that Phelan is interested in the deathness of the live. Her more nuanced argument is pitched against the "trap of visibility" by which "the real" and "representation" have been misrecognized, especially in twentieth-century identity politics, as coterminous. *Unmarked*, op. cit.: 6.

19 Ibid.: 5. Phelan was writing in 1993. Today we might act upon, or reperform, her question with an altered valence, given the fact that enhanced value is placed on immaterial labor in a twenty-first-century economy structured, increasingly, on affective services over (or even as) material goods. See Jon Erickson, *The Fate of the Object* (Ann Arbor: University of Michigan Press, 1995); Nicholas Ridout, "Performance in the Service Economy: Outsourcing and Delegation," in *Double Agent*, Claire Bishop and Sylvia Tramontana, eds. (London: Institute of Contemporary Arts, 2008) 126–31.

20 Diana Taylor, *The Archive and the Repertoire* (Durham, NC: Duke University Press, 2003). The "depreciation of live presence" is Auslander's term and he links it to the invention of technological implements for recording. For Auslander, live presence is both invented by technology, and, in that invention, simultaneously depreciated to the point that live bodies always already only come after, or cite, mediated precedents. Still, this does not lead Auslander to suggest that live bodies might (coming after) *record* media. Rather, he sees only "degradation" and "depreciation" along the lines of Baudrillard's paradigm of simulation. If "the mediatized replaces the live" and the live "incorporates the mediatized" such a mutuality might result in a revaluation of the live and an invitation to read the mediatized to be as much always already live as the live is always already mediatized. But this is not a direction preferred by Auslander, who remains nostalgically bound by the very binarized live/recorded binary he seems to resist. Auslander, *Liveness*, op. cit.: 36–9.

21 Predating Phelan's *Unmarked*, Sue-Ellen Case's important 1991 essay "Tracking the Vampire," *Differences* 3, no. 2, 1991: 1–20, is also key in this regard. Case reads for the heteronormative imperative that underscores and legislates the binarized borders marking living from dead in images and apparatus of representation. She makes very clear that the Platonic life/death binary opposition at the base of most Western ontologies is attended by a gender binary. On the matter of the inappropriateness of making "live" be antonymic to "dead," especially as regards theatre, see also Marvin Carlson, *The Haunted Stage* (Ann Arbor: University of Michigan Press, 2001).

22 Citations in this paragraph are from Auslander, *Liveness*, op. cit.: 54, 31. Phelan, *Unmarked*, op. cit.: 148, 152, 146.

23 Auslander fetishes the birth of technological reproduction as the birth of recording. He writes: "I want to emphasize that reproduction (recording) is the key issue. The Greek theatre may have been technologically mediated, if one subscribes to the theory that the masks acted as megaphones. What concerns me here, however, is technological reproduction. [. . .] I do not consider writing to be a form of recording in this context for several reasons. Scripts are blueprints for performances, not recordings of them, even though they may contain some information based on performance practice. Written descriptions and drawings or paintings of performances are not direct

transcriptions through which we access the performance itself, as aural and visual recording media are." *Liveness*, op. cit.: 52. There are worlds of disagreement between Auslander and Phelan in this regard, and between Auslander and many performance theorists who do not believe that the film, photograph, or audio recording of a performance can indicate aspects of the live any more than writing can. A recent example of the investment in the live as always only immediate is Erika Fischer-Lichte's *The Transformative Power of Performance*, which deploys the word "co-presence" and implicitly insists that it is only the living who can be co-present, despite the long history of thinking about theatre through thinking about ghosts. Fischer-Lichte, *The Transformative Power of Performance: A New Aesthetics* (New York: Routledge, 2008): 68–9. What interests me here, however, is that it is implicit in Auslander's statement that he, like Phelan and Fischer-Lichte, does not consider that live performance is itself already a means of recording in and through body-to-body transmission – what Diana Taylor might conversely situate as the recording mechanism of the repertoire, or Connerton, after Bergson, situate as body-memory – or a kind of habit-memory – certainly a durational and thus cross-temporal and non-immediate property of the live.

24 Auslander, *Liveness*, op. cit.: 51.

25 See Foreword, fn19, on "sedimented acts."

26 Mary Ann Doane, "Real Time: Instantaneity and the Photographic Imaginary," in *Stillness and Time: Photography and the Moving Image*, David Green, ed. (Brighton: Photoworks/Photoforum, 2006): 24, emphasis added.

27 Ibid.; see also the work of Nick Kaye on issues of liveness and time in relationship to performance and multi-media installation. Kaye, *Multi-Media: Video, Installation, Performance* (New York: Routledge, 2007).

28 Ibid.

29 Ibid.: 25.

30 Ibid. Contemporary investment in interactivity and immediacy in digital media parallels the thrall to a "co-presence" in theatre studies by which theorists such as Erika Fischer-Lichte re-mark performance as against media: necessarily living, immediate, and existing in an instantaneous "now" that is fundamentally shared between participants in the same space. As we see in Chapter 5, this orientation in theatre studies may in some ways respond to the history of photography and result from the limits of thinking about theatre in rigid distinction to photography. Fischer-Lichte insists that performance requires the co-presence of an actor and an audience – though the roles can be reversed – and she distinguishes this fundamentally from mediated performance. *The Transformative Power of Performance*, op. cit.: 38–74. Media theorist Mary Ann Doane's articulation of computer real time as manufacturing the "impression that something is happening *only once*" is not at all foreign to the theatre stage, where such an impression is sometimes overtly courted. And actors, too, might be acknowledged as among "the most sophisticated of repetition machines." Doane, "Real Time," op. cit.: 25. Such an accounting of theatre history might suggest, contra Fischer-Lichte, a more intermedial history of live performance in relation to media as well as a more malleable notion of co-presence informed by the complications of duration that resist determinate legislation of the boundaries of the "now."

31 Gertrude Stein, *Lectures in America*, op. cit.: 117, emphasis added.

32 Ibid.: 116.

33 Ibid.: 94, emphasis added.

34 Richard Schechner, "Theatre Criticism," *The Tulane Drama Review* 9, no. 3, 1965: 22, 24. See John Emigh's account of the genesis of Schechner's thought as it moved from theatre to performance in "Liminal Richard: A Prelude to Performance Studies" in *The Rise of Performance Studies: Rethinking Richard Schechner's Broad Spectrum*, James Harding and Cindy Rosenthal, eds. (New York: Palgrave, 2011).

35 Marcia B. Siegel, *At the Vanishing Point. A Critic Looks at Dance* (New York: Saturday Review Press, 1968): 1.

36 Richard Schechner, "TDR Comment: A Critical Evaluation of Kirby's Criticism of Criticism," *TDR: The Drama Review* 18, no. 4, 1974: 118.

37 Richard Schechner, "Performance Studies: The Broad Spectrum Approach," *TDR: The Drama Review* 32, no. 3, 1988: 4–6.

38 Herbert Blau, *Take Up The Bodies: Theater at the Vanishing Point* (Urbana: University of Illinois Press, 1982): 28.

39 See W. B. Worthen, "Drama, Performativity and Performance," *PMLA* 113, no. 5, 1998; and "Antigone's Bones," *TDR: The Drama Review* 52, no. 3, 2008. See also his *Drama: Between Poetry and Performance* (New York: Wiley Blackwell, 2010). For an example of how far scholars will take the "disappearance" trope, see Ellen MacKay, "Theatre as a Self-Consuming Art," *Theatre Survey* 49, 2009: 91–107.

40 Richard Schechner, *Between Theatre and Anthropology* (Chicago, IL: University of Chicago University Press, 1985): 50.

41 Phelan, *Unmarked*, op. cit.: 146.

42 Barbara Kirshenblatt-Gimblett, *Destination Culture: Tourism, Museums, and Heritage* (Berkeley: University of California Press, 1998): 30.

43 Joseph Roach, *Cities of the Dead: Circum-Atlantic Performance* (New York: Columbia University Press, 1996): 30.

44 José Esteban Muñoz, "Ephemera as Evidence: Introductory Notes to Queer Acts," *Women and Performance: A Journal of Feminist Theory* 8, no. 2, 1996: 10.

45 The most comprehensive book charting the development of performance studies to date is Shannon Jackson's *Professing Performance* (Cambridge: Cambridge University Press, 2004). See also Jon McKenzie, *Perform or Else: From Discipline to Performance* (New York: Routledge, 2001).

46 In 1985 Northwestern University's Department of Performance Studies was founded out of communications and the study of oral literatures. The work of Dwight Conquergood was germinal to this initiative, and though he did write of performance as "ephemeral," it was not disappearance from the visual per se that marked his investment as much as it was, after de Certeau, the "fugitivity" of the live. In 2002 he wrote: "Dominant epistemologies that link knowing with seeing are not attuned to meanings that are masked, camouflaged, indirect, embedded, or hidden in context. The visual/verbal bias of Western regimes of knowledge blinds researchers to meanings that are expressed forcefully through intonation, silence, body tension, arched eyebrows, blank stares, and other protective arts of disguise and secrecy – what de Certeau called 'the elocutionary experience of a fugitive communication.'" Conquergood, "Performance Studies: Interventions and Radical Research," *TDR: The Drama Review* 46, no. 2, 2002: 146. Shannon Jackson, who studied performance studies with Conquergood at Northwestern, wrote a brilliant and underutilized study at the cross-points between the archive and live historiography. Jackson's *Lines of Activity* troubles both the absolute "goneness" of the past and the self-evident "presentness" of ephemeral acts. *Lines of Activity: Performance, Historiography, Hull-House Domesticity* (Ann Arbor: University of Michigan Press, 2000). On trouble with the trope of the "fugitive," see Tavia Nyong'o, *The Amalgamation Waltz: Race, Performance, and the Ruses of Memory* (Minneapolis: University of Minnesota Press, 2009): 40–1 and 152–4.

47 A footnote on the re-do: The essay is here altered somewhat from the original publication – modifications that bear the marks of the essay's promiscuous afterlife. The essay was first published in the journal *Performance Research*. However, for some reason I received an unusual number of requests for the essay from readers who could not locate it – and requests for the essay increased after it was cited by Diana Taylor in *The Archive and the Repertoire* in 2003. Thus, more than any other of my writings, this essay has had an ethernet afterlife in the form of the manuscript changing hands, or jumping screens, in what seemed an irregular fashion. In the afterlife of the publication, I fairly regularly tripped in the delivery of my speech – if "delivery" is a

word that might be used not only for oral speaking but for sending and receiving a text. I made changes for publications in Italian and Spanish and another for republication in English. When the manuscript was occasionally requested, I sent out whichever latest modification I had made. My promiscuity resulted in now untrackable alterations. Why discuss the tracks of its errant travels? The resilient habit in performance and theatre studies of demarking "discourse" from "practice" – or "text" from "act" – too often resolidifies a faulty binary. I continue to be interested in how literature may in fact be orature (and orature, literature) – a live transmission despite the materiality of printing – in a long and ongoing story more about circulation than about archival stasis. More, that is, about *tripping* in the meantime. Less about "death of the author" than about call and response occasions of and for the cross-temporal live.

48 Richard Schechner, "Theatre Criticism," 1965, op. cit.: 22. Emphasis in original.
49 Marcia B. Siegel, *At the Vanishing Point*, 1968, op. cit.: 1.
50 Herbert Blau, *Take Up the Bodies*, 1982, op. cit.: 94.
51 Ibid.: 28.
52 Building explicitly on Phelan, Jane Blocker's *Where Is Ana Mendieta* provides an example of art history's application of the ephemerality of performance as informed through performance studies. Blocker employed the equation of performance with disappearance to suggest that performance is the antithesis of "saving" in *Where Is Ana Mendieta: Identity, Performativity, and Exile* (Durham, NC: Duke University Press, 1999): 134. See Blocker's own important complication of this position in her subsequent book, *What the Body Cost* (Minneapolis: University of Minnesota Press 2004): 105–7.
53 Jacques Le Goff, *History and Memory* (New York: Columbia University Press, 1992): xvii.
54 See Richard Thomas, *The Imperial Archive: Knowledge and the Fantasy of Empire* (New York: Verso, 1993). The articulation of Greek antiquity as forefathering history itself is mythic. The "disremembering" of other lineages ultimately served Eurocentric, geopolitical, racializing agendas. See Martin Bernal, *Black Athena* (New Brunswick, NJ: Rutgers University Press, 1989).
55 Jacques Derrida, *Archive Fever: A Freudian Impression* (Chicago, IL: University of Chicago Press, 1995): 2. In the late 1960s, reaching English readers in the early 1970s, Michel Foucault had expanded the notion of "the archive" beyond a material, architectural housing of documents and objects to include, more broadly, structures of enunciability at all. Foucault articulated "the archive" as essentially discursive – invested of *an investment in* preservation – determining not only the "system of enunciability" (what can be said) but also the duration of any enunciation (what is given to remain becomes *what can have been said*). An excerpt from Foucault's *The Archaeology of Knowledge* bears repeating: "The archive is first the law of what can be said, the system that governs the appearance of statements as unique events. But the archive is also that which determines that all these things said do not accumulate endlessly in an amorphous mass, nor are they inscribed in an unbroken linearity, nor do they disappear at the mercy of chance external accidents; but they are grouped together in distinct figures [. . .] The archive is not that which, despite its immediate escape, safeguards the event of the statement, and preserves, for future memories, its status as an escapee; it is that which, at the very root of the statement-event, and in that which embodies it, defines at the outset *the system of its enunciability*. Nor is the archive that which collects the dust of statements that have become inert once more, and which may make possible the miracle of their resurrection; it is that which defines the mode of occurrence of the statement-thing; it is *the system of its functioning*." In *The Archaeology of Knowledge*, trans. Alan Sheridan (London: Tavistock, 1972): 129, emphasis in original.
56 See Keith Piper's installation, *Relocating the Remains* (London: Institute of International Visual Artists, 1997). The work of Suzan-Lori Parks is also exemplary. See Harry Elam and Alice Rayner, "Unfinished Business: Reconfiguring History in Suzan-Lori

Parks's *The Death of the Last Black Man in the Whole Entire World*," *Theatre Journal* 46, no. 4, 1994: 447–61.

57 Kobena Mercer, "To Unbury the Disremembered Past: Keith Piper," in *New Histories* (exhibition catalogue), Milena Kalinovska, ed. (Boston, MA: Institute of Contemporary Arts, 1996): 165.

58 Paul Schimmel, "Leap Into the Void: Performance and the Object," in *Out of Actions: Between Performance and the Object*, Paul Schimmel, ed. (Los Angeles: Museum of Contemporary Art, 1998): 17.

59 Comments made at the panel "Documentation in the Absence of Text," during the conference "Performance and Text: Thinking and Doing," sponsored by the Department of Theatre Arts, Columbia University, New York, May 2–4, 1997.

60 See Jonas Barish, *The Antitheatrical Prejudice* (Berkeley: University of California Press, 1981); Samuel Weber, *Theatricality as Medium*, op. cit. That a distrust of mimesis should develop simultaneously with the development of archives in ancient Greece deserves greater analysis, especially given the fact that the first Greek archives did not house originals but seconds. The first archives were used to store legal documents that were not originals but official copies of text inscribed on stone monuments placed around the city. The documents were copies of stone markers that were themselves "mnemonic aids" – not, that is, the "thing" preserved. See Rosalind Thomas, *Literacy and Orality in Ancient Greece* (Cambridge: Cambridge University Press, 1992): 86–7. Thus the first archived documents *backed up* a performance-oriented memory intended to be encountered live in the form of monuments, art, and architecture. On the classical art of memory as performance-oriented, see Francis Yates, *The Art of Memory* (Chicago, IL: University of Chicago Press, 1966): 1–49.

61 Derrida, *Archive Fever*, op. cit.: 2.

62 See footnote 60 on mnemonic mapping. On social power over memory, Derrida writes: "The meaning of 'archive,' its only meaning, comes to it from the Greek *arkheion*: initially a house, a domicile, an address, the residence of the superior magistrates, the *archons*, those who commanded. The citizens who thus held and signified political power were considered to possess the right to make or to represent the law. On account of their publicly recognized authority, it is at their home, in that *place* which is their house (private house, family house, or employees' house), that official documents are filed." Derrida, *Archive Fever*, op. cit.: 2. But ancient archival practice is more complicated than Derrida lets on. In ancient Greece the word archive was not used to refer to the housing of original documents. See James P. Sickinger, *Public Records and Archives in Classical Athens* (Chapel Hill: University of North Carolina Press, 1999): 6. I have alluded to this briefly in footnote 60, but to complicate matters, the first official (though not the only) storeroom for documents in Ancient Greece was the Metroon – the sanctuary of the Mother of the Gods. The Metroon was established in part to bring some order to official documents that had been scattered in the keeping of the archons.

63 See Ann Laura Stoller, "Colonial Archives and the Arts of Governance," *Archival Science* 2, nos. 1&2, 2002: 87–109; and her *Along the Archival Grain: Epistemic Anxieties and Colonial Common Sense* (Princeton, NJ: Princeton University Press, 2009). See also Richard Thomas, *Imperial Archive*, op. cit.

64 Psychoanalysis certainly posits flesh as archive, but an inchoate and unknowing archive. Is it a given in all circumstances that body memory is "unknowing" and "blind"? See Rebecca Schneider, "Judith Butler in My Hands," in *Bodily Citations: Religion and Judith Butler*, Ellen Armour and Susan St. Ville, eds. (New York: Columbia University Press, 2006).

65 In his influential book *Orality and Literacy: The Technologizing of the Word*, Walter Ong makes the claim that because they are performance based, oral traditions do not leave "residue," make no "deposit," do not remain. Arguably, this claim is debunked by his own insistence that many habits from oral culture persist. *Orality and Literacy* (New

York: Methuen, 1982): 11. On the issue of body memory in general see Paul Connerton, *How Societies Remember* (Cambridge: Cambridge University Press, 1989). Connerton surprisingly situates bodily memory as extremely fixed and unchanging. This aspect is critiqued by Neil Jarman in *Material Conflicts: Parades and Visual Displays in Northern Ireland* (Oxford: Berg Publishers, 1997): 11. See also the work of Susan Leigh Foster, Mark Franko, Fred Moten.

66 Le Goff's work provides an example of the troubled leap from oral history to ritual to ethnicity and from ethnicity to "peoples without writing." Le Goff, *History and Memory*, op. cit.: 55.

67 Richard Thomas, *Imperial Archive*, 993, op. cit.: 11.

68 Cultural historians now accept popular and aesthetic representation generally as social modes of historicization, often under Maurice Halbwachs's rubric "collective memory." See Halbwachs, *On Collective Memory* (Chicago, IL: University of Chicago Press). Still, the process of approaching aesthetic production as valid historiography involves careful (and debated) delineation between "memory," "myth," "ritual," and "tradition" on the one hand and the implicitly more legitimate (or supposedly non-mythic) "history" on the other. See Michael Kammen. *Mystic Chords of Memory: The Transformation of Tradition in American Culture* (New York: Vintage Books, 1993): 25–32.

69 Le Goff, *History and Memory* op. cit.: 95–6.

70 Marvin Carlson, "Performing the Past: Living History and Cultural Memory" *Paragrana* 9, no. 2, 2000: 237–48. See also Tony Horwitz, *Confederates in the Attic: Dispatches from the Unfinished Civil War* (New York: Vintage, 1999): 7–8.

71 See Vanessa Agnew on the myriad problems that arise for historians who attempt to credit live reenactment as any kind of access to history or any kind of complement to the historical record. As discussed in Chapter 1, Agnew accuses reenactment of "theatre." She rather reductively associates theatre with one of its historical modes – romantic sentimentalism – rather than, say, associating theatre with Brechtian alienated historicization. Agnew's primary critique of living history and reenactment is that the focus on reenactors' experiences sentimentalizes and subjectivizes history. See Vanessa Agnew, "Introduction: What is Reenactment?" *Criticism* 46, no. 3, 2004: 335. But the case of the corpse is problematic. For, at least as described by Horwitz, *Confederates in the Attic*, 1999 op. cit.: 7–8, Hodge is not naïve enough to think that he fully experiences what it means to be a corpse, even if it is true that his (mock) fallen body may (mock) alarm other (mock) soldiers who come upon it on the (mock) battlefield.

72 Stefan Brecht, "Family of the f.p.: Notes on the Theatre of the Ridiculous," *TDR: The Drama Review* 13, no. 1, 1968: 120.

73 See Fred Moten and Charles Henry Rowell, "'Words Don't Go There': An Interview with Fred Moten," *Callaloo* 27, no. 4, 2004: 954–66.

74 Blau, *Take Up the Bodies*, op.cit.: 137.

75 See Schneider, "Judith Butler in My Hands," op. cit.

76 Derrida, *Archive Fever*, op. cit.: 95.

77 Ann Pellegrini, *Performance Anxieties: Staging Psychoanalysis, Staging Race* (New York: Routledge, 1997): 69.

78 See Schneider, "Hello Dolly Well Hello Dolly: The Double and Its Theatre," in *Psychoanalysis and Performance*, Peter Campbell and Adrian Kear, eds. (New York: Routledge, 2001).

79 Suzan-Lori Parks, *Death of the Last Black Man in the Whole Entire World*, in *The America Play and Other Works* (New York: Theatre Communications Group, 1995).

80 See Tavia Nyong'o, *Amalgamation Waltz*, op. cit.: 152–3, for engagement with oral history and "official" history in the example of Jefferson's descendents and the "hidden in plain sight" theory of quilting patterns. Nyong'o, reminding us fulsomely throughout his book of the race politics always sedimented in debates about history

and memory, writes that "at issue was less a choice between the archive and memory and more a context over black representative space in memory [. . .] less a competition between 'elite' and 'folk' knowledge and more of a competition between academic and mass culture over the pedagogic stakes of remembrance" (p. 153). Nyong'o's comments of the generative aspects of "myth," "error," and "mistake," and the palimpsest of racial politics that inform the stakes in mistake, are extremely useful as well.

81 See the chapter on Spiderwoman in Rebecca Schneider, *The Explicit Body in Performance* (New York: Routledge, 1997).

82 Suzan-Lori Parks, "Elements of Style" in *The America Play and Other Works*, op. cit.: 13 emphasis in original.

83 What follows is a partial list of mis-citations, which nevertheless cannot be considered "wrong." Jessica Santone, "Marina Abramović's *Seven Easy Pieces*: Critical Documentation Strategies for Preserving Art's History," *Leonardo* 41, no. 2, 2008: 147–52; Harvey Young, "The Black Body as Souvenir in American Lynching," *Theatre Journal* 57, no. 4, 2005: 639–57; Jennifer DeVere Brody, *Punctuation: Art, Politics, and Play* (Durham, NC: Duke University Press, 2008).

84 Diana Taylor, *The Archive and the Repertoire*, op. cit.: 36–7.

85 See Carolyn Kay Steedman, *Dust: The Archive and Cultural History* (New Brunswick, NJ: Rutgers University Press, 2002).

86 Diana Taylor, *The Archive and the Repertoire*, op. cit.: 37.

87 Ibid.: 37.

88 Ibid.: 8.

89 Ibid.: 36.

90 Ibid.: 22, 37.

91 Ibid.: 20.

92 Ibid.: 16.

93 See W. B. Worthen, "Shakespeare 3.0: The Remix," in *Alternative Shakespeares 3*, Diana Henderson, ed. (London: Routledge, 2007): 54–5, and "Antigone's Bones," op. cit. for a similar critique of the resilience of the binary in Taylor's *Archive and the Repertoire*.

94 Derrida, *Archive Fever*, op. cit.: 3.

95 Ibid.: 33–4.

96 Ibid.: 36.

97 Ibid.: 37.

98 Ibid.: 84–5.

99 For Derrida, the theory of psychoanalysis is a "theory of the archive and not only a theory of memory." *Archive Fever*, op. cit.: 19.

100 Ibid.: 61, emphasis in original.

101 Ibid.: 84.

102 See Roland Barthes, *Camera Lucida*, trans. Richard Howard (New York: Hill and Wang, 1982).

103 Stein, *Lectures in America*, op. cit.: 94.

104 Derrida's general proposition is that processes of signification in representation are "no longer conceivable on the basis of the opposition presence/absence" but rather engage the "generative movement in the play of differences" that are undecideable. Jacques Derrida, *Positions*, trans. Alan Bass (Chicago, IL: University of Chicago Press, 1981): 27.

4 Poor poor theatre

1 The Wooster Group, *Poor Theater: A Series of Simulacra* program, The Performing Garage, New York, 18 February–24 April, 2004.

2 Jerzy Grotowski, "*Tu es le fils de quelqu'un* [You are someone's son]," *TDR: The Drama Review* 31, no. 3, 1987: 30–41. See also Kermit Dunkelberg, "Confrontation,

Simulation, Admiration: The Wooster Group's *Poor Theater*." *TDR: The Drama Review* 49, no. 3, 2005: 43–57.

3 See Naomi Schor, *Reading in Detail: Aesthetics and the Feminine* (New York: Routledge, 1987). See also Sandra Gilbert and Susan Gubar's *The Madwoman in the Attic* for its effort to rethink Harold Bloom's thesis on the "anxiety of influence" as regards female authors who can not be "someone's son." *The Madwoman in the Attic: The Woman Writer and the Nineteenth-Century Literary Imagination* (New Haven, CT: Yale University Press, 1979). In the context of LeCompte, of course, the reference would be women directors. On feminist generationality and issues particular to feminist "lineage," see Robyn Wiegman, "Feminism's Apocalyptic Futures," *New Literary History* 31, no. 4, 2000: 805–25.

4 David Romàn, *Performance in America: Contemporary US Culture and the Performing Arts* (Durham, NC: Duke University Press 2005): 137–78.

5 On thinking through touch and negotiating borders between sameness and difference, see Carolyn Dinshaw, *Getting Medieval: Sexual Communities Pre- and Post-Modern* (Durham, NC: Duke University Press, 1999): 1–54. See also Laura U. Marks, *The Skin of the Film: Intercultural Cinema, Embodiment and the Senses* (Durham, NC: Duke University Press, 2000); and Eve Kosofsky Sedgwick, *Touching Feeling: Affect, Pedagogy, Performativity* (Durham, NC: Duke University Press, 2003). On the "touch" of trauma, see Ann Cvetkovich, *An Archive of Feelings: Trauma, Sexuality, and Lesbian Public Cultures* (Durham, NC: Duke University Press, 2003): 49–82.

6 Walter Benjamin, "The Task of the Translator," in *Illuminations*, trans. Harry Zohn (New York: Schocken Books, 1968): 78.

7 Marvin Carlson, *The Haunted Stage: The Theatre as Memory Machine* (Ann Arbor: University of Michigan Press, 2001).

8 This in itself is not unlike precedent Wooster Group works-in-progress where the footprint of a previous show, or some set structure of that show, remains on the stage of the "new" work-in-progress. See David Savran, *Breaking the Rules: The Wooster Group* (New York: Theatre Communications Group, 1988).

9 I am indebted to correspondence with the dramaturg, Sam Gold, about these details.

10 Kermit Dunkelberg situates the production succinctly writing: "I see the Wooster Group's production in light of the history of reception/rejection/appropriation of Grotowski's work in the United States. In the wake of Grotowski's first American workshop at New York University in 1967, Richard Schechner founded the Performance Group. In the mid-1970s, the Wooster Group grew out of the Performance Group, becoming an independent entity in 1980." Dunkelberg, "Confrontation, Simulation, Admiration," op. cit.: 43.

11 Jerzy Grotowski, *Towards a Poor Theatre* (New York: Simon and Schuster, 1968): 33–7, 77, 133. Grotowski's theatre sought the pure act, a search that still resonates as a certain heritage for performance art, often taking place today in art museums. See Rebecca Schneider and Gabrielle Cody, "General Introduction" to *Re:Direction* (New York: Routledge, 2001), for an account of the connections that might be charted from naturalism in theatre through Artaud and Grotowski to performance art.

12 Jerzy Grotowski, *Towards a Poor Theatre*, op. cit.: 19.

13 Philip Auslander, "Toward a Concept of the Political in Postmodern Theatre," *Theatre Journal* 39, no. 1, 1987: 20–34.

14 Personal correspondence with Sam Gold, July 2004.

15 In her essay "Between History and Memory: Auschwitz in Akropolis, Akropolis in Auschwitz," Magda Romanska tells us that Wyspianski's work on *Akropolis* (1904), in which cathedral statues come to life, led him to work simultaneously on *Hamlet*. Similarly, "*Akropolis* was not the only text by Wyspianski that Grotowski adapted; he also adapted *Studium o Hamlecie* (*A Study on Hamlet*) in 1964, which Wyspianski wrote around the same time as he wrote *Akropolis* (*Studium* was published in 1905, a year after *Akropolis*). [. . .] Grotowski, though, considered his adaptation of *Studium* a failed

project, and he did not include it in his list of accomplishments." Magda Romanska, "Between History and Memory: Auschwitz in *Akropolis, Akropolis* in Auschwitz," *Theatre Survey* 50, no. 2, 2009: 227, 248. That LeCompte went on to stage *Hamlet* after *Poor Theater* resonates with this history.

16 To think about this transposition further, the work of Giorgio Agamben might be helpful. On the "divine terror" of premodern art in which the "wonders" of the cathedral become paradigmatic, see *The Man Without Content* (Stanford, CA: Stanford University Press, 1999): 4, 34. For his argument that the concentration camp is the "biopolitical paradigm of the modern" see *Homo Sacer: Sovereign Power and Bare Life* (Stanford, CA: Stanford University Press, 1998): 117.

17 Elizabeth Hardwick, "The Theater of Grotowski," *New York Review of Books* 14, no. 3, February 12, 1970.

18 Ibid.

19 LeCompte told Kermit Dunkelberg in 2004 that she saw Grotowski's *Akropolis* in New York (where it was re-staged in 1969) and recalled thinking: "That's interesting stuff, but it's – you know, it's 'Polish drag.' It was something weird. It was beautiful, and Catholic, and male, and 'over there' somewhere." She was struck by the "intimacy" of *Akropolis*, particularly "the incredibly big performances next to very uncomfortable people" and how "wonderfully skilled" the actors were. Cited in Dunkelberg, "Confrontation, Simulation, Admiration," op. cit.: 44.

20 I am reminded of a passage I cited in the Foreword, from Michel de Certeau's *The Practice of Everyday Life:* "The passing faces on the street seem [. . .] to multiply the indecipherable and nearby secret of the monument" suggesting, as we return to in Chapter 5, that the stone and the live inter(in)animate each other in the pass. De Certeau, *The Practice of Everyday Life,* trans. Steven F. Rendall, (Berkeley: University of California Press, 1984): 15.

21 See Hal Foster, "Return of the Real," in *Return of the Real* (Cambridge, MA: MIT Press, 1996).

22 On the impossibility of "fixing" in general – both regarding language and bodily acts – see Judith Butler, *Excitable Speech: A Politics of the Performative* (New York: Routledge, 1997).

23 Richard Schechner, "Actuals: A Look into Performance Theory," in *The Rarer Action: Essays in Honor of Frances Ferguson,* Alan Cheuse and Richard Koffler, eds. (New Brunswick, NJ: Rutgers University Press, 1970): 97–135; Chris Thompson and Katarina Wieslien, "Pure Raw: Performance, Pedagogy, and (Re)Presentation, an Interview with Marina Abramović," *PAJ: Performing Arts Journal* 82, 2006: 39.

24 Jacques Derrida, *Archive Fever: A Freudian Impression* (Chicago, IL: University of Chicago Press, 1995): 37. This quote is unpacked in greater depth in Chapter 3.

25 Søren Kierkegaard, *Fear and Trembling/Repetition,* trans. Howard V. Hong and Edna H. Hong (Princeton, NJ: Princeton University Press, 1983): 131.

26 See Jon McKenzie, *Perform or Else: From Discipline to Performance* (New York: Routledge, 2001).

27 Richard Schechner, *The End of Humanism: Writings on Performance* (New York: PAJ Publications, 1982).

28 Richard Schechner, "Mainstream Theatre and Performance Studies," *TDR: The Drama Review* 44, no. 2, 2000: 6.

29 W. B. Worthen, "Shakespeare 3.0: Or Text Versus Performance, the Remix," in *Alternative Shakespeares 3,* Diana Henderson, ed. (London: Routledge, 2007): 68.

30 On a basic antitheatricality in modernity, functioning as a crucible for "resistance" to theatricality that simultaneously depends upon the theatre it resists, see Martin Puchner, *Stage Fright: Modernism, Antitheatricality and Drama* (Baltimore, MD: Johns Hopkins University Press, 2002): 2.

31 Richard Schechner, "Actuals" op. cit.: 99. I cite the original here. The passage was only slightly edited in subsequent editions of *Performance Theory* to add "happenings" to

the list of avant-gardes (see Richard Schechner, *Performance Theory*, New York: Routledge, 1988: 36). For his account of the word "actual" see also Richard Schechner, *Between Theater and Anthropology* (Chicago, IL: University of Chicago Press, 1985): 115, fn4.

32 On antitheatricality in Schechner's work in particular – and the "turf war," to quote David Savran, between performance studies and theatre studies – see Stephen J. Bottoms, "The Efficacy/Effeminacy Braid: Unpicking the Performance Studies/Theatre Studies Dichotomy," *Theatre Topics* 13, no. 2, 2003: 173–87. David Savran, "Choices Made and Unmade," *Theater* 31, no. 2, 2001: 89–107.

33 Schechner, "Actuals," op. cit.: 115–16.

34 See Pamela Lee, *Chronophobia: On Time in the Art of the 1960s* (Cambridge, MA: MIT Press, 2004). Grotowski provides an excellent example of the drive towards essentialism in "poor theatre" that so impressed Schechner. For Grotowski, the essential would result from "eliminating whatever proved superfluous." Grotowski, *Towards a Poor Theatre*, op. cit.: 19.

35 Schechner, "Actuals," op. cit.: 103. This sentence remains unedited across the editions, appearing the same in 2003: 32.

36 Mircea Eliade, *Rites and Symbols of Initiation* (New York: Harper and Row, 1965): 6.

37 Mircea Eliade, *The Sacred and the Profane: The Nature of Religion*, trans. Willard R. Trask (New York: Harcourt, 1959): 70.

38 Schechner, *Between Theater and Anthropology*, op. cit.: 35–6.

39 Schechner footnotes his earlier essay "Actuals" in *Between Theater and Anthropology* but is careful to let his sense of "actual" not extend to actual *history*. He writes that an event to be restored has "either been forgotten, never was, or is overlaid with so much secondary stuff that its actuality-in-history is lost." Schechner, *Between Theater and Anthropology*, op. cit.: 50. This is slightly confusing, when he has admitted on the same page that history is "what has been constructed out of events." Would not "actuality-in-history" already be an actuality *in* repetition? Restored behavior *is* actual, and actuality *is*, then, composed in and through the fore and aft of repetition.

40 Ibid.

41 Ibid.: 51.

42 Judith Butler, "Performative Acts and Gender Constitution: An Essay in Phenomenology and Feminist Theory," *Theatre History* 40, 1988: 519–38. Reprinted in *Performing Feminisms: Feminist Critical Theory and Theatre*, Sue-Ellen Case, ed., 270–82 (Baltimore, MD: Johns Hopkins University Press, 1990): 274.

43 Margaret Thompson Drewal has written on the paradoxical nature of this point regarding performance theory and Yoruban ritual. See *Yoruba Ritual: Performers, Play, Agency* (Bloomington: Indiana University Press, 1992).

44 Schechner, *Between Theater and Anthropology*, op. cit.: 92.

45 Schechner sums up his theories on make-believe versus make belief in *Performance Studies: An Introduction* (New York: Routledge, 2002): 35. On education as "make belief" one might reread Louis Althusser's important "Ideology and Ideological State Apparatuses" to invest "restored behavior" with a theory of the social in modernity. "Ideology and Ideological State Apparatuses (Notes Toward an Investigation)," in *Lenin and Philosophy and Other Essays*, trans. Ben Brewster (New York: Monthly Review Press, 1971): 127–88.

46 Victor Turner, *From Ritual to Theatre: The Human Seriousness of Play* (New York: PAJ Books, 1982); Richard Schechner, *Between Theater and Anthropology*, op. cit.; Richard Schechner, "From Ritual to Theatre and Back: The Structure/Process of the Efficacy-Entertainment Dyad," *Educational Theatre Journal* 26: 4, 1974: 455–81. See also Mircea Eliade, *The Myth of the Eternal Return* (Princeton, NJ: Princeton University Press, 2005 [1954]). Eliade, something of an essentialist, applied the term "eternal return" to what he saw as a universal religious belief in the ability to reverse or arrest time through myth and ritual. Earlier, Friedrich Nietzsche posited "eternal return" as

a fundamental question, the possibility of which haunts the modern. See Nietzsche's *The Gay Science: With a Prelude Rhymes and an Appendix of Songs*, trans. Walter Kaufmann (New York: Vintage, 1974) and *Thus Spoke Zarathustra*, trans. R. J. Hollingdale (New York: Penguin, 1961). See Martin Heidegger, *Nietzsche. Volume II: The Eternal Recurrence of the Same*, trans. David Farrell Krell (New York: Harper and Row, 1984). See Sven Lütticken's discussion of Nietzsche, Benjamin, and Deleuze on "eternal return" in the context of reenactment in Lütticken, "An Arena in Which to Reenact," in *Life Once More: Forms of Re-enactment in Contemporary Art*, Sven Lütticken, ed. (Rotterdam: Witte de With Institute, 2005): 43–5.

47 Fred Moten, "Not In Between: Lyric Painting, Visual History and the Postcolonial Future," *TDR: The Drama Review* 47, no. 1, 2003: 134.

48 On hyphen trouble, puntuation, intermediality and performance see Jennifer DeVere Brody, *Punctuation: Art, Politics, and Play* (Durham, NC: Duke University Press, 2008).

49 Debates about "relational" art are vital to this discussion. See Nicolas Bourriaud, *Relational Aesthetics* (Paris: Les Presses Du Réel, 1998); Claire Bishop, "Antagonism and Relational Aesthetics," *October* 110, 2004: 51–79; Stewart Martin, "Critique of Relational Aesthetics," *Third Text* 21 no. 4, 2007: 369–86; Shannon Jackson, *Social Works: Performing Publics* (New York: Routledge, 2011).

50 See Shannon Jackson, *Social Works*, op. cit.

51 Lucy Lippard, *Six Years: The Dematerialization of the Art Object, 1966–1972* (Berkeley: University of California Press, 1997). See also Julia Bryan-Wilson, *Art Workers: Radical Practice in the Vietnam Era.* (Berkeley: University of California Press, 2009): 94–5. On the phrase "dematerialization" as misleading, see Dorothea von Hantelmann, *How to Do Things with Art* (Zurich: JRP/Ringier, 2010): 144.

52 Carrie Lambert-Beatty, "Performance Police," unpublished paper presented at "Thinking Performance," The Guggenheim Museum, June 18, 2010.

53 Abramović cited in Chris Thompson and Katarina Weslien, "Pure Raw: Performance, Pedagogy, and (Re)Presentation, an Interview with Marina Abramović," *PAJ: Performing Arts Journal* 82, 2006: 29–50; Abramović cited in Fabio Cypriano, "Performance and Reenactment: Analyzing Marina Abramović's *Seven Easy Pieces*," Idanca.net, available online at http://idanca.net/lang/en-us/2009/09/02/performance-e-reencenacao-uma-analise-de-seven-eeasy-pieces-de-marina-abramovic/12156/ (written September 2009, accessed March 10, 2010).

54 See curator Klaus Biesenbach's comment in the MoMA instructional video, available online at http://www.moma.org/interactives/exhibitions/2010/marinaabramovic/conversation.html (accessed April 2010).

55 See Rebecca Schneider, "Patricide and the Passerby," in *Performance and the City*, D. J. Hopkins, Shelley Orr and Kim Solga, eds. (New York: Palgrave, 2009).

56 See Julia Bryan Wilson, *Art Workers: Radical Practice in the Vietnam War Era* (Berkeley: University of California Press, 2009), particularly the chapter on Lucy Lippard.

57 "The peculiar burden and problem of the theatre is that there is no *original artwork at all*." Richard Schechner, "Theatre Criticism," *The Tulane Drama Review* 9, no. 3, 1965: 22, emphasis in original.

58 For efforts at exact representation of original performance described as "slavish" versus "artistic," see Sven Lütticken, "Introduction," in *Life, Once More: Forms of Reenactment in Contemporary Art*, op. cit.: 5. Though Lütticken is not referencing theatre precisely here, in an ambitious essay titled "An Arena in which to Reenact," Lütticken appears to follow a Pollockian "distinction between authentic non-theatrical acts and 'phony' play-acting" in which play-acting becomes synonymous with the non-creative and unartistic. Indeed, throughout the essay, "acting" is linked distinctly with the passive neoliberal subject in postindustrial capitalism who uncritically performs a limited palette of affects. For Lütticken, *artistic* reenactment might interrupt this passivity, but not through the "slavish" mechanisms of exact repetition – in distinction to what I have been arguing above regarding the Wooster's Group's efforts in *Poor*

Theater. Lütticken, "An Arena in Which to Reenact," in *Life, Once More: Forms of Reenactment in Contemporary Art,* op. cit.: 21–3.

59 Guillermo Gómez-Peña, *Ethno-techno: Writings on Performance, Activism, and Pedagogy* (New York: Routledge, 2005): 26, emphasis added.

60 *Life, Once More: Forms of Reenactment in Contemporary Art.* Exhibit at the Witte de With Center for Contemporary Arts, Rotterdam, 2005. The citation is taken from the website project description at http://www.wdw.nl/project.php?id=36. The text echoes a similar reference to Pollock in Sven Lütticken, "An Arena in Which to Reenact," op. cit.: 21–3.

61 Philip Auslander, "The Performativity of Performance Documentation," *PAJ: A Journal of Performance and Art* 28, no. 3, 2006: 2; Nancy Spector, "Seven Easy Pieces," in *Marina Abramović: The Artist Is Present,* Klaus Biesenbach, ed. (New York: The Museum of Modern Art, 2010): 39.

62 See the promotional "product description" for the first edition of Marina Abramović, *Seven Easy Pieces* (New York: Charta, 2007) on Amazon.com. Spector, op cit.: 39.

63 Cited in Jennifer Allen, "Performance Anxiety: On 'A Little Bit of History Repeated,'" *Artforum,* March 2002: 42, emphasis added.

64 Ibid.

65 Ibid., emphasis added.

66 See Julia Bryan-Wilson, *Art Workers,* op. cit., especially 94–5. In 1976 artist Carl Andre referred to artists' labor in relation to the museum as "slave practice" (a term that Bryan-Wilson discusses for its problems and blindspots). Given the investment in labor so prevalent in 1960s–1970s performance-based work (including among feminist artists who often explored "women's work") the question can be raised as to whether, contra Lütticken, Hoffmann, and Gómez-Peña, the explicit hire of performers might actually touch something true about the pieces – at the level, even, of critique. Cited in Bryan-Wilson, *Art Workers,* op. cit.: 36.

67 Grotowski discusses the actor's "sacrifice" in *Towards a Poor Theatre,* op. cit.: 256. At first glance, "sacrifice," with its religious overtones, seems antithetical to the materialist critique of labor under capitalism. However, Marx was clear on the connection, even using the word "sacrifice" to describe the situation for the alienated worker. In *The Economic and Philosophical Manuscripts of 1844,* Marx writes: "First, the fact that labor is external to the worker, i.e., it does not belong to his intrinsic nature; that in his work, therefore, he does not affirm himself but denies himself, does not feel content but unhappy, does not develop freely his physical and mental energy but mortifies his body and ruins his mind. The worker therefore only feels himself outside his work, and in his work feels outside himself. He feels at home when he is not working, and when he is working he does not feel at home. His labor is therefore not voluntary, but coerced; it is *forced labor.* It is therefore not the satisfaction of a need; it is merely a means to satisfy needs external to it. Its alien character emerges clearly in the fact that as soon as no physical or other compulsion exists, labor is shunned like the plague. External labor, labor in which man alienates himself, is a labor of self-sacrifice, of mortification. Lastly, the external character of labor for the worker appears in the fact that it is not his own, but someone else's, that it does not belong to him, that in it he belongs, not to himself, but to another. Just as in religion the spontaneous activity of the human imagination, of the human brain and the human heart, operates on the individual independently of him – that is, operates as an alien, divine or diabolical activity – so is the worker's activity not his spontaneous activity. It belongs to another; it is the loss of his self." Marx, *The Economic and Philosophical Manuscripts of 1844,* in *Karl Marx: A Reader,* Jon Elster, ed., 35–46 (Cambridge: Cambridge University Press, 1986): 39–40. Marx's articulation of "forced labor" might ring in relevant ways with the trouble some curators have with "slavish" imitation and the "actor for hire" issue that haunts artwork composed of delegated performances today. Marx is working on a model of authenticity (an authentic self that can be lost) that resembles the drive for

the purity of performance articulated by Abramović. The *outsourced* "pure" performer, in this context, would seem an oxymoron. Grotowski's actors make their "sacrifice" explicit as labor – and, in the context of the prison, their labor re-performs "forced labor." In LeCompte's reenactment, imitation is so overt that it might court Lütticken's or Andre's description as "slavish." Their performances are, in Brecht's sense after Marx, alienated. More should be done with the problems and promises of explicitly alienated (or realienated) performance in reenactment, especially as concerns the trouble with the outsourced "actor for hire."

68 Dorothea von Hantelmann, *How to Do Things with Art*, op. cit.: 137, emphasis added.

69 One such example appears in "Art world drama! Tino Sehgal calls The New York Times 'crass.'" Available on line at http://www.wmagazine.com/w/blogs/editorsblog/2010/02/04/art-world-drama-tino-seghal-ca.htm#ixzz0uF510D2y.

70 Arthur Lubow, "Making Art Out of an Encounter," *The New York Times Magazine*, January 15, 2010: 24.

71 On "scriptive things" see Robin Bernstein, "Dances with Things: Material Culture and the Performance of Race," *Social Text* 27, no. 4, 2010: 67–94, discussed at greater length in Chapter 5.

72 Dorothea von Hantelmann, *How to Do Things With Art*, op. cit.: 150.

73 Frazer McIvor, "Tino Sehgal's Living Sculptures" in the webzine *Escape in to Life*, February 11, 2010. Available online at http://www.escapeintolife.com/art-reviews/tino-sehgal-living-sculptures/ (accessed February 20, 2010).

74 The full text on the website reads: "In an endeavor to transmit the presence of the artist and make her historical performances accessible to a larger audience, the exhibition includes the first live re-performances of Abramović's works by *other people* ever to be undertaken in a museum setting. In addition, a new, original work performed by Abramović will mark the longest duration of time that she has performed a single solo piece. [. . .] All performances, one of which involves viewer participation, will take place throughout the entire duration of the exhibition, starting before the Museum opens each day and continuing until after it closes, to allow visitors to experience the timelessness of the works" (emphasis added). The names of the "other people" are listed separately near the bottom of the website. The "viewer participation" piece was Abramović's new work, in which she sat stone still in a floor-length gown, allowing spectators to, one by one, sit opposite her. Available online at http://www.moma.org/visit/calendar/exhibitions/965 (accessed May 22, 2010).

75 Claire Bishop, "Outsourcing Authenticity? Delegated Performance in Contemporary Art," in *Double Agent*, Claire Bishop and Sylvia Tramontana, eds. (London: Institute of Contemporary Arts, 2008): 119.

76 On this question see Nicholas Ridout, "Performance in the Service Economy: Outsourcing and Delegation," in *Double Agent*, op. cit.: 126–31. Ridout draws on Jon Erickson who makes observations on this point in *The Fate of the Object: From Modern Object to Postmodern Sign in Performance, Art, and Poetry* (Ann Arbor: University of Michigan Press, 1995).

5 Still living

1 Roland Barthes, *Camera Lucida* (New York: Hill and Wang, 1981): 32. The other epigraph is Jacques Derrida, "The Deaths of Roland Barthes," in *The Work of Mourning*, trans. Pascale-Anne Brault (Chicago: University of Chicago Press, 2003): 41.

2 Gertrude Stein, *Lectures in America* (New York: Random House, 1935): 94; Edward Gordon Craig, *On the Art of the Theatre*, (New York: Theatre Arts Books, 1911): 74–5.

3 Jacques Derrida, "The Deaths of Roland Barthes," op. cit.: 52.

4 Cited in Victor Burgin, *In/Different Places: Place and Memory in Visual Culture* (Berkeley: University of California Press, 1996): 85.

5 Jonathan Crary, *Techniques of the Observer: On Vision and Modernity in the 19th Century* (Cambridge MA: MIT Press, 1991): 1.

6 See Rosalind Krauss, "Reinventing the Medium," *Critical Inquiry* 25, 1999: 289–305. See also Mary Ann Doane, "Real Time: Instantaneity and the Photographic Imaginary," in *Stillness and Time: Photography and the Moving Image,* David Green, ed. (Brighton: Photoworks/Photoforum, 2006).

7 There are exceptions. See for example the excellent collection *Acting the Part: Photography As Theatre*, Lori Pauli, ed. (New York: Merrell, 2006).

8 Doane reminds her readers of the frequent reliance on death as a means for academics to orient photography's relationship to time as frozen in the photograph and, as arrested, irretrievable. André Bazin writes that photographic technology "embalms time, rescuing it simply from its proper corruption" while Thierry de Duve uses the word "petrified." See Mary Ann Doane, *The Emergence of Cinematic Time* (Cambridge: Harvard University Press, 2002): 3, 209. We can recall as well Walter Benjamin's reference to photography's "posthumous" shock in "On Some Motifs in Baudelaire," *Illuminations* (New York: Schocken Books, 1969): 175. Eduardo Cadava underscores the privileged point of death in photography in his essay "Words of Light: Theses on the Photography of History," *Diacritics* 2, nos. 3/4, 1992: 85–114 (expanded in 1998 to a book by the same title). The over-privileging of death as the primary property of the photograph is largely the result of the conviction that a photograph "survives," circulating, much like writing, beyond the so-called death of the author. Rather, as Julia Hell has written after W. G. Sebald, "the belief that clings so tenaciously to the medium, i.e., that the photograph 'captures' the object, is an actual emanation of it." Julia Hell, "The Angel's Enigmatic Eyes, or The Gothic Beauty of Catastrophic History in W. G. Sebald's 'Air War and Literature,'" *Criticism* 46, no. 3, 2004: 361–92. The conviction that photography captures "this here now" to become "that there then" assumes that the "here now" is non-recurrent, not cross-temporal, and not of multiple or variable duration. This position assumes that a photo will, as Cadava writes, "continue to evoke what is no longer there" and thus that viewers will be recipient of the evocation "no longer" and somehow able to experience the photographed as absent in a future that is both contained in the photograph and, oddly, beyond it (Cadava, "Words of Light": 92). The privileging of absence as a given is debatable. Sebald writes that photography is "addicted" to death (cited in Hell: 387). This "addiction" may indeed be on the part of modernist habit of thought about photography, rather than a condition of photography itself.

9 See Judith Butler, *Frames of War – When Is Life Grievable?* (New York: Verso, 2009).

10 On the intersecting deployments of fiction, aesthetics, and theatricality in war, terrorism, and torture see Diana Taylor, *Disappearing Acts* (Durham, NC: Duke University Press, 1997); Michael Taussig, *The Nervous System* (New York: William Morrow, 1991); and Saidya Hartman, *Scenes of Subjection: Terror, Slavery and Self-Making in Nineteenth-Century America* on the "obscene theatricality of the slave trade" (Oxford: Oxford University Press, 1997): 17. On the problem of over-reading the Abu Ghraib images for theatricality, or under-reading theatricality's culpability in the real, see Jasbir K. Puar, "On Torture: Abu Ghraib," *Radical History Review* 93, 2005: 13–38.

11 On staging in war photography see Susan Sontag, *Regarding the Pain of Others* (New York: Picador, 2004). See also Philip Gefter, *Photography After Frank* (New York: Aperture, 2009).

12 To illustrate the circulatory structures by which persons become subjects of the broader social networks they inhabit, Louis Althusser gives the example of a police officer shouting "Hey, you there!" to a passer-by in public. Hearing the call, the passer-by turns around, and "by this mere one-hundred-and-eighty-degree physical conversion, he becomes a *subject.*" Althusser, "Ideology and Ideological State

Apparatuses (Notes Toward an Investigation)," in *Lenin and Philosophy, and Other Essays*, 127–88 (New York: Monthly Review Press, 1971): 174, emphasis in original. The notion that a subject can be interpellated through various mediums (film, photography, literature) has been productively applied by cultural studies, gender studies, and media theory. Media theorists have often used Althusser's concept of interpellation to discuss how consumers are hailed by images and other "media texts" (as well as by language), and "subjected" to the habits of reception that become ritualized architectures of engagement. It is fascinating for this study that Althusser terms this policeman/passer-by scene his "little theoretical theatre." In this way, he explains hailing through the fictions of temporal sequence, and connects temporal sequence to the fictions of theatre: "Naturally for the convenience and clarity of my little theoretical theatre I have had to present things in the form of a sequence, with a before and an after, and thus in the form of a temporal succession. [. . .] But in reality these things happen *without any succession*. The existence of ideology and the hailing or interpellation of individuals as subjects are one and the same thing" (p. 174, emphasis added). The theatre produces a fiction of temporal sequence, but the *theatricality* of the scene belies a syncopated, multiple, or non-successive time. See the brilliant exegesis of this passage in Ann Pellegrini's essay "(Laughter)," in *Psychoanalysis and Performance*, Patrick Campbell and Adrian Kear, eds. (New York: Routledge, 2001).

13 Craig Owens, "Posing," in *Beyond Recognition* (Berkeley: University of California Press, 1994).

14 Robin Bernstein, "Dances with Things: Material Culture and the Performance of Race" *Social Text* 27, no. 4, 67–94, 2009: 68.

15 On the camera as a "thing" in the scene see Bernstein, "Dances with Things," op. cit.: 87.

16 See Toni Morrison, *Lecture and Speech of Acceptance, upon the Award of the Nobel Prize for Literature, Delivered in Stockholm on the Seventh of December, Nineteen Hundred and Ninety-Three* (New York: Knopf, 1994): 30.

17 Sue-Ellen Case, "Tracking the Vampire," *Differences* 3, no. 2, 1991: 1–20. As to the queer implications in decentering the life/death binary, and especially *vis à vis* cross-temporality and historiography, I am indebted to Carolyn Dinshaw's thoughts on simultaneity in *Getting Medieval: Sexualities and Communities, Pre- and Postmodern* (Durham, NC: Duke University Press, 1999). On Civil War era attitudes toward and practices of photography that disregard a strict life/death binary, such as "spectral photography," see Molly McGarry, *Ghosts of Futures Past: Spiritualism and the Politics of Nineteenth-Century America* (Berkeley: University of California Press, 2008).

18 Richard Schechner, *Between Theater and Anthropology* (Chicago, IL: University of Chicago Press, 1985): 50.

19 Siegfried Kracauer, "Photography," in *The Mass Ornament*, trans. Thomas Y. Levin (Cambridge: Harvard University Press, 1995).

20 Mary Ann Doane, *The Emergence of Cinematic Time*, op. cit.: 105.

21 Myriad performance artists over the twentieth century have troubled this proposition by creating "durational" events that explore a kind of ongoing quality to performance, unsettling easy distinctions between that which is live and passing and that which remains. On the temporality of the still see Henry Sayre, *The Object of Performance: The American Avant-Garde Since 1970* (Chicago, IL: University of Chicago Press, 1989), and his essay "In the Space of Duration" in *Live: Art and Performance*, Adrian Heathfield, ed. (London: Tate Publishing, 2004).

22 See Diana Taylor, *Disappearing Acts* (Durham, NC: Duke University Press, 1997). The artwork of Miriam Ghani and Chitra Ganesh is also important in this regard. See their project "Index of the Disappeared." Available online at http://www.kabul-reconstructions.net/disappeared/.

23 Amelia Jones, "The 'Eternal Return': Self-Portrait Photography as a Technology of Embodiment," *Signs* 27, no. 4, 947–78, 2002: 949.

24 Ibid.: 951.

25 André LePecki, *Exhausting Dance: Performance and the Politics of Movement* (New York: Routledge, 2006): 15, emphasis in original.

26 Homi Bhabha's notion of the time-lag is indebted to the writings of Roland Barthes and Walter Benjamin on photography and theatre. For Bhabha, "It is the function of the lag to slow down the linear, progressive time of modernity to reveal its 'gesture', its tempi, 'the pauses and stresses of the whole performance'. This can only be achieved – as Walter Benjamin remarked of Brecht's epic theatre – by damming the stream of real life, by bringing the flow to a standstill in a reflux of astonishment. When the dialectic of modernity is brought to a standstill, then the temporal action of modernity – its progressive, future drive – is staged, revealing 'everything that is involved in the act of staging per se'. This slowing down, or lagging, impels the 'past', projects it, gives its 'dead' symbols the circulatory life of the 'sign' of the present, of passage, the quickening of the quotidian. Where these temporalities touch contingently, their spatial boundaries metonymically overlapping, at that moment their margins are lagged, sutured, by the indeterminate articulation of the 'disjunctive' present. *Time-lag keeps alive the making of the past.*" Homi K. Bhabha, *The Location of Culture* (London: New York: Routledge, 1994): 253–4, emphasis in original.

27 It is worth noting that the word "theatricality" was first coined in 1837 and the word "photography" in 1834 (with the official "invention" in 1939). See Tracy Davis, "Theatricality and Civil Society" in *Theatricality*, Tracy Davis and Thomas Postlewait, eds. (Cambridge: Cambridge University Press, 2004): 127. See Geoffrey Batchen, "The Naming of Photography: 'A Mass of Metaphor,'" *History of Photography* 17, no. 1, 1993: 22–32.

28 I dwell on Western theatrical roots, not to suggest that photography can only be read in relation to Western practices, but because the after-effect of the Greek *theatron* (place for viewing) on Western "symbolic form" has been enormous. See Erwin Panofsky, *Perspective as Symbolic Form*, trans. Christopher S. Wood (New York: Zone Books, 1991). The replay of Hellenic architecture in Vitruvius's Roman *De architectura*, and the long life of the "screen" and "scene" are what interest me here. However, it is imperative to remember that Western theatre history, with its "mainstage" privileging of bicameral or screenal vision, is not a universal theatrical form, and not a singular heritage even within the West. On the "mainstage" aspect of Western theatre history see Susan Bennett, "Decomposing History (Why Are There So Few Women in Theatre History)," in *Theorizing Practice: Redefining Theatre History*, W. B. Worthen and Peter Holland, eds. (London: Palgrave McMillan, 2003) 71–87. Western theatre history generally produces a more ocularcentric narrative than theatre history considered globally, or histories of "performance" arts. I say "Western" too, to avoid universal and transhistorical claims about the science of perspective. The tendency in much scholarship to universalize perspective to human vision and to thereby naturalize the screen should be chastened by the following passage by Indra Kagis McEwen, scholar of Vitruvius: "The transhistorical voice that many English-speaking historians continue to hear in Vitruvius may sound universal precisely because it is Roman. Which is precisely what apologists for the imperial Roman order, Vitruvius among them, intended." McEwen, *Vitruvius: Writing the Body of Architecture* (Cambridge, MA: MIT Press, 2003): 5.

29 On this question, see Laurence Senelick, "Early Photographic Attempts to Record Performance Sequence," *Theatre Research International* 22, no. 3, 1997: 255–64.

30 See Tavia Nyong'o, "Carnivalizing Time," in *Amalgamation Waltz: Race, Performance and the Ruses of Memory* (Minneapolis: University of Minnesota Press, 2009): 135–66.

31 To argue against historical rupture might suggest historical continuity, as if theatre, for instance, had some long and unbroken, unified history "behind" photography. Such an argument would miss the point. It may be useful to cite Michel de Certeau on Western historiography's obsession with death and investment in rupture: "In their

respective turns, each 'new' time provides the place for a discourse considering whatever preceded it to be dead [. . .] The labor designated by this breakage is self-motivated. In the past from which it is distinguished it promotes a selection between what can be understood and what must be forgotten in order to obtain the representation of a present intelligibility. But whatever this new understanding of the past holds to be irrelevant – shards created by the selection of materials, reminders left aside by an explication – comes back, despite everything, on the edges of discourse or in its rifts and crannies." De Certeau, *The Writing of History* (New York: Columbia University Press, 1988): 4. See also Jacques Derrida, *Positions*, trans. Alan Bass (Chicago, IL: University of Chicago Press, 1981): 24, on the trouble with an either/or, continuity or rupture model.

32 Carolyn Dinshaw has inspired me on this potential. See Dinshaw, "Introduction: Touching the Past," *Getting Medieval*, op. cit.: 1–54.

33 George Kernodle, *From Art to Theatre: Form and Convention in the Renaissance* (Chicago, IL: Chicago University Press, 1944): 13, 15.

34 Ibid.: 29, see also 36, 39.

35 Michel de Certeau, *The Practice of Everyday Life* (Berkeley: University of California Press, 1984): 15. For a close reading of this sentence see my "Patricide and the Passerby," in *Performance and the City*, D. J. Hopkins, Shelley Orr and Kim Solga, eds. (New York: Palgrave, 2009).

36 George Kernodle, *From Art to Theatre*, op. cit.: 65. See also George Kipling, *Enter the King* (Oxford: Clarendon Press, 1998): 264–80.

37 Kipling, *Enter the King*, op. cit.: 275.

38 See Jody Enders, *The Medieval Theatre of Cruelty* (Ithaca, NY: Cornell University Press, 1999): 189, on the practice of casting actual workers in parts signifying the profession played. This practice is also often evident in Civil War reenactment. In Lincoln, RI, in 2005 at a reenactment at Chase Farm, a prominent piece of the reenactment was a field hospital where, we were told, "actual surgeons and nurses" were performing reenactments of amputations. Available online at http://www.hearthside house.org/photos/civil.war.html. See Figure 1.1.

39 On "preenactment" and tableaux vivants see Kernodle, *From Art to Theatre*, op. cit.: 39, 56. See also Hans Belting on the prospective, or preenactment, nature of cultic medieval memory in *Likeness and Presence: A History of the Image Before the Era of Art*, trans. Edmund Jephcott (Chicago, IL: University of Chicago Press, 1994): 10.

40 Hans Belting, *Likeness and Presence*, op. cit.: 4–10.

41 See essays by Jean Fisher, Lynne Cooke, and Raymond Belleur that take up James Coleman's installation *Living and Presumed Dead* in *James Coleman*, George Baker, ed. (Cambridge, MA: MIT Press, 2003). See Dorothea von Hantelmann on Coleman's performativity and theatricality in *How To Do Things with Art* (Zurich, JRP/Ringier, 2010): 24–69.

42 Geoffrey Batchen performs an interesting reading of the "death" factor in photography in relation to other media in *Burning with Desire: The Conception of Photography* (Cambridge, MA: MIT Press, 1997): 204–16.

43 Barbara Hodgdon, "Photography, Theatre, Mnemonics; or, Thirteen Ways of Looking at a Still," in *Theorizing Practice: Redefining Theatre History*, W. B. Worthen and Peter Holland, eds., 88–119 (London: Palgrave Macmillan, 2003): 89.

44 See Amelia Jones, "'Presence' in Absentia: Experiencing Performance Art as Documentation," *Art Journal* 56, no. 4, 1997: 11–18.

45 Edward Gordon Craig, *On the Art of the Theatre*, op. cit.: 74.

46 Craig admonishes theatre artists to abjure the dangerous artifice of "life" in favor of the safer terrain of "death." Antonin Artaud would seem to agree. In 1938, *The Theatre and Its Double* called for theatre-makers to seek danger. For him, as for Craig, the danger was, explicitly, life. The difference was only that Artaud sought danger.

Artaud, *The Theatre and Its Double*, trans. Mary Caroline Richards (New York: Grove Press, 1958): 10, 42.

47 W. B. Worthen, *Modern Drama and the Rhetoric of Theater* (Berkeley: University of California Press, 1992): 194. Of course, there are many examples from modern theatre history of the use of photography and film on stage. An early example is Dion Boucicault's 1859 American melodrama *The Octoroon*. The opening of Adam Sonstegard's essay "Performing Remediation: The Minstrel, The Camera, and *The Octoroon*" (*Criticism* 48, no. 3, 2006: 375–95) gives a hint at the complexity of the complicity between photography and theatricality in this drama: "On the eve of [the Civil War], the first conflict America would wage in part with photographic images, the first actor to play a photographer debuted on the American stage. [. . .] His camera recorded one character's murder of a character in blackface; his apparatus got smashed to pieces by a character dressed as an Indian brave; and a photograph, found within his apparatus, came to 'prove' the murderer's guilt. [. . .] During that debut, one medium, a stage performance, including minstrelsy and playing out before an audience, participated in constructing another medium, photography."

48 Konstantin Stanislavky, *An Actor Prepares*, translated by Elizabeth Hapgood (New York: Routledge, 1989 [1936]): 36–7, emphasis added.

49 W. B. Worthen, *Modern Drama*, op. cit.: 12. Consider also the theatre of German director Erwin Piscator who used photography and film on stage in the 1920s. He termed on-stage photography and film "*living* scenery." Thus, again, the reference to photographic media as *living*, by which Piscator arguably meant linked to "immediate" or "concrete" reality. Cited in John Willett, *The Theatre of Erwin Piscator* (London: Methuen, 1986): 60.

50 This is also the central conceit of Michelangelo Antonioni's 1966 film *Blow-Up*, a film about photography, the pose, violence, and the surrogate labor of modeling affect in the realm of commodities. *Blow-Up* is oddly punctuated by rowdy miscreant mimes who seem to randomly interrupt plot, and course through the city streets as if revenant of medieval carnival. They recur, without explanation, throughout the film, both counter to the story and syncopated with it, at all times anachronistic and anamorphic (as when an older medium recurs in a newer one, distorted and challenging the new medium it also grounds). The Greek root of anamorphosis signifies "formed again" – suggesting that the word is particularly suited to reenactment as a practice.

51 In 2007 artist Daniel Peltz took a series of cameraless images at the Vasa Museum in Stockholm in a piece titled *Cameraless Video*. Interested in the "bodily performance of digital photography," Peltz moved around the museum *as if* he had a video camera, miming the presence of that camera by using his body in camera-legible poses. The documentation (there was a camera present shooting Peltz's cameralessness) suggests the ways that "the camera" is a scriptive thing, and even (like a mimed object) a thingless thing, extending the notion of apparatus beyond the mechanical and into the performative. The live/mime/present/absent/image-capture/performance knottiness of this situation compels thought, reminiscent of the *collaboration* between Nadar and Deburau. See the piece documented at http://www.risd.tv/dpeltz/cameralessvideos. html.

52 Arthur C. Danto, "Photography and Performance: Cindy Sherman's Stills," in Cindy Sherman, *Cindy Sherman: Untitled Film Stills*, 5–14 (Munich: Schirmer, 1990): 8.

53 See Jennifer Blessing's edited volume *A Rose is a Rose is a Rose: Gender Performance in Photography* (New York: Guggenheim Museum, 2006).

54 Jean-Luc Godard and Jean-Pierre Gorin, *Letter to Jane: An Investigation about a Still*, is a postscript film to their feature *Tout va bien* (Anouchka Films, 1972). The short film is a voice-over commentary, largely centered on an image of Fonda first published in *Paris Match* in 1972.

55 Discourse on this problem is voluminous. See the 1929 essay by Joan Riviere, "Womanliness as Masquerade," *International Journal of Psycho-Analysis* 10: 303–13. See

Simone de Beauvoir, *The Second Sex* (trans. H. M. Parshley, New York: Vintage, 1954) and the massive literature that began to collect across the century under the rubric "feminist theory," much of which is concerned with the problem of the mimetic capacities of the double. Indeed, it would be possible to argue that "reenactment" has a profoundly feminist history, and to explore how its genesis as a site of fascination in the art world has roots deep in the work of feminist artists and scholars who began to think of the body as stage, and in so thinking, began to wrestle productively with precedent by performatively replaying gesture, act, scenario, and image for criticism and revision. See Luce Irigaray, *Speculum of the Other Woman* (Ithaca, NY: Cornell University Press, 1985); Teresa de Lauretis, *Technologies of Gender* (Bloomington: Indiana University Press, 1987); Elin Diamond, *Unmaking Mimesis* (New York: Routledge, 1997); Amelia Jones, *Body/Art: Performing the Subject* (Minneapolis: University of Minnesota Press, 1998).

56 Danto's remarks on how Sherman could not be considered similar to Rembrandt were published in 1990, "Photography and Performance," op. cit.: 9, emphasis added. The year before that, Sherman had created her "History Portraits in the style of Old Masters" in which she photographed herself as if a series of oil paintings. Did Danto know of this work before they were exhibited at Metro Pictures in January 1990? He would publish the accompanying essay to the Rizzoli publication of the History Portrait Series one year later, in which comparison with Rembrandt would be required. In that text, Danto remarks that Sherman is "like some astonishing Houdini." Arthur C. Danto, "Post Masters and Post Modern: Cindy Sherman's *History Portraits*," in *Cindy Sherman: History Portaits* (New York: Rizzoli, 1991). As an aside, one cannot help but wonder whether the artist Yasumasa Morimura read Danto on Sherman, and contemplated Danto's inability to read Sherman as other than an actress, since in Morimura's own replay of Sherman's style he seems, in Donald Kuspit's words, "to favor Rembrandt particularly." Kuspit, "Art's Identity Crisis: Yasumasa Morimura's Photographs," in *Daughters of Art History: The Photographs of Yasumasa Morimura* (New York: Aperture, 2003): 9. By 2003, note that Peter Schjeldahl could reverse the line of descent and label Rembrandt a "seventeenth-century Cindy Sherman." Schjeldahl, "Story Line: Rembrandt in Boston," *The New Yorker*, November 10, 2003: 122.

57 Three years earlier in 1987 in *The Nation*, Danto published what appears to be the opposite statement: "Sherman's face must by now be the second most widely known face in the art world, despite its happy indistinction. She is surpassed in familiarity only by Warhol." Arthur C. Danto, "Cindy Sherman," *The Nation*, August 15/22 1987: 134–7. But these two claims – that no one can recognize her and that she is recognizable everywhere – are perhaps not contradictory, as Godard and Gorin made clear in the case of Fonda, for, to Danto, she is primarily "an astonishing actress" in the "standard way of women" and *not* a photographer. The alignment with Warhol might also remind us to read for a basic heteronormative gender panic surrounding intermediality.

58 A June 6, 2006 press release for a 2006–7 retrospective of Sherman's work organized by Jeu de Paume, Paris, and co-produced with the Kunsthaus Bregenz, the Louisiana Museum of Modern Art, Humlebæk, Denmark, and the Martin-Gropius-Bau, Berlin, stated of Sherman's *Civil War* series: "The Civil War is, of course, a reference to the conflict between the northern and southern American states from 1861 to 1865 [. . .] but it also is the war that continues to rage throughout the modern world, the anonymous, everyday violence whose consequences are seen in tiny 'forgotten' wars, news reports and morgues all over the world." This is an odd claim, but might resonate with the argument in Tiqqun, *Introduction to Civil War*, though Tiqqun does *not* universalize the US conflict. The retrospective also stated, somewhat inexplicably, that the *Civil War* series was a "logical extension of the *Sex Pictures*," though the *Sex*

Pictures series followed the *Civil War* series by one year. Might it be that the curators were purposefully running the clock backwards?

59 Relative to this point, Sally Mann's photographs of the Civil War battlefield at Antietam, shot with pin-hole cameras, result in a reenactment at the level of photographic form. The material document itself – the record – poses itself again as re-record in a syncopated temporal uncanny. These are not reenactments of a civil war battle re-staged across bodies in again time. Rather, these images offer a reenactment of the photograph itself, as rephotography, or redocument. See Sally Mann, *What Remains* (New York: Bulfinch Press, 2003). Robert Longo explored this ground in his *Seeing the Elephant* series of photographs of Civil War reenactors from 2002. For an even earlier, related exploration see Warren Neidich, *American History Reinvented* (NewYork: Aperture, 1989). Neidich's project is critical, asking his viewer to recognize a collective habituation to history *as* photographic image, as he shoots images from before the invention of the camera. A project related to Mann's, Longo's, and Neidich's is the "personal" homage of Kris Kristopherson, who attempts to honor his Confederate ancestors (and to continue their fight) through photographing Civil War reneactors in images that attempt to pass as period. The critical nature of Longo's and Neidich's more materialist projects and the romantic, commemorative nature of Kristopherson's are interesting to compare, as both use similar means to arrive at what certainly are radically dissimilar aims. Kristopherson, *Not Shall Your Glory Be Forgot* (New York: St. Martin's Press, 1999). The question of reenactment as redocumentation is also addressed in Chapter 4.

60 Craig Owens, "The Allegorical; Impulse: Toward a Theory of Postmodernism, Part 2," in *Beyond Recognition* (Berkeley: University of California Press, 1994): 84.

61 Craig Owens, "Posing," op. cit.: 215.

62 Jacques Derrida, *Positions* op. cit.: 27.

63 Toni Morrison, *Lecture*, op. cit.: 30. For further analysis of "in your hands," see Judith Butler, *Excitable Speech* (New York: Routledge, 1997): 6–13; and a critique of Butler's analysis in Rebecca Schneider, "Judith Butler in My Hands," in *Bodily Citations: Religion and Judith Butler*, Ellen Armour and Susan St. Ville, eds. (New York: Columbia University Press, 2006).

64 See the 1995 series, "Actress Through the Looking Glass" published in Yasumasa Morimura, *Yasumasa Morimura: On Self-Portait: Through the Looking Glass* (Amsterdam: Reflex Editions, 2007).

65 Yasumasa Morimura, *Daughter of Art History: Photographs of Yasumasa Morimura* (New York: Aperture: 2005). See also Joonsung Yoon, "Seeing His Own Absence: Culture and Gender in Yasusmasa Morimura's Photographic Self-Portraits," *Journal of Visual Art Practice* 1, no. 3, 2001: 162–9; and Paul B. Franklin, "Orienting the Asian Male Body in the Photography of Yasumasa Morimura," in Brenda Bright, ed., *The Passionate Camera: Photography and Bodies of Desire* (New York: Routledge, 1998) 233–47.

66 Donald Kuspit, "Art's Identity Crisis," op. cit.: 8, emphasis added.

67 Ibid.: 9.

68 Michael Fried, "Art and Objecthood," in *Minimal Art*, Gregory Battock, ed. (Berkeley: University of California Press, 1995 [1967]): 142.

69 Homi Bhabha, "Of Mimicry and Man: The Ambivalence of Colonial Discourse," *The Location of Culture* (New York: Routledge, 1994).

70 The "difference" of the "not quite" becomes a detail at the level of performance mode. Sometimes the photograph gives away extremely minor manipulations of what are not always material bodily details (though affects should not be considered non-bodily, even if seemingly immaterial). Rather, a detail may simply imply just a "certain something" that is not quite right, or "just too posed" or "overtly theatrical" – a theatricality that both creates *and* gives the scene away as faux. Here, affective stances and the minor disputations of passing (or not-passing) become the immaterial

labor of critique passed across the body. This is the resistant labor of the (otherwise shown as compliant) passer-by in relation to the monumentality of habituation to gendered representation that precedes her.

71 I take the word "scenario" from Diana Taylor's *The Archive and the Repertoire*, op. cit.: 17. Taylor makes a compelling argument for the use of this word while simultaneously theorizing the relationship between theatricality and scenario in the context of colonial conquest and its reiterative repetitions. See also her essay "Afterword: War Play," *PMLA* 124, no. 5, 2009: 1886–95.

72 Cadava, "Words of Light," op. cit.: 84–114, especially 89–92.

73 Walter Benjamin, "A Small History of Photography," in *One-Way Street and Other Writings*, trans. Edmund Jephcott and Kingsley Shorter (London: New Left Books, 1979 [1931]): 243.

74 Ibid.: 243.

75 Ibid.: 242.

76 Ibid.: 242–3, emphasis in original.

77 On phonic materiality, see Chapter 3, "Visible Music," in Fred Moten's *In the Break: The Aesthetics of the Black Radical Tradition* (Minneapolis: University of Minnesota Press, 2003). I am also indebted to conversations with Harvey Young on stillness and the "futured." See Young, *Embodying Black Experience: Stillness, Critical Memory, and the Black Body* (Ann Arbor: University of Michigan Press, 2010).

78 On the homophobic logic of shame in the narratives surrounding these images see Puar, "On Torture: Abu Ghraib," op. cit.

79 Moten, *In the Break*, op. cit.: 202.

80 Moten suggests that the image of Till can be *listened to*, and likens it to the "pain" (i.e., the aestheticization of feeling) in the blues. He writes, "You have to think about the fact that an aesthetic appropriation could be said to desacrilize the legacy of lynchings, precisely by way of an 'alchemizing' that seems to fetishize or figure on the literal, on the absolute fact and reality of so many deaths while, at the same time, continually opening the possibility of redemption in out sensuality." Moten, *In the Break*, op. cit.: 197. It is hard to know precisely what Moten means by "out sensuality," as his writing often begins to mirror the lyric and cut of the blues he thinks through – his writing itself becomes the sensuality he writes of and it slips and slides into its own cracks. But if his writing is his riff on the photograph of Emmet Till – if it is mourning and homonymic morning – then he is performing the movement of the image of which he writes, he is putting it into passage and multiplying its secrets. He is singing the photo into the break.

81 Rosalind Krauss outlines a progression from the modernist drive for the "specificity" of distinct art forms toward the post-medium condition she celebrates as "differential specificity." As opposed to the postmodern (which can be defined by a soupy and apolitical loss of specificity), Krauss celebrates post-medium as work that critically engages the outmoded forms it re-combines. For Krauss, thus, the post-medium condition is necessarily cross-temporal and composed in a materialist history. Krauss's post-medium condition might resonate with my reading of Moten here. However, in her 1999 essay "Reinventing the Medium," discussed later in this chapter, Krauss displays a nostalgia for "pure form" that is not consonant with what I take to be Moten's drive. Rosalind Krauss, *A Voyage on the North Sea: Art in the Age of the Post-Medium Condition* (London: Thames & Hudson, 2000).

82 Moten's "itineracy" might be read beside de Certeau's investment in dispersal. Interested in the ways that users use images, de Certeau presents an argument for shifting the site of meaning off any image itself, or any individual viewer him/herself, and onto (social) relationality cast into a future of live engagement with the image or object in which users "make innumerable and infinitesimal transformations of and within the dominant cultural economy in order to adapt it to their own interests and their own rules." De Certeau is interested in what is "made" of an image or an object

through engagement and so he writes of a kind of fugitivity of the image in that usage is "scattered" or "dispersed." *Practice of Everyday Life*, op. cit.: xi–xiv, 15.

83 Moten, *In the Break*, op. cit.: 197.
84 Krauss, "Reinventing the Medium," op. cit.: 293.
85 Ibid.: 292–4.
86 Ibid.: 290.
87 Ibid.: 295.
88 Ibid.: 296. See also Krauss, *A Voyage on the North Sea*, op. cit.
89 Krauss, "Reinventing the Medium," op. cit.: 296.
90 Ibid.: 295, 298.
91 Later Coleman works, such as, *INITIALS* (1994) retain the citational theatricality and the aspect of procession via the material support of the still photograph and the slide projector. *INITIALS* shows a group of people who have all come for a photographic appointment. The scene is set in rooms adjacent to an operating theatre. The sequences of still pictures show the protagonists preparing themselves for the camera, rehearsing for their poses, and forming different groupings. See Dorothea von Hantelmann, *How to Do Things With Art*, op. cit.: 24–68.
92 Krauss, *A Voyage to the North Sea*, op. cit.: 56. "Reinventing the Medium," op. cit.: 304, 305, emphasis added.
93 Batchen, op. cit.: 160.
94 Cited in Michael Sapir, "The Impossible Photograph: Hippolyte Bayard's Self-Portrait as a Drowned Man," *MFS: Modern Fiction Studies* 40, no. 3, 1994: 623, emphasis added.
95 Julia Ballerini, "Recasting Ancestry: Statuettes as Imaged by Three Inventors of Photography," in *The Object as Subject: Studies in the Interpretation of Still Life*, Anne W. Lowenthal, ed. (Princeton, NJ: Princeton University Press, 1996).

And back – Afterword

1 Allison Smith, "Public Art Fund Presents *The Muster*, A Project by Allison Smith," http://www.themuster.com/.
2 Ann Pellegrini, "After Sontag: Future Notes on Camp," in *A Companion to Lesbian, Gay, Bisexual, Transgender, and Queer Studies*, George E. Haggerty and Molly McGarry, eds. (London: Blackwell, 2007) 168–93.
3 Ibid.: 176; Allison Smith, "Public Address," in *Ahistoric Occasion: Artists Making History*, Nato Thompson, ed. (North Adams, MA: Mass MOCA, 2007): 107.
4 This paragraph is meant to syncopate but not replicate Giorgio Agamben, *State of Exception*, trans. Kevin Attell (Chicago, IL: The University of Chicago Press, 2005).
5 Allison Smith, "*The Muster*," op. cit.
6 On the Protestantism of the so-called secular, see Janet R. Jakobsen and Ann Pellegrini, "Times Like These," in *Secularisms*, Janet R. Jakobsen and Ann Pellegrini, eds. (Durham, NC: Duke University Press, 2008) 1–36.
7 Allison Smith, "Public Address," op. cit.: 107.
8 I borrow Luce Irigaray's term "hom(m)o-social" by which she refers to structures of identification recognizing the "sameness" of masculine privilege at base. See Luce Irigaray, "When the Goods Get Together," in *New French Feminisms*, Elaine Marks and Isabelle de Courtivron, eds. (New York: Schocken Books, 1981) 99–110. On Irigaray's use of this term, see Eve Kosofsky Sedgwick, *Between Men: English Literature and Male Homosocial Desire* (New York: Columbia University Press, 1985).
9 Allison Smith, "Public Address," op. cit.: 109.
10 Jasbir K. Puar, "Queer Times, Queer Assemblages," *Social Text* 23, nos. 3–4, 2005: 121–39. See also her *Terrorist Assemblages: Homonationalism in Queer Times* (Durham, NC: Duke University Press, 2007).

11 Puar draws here on Gilles Deleuze to argue for queer assemblage versus inter-sectionality. Like Patricia Cough and others invested in critical thinking about networks of affect, Puar argues for a shift away from mapping for identity politics toward reading for affective networks of cross-affiliate implication in shifting terrains of identity politics. The argument is that "identity" tends to fix and root subjects, where reading for affective networks or (mimetic) affiliation and exchange allows for the complexity of cross-affiliation in shifting political landscapes. See Puar "Queer Times," op. cit.: 122, 127.

12 Ibid.: 127–8.

13 Ibid.: 131. For an analysis of states and performances of feeling in excess of the national see José Esteban Muñoz, "Feeling Brown and Affect in Ricardo Bracho's *The Sweetest Hangover* (and Other STDs)," *Theatre Journal* 52, no. 1, 2000: 67–79.

14 Janet R. Jakobsen and Ann Pellegrini, "Times Like These," op. cit.: 28.

15 Janet R. Jakobsen and Ann Pellegrini, "Dreaming Secularism," introduction to special issue "World Secularisms at the Millennium," Janet R. Jakobsen and Ann Pellegrini, eds., *Social Text* 18, no. 3, 1–27, 2000: 24.

16 See my chapter "Seeing the Big Show" on counter-memory and Spiderwoman Theatre in Rebecca Schneider, *The Explicit Body in Performance* (New York: Routledge, 1997): 153–75.

17 Allison Smith, "Public Address," op. cit.: 107.

18 Pellegrini, "After Sontag: Future Notes on Camp," op. cit.: 178.

19 Elizabeth Freeman, "Packing History, Count(er)ing Generations," *New Literary History* 31, no. 4, 727–44, 2000: 742.

20 The Cherokee handbag refers to "relative pain" in Chapter 1. "Terrorist drag" resonates with my work on "binary terror" in feminist performance art in *The Explicit Body in Performance*, op. cit.: 12–42, and the work of José Esteban Muñoz on "terrorist drag" in *Disidentifications: Queers of Color and the Performance of Politics* (Minneapolis: University of Minnesota Press, 1999): 93–115. See also Shane Vogel on "terror drag" in "Where Are We Now? Queer World Making and Cabaret Performance," *GLQ: A Journal of Lesbian and Gay Studies* 6, no. 1, 29–60, 2000: 43.

21 Rosalyn Deutsche, "Not-Forgetting: Mary Kelly's Love Songs," *Grey Room* 24, 26–37, 2006: 33. See also Susan Richmond, "'From Stone to Cloud': Mary Kelly's Love Songs and Feminist Intergenerationality," *Feminist Theory* 11, no. 1, 2010: 57–78.

22 Lynne Cooke, "A Tempered Agnosia," in *James Coleman*, George Baker, ed., 113–38 (Cambridge, MA: MIT Press, 2003): 124.

23 The intersection between circulating news and still portraiture that Coleman's *Line of Faith* cites (and troubles) puts him in the company of photographers like Thomas Ruff and Christian Boltanski who have exhibited newspaper images, devoid of their captions, as art, inviting critical thought about the relationship between image and venue as images circulate, or move, between contexts and across time.

24 Raymond Bellour, "The Living Dead (*Living and Presumed Dead*)," in *James Coleman*, George Baker, ed., 57–72 (Cambridge, MA: MIT Press, 2003): 57.

25 Howard Zinn, *A Power Governments Cannot Suppress* (San Francisco, CA: City Light Books, 2007): 11–12.

26 Ibid.

27 The *Port Huron Project* entailed six reenactments staged between 2006 and 2008. Speeches by Coretta Scott King, Paul Potter, and Howard Zinn were the first three in the series. Creative Time then commissioned three more – César Chávez, Angela Davis, and Stokely Carmichael – to accompany *Democracy in America*, a large-scale exhibition at New York City's Park Avenue Armory. In each case, the speech was reenacted at the same spot where it first took place – from Boston and New York and Washington to Los Angeles and Oakland, California. The project is named for Tom Hayden's Port Huron Statement of 1962, a germinal manifesto of the New Left.

28 Similarly, I brought out an essay "Protesting Now and Again" that took place more than once under the same title. A version appears in *Mark Tribe, The Port Huron Project:*

Reenactments of New Left Protest Speeches (Milan: Edizioni Charta, 2010), and another in *TDR: The Drama Review* 54, no. 2, 7–11, and a third online as part of Red Channels' "Overcoming Silence" series at http://redchannels.org/writings/RC003/RC003_protest.html. No version can be said to be "the original." All are simultaneous "takes" on the *Port Huron Project*, appearing with minor differences. My thanks to *TDR*, Mark Tribe, and Edizioni Charta for allowing this less-than-usual scholarly practice of simultaneous publication.

29   See Mark Tribe, "Introduction," in *The Port Huron Project: Reenactments of New Left Protest Speeches* (Milan: Edizioni Charta, 2010): 7. On resisting "left melancholy" see Wendy Brown, "Resisting Left Melancholy," *Boundary 2* 26, no. 3, 1999: 19–27.

30   Howard Zinn, *Declarations of Independence: Cross-Examining American Ideology* (New York: Perennial, 1990): 7.

31   Mark Tribe, "Introduction," op. cit.: 8, emphasis added.

32   Videos of the Port Huron reenactments, including Davis's re-speech, can be found at http://www.marktribe.net/art/port-huron-project/.

33   See Sharon Hayes, *After Before – In the Near Future* (New York: Art In General, 2008). See also *History is Ours: Art by Andrea Geyer and Sharon Hayes*, Konrad Bitterli, ed. (Heidelberg: Kehrer Verlag, 2010).

34   Raymond Williams, *Keywords: A Vocabulary of Culture and Society* (Oxford: Oxford University Press, 1985 [1976]): 270.

35   On the limits of the "American" denigration of nostalgia as compared with the cross-temporal and visceral promise in the Greek root, see C. Nadia Seremetakis, *The Senses Still: Perception and Memory as Material Culture in Modernity* (Boulder, CO: Westview Press, 1994): 4. Also see Julia Bryan-Wilson on nostalgia in Tribe's work in "Sounding the Fury: Kirsten Forkert and Mark Tribe," *Artforum* 46, no. 5 (January), 2008: 95–6.

36   Paige Sarlin, "New Left-Wing Melancholy: Mark Tribe's 'The Port Huron Project' and the Politics of Reenactment," *Framework* 50, nos. 1 & 2, 139–57, 2009: 141.

37   Ibid.: 153.

38   Rosalind Krauss, *A Voyage on the North Sea: Art in the Age of the Post-Medium Condition* (London: Thames & Hudson, 2000): 56. See the discussion on differential specificity in Chapter 5.

39   Julia Bryan-Wilson, *Art Workers: Radical Practice in the Vietnam Era*, op. cit.: 11, emphasis added.

Bibliography

Abramović, Marina 2007 *Seven Easy Pieces*. New York: Charta.

Abramović, Marina and Tania Bruguera 2009 "Conversation: Abramović and Bruguera," in Steven Maddoff (ed.) *Art School (Propositions for the 21st Century)*. Cambridge, MA: MIT Press, 177–88.

Agamben, Giorgio 1998 *Homo Sacer: Sovereign Power and Bare Life*. Stanford, CA: Stanford University Press.

Agamben, Giorgio 1999 *The Man Without Content*. Stanford, CA: Stanford University Press.

Agamben, Giorgio 2005 *State of Exception*. Translated by Kevin Attell. Chicago, IL: University of Chicago Press.

Agnew, Vanessa 2004 "Introduction: What is Reenactment?" *Criticism* 46, no. 3: 327–39.

Agnew, Vanessa 2007 "History's Affective Turn: Historical Reenactment and Its Work in the Present." *Rethinking History* 11, no. 3: 299–312.

Ahmed, Sara 2004 *The Cultural Politics of Emotion*. New York: Routledge.

Alcock, Susan E. 2002 *Archaeologies of the Greek Past: Landscape, Monuments, and Memories*. New York: Cambridge University Press.

Alexie, Sherman 1993 "Crazy Horse Speaks," in *Old Shirts and New Skins*. Los Angeles, CA: UCLA American Indian Studies Center Publications.

Allain, Paul and Jen Harvie 2006 *Routledge Companion to Theatre and Performance*. New York: Routledge.

Allen, Jennifer 2002 "Performance Anxiety: On 'A Little Bit of History Repeated.'" *Artforum*, March.

Althusser, Louis 1971 "Ideology and Ideological State Apparatuses (Notes Toward an Investigation)," in *Lenin and Philosophy and Other Essays*. Translated by Ben Brewster. New York: Monthly Review Press, 127–88.

Anderson, Jack 1987 "Stage: 'Cross Way Cross,' A Journey." *The New York Times*. Sunday, March 1.

Anderson, Jay 1984 *Time Machines: The World of Living History*. Nashville, KY: American Association for State and Local History.

Arns, Inke 2007 "History Will Repeat Itself," in Inke Arns and Gabriele Horn (eds.) *History Will Repeat Itself: Strategies of Re-Enactment in Contemporary (Media) Art and Performance*. Frankfurt: Revolver, 36–63.

Artaud, Antonin 1958 *The Theatre and Its Double*. Translated by Mary Caroline Richards. New York: Grove Press.

Auslander, Philip 1987 "Toward a Concept of the Political in Postmodern Theatre." *Theatre Journal* 39, no. 1: 20–34.

Auslander, Philip 1997 *From Acting to Performance: Essays in Modernism and Postmodernism*. New York: Routledge.

Auslander, Philip 1999 *Liveness: Performance in a Mediatized Culture*. New York: Routledge.

Auslander, Philip 2006 "The Performativity of Performance Documentation." *PAJ: A Journal of Performance and Art* 28, no. 3: 1–10.

Austin, J. L. 1955 *How to Do Things with Words*. Cambridge, MA: President and Fellows of Harvard College.

Baker, George, ed. 2003 *James Coleman*. Cambridge, MA: MIT Press.

Ballerini, Julia 1996 "Recasting Ancestry: Statuettes as Imaged by Three Inventors of Photography," in Anne W. Lowenthal (ed.) *The Object as Subject: Studies in the Interpretation of Still Life*. Princeton, NJ: Princeton University Press.

Balme, Christopher 2007 *Pacific Performances: Theatricality and Cross-Cultural Encounter in the South Seas*. New York: Palgrave.

Bank, Rosemarie K. 1997 *Theatre Culture in America, 1825–1860*. New York: Cambridge University Press.

Baraka, Amiri (LeRoi Jones) 1968 *Black Music*. New York: William Morrow.

Barba, Eugenio 2005 *A Dictionary of Theatre Anthropology*, second edition. New York: Routledge.

Barish, Jonas 1981 *The Antitheatrical Prejudice*. Berkeley: University of California Press.

Barthes, Roland 1981 *Camera Lucida: Reflections on Photography*. Translated by Richard Howard. New York: Hill and Wang.

Batchen, Geoffrey 1993 "The Naming of Photography: 'A Mass of Metaphor.'" *History of Photography* 17, no. 1: 22–32.

Batchen, Geoffrey 1997 *Burning With Desire: The Conception of Photography*. Cambridge, MA: MIT Press.

Bateson, Gregory 1983 "A Theory of Play and Fantasy," in Gregory Bateson, *Steps to an Ecology of Mind: Collected Essays in Anthropology, Psychiatry, Evolution, and Epistemology*. New York: Ballantine, 177–93.

Bellour, Raymond 2003 "The Living Dead (*Living and Presumed Dead*)," in George Baker (ed.) *James Coleman*. Cambridge, MA: MIT Press, 57–72.

Belting, Hans 1994 *Likeness and Presence: A History of the Image Before the Era of Art*. Translated by Edmund Jephcott. Chicago, IL: University of Chicago Press.

Benjamin, Andrew 1997 *Present Hope: Philosophy, Architecture, Judaism*. New York: Routledge.

Benjamin, Walter 1969 *Illuminations*. Translated by Harry Zohn. New York: Schocken Books.

Benjamin, Walter 1979 *One-Way Street and Other Writings*. Translated by Edmund Jephcott and Kingsley Shorter. London: New Left Books.

Benjamin, Walter 2008 *The Work of Art in the Age of its Technological Reproducibility*. Cambridge, MA: Harvard University Press.

Bennett, Lerone, Jr. 2000 *Forced Into Glory: Abraham Lincoln's White Dream*. Chicago, IL: Johnson Publishing Company.

Bennett, Susan 2003 "Decomposing History (Why Are There So Few Women in Theatre History?)," in W. B. Worthen and Peter Holland (eds.) *Theorizing Practice: Redefining Theatre History*. London: Palgrave Macmillan, 71–87.

Bergson, Henri 1988 *Matter and Memory*. Translated by M. N. Paul and W. S. Palmer. New York: Zone Books.

Bergson, Henri 2001 "Time as Lived Duration" from *Duration and Simultaneity*, in Charles M. Sherover (ed.) *The Human Experience of Time*. Evanston, IL: Northwestern University Press, 219–38.

Bernal, Martin 1989 *Black Athena: The Afro–Asiatic Roots of Classical Civilization.* New Brunswick, NJ: Rutgers University Press.

Bernstein, Robin 2009 "Dances With Things: Material Culture and the Performance of Race." *Social Text* 27, no. 4: 67–94.

Bhabha, Homi, ed. 1990 *Nation and Narration.* New York: Routledge.

Bhabha, Homi 1994 *The Location of Culture.* New York: Routledge.

Biesenbach, Klaus, ed. 2010 *Marina Abramović: The Artist Is Present.* New York: The Museum of Modern Art.

Bishop, Claire 2004 "Antagonism and Relational Aesthetics." *October* 110: 51–79.

Bishop, Claire 2008 "Outsourcing Authenticity? Delegated Performance in Contemporary Art," in Claire Bishop and Sylvia Tramontana (eds.) *Double Agent.* London: Institute of Contemporary Arts, 110–25.

Bitterli, Konrad, ed. 2010 *History is Ours: Art by Andrea Geyer and Sharon Hayes.* Heidelberg: Kehrer Verlag.

Blau, Herbert 1982 *Take up the Bodies: Theater at the Vanishing Point.* Urbana, IL: University of Illinois Press.

Blessing, Jennifer, ed. 2006 *A Rose is a Rose is a Rose: Gender Performance in Photography.* New York: Guggenheim Museum.

Blight, David 2002 *Race and Reunion: The Civil War in American Memory.* Cambridge, MA: Harvard University Press.

Blocker, Jane 1999 *Where Is Ana Mendieta: Identity, Performativity, and Exile.* Durham, NC: Duke University Press.

Blocker, Jane 2004 *What the Body Cost: Desire, History, and Performance.* Minneapolis: University of Minnesota Press.

Blocker, Jane 2005 "Binding to Another's Wound: Of Weddings and Witness," in Gavin Butt (ed.) *After Criticism: New Responses to Art and Performance.* New York: Blackwell, 48–64.

Blocker, Jane 2009 *Seeing Witness: Visuality and the Ethics of Testimony.* Minneapolis: University of Minnesota Press.

Borneman, John 2004 "Introduction: Theorizing Regime Ends," in John Borneman (ed.) *Death of the Father: An Anthropology of the End in Political Authority.* New York: Berghahn Books, 1–32.

Bottoms, Stephen 2003 "The Efficacy/Effeminacy Braid: Unpicking the Performance Studies/Theatre Studies Dichotomy." *Theatre Topics* 13, no. 2: 173–87.

Bourriaud, Nicolas 1998 *Relational Aesthetics.* Paris: Les Presses Du Réel.

Bowan, Kate 2010 "R. G. Collingwood, Historical Reenactment, and the Early Music Revival," in Iain McCalman and Paul A. Pickering (eds.) *Historical Reenactment: From Realism to the Affective Turn.* New York: Palgrave MacMillan, 134–58.

Brecht, Stefan 1968 "Family of the f.p.: Notes on the Theatre of the Ridiculous." *The Drama Review* 13, no. 1: 117–41.

Brennan, Teresa 2004 *The Transmission of Affect.* Ithaca, NY: Cornell University Press.

Brody, Jennifer DeVere 2008 *Punctuation: Art, Politics, and Play.* Durham, NC: Duke University Press.

Brown, Wendy 1999 "Resisting Left Melancholy." *Boundary 2* 26, no. 3: 19–27.

Bryan-Wilson, Julia 2008 "Sounding the Fury: Kirsten Forkert and Mark Tribe." *Artforum* 46, no. 5 (January): 95–6.

Bryan-Wilson, Julia 2009 *Art Workers: Radical Practice in the Vietnam War Era.* Berkeley: University of California Press.

Bruner, Edward M. 1994 "Abraham Lincoln as Authentic Reproduction: A Critique of Postmodernism." *American Anthropologist* 96, no. 2: 397–415.

Buchli, Victor, and Gavin Lucas 2001 "The Absent Present: Archaeologies of the Contemporary Present," in Victor Buchli and Gavin Lucas (eds.) *Archaeologies of the Contemporary Past.* New York: Routledge, 3–18.

Burgin, Victor 1996 *In/Different Places: Place and Memory in Visual Culture.* Berkeley: University of California Press.

Burke, Peter 2005 "Performing History: The Importance of Occasions." *Rethinking History* 9, no. 1: 35–52.

Butler, Judith 1990 *Gender Trouble: Feminism and the Subversion of Identity.* New York: Routledge.

Butler, Judith 1990 "Performative Acts and Gender Constitution: An Essay in Phenomenology and Feminist Theory," in Sue-Ellen Case (ed.) *Performing Feminisms: Critical Theory and Theatre.* Baltimore, MD: Johns Hopkins University Press, 270–82.

Butler, Judith 1997 *Excitable Speech: A Politics of the Performative.* New York: Routledge.

Butler, Judith 2009 *Frames of War – When Is Life Grievable?* New York: Verso.

Cadava, Eduardo 1992 "Words of Light: Theses on the Photography of History." *Diacritics* 22, nos. 3/4: 85–114.

Campany, David 2006 "Posing, Acting, Photography," in David Green and Joanna Lowry (eds.) *Stillness and Time: Photography and the Moving Image.* Brighton: Photoworks/ Photoforum, 97–112.

Carlson, Marvin 2000 "Performing the Past: Living History and Cultural Memory." *Paragrana* 9, no. 2: 237–48.

Carlson, Marvin 2001 *The Haunted Stage: The Theatre as Memory Machine.* Ann Arbor: University of Michigan Press.

Caronia, Antonio, Janez Janša and Domenico Quaranta, eds. 2009 *Re:Akt: Reconstruction, Re-enactment, Re-porting.* Italy: F.P. Editions.

Carriger, Michelle Liu 2010 "Historionics: Neither Here Nor There with Historical Reality TV." *Journal of Dramatic Theory and Criticism* 24, no. 2: 135–50.

Caruth, Cathy 1996 *Unclaimed Experience: Trauma, Narrative, and History.* Baltimore, MD: Johns Hopkins University Press.

Case, Sue-Ellen 1991 "Tracking the Vampire." *Differences* 3, no. 2: 1–20.

Case, Sue-Ellen and Jeanie K. Forte 1985 "From Formalism to Feminism." *Theater* 16, no. 2: 62–5.

Chakrabarty, Dipesh 1997 "The Time of History and the Times of the Gods," in Lisa Lowe and David Lloyd (eds.) *The Politics of Culture in the Shadow of Capital.* Durham, NC: Duke University Press, 35–60.

Chow, Rey 1991 *Women and Chinese Modernity: The Politics of Reading Between East and West.* Minneapolis: University of Minnesota Press.

Clarke, Paul and Julian Warren 2009 "Ephemera: Between Archival Objects and Events." *Journal of the Society of Archivists* 30, no. 1: 45–66.

Clough, Patricia, ed. 2007 *The Affective Turn: Theorizing the Social.* Durham, NC: Duke University Press.

Connerton, Paul 1989 *How Societies Remember.* New York: Cambridge University Press.

Conquergood, Dwight 2002 "Performance Studies: Interventions and Radical Research." *TDR: The Drama Review* 46, no. 2: 145–56.

Cook, Alexander 2004 "The Use and Abuse of Historical Reenactment: Thoughts on Recent Trends in Public History." *Criticism* 46, no. 3: 487–96.

Cooke, Lynne 2003 "A Tempered Agnosia," in George Baker (ed.) *James Coleman.* Cambridge, MA: MIT Press, 113–38.

Craig, Edward Gordon 1911 [1905] *On the Art of the Theatre.* New York: Theatre Arts Books.

Crary, Jonathan 1991 *Techniques of the Observer: On Vision and Modernity in the 19th Century.* Cambridge, MA: MIT Press.

Cvetkovich, Ann 2003 *An Archive of Feelings: Trauma, Sexuality, and Lesbian Public Cultures.* Durham, NC: Duke University Press.

Cypriano, Fabio 2009 "Performance and Reenactment: Analyzing Marina Abramović's *Seven Easy Pieces.*" Idanca.net. Available online at http://idanca.net/lang/en-us/2009/09/02/performance-e-reencenacao-uma-analise-de-seven-eeasy-pieces-de-marina-Abramović/12156/ (accessed March 10, 2010).

Daly, Ann 1987 "Cross Way Cross." *High Performance* 38: 74.

Danto, Arthur C. 1987 "Cindy Sherman." *The Nation.* August 15/22: 134–7.

Danto, Arthur C. 1990 "Photography and Performance: Cindy Sherman's Stills," in Cindy Sherman, *Cindy Sherman: Untitled Film Stills.* Munich: Schirmer, 5–14.

Danto, Arthur C. 1991 "Post Masters and Post Modern: Cindy Sherman's *History Portraits,*" in *Cindy Sherman: History Portraits.* New York: Rizzoli.

Davis, Tracy 2004 "Theatricality and Civil Society," in Tracy Davis and Thomas Postlewait (eds.) *Theatricality.* New York: Cambridge University Press, 127–55.

Davis, Tracy and Thomas Postlewait, eds. 2004 *Theatricality.* New York: Cambridge University Press.

de Beauvoir, Simone 1989 [1952] *The Second Sex.* Translated by H. M. Parshley. New York: Vintage.

de Certeau, Michel 1984 *The Practice of Everyday Life.* Translated by Steven F. Rendall. Berkeley: University of California Press.

de Certeau, Michel 1988 *The Writing of History.* New York: Columbia University Press.

de Groot, Jerome 2008 *Consuming History: Historians and Heritage in Contemporary Popular Culture.* New York: Routledge.

de Lauretis, Teresa 1985 "Desire in Narrative," in *Alice Doesn't: Feminism, Semiotics, Cinema.* Bloomington: Indiana University Press, 103–57.

de Lauretis, Teresa 1987 *Technologies of Gender: Essays on Theory, Film, and Fiction.* Bloomington: Indiana University Press.

Deller, Jeremy 2002 *The English Civil War: Part II.* London: Artangel.

Deloria, Philip J. 1999 *Playing Indian.* New Haven, CT: Yale University Press.

Derrida, Jacques 1981 *Positions.* Translated by Alan Bass. Chicago, IL: University of Chicago Press.

Derrida, Jacques 1994 *Specters of Marx: The State of the Debt, The Work of Mourning , and the New International.* Translated by Peggy Kamuf. New York: Routledge.

Derrida, Jacques 1995 *Archive Fever: A Freudian Impression.* Chicago, IL: University of Chicago Press.

Derrida, Jacques 2003 "The Deaths of Roland Barthes," in *The Work of Mourning.* Translated by Pascale-Anne Brault. Chicago, IL: University of Chicago Press.

Deutsche, Rosalyn 2006 "Not-Forgetting: Mary Kelly's Love Songs." *Grey Room* 24: 26–37.

Diamond, Elin 1988 "Brechtian Theory/Feminist Theory: Toward a Gestic Feminist Criticism." *TDR: The Drama Review* 32, no. 1: 82–94.

Diamond, Elin 1997 *Unmaking Mimesis: Essays on Feminism and Theatre.* New York: Routledge.

Dickey, Stephen 2006 "Lincoln and Shakespeare." Available online at http://www.shakespeareinamericanlife.org/identity/politicians/presidents/pick/lincoln/lincoln_shakespeare_2.cfm (accessed August 3, 2009).

Dinshaw, Carolyn 1999 *Getting Medieval: Sexual Communities Pre- and Post-Modern.* Durham, NC: Duke University Press.

Doane, Mary Ann 2002 *The Emergence of Cinematic Time: Modernity, Contingency, The Archive.* Cambridge, MA: Harvard University Press.

Doane, Mary Ann 2006 "Real Time: Instantaneity and the Photographic Imaginary," in David Green (ed.) *Stillness and Time: Photography and the Moving Image.* Brighton: Photoworks/ Photoforum, 23–38.

Dolan, Jill 1985 *The Feminist Spectator as Critic.* Ann Arbor: University of Michigan Press.

Drewal, Margaret Thompson 1992 *Yoruba Ritual: Performers, Play, Agency.* Bloomington, IN: Indiana University Press.

Drukman, Steven 1995 "Suzan-Lori Parks and Liz Diamond: Do-a-Diddly-Dit-Dit." *TDR: The Drama Review* 39: no. 3: 56–73.

Duara, Prasenjit 1995 *Rescuing History from the Nation.* Chicago, IL: University of Chicago Press.

Dunkelberg, Kermit 2005 "Confrontation, Simulation, Admiration: The Wooster Group's *Poor Theater.*" *TDR: The Drama Review* 49, no. 3: 43–57.

Durkheim, Emile 1987 *Suicide.* Translated by John A. Spaulding. New York: Free Press.

Durkheim, Emile 2008 *The Elementary Forms of Religions Life.* Translated by Carol Cosman. New York: Oxford University Press.

Elam, Harry J., Jr. and Alice Rayner 1994 "Unfinished Business: Reconfiguring History in Suzan-Lori Parks's *The Death of the Last Black Man in the Whole Entire World.*" *Theatre Journal* 46, no. 4: 447–61.

Eliade, Mircea 1959 *The Sacred and the Profane: The Nature of Religion.* Translated by Willard R. Trask. New York: Harcourt, Brace, Jovanovich.

Eliade, Mircea 2005 *The Myth of the Eternal Return.* Princeton, NJ: Princeton University Press.

Emigh, John 2011 "Liminal Richard: A Prelude to Performance Studies," in James Harding and Cindy Rosenthal (eds.) *The Rise of Performance Studies: Rethinking Richard Schechner's Broad Spectrum.* New York: Palgrave Macmillan.

Enders, Jody 1999 *The Medieval Theater of Cruelty: Rhetoric, Memory, Violence.* Ithaca, NY: Cornell University Press.

Erickson, Jon 1995 *The Fate of the Object: From Modern Object to Postmodern Sign in Performance, Art, and Poetry.* Ann Arbor: University of Michigan Press.

Fabian, Johannes 1983 *Time and the Other: How Anthropology Makes Its Object.* New York: Columbia University Press.

Féral, Josette, ed. 2002 "Theatricality." Special issue of *SubStance* 31, nos. 2, 3.

Fischer-Lichte, Erika 1995 "Introduction" to "Theatricality: A Key Concept in Theatre and Cultural Studies." *Theatre Research International* 20, no. 2: 97–105.

Fischer-Lichte, Erika 2008 *The Transformative Power of Performance: A New Aesthetics.* Translated by Saskia Iris Jain. New York: Routledge.

Forgie, George B. 1981 *Patricide in the House Divided.* New York: W. W. Norton.

Foster, Hal 1996 *The Return of the Real: Art and Theory at the End of the Century.* Cambridge, MA: MIT Press.

Foster, Susan Leigh, ed. 1995 *Choreographing History.* Bloomington: Indiana University Press.

Foucault, Michel 1972 *The Archaeology of Knowledge and the Discourse on Language.* Translated by Alan Sheridan. London: Tavistock.

Foucault, Michel 1977 *Language, Counter-Memory, Practice.* Ithaca, NY: Cornell University Press.

Fradenberg, Louise and Carla Freccero 1996 "Caxton, Foucault, and the Pleasures of History," in Louise Fradenberg and Carla Freccero (eds.) *Premodern Sexualities.* New York: Routledge.

Franklin, Paul B. 1998 "Orienting the Asian Male Body in the Photography of Yasumasa Morimura," in Brenda Bright (ed.) *The Passionate Camera: Photography and Bodies of Desire*. New York: Routledge, 233–47.

Franko, Mark and Annette Richards, eds. 2000 *Acting on the Past: Historical Performance Across the Disciplines*. Middletown, CT: Wesleyan University Press.

Freccero, Carla 2006 *Queer/Early/Modern*. Durham, NC: Duke University Press.

Freeman, Elizabeth 2000 "Packing History, Count(er)ing Generations." *New Literary History* 31, no. 4: 727–44.

Freeman, Elizabeth 2005 "Time Binds, or Erotohistory." *Social Text* 23, nos. 3–4: 57–68.

Freeman, Elizabeth, ed. 2007 "Queer Temporalities." A Special issue of *GLQ: A Journal of Lesbian and Gay Studies* 13, nos. 2–3.

Freud, Sigmund 1955 *Moses and Monotheism*. Translated by Katherine Jones. New York: Vintage.

Freud, Sigmund 1958 "Remembering, Repeating, and Working-Through." Translated by James Strachey. *The Standard Edition of the Complete Psychological Works of Sigmund Freud*, Volume 12. New York: Hogarth Press.

Freud, Sigmund 1990 *Beyond the Pleasure Principle*. Translated by James Strachey. New York: Norton.

Fried, Michael 1995 [1967] "Art and Objecthood." Reprinted in Gregory Battock (ed.) *Minimal Art*. Berkeley: University of California Press.

Fuchs, Elinor 2002 "Reading for Landscape: The Case of American Drama," in Elinor Fuchs and Una Chaudhuri (eds.) *Land/Scape/Theater*. Ann Arbor: University of Michigan Press, 30–50.

Garber, Marjorie 2005 *Shakespeare After All*. New York: Anchor.

Garner, Stanton B. 1994 *Bodied Spaces: Phenomenology and Performance in Contemporary Drama*. Ithaca, NY: Cornell University Press.

Geertz, Clifford 1977 *The Interpretation of Cultures*. New York: Basic Books.

Gefter, Philip 2009 *Photography After Frank*. New York: Aperture.

Gilbert, Sandra and Susan Gubar 1979 *The Madwoman in the Attic: The Woman Writer and the Nineteenth-Century Literary Imagination*. New Haven, CT: Yale University Press.

Godard, Jean-Luc and Jean-Pierre Gorin 1972 *Letter to Jane: An Investigation about a Still*. Film. Postscript to *Tout va bien*. Anouchka Films.

Goffman, Erving 1986 *Frame Analysis*. Lebanon, NH: Northeastern University Press.

Gold, Sam 2004 Personal correspondence. July 1, 4.

Goldberg, Marianne 1988/89 "Turning History Around: Linda Mussmann's *Chronicles*." *Women and Performance* 4, no. 1: 150–6.

Golub, Spencer 1994 *The Recurrence of Fate: Theatre and Memory in Twentieth-Century Russia*. Iowa City: University of Iowa Press.

Gómez-Peña, Guillermo 2005 *Ethno-Techno: Writings on Performance, Activism, and Pedagogy*. New York: Routledge.

Gopnik, Adam 2007 "Angels and Ages: Lincoln's Language and its Legacy. *The New Yorker*, May 28.

Gopnik, Adam 2009 *Angels and Ages: A Short Book about Darwin, Lincoln, and Modern Life*. New York: Knopf.

Gordon, Avery F. 1997 *Ghostly Matters: Haunting and the Sociological Imagination*. Minneapolis: University of Minnesota Press.

Gorton, Kristyn 2007 "Theorizing Emotion and Affect: Feminist Engagements." *Feminist Theory* 8, no. 3: 333–48.

Greenaway, Twilight n.d. "Miranda July: Performance." *Curve Magazine*. Available online at http://backup.curvemag.com/Detailed/85.html (accessed October 11, 2002).

Greenblatt, Stephen 1988 *Shakespearean Negotiations*. Berkeley: University of California Press.

Grotowski, Jerzy 1968 *Towards a Poor Theatre*. New York: Simon and Schuster.

Grotowski, Jerzy 1987 "*Tu es le fils de quelqu'un* [You are someone's son]." *TDR: The Drama Review* 31, no. 3: 30–41.

Grosz, Elizabeth 2005 *Time Travels: Feminism, Nature, Power*. Durham, NC: Duke University Press.

Halberstam, Judith 2005 *In a Queer Time and Place*. New York: New York University Press.

Halbwachs, Maurice 1992 *On Collective Memory*. Chicago, IL: University of Chicago Press.

Hammond, Harmony 1984 "Hearing and Seeing: Linda Mussmann and Ann Wilson on Creating Nonnarrative Theater." *Heresies* 17: 89–93.

Handler, Richard and William Saxton 1988 "Dyssimulation: Reflexivity, Narrative, and the Quest for Authenticity in 'Living History.'" *Cultural Anthropology* 3, no. 2: 242–60.

Hardwick, Elizabeth 1970 "The Theater of Grotowski." *New York Review of Books* 14, no. 3, February 12.

Hartman, Saidiya 1997 *Scenes of Subjection: Terror, Slavery, and Self-Making in Nineteenth-Century America*. New York: Oxford University Press.

Hayes, Sharon 2008 *After Before – In the Near Future*. New York: Art In General.

Heathfield, Adrian, ed. 2004 *Live: Art and Performance*. London: Tate Publishing.

Heidegger, Martin 1984 *Nietzsche. Volume II: The Eternal Recurrence of the Same*. Translated by David Farrell Krell. New York: Harper and Row.

Hell, Julia 2004 "The Angel's Enigmatic Eyes, or The Gothic Beauty of Catastrophic History in W. G. Sebald's 'Air War and Literature.'" *Criticism* 46, no. 3: 361–92.

Hertz, Betti-Sue 2008 "Eleanor Antin's Transpositions: A Feminist View of Academic Painting in the Age of Digital Photography," in Betti-Sue Hertz (ed.) *Eleanor Antin: Historical Takes*. San Diego, CA: San Diego Museum of Art, 81–91.

Hodgdon, Barbara 2003 "Photography, Theatre, Mnemonics; or, Thirteen Ways of Looking at a Still," in W. B. Worthen and Peter Holland (eds.) *Theorizing Practice: Redefining Theatre History*. London: Palgrave Macmillan, 88–119.

Horwitz, Tony 1999 *Confederates in the Attic: Dispatches from the Unfinished Civil War*. New York: Vintage.

Hoyne, Alina 2009 "Doing It Again: Re-enactment in Contemporary British Art (1996–2007)." Ph.D. dissertation. School of Culture and Communications, University of Melbourne, February.

Hungerford, Amy 2001 "Memorizing Memory." *The Yale Journal of Criticism* 14, no.1: 67–92.

Iles, Chrissie 2010 "Marina Abramović and the Public: A Theater of Exchange," in Klaus Biesenbach (ed.) *Marina Abramović: The Artist Is Present*. New York: The Museum of Modern Art, 40–3.

Irigaray, Luce 1981 "When the Goods Get Together," in Elaine Marks and Isabelle de Courtivron (eds.) *New French Feminisms*. New York: Schocken Books, 99–110.

Irigaray, Luce 1985 *Speculum of the Other Woman*. Ithaca, NY: Cornell University Press.

Irigaray, Luce 1993 *An Ethics of Sexual Difference*. Translated by Carolyn Burke and Fill Gillian. Ithaca, NY: Cornell University Press.

Jackson, Shannon 2000 *Lines of Activity: Performance, Historiography, and Hull-House Domesticity*. Ann Arbor: University of Michigan Press.

Jackson, Shannon 2004 *Professing Performance: Theatre in the Academy from Philology to Performativity*. New York: Cambridge University Press.

Jackson, Shannon 2011 *Social Works: Performing Publics*. New York: Routledge.

Jakobsen, Janet R. and Ann Pellegrini 2000 "Dreaming Secularism." Introduction to special issue "World Secularisms at the Millennium." *Social Text* 18, no. 3: 1–27.

Jakobsen, Janet R. and Ann Pellegrini 2008 "Times Like These," in Janet Jakobsen and Ann Pellegrini (eds.) *Secularisms*. Durham, NC: Duke University Press, 1–36.

Jameson, Fredric 1988 "Postmodernism and Consumer Society," in E. Ann Kaplan (ed.) *Postmodernism and Its Discontents*. London: Verso.

Jameson, Fredric 1991 *Postmodernism, Or, the Cultural Logic of Late Capitalism*. Durham, NC: Duke University Press.

Jarman, Neil 1997 *Material Conflicts: Parades and Visual Displays in Northern Ireland*. Oxford: Berg Publishers.

Jay, Martin 2006 *Songs of Experience: Modern American and European Variations on a Universal Theme*. Berkeley: University of California Press.

Jones, Amelia 1997 "'Presence' in Absentia: Experiencing Performance Art as Documentation." *Art Journal* 56, no. 4: 11–18.

Jones, Amelia 1998 *Body/Art: Performing the Subject*. Minneapolis: University of Minnesota Press.

Jones, Amelia 2002 "The 'Eternal Return': Self-Portrait Photography as a Technology of Embodiment." *Signs: Journal of Women in Culture and Society* 27, no. 4: 947–78.

Jones, Meta Du Ewa 2002 "Jazz Prosodies: Orality and Textuality." *Callaloo* 25, no. 1: 66–91.

Jost, François 1978 "John Wilkes Booth and Abraham Lincoln: The Reenactment of a Murder." *MLN* 93, no. 3: 503–5.

Judt, Tony 2008 "What Have We Learned, If Anything?" *The New York Review of Books* 55, no. 7, May 1.

Kammen, Michael 1993 *Mystic Chords of Memory: The Transformation of Tradition in American Culture*. New York: Vintage Books.

Kauffman, Michael W. 2004 *American Brutus: John Wilkes Booth and the Lincoln Conspiracies*. New York: Random House.

Kaye, Nick 2000 *Site-Specific Art: Performance, Place, Documentation*. New York: Routledge.

Kaye, Nick 2007 *Multi-Media: Video, Installation, Performance*. New York: Routledge.

Keats, John 2005 [1817] "Letter from John Keats to Benjamin Bailey, 22 November 1817," in Duncan Wu (ed.) *Romanticism: An Anthology*. London: Blackwell, 1349–51.

Kernodle, George 1944 *From Art to Theatre: Form and Convention in the Renaissance*. Chicago, IL: Chicago University Press.

Kierkegaard, Søren 1983 *Fear and Trembling/Repetition*. Translated by Howard V. Hong and Edna H. Hong. Princeton, NJ: Princeton University Press.

Kino, Carol 2010 "A Rebel Form Gains Favor. Fights Ensue." *The New York Times*, March 14: AR25.

Kipling, George 1998 *Enter the King: Theatre, Liturgy, and Ritual in the Medieval Civic Triumph*. Oxford: Clarendon Press.

Kirshenblatt-Gimblett, Barbara 1998 *Destination Culture: Tourism, Museums, and Heritage*. Berkeley: University of California Press.

Klein, Kerwin Lee 2000 "On the Emergence of Memory in Historical Discourse." Special issue, "Grounds for Remembering." *Representations* 69: 127–50.

Kostelanetz, Richard 1981 "Robert Wilson, Richard Foreman, Linda Mussmann: A Symposium on Writing and Performance." *New York Arts Journal* 25–6: 4–9.

Kracauer, Siegfried 1995 "Photography." Republished in *The Mass Ornament*. Translated by Thomas Y. Levin. Cambridge, MA: Harvard University Press.

Krauss, Rosalind 1999 "Reinventing the Medium." *Critical Inquiry* 25, no. 2: 289–305.

Krauss, Rosalind 2000 *A Voyage on the North Sea: Art in the Age of the Post-Medium Condition.* London: Thames & Hudson.

Kristopherson, Kris 1999 *Not Shall Your Glory Be Forgot.* New York: St. Martin's Press.

Kruger, Barbara 1990 *Love for Sale: The Words and Pictures of Barbara Kruger.* New York: Harry N. Abrams.

Kuspit, Donald 2003 "Art's Identity Crisis: Yasumasa Morimura's Photographs," in *Daughters of Art History: The Photographs of Yasumasa Morimura.* New York: Aperture, 7–11.

Lambert-Beatty, Carrie 2010 "Performance Police." Unpublished paper presented at "Thinking Performance," a symposium sponsored by the Guggenheim Museum, New York, June 18.

Lee, Pamela 2004 *Chronophobia: On Time in the Art of the 1960s.* Cambridge, MA: MIT Press.

Le Goff, Jacques 1992 *History and Memory.* Translated by Steven Rendall and Elizabeth Claman. New York: Columbia University Press.

LeMenager, Stephanie 2007 *Manifest and Other Destinies: Territorial Fictions of the Nineteenth-Century United States.* Lincoln: University of Nebraska Press.

LePecki, André 2006 *Exhausting Dance: Performance and the Politics of Movement.* New York: Routledge.

Lincoln, Abraham 1989 "Abraham Lincoln to James H. Hackett, August 17, 1863," in *Lincoln, Speeches and Writings 1859–1865.* New York: Library of America.

Lingis, Alphonso 1994 "The Society of Disremembered Body Parts," in Constantin Boundas and Dorothea Olkowski (eds.) *Deleuze and the Theatre of Philosophy.* New York: Routledge.

Lippard, Lucy 1997 *Six Years: The Dematerialization of the Art Object, 1966–1972.* Berkeley: University of California Press.

Lorde, Audre 1984 "The Master's Tools Will Never Dismantle the Master's House," in *Sister Outsider: Essays and Speeches.* Trumansburg, NY: The Crossing Press, 110–14.

Love, Heather 2009 *Feeling Backward: Loss and the Politics of Queer History.* Cambridge, MA: Harvard University Press.

Lowenthal, David 1999 *The Past is a Foreign Country.* New York: Cambridge University Press.

Lowenthal, David 2002 "The Past as a Theme Park," in Terence Young and Robert Riley (eds.) *Theme Park Landscapes: Antecedents and Variations.* Washington, DC: Dumbarton Oaks, 11–23.

Lubow, Arthur 2010 "Making Art Out of an Encounter." *The New York Times Magazine,* January 15.

Lucas, Gavin 2004 "Modern Disturbances: On the Ambiguities of Archaeology." *Modernism/modernity* 11, no. 1: 109–20.

Luciano, Dana 2007 *Arranging Grief: Sacred Time and the Body in Nineteenth-Century America.* New York: New York University Press.

Lütticken, Sven 2002 "An Arena in Which to Reenact," in Sven Lütticken (ed.) *Life Once More: Forms of Re-enactment in Contemporary Art.* Rotterdam: Witte de With Institute, 17–60.

Lütticken, Sven 2005 "Introduction," in Sven Lütticken (ed.) *Life Once More: Forms of Re-enactment in Contemporary Art.* Rotterdam: Witte de With Institute, 5–8.

MacKay, Ellen 2009 "Theatre as a Self-Consuming Art." *Theatre Survey* 49: 91–107.

Magelssen, Scott 2007 *Living History Museums: Undoing History Through Performance.* Lanham, MD: Scarecrow Press.

Malkin, Jeanette 1999 *Memory-Theatre and Postmodern Drama.* Ann Arbor: University of Michigan Press.

Mann, Sally 2003 *What Remains.* New York: Bulfinch Press.

Marks, Laura U. 2000 *The Skin of the Film: Intercultural Cinema, Embodiment, and the Senses*. Durham, NC: Duke University Press.

Martin, Stewart 2007 "Critique of Relational Aesthetics." *Third Text*, 21, no. 4: 369–86.

Marx, Karl 1913 *The Eighteenth Brumaire of Louis Bonaparte*. Translated by Daniel De Leon. Ann Arbor, MI: C. H. Kerr, 9–10.

Marx, Karl 1972 *The Grundrisse*. Translated by David McLellan. New York: Harper and Row.

Marx, Karl 1986 *The Economic and Philosophical Manuscripts of 1844*, excerpted in Jon Elster (ed.) *Karl Marx: A Reader*. New York: Cambridge University Press, 35–46.

Massumi, Brian 2002 *Parables for the Virtual: Movement, Affect, Sensation*. Durham, NC: Duke University Press.

McCalman, Iain, and Paul A. Pickering, eds. 2010 *Historical Reenactment: From Realism to the Affective Turn*. New York: Palgrave Macmillan.

McEwen, Indra Kagis 2003 *Vitruvius: Writing the Body of Architecture*. Cambridge, MA: MIT Press.

McGarry, Molly 2008 *Ghosts of Futures Past: Spiritualism and the Politics of Nineteenth-Century America*. Berkeley: University of California Press.

McIvor, Frazer 2010 "Tino Sehgal's Living Sculptures," in the webzine *Escape into Life*, February 11. Available online at http://www.escapeintolife.com/art-reviews/tino-sehgal-living-sculptures/ (accessed February 20, 2010).

McKenzie, Jon 2001 *Perform or Else: From Discipline to Performance*. New York: Routledge.

Melville, Herman 1970 *White-Jacket: Or, the World on a Man-of-War*. Evanston, IL: Northwestern University Press.

Mercer, Kobena 1996 "To Unbury the Disremembered Past: Keith Piper," in Milena Kalinovska (ed.) *New Histories*. Boston, MA: Institute of Contemporary Arts.

Merleau-Ponty, Maurice 1969 *The Visible and the Invisible*. Translated by Alphonso Lingis. Evanston, IL: Northwestern University Press.

Miller, Richard 2009 Newsletter of the Association of Lincoln Presenters (March). Available online at http://www.lincolnpresenters.net.

Morimura, Yasumasa 2005 *Daughter of Art History: Photographs of Yasumasa Morimura*. New York: Aperture.

Morimura, Yasumasa 2007 *Yasumasa Morimura: On Self-Portait: Through the Looking Glass*. Amsterdam: Reflex Editions.

Morrison, Toni 1994 *Lecture and speech of acceptance, upon the award of the Nobel prize for literature, delivered in Stockholm on the seventh of December, nineteen hundred and ninety-three*. New York: Knopf.

Morrison, Toni 2006 *Beloved*. New York: Everyman's Library.

Moten, Fred 2003 "Not In Between: Lyric Painting, Visual History, and the Postcolonial Future." *TDR: The Drama Review* 47, no.1: 127–48.

Moten, Fred 2003 *In the Break: The Aesthetics of the Black Radical Tradition*. Minneapolis: University of Minnesota Press.

Moten, Fred and Charles Henry Rowell 2004 "'Words Don't Go There': An Interview with Fred Moten." *Callaloo* 27, no. 4: 954–66.

Mulvey, Laura 1975 "Visual Pleasure and Narrative Cinema." *Screen* 16, no. 3: 6–18.

Mulvey, Laura 2006 *Death 24× a Second: Stillness and the Moving Image*. New York: Reaktion Books.

Muñoz, José Esteban 1996 "Ephemera as Evidence: Introductory Notes to Queer Acts." *Women and Performance: A Journal of Feminist Theory* 8, no. 2: 5–16.

Muñoz, José Esteban 1999 *Disidentifications: Queers of Color and the Performance of Politics*. Minneapolis: University of Minnesota Press.

Muñoz, José Esteban 2000 "Feeling Brown and Affect in Ricardo Bracho's The Sweetest Hangover (and Other STDs)." *Theatre Journal* 52, no.1: 67–79.

Mussmann, Linda 1987 "If Kansas Goes." Unpublished play.

Mussmann, Linda 1988/89 "*Cross Way Cross: Civil War Chronicles*, Part III." *Women and Performance* 4, no. 1: 88–149.

Nealon, Chris 2001 *Foundlings: Lesbian and Gay Historical Emotion Before Stonewall*. Durham, NC: Duke University Press.

Neidich, Warren 1989 *American History Reinvented*. New York: Aperture.

Ngũgĩ wa Thiong'o 2007 "Notes Toward a Performance Theory of Orature." *Performance Research* 12, no. 3: 4–7.

Nietzsche, Friedrich 1961 *Thus Spoke Zarathustra*. Translated by R. J. Hollingdale. New York: Penguin.

Nietzsche, Friedrich 1974 *The Gay Science: With a Prelude in Rhymes and an Appendix of Songs*. Translated by Walter Kaufmann. New York: Vintage.

Nietzsche, Friedrich 2009 *On the Genealogy of Morals*. Translated by Douglas Smith. New York: Oxford University Press.

Nyong'o, Tavia 2009 *The Amalgamation Waltz: Race, Performance, and the Ruses of Memory*. Minneapolis: University of Minnesota Press.

Ong, Walter 1982 *Orality and Literacy: The Technologizing of the Word*. New York: Methuen.

O'Quinn, Jim 1980 "Linda Mussmann's Time and Space Limited Theater." *TDR: The Drama Review* 24, no. 2: 17–84.

O'Sullivan, John L. 1839 "The Great Nation of Futurity." *United States Magazine and Democratic Review* 6, no. 23 (November): 426–30.

Owens, Craig 1994 *Beyond Recognition: Representatoin, Power, and Culture*. Berkeley: University of California Press.

Panofsky, Erwin 1991 *Perspective as Symbolic Form*. Translated by Christopher S. Wood. New York: Zone Books.

Parks, Suzan-Lori 1995 *The America Play and Other Works*. New York: Theatre Communications Group.

Parks, Suzan-Lori 1995 "Elements of Style," in *The America Play and Other Works*. New York: Theatre Communications Group, 6–18.

Parks, Suzan-Lori 1999 *Topdog/Underdog*. New York: Theatre Communications Group.

Pauli, Lori, ed. 2006 *Acting the Part: Photography As Theatre*. New York: Merrell Publishers.

Pearson, Mike and Michael Shanks 2001 *Theatre/Archaeology: Disciplinary Dialogues*. New York: Routledge.

Pellegrini, Ann 1997 *Performance Anxieties: Staging Psychoanalysis, Staging Race*. New York: Routledge.

Pellegrini, Ann 2001 "(Laughter)," in Patrick Campbell and Adrian Kear (eds.) *Psychoanalysis and Performance*. New York: Routledge, 177–91.

Pellegrini, Ann 2007 "After Sontag: Future Notes on Camp," in George E. Haggerty and Molly McGarry (eds.) *Companion to Lesbian, Gay, Bisexual, Transgender, Queer Studies*. London: Blackwell, 168–93.

Phelan, Peggy 1988 Unpublished paper delivered at post-performance discussion of Time and Space Limited Theater's *Mary Surratt*. Village Community School, New York, February 12.

Phelan, Peggy 1990 "Serrano, Mapplethorpe, the NEA, and You: Money Talks." *TDR: The Drama Review* 34, no. 1: 4–15.

Phelan, Peggy 1991 "Money Talks, Again." *TDR: The Drama Review* 35, no. 3: 131–41.

Phelan, Peggy 1993 *Unmarked: The Politics of Performance*. New York: Routledge.

Piper, Keith 1997 *Relocating the Remains*. London: Institute of International Visual Artists.

Posner, Dassia N. 2009 "A Theatrical Zigzag: Doctor Dappertutto, Columbine's Veil, and the Grotesque." *Slavic and East European Performance* 29, no. 3: 43–53.

Puar, Jasbir K. 2005 "Queer Times, Queer Assemblages." *Social Text* 23, nos. 3–4: 121–39.

Puar, Jasbir K. 2005 "On Torture: Abu Ghraib." *Radical History Review* 93: 13–38.

Puar, Jasbir K. 2007 *Terrorist Assemblages: Homonationalism in Queer Times*. Durham, NC: Duke University Press.

Puchner, Martin 2002 *Stage Fright: Modernism, Antitheatricality, and Drama*. Baltimore, MD: Johns Hopkins University Press.

Purvis, Jennifer 2004 "Grrrls and Women Together in the Third Wave: Embracing the Challenges of Intergenerational Feminism(s)." *NWSA Journal* 16, no. 3: 93–123.

Quinn, Richard 2000 "The Creak of Categories: Nathaniel Mackey's '*Strick: Song of the Andoumboulou 16–25*.'" *Callaloo* 23, no. 2: 608–20.

Rainer, Yvonne 1985 "More Kicking and Screaming from the Narrative Front/ Backwater." *Wide Angle* 7, nos. 1 & 2: 8–12.

Rayner, Alice 1994 *To Act, To Do, To Perform: The Phenomenology of Action*. Ann Arbor: University of Michigan Press.

Rayner, Alice 2006 *Ghosts: Death's Double and the Phenomena of Theatre*. Minneapolis: University of Minnesota Press.

Renan, Ernst 1989 "What is a Nation?," reprinted in Homi Bhabha (ed.) *Nation and Narration*. New York: Routledge.

Reynolds, Bryan 2002 *Becoming Criminal: Transversal Performance and Cultural Dissidence in Early Modern England*. Baltimore, MD: Johns Hopkins University Press.

Rich, Adrienne 1979 "When We Dead Awaken: Writing as Re-vision," in *On Lies, Secrets, and Silence*. New York: W. W. Norton, 33–49.

Richmond, Susan 2010 "'From Stone to Cloud': Mary Kelly's Love Songs and Feminist Intergenerationality." *Feminist Theory* 11, no. 1: 57–78.

Ricoeur, Paul 2004 *Memory, History, Forgetting*. Translated by Kathleen Blamey and David Pellauer. Chicago, IL: University of Chicago Press.

Ridout, Nicholas 2006 *Stage Fright, Animals, and Other Theatrical Problems*. New York: Cambridge University Press.

Ridout, Nicholas 2008 "Performance in the Service Economy: Outsourcing and Delegation," in Claire Bishop and Sylvia Tramontana (eds.) *Double Agent*. London: Institute of Contemporary Arts, 126–31.

Riviere, Joan 1929 "Womanliness as Masquerade." *International Journal of Psycho-Analysis* 10: 303–13.

Roach, Joseph 1996 *Cities of the Dead: Circum-Atlantic Performance*. New York: Columbia University Press.

Robinson, Marc 2002 "Robert Wilson, Nicolas Poussin, and Lohengrin," in Elinor Fuchs and Una Chaudhuri (eds.) *Land/Scape/Theater*. Ann Arbor: University of Michigan Press, 159–85.

Rokem, Freddie 2000 *Performing History: Theatrical Representations of the Past*. Iowa City: University of Iowa Press.

Romàn, David 2005 *Performance in America: Contemporary US Culture and the Performing Arts*. Durham, NC: Duke University Press.

Romanska, Magda 2009 "Between History and Memory: Auschwitz in *Akropolis*, *Akropolis* in Auschwitz." *Theatre Survey* 50, no. 2: 223–50.

Roth, Stacy F. 1998 *Past Into Present: Effective Techniques for First-Person Historical Interpretation.* Chapel Hill, NC: University of North Carolina Press.

Ruane, Michael E. 2009 "Lots of Lincolns Bring Honest Abe's Ethics to Town." *The Washington Post*, April 19.

Rushton, Steve 2004 *The Milgram Re-Enactment.* Maastricht: Eyck Academie.

Samuels, Shirley, ed. 1992 *The Culture of Sentiment: Race, Gender and Sentimentality in 19th-Century America.* New York: Oxford University Press.

Samuels, Shirley 2004 *Facing America: Iconography and the Civil War.* New York: Oxford University Press.

Santayana, George 1905 *The Life of Reason.* New York: Charles Scribner's Sons.

Santone, Jessica 2008 "Marina Abramović's *Seven Easy Pieces*: Critical Documentation Strategies for Preserving Art's History." *Leonardo* 41, no. 2: 147–52.

Sapir, Michael 1994 "The Impossible Photograph: Hippolyte Bayard's Self-Portrait as a Drowned Man." *MFS: Modern Fiction Studies* 40, no. 3: 619–29.

Sarlin, Paige 2009 "New Left-Wing Melancholy: Mark Tribe's 'The Port Huron Project' and the Politics of Reenactment." *Framework* 50, nos. 1 & 2: 139–57.

Savran, David 1988 *Breaking the Rules: The Wooster Group.* New York: Theatre Communications Group.

Savran, David 2001 "Choices Made and Unmade." *Theater* 31, no. 2: 89–107.

Sayre, Henry 1989 *The Object of Performance: The American Avant-Garde Since 1970.* Chicago, IL: University of Chicago Press.

Sayre, Henry 2004 "In the Space of Duration," in Adrian Heathfield (ed.) *Live: Art and Performance.* London: Tate Publishing, 38–45.

Schechner, Richard 1965 "Theatre Criticism." *The Tulane Drama Review* 9, no. 3: 13–24.

Schechner, Richard 1970 "Actuals: A Look into Performance Theory," in Alan Cheuse and Richard Koffler (eds.) *The Rarer Action: Essays in Honor of Frances Ferguson.* New Brunswick, NJ: Rutgers University Press, 97–135.

Schechner, Richard 1974 "From Ritual to Theatre and Back: The Structure/Process of the Efficacy–Entertainment Dyad." *Educational Theatre Journal* 26, no. 4: 455–81.

Schechner, Richard 1974 "TDR Comment: A Critical Evaluation of Kirby's Criticism of Criticism." *TDR: The Drama Review* 18, no. 4: 116–18.

Schechner, Richard 1982 *The End of Humanism: Writings on Performance.* New York: PAJ Publications.

Schechner, Richard 1985 *Between Theater and Anthropology.* Chicago, IL: University of Chicago Press.

Schechner, Richard 1988 *Performance Theory.* New York: Routledge.

Schechner, Richard 1988 "Performance Studies: The Broad Spectrum Approach." *TDR: The Drama Review* 32, no. 3: 4–6.

Schechner, Richard 2000 "Mainstream Theatre and Performance Studies." *TDR: The Drama Review* 44, no. 2: 4–6.

Schechner, Richard 2002 *Performance Studies: An Introduction.* New York: Routledge.

Schechner, Richard 2010 "There's Something Happenin' Here . . ." *TDR: The Drama Review* 54, no. 2: 12–17.

Schimmel, Paul 1998 "Leap Into the Void: Performance and the Object," in Paul Schimmel (ed.) *Out of Actions: Between Performance and the Object.* Los Angeles, CA: Museum of Contemporary Art, 17–120.

Schjeldahl, Peter 2003 "Story Line: Rembrandt in Boston." *The New Yorker*, November 10.

Schneider, Bethany 2010 "Thus, Always: Julius Caesar and Abraham Lincoln," in Madhavi Menon (ed.) *Shakesqueer.* Durham, NC: Duke University Press.

Schneider, Rebecca 1997 *The Explicit Body in Performance*. New York: Routledge.

Schneider, Rebecca 2001 "Performance Remains." *Performance Research* 6, no. 2: 100–8.

Schneider, Rebecca 2001 "Hello Dolly Well Hello Dolly: The Double and Its Theatre," in Patrick Campbell and Adrian Kear (eds.) *Psychoanalysis and Performance*. New York: Routledge, 94–114.

Schneider, Rebecca 2004 "Solo Solo Solo," in Gavin Butt (ed.) *After Criticism: New Responses to Art and Performance*. London: Blackwell Press, 23–47.

Schneider, Rebecca 2006 "Judith Butler in My Hands," in Ellen Armour and Susan St. Ville (eds.) *Bodily Citations: Religion and Judith Butler*. New York: Columbia University Press, 225–51.

Schneider, Rebecca 2006 Interviews collected between 1999 and 2006 with Civil War Reenactors. Unpublished.

Schneider, Rebecca 2009 "Patricide and the Passerby," in D. J. Hopkins, Shelley Orr and Kim Solga (eds.) *Performance and the City*. New York: Palgrave Macmillan, 51–67.

Schneider, Rebecca 2010 "Protest Now and Again," in Mark Tribe (ed.) *The Port Huron Project: Reenactments of New Left Protest Speeches*. New York: Charta.

Schneider, Rebecca 2010 "Protest Now and Again." *TDR: The Drama Review* 54, no. 2: 7–11.

Schneider, Rebecca and Gabrielle Cody 2001 "General Introduction," in Rebecca Schneider and Gabrielle Cody (eds.) *Re:Direction: A Theoretical and Practical Guide*. New York: Routledge.

Scott, Joan Wallach 1991 "The Evidence of Experience." *Critical Inquiry* 17, no. 4: 773–97.

Schor, Naomi 1987 *Reading in Detail: Aesthetics and the Feminine*. New York: Routledge.

Sedgwick, Eve Kosofsky 1985 *Between Men: English Literature and Male Homosocial Desire*. New York: Columbia University Press.

Sedgwick, Eve Kosofsky 2003 *Touching Feeling: Affect, Pedagogy, Performativity*. Durham, NC: Duke University Press.

Senelick, Laurence 1997 "Early Photographic Attempts to Record Performance Sequence," *Theatre Research International* 22, no. 3: 255–64.

Seremetakis, C. Nadia, ed. 1993 *The Senses Still: Perception and Memory as Material Culture in Modernity*. Boulder, CO: Westview Press.

Serres, Michel 2007 *The Parasite*. Minneapolis: University of Minnesota Press.

Shakespeare, William 1963 *The Tragedy of Hamlet, Prince of Denmark*. New York: Signet Classic.

Shimakawa, Karen 2004 "The Things We Share: Ethnic Performativity and 'Whatever Being.'" *The Journal of Speculative Philosophy* 18, no. 2: 149–60.

Sickinger, James P. 1999 *Public Records and Archives in Classical Athens*. Chapel Hill, NC: University of North Carolina Press.

Siegel, Marcia B. 1968 *At the Vanishing Point. A Critic Looks at Dance*. New York: Saturday Review Press.

Smith, Allison 2007 "Public Address," in Nato Thompson (ed.) *Ahistoric Occasion: Artists Making History*. North Adams, MA: Mass MOCA, 102–13.

Smith, Allison 2007 *The Muster*. New York: Public Art Fund.

Smith, Allison 2007 "The Muster," in Nato Thompson (ed.) *Ahistoric Occasion: Artists Making History*. North Adams, MA: Mass MOCA.

Smith, Mark M. 2000 "Listening to the Heard Worlds of Antebellum America." *Journal of the Historical Society* 1, no. 1: 65–99.

Smith, Wes 1993 "Land of Lincolns." *Chicago Tribune*. "Tempo" section. January 27.

Snow, Stephen Eddy 1993 *Performing the Pilgrims: A Study of Ethnohistorical Role-Playing at Plimoth Plantation*. Jackson: University Press of Mississippi.

Sonstegard, Adam 2006 "Performing Remediation: The Minstrel, The Camera, and *The Octoroon.*" *Criticism* 48, no. 3: 375–95.

Sontag, Susan 1990 [1966] "Notes on Camp," in *Against Interpretation and Other Essays*. New York: Anchor Books, 275–92.

Sontag, Susan 2004 *Regarding the Pain of Others*. New York: Picador.

Spector, Nancy 2010 "*Seven Easy Pieces*," in Klaus Biesenbach (ed.) *Marina Abramović: The Artist Is Present*. New York: The Museum of Modern Art, 37–9.

Stallybrass, Peter 2001 "Well-Grubbed, Old Mole: Marx, *Hamlet*, and the Unfixing of Representation," in Jean E. Howard and Scott Cutler Shershow (eds.) *Marxist Shakespeares*. New York: Routledge, 16–30.

Stanislavsky, Konstantin 1989 *An Actor Prepares*. Translated by Elizabeth Hapgood. New York: Routledge.

Stanton, Cathy and Stephen Belyea 2000 "'Their Time Will Yet Come': African American Presence in Civil War Reenactment," in Martin Henry Blatt, Thomas J. Brown and Donald Yakovone (eds.) *Hope and Glory: Essays on the Legacy of the 54th Massachusetts Regiment*. Amherst: University of Massachusetts Press, 253–74.

Steedman, Carolyn Kay 2002 *Dust: The Archive and Cultural History*. New Brunswick, NJ: Rutgers University Press.

Stein, Gertrude 1935 *Lectures in America*. New York: Random House.

Stein, Gertrude 1995 [1925] *The Making of Americans*. Normal, IL: Dalkey Archive Press.

Stephanson, Anders 1995 *Manifest Destiny: American Expansionism and the Empire of Right*. New York: Hill and Wang.

Stewart, Kathleen 2007 *Ordinary Affects*. Durham, NC: Duke University Press.

Stoller, Ann Laura 2002 "Colonial Archives and the Arts of Governance." *Archival Science* 2, nos. 1&2: 87–109.

Stoller, Ann Laura 2009 *Along the Archival Grain: Epistemic Anxieties and Colonial Common Sense*. Princeton, NJ: Princeton University Press.

Swanson, James L. 2006 *Manhunt*. New York: William Morrow.

Taussig, Michael 1991 *The Nervous System*. New York: Routledge.

Taylor, Diana 1997 *Disappearing Acts*. Durham, NC: Duke University Press.

Taylor, Diana 2003 *The Archive and the Repertoire: Performing Cultural Memory in the Americas*. Durham, NC: Duke University Press.

Taylor, Diana 2009 "Afterword: War Play." *PMLA* 124, no. 5: 1886–95.

Taylor, Diana, ed. 1994 *Negotiating Performance: Gender, Sexuality, and Theatricality in Latin/o America*. Durham, NC: Duke University Press.

Terdiman, Richard 1993 *Present Past: Modernity and the Memory Crisis*. Ithaca, NY: Cornell University Press.

Thomas, Richard 1993 *The Imperial Archive: Knowledge and the Fantasy of Empire*. New York: Verso.

Thomas, Rosalind 1992 *Literacy and Orality in Ancient Greece*. New York: Cambridge University Press.

Thompson, Chris and Katarina Weslien 2006 "Pure Raw: Performance, Pedagogy, and (Re)Presentation, an interview with Marina Abramović." *PAJ: Performing Arts Journal* 82: 29–50.

Thompson, Joseph 2007 "Foreword," in Nato Thompson (ed.) *Ahistoric Occasion: Artists Making History*. North Adams, MA: Mass MOCA, 8–9A.

Thompson, Nato, ed. 2007 *Ahistoric Occasion: Artists Making History*. North Adams, MA: Mass MOCA.

Time and Space Limited 1988 "*Civil War Chronicles*." Press release.

Tiqqun 2010 *Introduction to Civil War*. Translated by Alexander R. Galloway and Jason E. Smith. New York: Semiotext(e).

Tivers, Jacqueline 2002 "Performing Heritage: The Use of Live 'Actors' in Heritage Presentations." *Leisure Studies* 21, nos. 3 & 4: 187–200.

Tribe, Mark 2010 *The Port Huron Project: Reenactments of New Left Protest Speeches*. Milan: Edizioni Charta.

Turner, Rory 1990 "Bloodless Battles: The Civil War Reenacted." *TDR: The Drama Review* 34, no. 4: 123–36.

Turner, Victor 1982 *From Ritual to Theatre: The Human Seriousness of Play*. New York: PAJ Books.

Vizenor, Gerald, ed. 2008 *Survivance: Narratives of Native Presence*. Lincoln: Nebraska University Press.

Vogel, Shane 2000 "Where Are We Now? Queer World Making and Cabaret Performance." *GLQ: A Journal of Lesbian and Gay Studies* 6, no. 1: 29–60.

von Hantelmann, Dorothea 2007 *How to Do Things With Art*. Zurich: JRP/Ringier.

Warhol, Andy and Pat Hackett 1980 *POPism*. New York: Harcourt, Brace.

Weber, Samuel 2004 *Theatricality as Medium*. New York: Fordham University Press.

Weiss, Marta 2006 "Staged Photography in the Victorian Album," in Lori Pauli (ed.) *Acting the Part: Photography As Theatre*. New York: Merrel.

Wernz, Stanley 2009 Email correspondence. October 11.

White, Hayden 1980 "The Value of Narrativity in the Representation of Reality," in W. J. T. Mitchell (ed.) *On Narrative*. Chicago, IL: University of Chicago Press, 1–24.

Whitman, Walt 1897 *Complete Prose Works*. New York: D. McKay.

Wiegman, Robyn 2000 "Feminism's Apocalyptic Futures." *New Literary History* 31, no. 4: 805–25.

Willett, John 1986 *The Theatre of Erwin Piscator*. New York: Methuen.

Williams, Raymond. 1985 *Keywords: A Vocabulary of Culture and Society*. New York: Oxford University Press.

Wills, Garry 1993 *Lincoln at Gettysburg: The Words that Remade America*. New York: Simon and Schuster.

Woolfork, Lisa 2008 *Embodying American Slavery in Contemporary Culture*. Bloomington: University of Indiana Press.

Wooster Group 2004 *Poor Theater: A Series of Simulacra*. Program. The Performing Garage, New York, 18 February–24 April.

Worthen, W. B. 1992 *Modern Drama and the Rhetoric of Theater*. Berkeley: University of California Press.

Worthen, W. B. 1997 *Shakespeare and the Authority of Performance*. New York: Cambridge University Press.

Worthen, W. B. 1998 "Drama, Performativity, and Performance." *PMLA* 113, no. 5: 1093–1107.

Worthen, W. B. 2007 "Shakespeare 3.0: Or Text Versus Performance, the Remix," in Diana Henderson (ed.) *Alternative Shakespeares 3*. New York: Routledge, 54–5.

Worthen, W. B. 2008 "Antigone's Bones." *TDR: The Drama Review* 52, no. 3: 10–33.

Worthen, W. B. 2010 *Drama: Between Poetry and Performance*. New York: Wiley Blackwell.

Wu, Duncan 2006 *Romanticism: An Anthology*. Oxford: Blackwell.

Yates, Frances 1966 *The Art of Memory*. Chicago, IL: University of Chicago Press.

Yoon, Joonsung 2001 "Seeing His Own Absence: Culture and Gender in Yasusmasa Morimura's Photographic Self-Portaits." *Journal of Visual Art Practice* 1, no. 3: 162–9.

Young, Elizabeth 1999 *Disarming the Nation: Women's Writing and the American Civil War*. Chicago, IL: University of Chicago Press.

Young, Harvey 2005 "The Black Body as Souvenir in American Lynching." *Theatre Journal* 57, no. 4: 639–57.

Young, Harvey 2010 *Embodying Black Experience: Stillness, Critical Memory, and the Black Body*. Ann Arbor: University of Michigan Press.

Zak, Dan 2007 "Local Reenactment Groups Try to Keep It Real." *The Washington Post*. July 1: M06.

Zdroj, John 2008 "What's It Like Being a Reenactor?" 2nd Missouri Cavalry C.S.A. Available online at http://members.tripod.com/2ndmocavcsa/id17.htm (accesssed October 2008).

Zezima, Kate 2006 "When Soldiers Go to War, Flat Daddies Hold Their Place at Home." *The New York Times*. September 30.

Zinn, Howard 1990 *Declarations of Independence: Cross-Examining American Ideology*. New York: Perennial.

Zinn, Howard 2002 "The Others." *The Nation*. 11 February: 16–20.

Zinn, Howard 2007 *A Power Governments Cannot Suppress*. San Francisco, CA: City Lights Books.

Žižek, Slavoj 1991 "Grimaces of the Real, or When the Phallus Appears." *October* 58, no. 1: 44–68.

Žižek, Slavoj 2009 *First as Tragedy, Then as Farce*. New York: Verso.

Index

Page numbers in **bold** refer to illustrations

A Little Bit of History Repeated 132–3
A Power Governments Cannot Suppress (Zinn) 179
"A Rebel Form Gains Favor. Fights Ensue"
  (Kino) 3–5
"A Small History of Photography"
  (Benjamin) 161–2, 164–5
Abramović, Marina 3–7, **5**, 13, 15, 28, 29,
  123, 129, 130, 132, 135, 136, 188n13,
  188n16
Abu Ghraib prison, Iraq 139–40, 160–4, 168
activism and activists 12, 27, 152, 169, 175,
  179–86
actressization 157
actual, the 15, 50, 57, 116, 123, 125–7, 180,
  218n39
"Actuals" (Schechner) 116, 123, 125–6, 180
Adoration of the Mystic Lamb, The (van Eyck)
  146–8, **147**
Adorno, Theodor 129, 135, 136
affect: jump of 36–7, 75, 135, 178, 183; labor
  of 137; transmission of 11, 191n46
affect-assemblages 66
affective engagement 50–1
affective turn, the 35–6
African Americans 11, 55–6, 197n25, 204n23
againness 6, 50
Agamben, Giorgio 217n16, 230n4
Agnew, Vanessa 35, 47, 214n71
"Ahistoric Occasion," exhibition 26–7
Ahmed, Sara 36–7
Akropolis (Wyspianski) 112–13, 114–15,
  116–21, **118**, 124, 130, 216n15
Allain, Paul 89
Allen, Jennifer 133
Althusser, Louis 222n12
*Amalgamation Waltz: Race, Performance, and the
  Ruses of Memory* (Nyong'o) 17
ambivalence 8, 133, 143, 159
America Play, The (Parks) 64, 64–70, 66–70,
  84, 105, 180, 185

American History Reinvented (Neidich) 228n59
American Revolution, the 23
An Actor Prepares (Stanislavsky) 149
anachronism 8, 42, 53, 53–4, 60, 92, 171,
  180, 184, 186
Andre, Carl 220n66
Angel of Mercy, The (Antin) **74**, 75
Antietam, battle of, reenactment 55,
  228n59
Antin, Eleanor 29, **74**, 75, 205n47
antitheatricality 99, 125, 129, 148, 204n30,
  217n30, 218n32
Antonioni, Michelangelo 226n50
appropriation art 15, 29, 123, 130, 151, 164,
  187n3
Archaeology of Knowledge, The (Foucault) 212n55
archival drag 14, 75
archive, the 97–9, 103, 106–10, 212n55,
  213n62, 213n64; *coup de théâtre* 108–10;
  performing 99–102; as performance 108
Archive and the Repertoire, The (Taylor) 91, 96,
  105–8, 209n20
archive culture 97, 130
Archive Fever (Derrida) 107–10, 123
Aristotle 18, 40, 44
Arns, Inke 27–8
art: dematerialization of 129
"Art and Objecthood" (Fried) 159
art history, theatre of 158
art reenactment 12–13, **12**
Artaud, Antonin 225n46
Artist is Present, The (Abramović) 3–5, 28–9,
  130, 135, 136, 188n13
Association of Lincoln Presenters (ALP) 32,
  45–9, **46**
Auslander, Philip 91, 92, 116, 132, 208n16,
  209n20, 209n23
Austin, J. L. 68–9, 127
authenticity 9, 13, 30, 45, 47, 54, 55–6, 86,
  121, 137

Ballard, J. G. 72–3
Ballerini, Julia 167
Bandit Princess, The (Tashiro) 78
Bank, Rosemarie K. 26
Baraka, Amiri (LeRoi Jones) 204n21
Barba, Eugenio 10, 14
Barney, Tina 29
Barthes, Roland 110, 138, 143–4, 164, 165,
    224n26
Batchen, Gregory 166, 167, 225n42
Battle at Orgreave (Deller) 3, 28
battle reenactment 2–3, 7, 13, 24, 45, 54,
    101, 187n1
Bayard, Hippolyte 165–7, **166**
being 105
Bellour, Raymond 178
belonging 32, 46, 60
Beloved (Morrison) 189n18
Belting, Hans 147–8
Belyea, Stephen 55–6
Benjamin, Walter 17, 37, 61–2, 94, 113, 160,
    161–2, 164–5, 197n20, 222n8, 224n26
Bergson, Henri 41, 90, 110, 208n6
Berlant, Lauren 35
Bernstein, Robin 141
"Between History and Memory: Auschwitz in
    Akropolis, Akropolis in Auschwitz"
    (Romanska) 216n15
Between Theatre and Anthropology (Schechner)
    124, 126–7, 218n39
betweenness 124, 128, 129, 164
Bhabha, Homi 14, 30, 159–60, 191n43,
    224n26
Biesenbach, Klaus 3–7, 130, 135
Bishop, Claire 137
black representational space 18
blackface minstrel routines 55
Blau, Herbert 94–5, 98, 102
Blessing, Jennifer 4
Blight, David 11
Blocker, Jane 190n27, 201n71, 201n73,
    212n52
Blow-Up, Antonioni 226n50
Blue Scene Grey (Mussmann) 75–6, 80, 82
bodily memory 11, 37–9
Boltanski, Christian 231n23
Booth, John Wilkes 61–3
Borneman, John 203n12
Boston 24–5, 25
Brecht, Stefan 101
Brennan, Teresa 11, 36, 191n46
Brody, Jennifer DeVere 128–9
Brook, Peter 119
Bruce, Claudia **71**, 73, 75, 76, 77, 78, 83–4,
    86
Bruguera, Tania 3
Brutus, Marcus Junius 61–2, 63, 202n3,
    203n10

Bryan-Wilson, Julia 133, 185–6, 220n66
Büchner, Georg 78
Burgess, Lauren Cook 55, 190n25
Bush, George W. 11, 171
Butler, Judith 7, 127, 189n20

Cadava, Eduardo 161, 222n81
call to art/arms 169–73
Camera Lucida (Barthes) 138, 143–4
camera obscura 144–5
Cameraless Video (Peltz) 226n51
camp 74, 101
camp performance 46, 112, 170
capitalism 173–4
Carlson, Marvin 101, 114
Caruth, Cathy 102
Case, Sue-Ellen 79, 141–2, 209n21
Chakrabarty, Dipesh 35
Chase Farm Civil War reenactment 51–2,
    52, 225n38
chiasmus 67, 71, 75, 143–4
chronopolitics 173–4
Cieslak, Ryszard 125
cinema 94, 142, 178, 207n61
citation 10, 14–15, 63, 69, 75, 90, 121, 126,
    185
Cities of the Dead (Roach) 62–3, 95–6
Civil War Chronicles (Mussmann) 74, 75–7, 78,
    79–80, 81, 82
Civil War (Sherman) 154, **156**, 227n58
CIVIL warS (Wilson) 63
Cleveland Plain Dealer 60
Clinton, Hillary 70
Clough, Patricia 35
Cocteau, Jean 138
Coleman, James 148, 165, 177–8, 230n91,
    231n23
complicity 156, 163
*Confederates in the Attic: Dispatches from the
    Unfinished Civil War* (Horwitz) 54–5
Connerton, Paul 43, 190n33, 193n64,
    197n21
Conquergood, Dwight 211n46
conservation 5
contingency 96, 161–2
Continuous Project – Altered Daily (Rainer) 2–3
Cook, Alexander 35
Cooke, Lynne 177
copy, the 6, 10, 18, 64, 68, 86
copyright 6, 131
Cough, Patricia 231n11
counter-memory 101, 105
Craig, Edward Gordon 138, 148–9, 225n46
Crary, Jonathan 139, 144
Crash (Ballard) 72–3
creation 15–16, 98
Crewdson, Gregory 29
critical theory 192n56

Cross Way Cross (Mussmann) 64, 71–5, **71**, 76,
    81, 82, 83, 83–6, **85**, 185
cross-dressing 74–5, 189n25
cross-temporality 14, 37, 42, 57
Cuenca, Lilibeth 3
Culps Hill, Battle for, reeenactment 33, 121;
    Field Notes 57–9
Cut Piece (Ono) 28, 132

dance 94–5, 108–9, 122, 131–7
Danto, Arthur C. 151–60, 164, 227n56,
    227n57
Danton's Death (Büchner) 78
*Daughter of Art History: Photographs of Yasumasa
    Morimura* (Morimura) 157
Davis, Angela 181
Davis, Tracy 224n27
de Beauvoir, Simone 180
de Certeau, Michel 145, 163, 224n31,
    229n82
de Lauretis, Teresa 79, 206n52
death 7, 54, 102–4, 138, 143–4, 148–9, 178,
    209n18, 224n31
*Death of the Last Black Man in the Whole Entire
    World* (Parks) 103
Deleuze, Gilles 35, 231n11
Deller, Jonathan 3, 28
Democracy in America (Tribe) 231n27
Derrida, Jacques 93, 95, 97, 103, 104,
    107–10, 123, 138, 156–7, 213n62,
    215n104
"Desire in Narrative" (de Lauretis) 79
detail: attention to 55; not quite 160, 228n70;
    precise 154; unanticipated 51, 51–2, **52**,
    60
Deutsche, Rosalyn 176
Diamond, Elin 75
Dickey, Stephen 47–8
Dickinson, Emily 44
Dickinson, Rod 13, 16, 28, 190n36
difference 86; and authenticity 30; of the not
    quite 160, 228n70
digital media 210n30
Dinshaw, Carolyn 18, 35
disappearance 97–9, 98–9, 102–4, 105; and
    ephemerality 95–6; of live performance
    29, 39; memory and 100; of the past 53;
    and photography 143; remains and 102–3
Disappearing Acts (Taylor) 105
Doane, Mary Ann 93–4, 142, 210n30,
    222n8
documents and documentation 10, 28–9, 97,
    98, 99–100, 107, 132
Dolan, Jill 218n52
Donne, John 1, 7, 189n21
Door/Window/Room (Mussmann) 78
double negative, aesthetic of the 75
dramatic theatre 90

Dunkelberg, Kermit 216n10
duration 188n16, 208n6
durational events 223n12
Durkheim, Emile 38
"Dyssimulation: Reflexivity, Narrative, and
    the Quest for Authenticity in 'Living
    History'" (Handler and Saxton) 200n61

Edsall, Mary 99
Eighteenth Brumaire of Louis Bonaparte, The
    (Marx) 42–3
Elementary Forms of Religious Life, The
    (Durkheim) 38
Eliade, Mircea 126
*Embodying American Slavery in Contemporary
    CultureEmbodying American Slavery in
    Contemporary Culture* (Woolfork) 13
Emergence of Cinematic Time, The (Doane) 222n8
emotion, stickiness of 36
emotional engagement 35
enactment 96, 190n33
End of Humanism, The (Schechner) 124
"Ephemera as Evidence: Introductory Notes
    to Queer Acts" (Muñoz) 96, 105
ephemerality 94–7, 98
errors 42, 45, 53, 105–7, 181–2, 186;
    acceptable levels of 54–5; everywhere of
    8; Lincoln's beard 69–70; of theatricality
    43
event afterlife 29–30
"The Evidence of Experience" (Scott) 195n9
exactitude 13, 182
*Exhausting Dance: Performance and the Politics of
    Movement* (LePecki) 143
experience as historical knowledge 2, 195n9
Explicit Body in Performance, The (Schneider) 9
"Exstasie, The" (Donne) 7

Fabian, Johannes 38
fabricators 54–5
Fanon, Franz 14, 191n43
faux 52; and real 41, 43
feel, the 50–1
feminism 4, 9, 75, 79, 207n61
feminist art 9
feminist theory 227n55
feminization 157
Field Hospital reenactment **34**
film 93, 207n61
Fischer-Lichte, Erika 209n23
Firestone, Shulamith 15
Firincioglu, Semih 76
Fliakos, Ari 112
Fly (Ono) 45
Fonda, Jane 152–3, **153**
footprints 11, 45, 112, 113–14, 115, 199n42
Foreman, Richard 76
forgetting 22–3, 26, 124

Forgie, George B. 23
formalism 78
Forsythe, William 122
Foster, Hal 194n3
Foster, Susan Leigh 213n65
Forte, Jeanie K. 79
Foucault, Michel 17–18, 92, 97, 102, 212n55
Fradenberg, Louise 35
Freccero, Carla 35
Freeman, Elizabeth 14–15, 30, 35, 37, 75, 174, 176, 191n46
Freud, Sigmund 44, 63, 92, 102, 103, 192n62
Fried, Michael 5, 17, 159, 165, 208n9
From Ritual to Theatre (Turner) 127–8
fugitive moments 180
fugitive time 180
futurity 25

Gardner, Alexander 140
gaze 78, 80
Geertz, Clifford 202n7
gender 55, 74–5, 79–80, 152–4, 157–60, 189n20
gestic cloning 112
Gettysburg (town) 20, **20**, **21**, 25, 192n58
Gettysburg, Battle of, reenactment 56–7, **56**
Gettysburg Address 20, 21–2, **21**, 192n58
Gettysburg reunion, 1913 11
ghost notes 65
Go Between Gettysburg (Mussmann) 76
Godard, Jean-Luc 152
Goffman, Erving 198n31
Gold, Sam 117
Gómez-Peña, Guillermo 131, 132
Gopnik, Adam 48, 48–9
Gorin, Jean-Pierre 152
Granier, Charles 140
Greek theatre 145
Grotowski, Jerzy 111–12, 114, 115–16, 118–19, 124, 125–6, 130, 133, 216n11, 218n34, 220n67
Guggenheim, the 3, 4, 133
Gulf War 172

habit 41
Halberstam, Judith 35
Halbwachs, Maurice 214n68
Hamlet (Shakespeare) 66, 87–9, 109, 110, 115
Hamlet (Wooster Group) 13, 16, **16**, 115
Handler, Richard 200n61
Hardwick, Elizabeth 119–20
Harvie, Jen 89
Hayes, Sharon 176–7, 182, **183**
Hegel, Georg 42–3, 44
Heidegger, Martin 95
heritage 111–12

heritage industry 127
Hertz, Betti-Sue 75
historical event, ghost notes 65
historical facticity, criticism of 99
historical materialism 197n20
historical memory 17
historical moments 49
historical narrative 85–6
historical specificity 93–4
historical tableau 73
historicism 197n20
historicization 75
historiography 214n68
history 6, 25, 97; as activity 44; belonging 32; camp 176; cannibalizing of 25–6; engagement with 64; Great Hole of 66, 69, 76; hauntingness of 60; keeping alive 39–42; lessons of 39–40; mistakes of 42; Native American view of 26; oral 100–1, 214n80; reading 104; reencountering 42–5; returns of 86; sense of 38; theatricality 32–3, 43; touching 126–7
History Portraits / Old Masters (Sherman) 154, **155**
History Will Repeat Itself 27–8
Hodgdon, Barbara 148, 151
Hodge, Robert Lee 101
Hoffmann, Jens 132–3
Horwitz, Tony 54–5
How Societies Remember (Connerton) 43, 190n33

ideality 30, 47, 99, 131
identicality 18, 101
identity 36, 231n11
If Kansas Goes (Mussmann) 75, 81, 82
Iles, Chrissie 5, 188n13
image capture. *see* photography
images, live power of 147–8
imitation 15–16, 123, 129, 131, 132
immediacy 91, 208n14, 210n30
immersion 13–14
In the Break (Moten) 160
In the Near Future (Hayes) 182–3, **183**
in-betweenness 128–9
INITIALS (Coleman) 230n91
instruction art 45
interactivity 93, 210n30
inter(in)animation 1, 7, 130, 138, 160–4, 168
intermediality 159, 160, 164, 210n30
interpellation 223n12
interpretation 13, 15, 17–18, 30
in-time performance art work 29
Iraq 171, 172
Iraq Veterans Against the War 184–5
Irigaray, Luce 67
itineracy 229n82

Jackson, Shannon, 191n49, 195n5, 211n45, 211n46
Jakobsen, Janet 35, 173–4
James, C. L. R. 128
Jameson, Fredric 25–6, 38, 39
Janša, Janez 3, 187n2
jazz 65–6, 204n21
jazz poetics 65
Johnson, Catherine 99
Johnson, J. Seward, Jr 20, **20**
Jones, Amelia 4, 142–3
Jones, Meta Du Ewa 65
Jonestown Re-Enactment (Dickinson) 28
Judt, Tony 24
Julius Caesar 61–2, 63, 203n10
Julius Caesar (Shakespeare) 61–2
July, Miranda 32–3, 49–50

Karasu, Bozkurt 122
Keats, John 204n18
Kelly, Mary 176–7, 178
Kennedy, Adrienne 66
Kernodle, George 145
Kierkegaard, Søren 113, 123
Kino, Carol 3–5, 28
Kipling, George 146
Kirshenblatt-Gimblett, Barbara 95
Kiss (Sehgal) 133–7, 137
knowledge 18, 100–1, 104, 106
Krauss, Rosalind 94, 164–5, 168, 177, 185, 229n81
Kristopherson, Kris 228n59
Kruger, Barbara 9
Kuspit, Donald 157–9

labor: Marxist critique of 220n67; in (re)performance 133–7
labor for hire 131, 133, 136–7, 220n66
Laboratorium Theatre 112
Lacan, Jacques 140, 156
Lambert-Beatty, Carrie 129–30
landscape plays 66
language 68–9
Le Goff, Jacques 97, 100
Le Roy, Xavier 2–3
"Leap into the Void" (Schimmel) 98
Leaves of Grass (Whitman) 86
LeCompte, Elizabeth 111–12, 115, 121, 123–4, 127, 128, 130, 217n19
Lectures in America (Stein) 94; "Plays" 65–6
Lee, Nikki S. 29
LePecki, André 134, 143
Letter to Jane: An Investigation About a Still (Godard and Gorin) 152
Levine, Sherrie 15, 29, 123
Life, Once More: Forms of Reenactment in Contemporary Art 131–2
Life of Reason, The (Santayana) 40

Lima, Laura 133
liminality 14, 125
Lincoln, Abraham 8, 20, 21–2, **21**, 23, 47–8, 192n58; *The America Play* portrayal 66–70, **68**; assassination 61–4; *Cross Way Cross* portrayal 71–5, 83–6; declaration of war 171; portraying 64; *Topdog/Underdog* portrayal 64–6
Lincoln Speak (Mussmann) 76
Line of Faith (Coleman) 177–8, 231n23
linear time 26, 27, 29–31, 35, 42, 53, 89, 92, 108–9, 142, 174
Lingis, Alphonso 36
Lippard, Lucy 129
live art 1, 129
live performance 89–90, 90–4, 182, 197n21, 208n16; definition 90; disappearance of 29, 39; remains 97–8
live presence 209n20
liveness 9, 29, 89, 90–4, 129, 132, 138, 148–9, 177–8, 183
Liveness: Performance in a Mediatized Culture (Auslander) 91, 92
Living and Presumed Dead (Coleman) 165, 178
living art 149
living history 2, 9, 13, 47, 101, 127, 154, 187n1, 214n71
living memory 23, 193n64
living remains 102–4
living stills 73
living tableaux. *see* tableaux vivants
Longo, Robert 228n59
loss: challenge to 102; instituted 103; sense of 24
Love, Heather 35, 37
Love Diamond (July) 49
Lowenthal, David 25
Lubow, Arthur 134–5, 137
Luciano, Dana 35, 45–6
Ludlam, Charles 101
Lütticken, Sven 131, 131–2, 219n58

Mackey, Nathaniel 65
Maeterlinck, Maurice 149
Magelssen, Scott 47
Making of Americans, The (Stein) 23
Manifest Destiny 193n65
Mann, Sally 228n59
Marranca, Bonnie 78
Marx, Karl 42–4, 220n67
Mary Surratt (Mussmann) 76, 83
masculinity 9
masks 109–10
masquerade 30
Massachusetts Museum of Contemporary Art (Mass MOCA) 26–7
Massumi, Brian 35, 36
materiality 105

Matter and Memory (Bergson) 208n6
McIvor, Frazer 136
meantime 87–90, 90
medial specificity 6, 94, 129–30, 136, 139, 159, 163–8
medical reenactment **34**, 35, 52–3
mediums, interweave of 83–4
Melville, Herman 23
memory 6, 21–3, 99, 213n62; academic study 38; bodily 11, 37–9; and disappearance 100; historical 17; keeping alive 100; living 193n64; performance as 100; sense of 38; transgenerational 59, 174
memory industry 2
Mendieta, Ana 3
Mercer, Kobena 98
Merleau-Ponty, Maurice 37, 67
method acting 55
Milgram Re-enactment (Dickinson) 13, 16, 28, 190n36
Miller, Matthew Floyd **179**, 184
mimesis 18, 30–1, 44, 55, 143, 213n60
mimicry 159–60
mind/body split 35
minimalist art 5–6
mise en scene 10
misremembering 42
modern historical consciousness 35
modernity 100, 224n26
Montgomery, Reggie **68**
monument, the 7, 132, 137, 145, 163
Morimura, Yasumasa 29, 157–60, **157**, **158**
Morrison, Toni 6, 18, 157, 163, 168, 189n18
Moses and Monotheism (Freud) 63
Moten, Fred 1, 7, 128, 160, 163, 168, 189n21, 229n80, 229n82
Mulvey, Laura 78
Muñoz, José Esteban 96, 105
Museum of Modern Art (MoMA) 3, 3–5, 28–9, 130, 133, 136
musicality 40–1
Mussmann, Linda 64, 104, 206n58; *Blue Scene Grey* 75–6, 80, 82; *Civil War Chronicles* 75–7, 78, 79–80, 81, 82; *Cross Way Cross* 71–5, 76, 81, 82, 83, 83–6, 185; denial of narrative 78; formalism 78; *If Kansas Goes* 75, 81, 82; productions 77; theater 76–80
Muster, The (Smith) 2, 12–13, **12**, 19, 137, 169–73, **170**, 176, 186
"Myself 1854" (Antin) **74**, 75

Nadar, Felix 150–1, **150**, 165
narrative 75, 76, 206n52; denial of 78; historical 85–6
narrative directives 85
nation creation 193n63
National Civil War Field Music School 40

Native Americans 22–3, 24, 26, 201n73, 204n23
Nealon, Chris 35
Nebraska of Questions, The (Mussmann) 78
negative capability 65, 204n18
Neidich, Warren 228n59
"Never Mind the Pollock" (Cuenca) 3
New Criticism 7
New Formalism 79
New York University, Department of Performance Studies 94–6, 124
Nicholson, Linda 35
Nietzsche, Friedrich 22, 28, 80, 102
"Nietzsche, Genealogy, History" (Foucault) 17–18
non-syncopated time 93
Nora, Pierre 100
Northwestern University, Department of Performance Studies 211n46
Notion Nanny Project (Smith) 19
not not *see* double negative
now, challenge of 181–3, 186
Nude with Skeleton (Abramović) **5**
Nyong'o, Tavia 17, 18, 214n80

Obama, Barack 11, 70, 171
object-based art 131
ocular hegemony 98
"Of Mimicry and Man: The Ambivalence of Colonial Discourse" (Bhabha) 159–60
Ong, Walter 213n65
Ono, Yoko 28, 45, 132
oral archives 99
oral history 100–1, 214n80
oral traditions 213n65
orality 65
Orality and Literacy: The Technologizing of the Word (Ong) 213n65
orature 197n25
originality 30, 131
O'Sullivan, John 21, 22–4, 26
O'Sullivan, Timothy 140
outsourced authenticity 137
Owens, Craig 140, 156

"Packing History, Count(er)ing Generations" (Freeman) 14
pain, relative 53, 59
Paris Match 152
Parks, Suzan-Lori 64, 64–70, 76, 84, 86, 103, 104, 105, 180, 185, 203n17
parody 43, 73–5, 174
participation 9, 19, 113, 135–7
passing, the 7, 135–6
past, the 14–15; cultural environment 19–26; disappearance of 53; disruption of the present 15; engagement with 35; in the future 22; keeping alive 37, 39–42;

learning from 40; lessons of 39–40;
participation in 19; pastness of 33, 37, 60;
stages 46; stickiness 36–7; theatricality 47;
as trace 45
Patricide in the House Divided (Forgie) 23
patricidic culture 61, 62, 63, 203n12
Peirce, C. S. 11
Pellegrini, Ann 35, 103–4, 170, 173–4,
175–6, 184
Peltz, Daniel 226n51
performance art 1, 15–16, 55, 131; challenge
5; and war 3–7
Performance Group 113, 115
"Performance Police" Lambert-Beatty
129–30
performance practice 100–1, 107
"Performance Remains" 105–6
Performance Research 106
performance studies 124, 125, 127–8, 129
Performance Theory (Schechner) 125
performative trace, the 102
performative turn, the 35
performativity, paradoxes 10
performing body, as labor for hire 131, 133,
136–7
perspective 78–9, 80
Phaedrus (Plato) 38
Phelan, Peggy 91, 92, 95, 98, 105, 142,
207n62, 209n18
photography 1, 7, 28, 29, 93–4, 133, 138–9,
228n59; Abu Ghraib prison images
160–4, 168; development of 144; and
disappearance 143; futures subsistence in
161–2; liveness 148–9, 177–8; medial
specificity 163–4, 164–7, 168, 229n80;
mimetic capacity 164; not quite details
160, 228n70; and performance 142, 148,
151–60, **151**, **153**, **155**, **156**, **157**, **158**,
168; poses 141; practices 140–3; reading
141–2, 163–4; and reappearance 143;
and retrievable time 139–40; self-portrait
142–3; staged 139–40, 165–7, **166**; and
theatre 143–4, 144–5, 148–51, **150**,
159–60, 168, 226n47; and time 222n8;
the viewer and 140
"Photography and Performance" (Danto)
227n56
photo-performance reenactment 29, 75
Pierrot the Photographer (Nadar) 150–1, **150**, 165
Piscator, Erwin 226n49
placedness 17
plastiques 115
Plato 5, 17, 18, 38
play, seriousness of 14
Plimoth Plantation 127
policing of performance 129–30
political stakes 2
politics 9

Pollock, Jackson 131–2
Poor Theater (Wooster Group) 13, 16, 111–23,
123, 137, 138; close 122–3; performance
113–23, **117**, **120**; program 113;
reenactment of *Akropolis* 112–13, 114–15,
116–21, 124; second half 122; stage 114;
temporal dislocation 122
poor theatre 115–16, 122, 132, 218n34
pop culture 28
popular cultural reenactments 26–8
Port Huron Project (Tribe) 28, 179–86, **179**,
181, 231n27
poses 73, 90, 161; reenactive 151–60
Positions (Derrida) 156–7
*Postmodernism, or, the Cultural Logic of Late
Capitalism* (Jameson) 25–6
postmodernity 38
poststructural theory 95
Potts, Michael **68**
Practice of Everyday Life, The (de Certeau) 145
Pratt, Greta 27
precedent art, 2–4, 13, 16, 28, 111
precision 13, 15–17, 16
present, the 92
presentness 121
preservation 37, 106, 108
protest 179–86
psychoanalysis 213n64
psychoanalytic trauma theory 22
Puar, Jasbir K. 173, 175, 231n11
Puchner, Martin 125
Punctuation: Art, Politics, and Play (Brody) 128–9

queer historiography 18
queer times 172–5
queerness 172–5

"'Race,' Time, and the Revision of
Modernity" (Bhabha) 191n43
Rainer, Yvonne 2–3, 78
Rayner, Alice 202n1, 204n24
reactualization 126
real, and faux 41, 43
real time 92–4
reappearance 143
"Recasting Ancestry: Statuettes as Imaged by
Three Inventors of Photography"
(Ballerini) 167
recognition 156, 160
reconstruction 3, 62
recording 89–90
recurrence 29, 30, 37, 47, 50, 53
reenactive poses 151–60
reenactment 32–3, 187n1; Agnew's critique
214n71; art 12–13, **12**; artistic 219n58;
definition 2, 29; experience of 2; logic of
17; musicality 40–1; paradoxes 10;
political stakes 2; practices 13–14;

reencountering history 42–3; scope 2; temporal contingencies 96
reenactment art 17, 28, 29
reenactment photography projects 228n59
reenactors 12–19; affective engagement 50–1; African American 55–6; and authenticity 45; casting 225n38; gender crossing 55, 189n25; hardcore 13–14, 54–5; keeping the past alive 33–9; labor 136–7; motivation 33–42, 100, 175, 200n63; and the past 32; period rush 35; validity claims 51
"Reinventing the Medium" (Krauss) 164–5
reiteration 10
reiterative acts 37–8
relative pain 53, 59
remains 33, 37, 97–8; in difference 104–5; and disappearance 102–3; living 102–4; ritual 147; visible 99
remembering 11, 23, 26, 32, 40, 43
rememory 6, 189n18
reminiscence 26
Renaissance, the 144
Renan, Ernst 193n63
"Repeating, Remembering, and Working Through" (Freud) 192n62
re-performance 3, 4, 6, 129–37
repertoire, the 107, 108
repetition 2, 10, 66, 102, 105, 107, 113, 147
re-placedness 17
replication 112–13, 121, 126–7
representational practice 10
reproducibility 16–17
restored behavior 10, 14, 126
retrievable time 139–40
"Return Visit" (Johnson) 20, **20**
reversibility 37
re-vision 6–7
revision 66
Rhode Island, Civil War reenactment 139, 140
Rich, Adrienne 6–7, 18
Rich Theatre 116
Richards, I. A. 7
Ricoeur, Paul 38
Ridout, Nicholas 191n49, 194n3, 221n19
ritual 14, 100, 103, 125, 147, 202n9
ritual repetition 104
Riviere, Joan 226n55
Roach, Joseph 62–3, 95–6
Robinson, Marc 63
Romàn, David 14, 75, 112, 176
Roman Republic 63
Roman theatre 145, 203n13
Romanska, Magda 216n15
Rose, Tracey 132
Routledge Companion to Theatre and Performance (Allain and Harvie) 89

Ruff, Thomas 231n23

Santayana, George 40, 42, 44
Sarlin, Paige 184–6
Savran, David 216n8, 218n32
Saxton, William 200n61
Sayre, Henry 208n14, 223n21
Schechner, Richard 10, 14, 15, 30, 94, 95, 98, 113, 115, 123, 124–8, 131, 142, 218n32, 218n39
Schimmel, Paul 98
Scott, Joan Wallach 195n9
scriptive things 135
sculpture 1, 135, 145, 167
secular time 35
Secularisms (Pellegrini and Jakobsen) 174
Sedgwick, Eve Kosofsky 35
sedimentation 189n20
sedimented acts 7, 92, 127
seeing 80
Seeing the Elephant (Longo) 228n59
Sehgal, Tino 133–7
Self-Portrait as a Suicide (Bayard) 165–7, **166**
Senelick, Laurence 224n29
sentimentality 199n47
Seremetakis, Nadia 143
service economy 137
Seven Easy Pieces (Abramović) 4, 132
Sex Pictures (Sherman) 154
sexual fetishism 72–3
Shakespeare, William 48, 61–2, 66, 87–9, 109, 110, 115, 200n52
Shepherd, Scott 112, 115
Sherman, Cindy 148, 151–6, **151**, **155**, **156**, 159–60, 160, 164, 227n56, 227n58
Shonibare, Yinka 29
Shulie (Subrin) 15, 16
Siegel, Marcia B. 94
Simpson, Lorna 29
simultaneous temporal registers 8
simultaneous time 90
slave auction reenactments 13
slave practice 220n66
Smith, Allison 2, 12–13, **12**, 19, 27, 136–7, 169–73, **170**, 175, 176, 186
social life 202n9
Socrates 38
Sonstegard, Adam 226n47
Sontag, Susan 170, 175, 184
sounding 65
specific, loss of the 185
spectators 14, 195n4
Specters of Marx (Derrida) 109
Spector, Nancy 4, 132
Stallybrass, Peter 43
Stanislavsky, Konstantin 149–50, 157
Stanton, Cathy 55–6
statuary 1, 135, 145, 167

Stein, Gertrude 6, 23, 31, 63, 65–6, 76, 88–9, 92, 94, 110, 113, 138, 204n23
stickiness 36–7
still, the 75, 94, 139–49, 156, 161, 178
still-act, the 143
stillness 73, 90, 143
Stoller, Ann Laura 100
Stonewall riots, the 172
Subrin, Elisabeth 15, 16, 83
substitution, performative acts of 62–3
Suicide (Durkheim) 38
surrogacy 96, 133
surrogate authentic, the 137
surrogation 62–3
Swan Tool (July) 49
Swanson, James L. 202n4
syncopated time 1, 2, 6, 81, 87–90, 102

tableaux vivants 73, 144, 145–8, **147**, 161, 178; *The Adoration of the Mystic Lamb* 146–8, **147**
Taggart, James 119
Take Up the Bodies: Theatre at the Vanishing Point (Blau) 102
"Taps" 40–1
Tashiro, Kikue 78
"The Task of the Translator," (Benjamin) 113
Taussig, Michael 95
Taylor, Diana 39, 91, 92, 96, 105, 105–8, 197n21, 209n20
TDR: The Drama Review 111, 124, 128
technical reproduction 118
technological reproduction, birth of 209n23
Technologies of Gender (de Lauretis) 206n52
temporal contingencies 96
temporal drag 14, 30, 75, 141, 154, 176
temporal lag 14, 30
temporal recurrence 2, 17
temporal repetition 2
temporal slippage 57
temporal specificity 172
temporality 1, 3, 30, 89, 208n9
Terrorist Assemblages (Puar) 173
terrorists 173, 175, 176
text 90, 106; rewriting 87–8
texuality 65
"The 'Eternal Return': Self-Portrait Photography as a Technology of Embodiment" (Jones) 142–3
Theater of the Ridiculous 101
theatre 46, 47, 48, 62–3, 64, 89, 94, 97–8, 131; and photography 143–4, 144–5, 148–51, **150**, 168, 226n47, 226n49
theatre events 1
Theatre of Images 78
theatre-going, ritual properties of 113
theatrical acts 1

theatrical reproducibility 17
theatrical time 93
theatricality 5–6, 6, 10, 18, 29, 30, 32–3, 47, 108, 224n27; errors of 43; of history 32–3, 43; hollow 68–9; recognition of againness 50; resistance to 130; special 69
theme parks 25
"Theses on the Philosophy of History" (Benjamin) 197n20
This Objective of that Object (Sehgal) 136
Thompson, Joseph 26–7
Till, Emmett 163, 229n80
time 6, 23, 207n62, 208n9; chiasmatic nature of 67; chronopolitics 173–4; crossing 9; fugitive 180; as geography 63; idealized 55; linear 26, 27, 29–31, 35, 42, 53, 89, 92, 108–9, 142, 174; nonlinear 178; non-syncopated 93; and photography 222n8; real 92–4; recurrence 51; retrievable 139–40; secular 35; simultaneous 90; syncopated 1, 2, 6, 81, 87–90, 102; theatrical 93; touching 35
Time and Space Limited Theatre (TSL) 76, 77
time lag 143, 224n26
time travel 50
time travel industry 24–6
timelessness 131
Tipton, Jennifer 117
To My Little Sister: For Cindy Sherman (Morimura) 157, **157**
Topdog/Underdog (Parks) 64–6, 203n17
touching time 35
Towards a Poor Theatre (Grotowski) 115–16, 119, 216n11, 220n67
"Tracking the Vampire" (Case) 141–2, 209n21
tragedy 42–4
Transformative Power of Performance, The (Fischer-Lichte) 210n30
transgenerational memory 59, 174
Transmission of Affect, The (Brennan) 191n46
trauma 44, 102, 192n62
trauma studies 38
trench art 13, 171
Tribe, Mark 28, 179–86
Turner, Victor 14, 125, 127–8
twice-behaved behavior 10, 14, 92, 127

United States Civil War 7–8, 11, 24, 26; Colored Troops 197n25; declaration of war 171; tragedy 47–8
United States Civil War reenactment 1, 3, **8**; and art 7–11; casting 225n38; Colored Troops 197n25; complexities 8–9; emergence of 8, 11; as imprint 39; keeping history alive 39–42; keeping the past alive 33–9; musicality 40–1;

photography 228n59; reenactors 12–19; remembering 11; understanding 41–2
United States of America: battlefields 22–3, 26; cultural environment 19–26; innocence 24; lack of memory 22–3
Unmarked: The Politics of Performance (Phelan) 91, 92
Untitled Film Stills (Sherman) 151–6, **151**, 160
US imaginary, the 3
Uses and Abuses of History (Nietzsche) 28

Valk, Kate 112
vanishing point, the 94–5, 97
verisimilitude 182
Vietnam War 185–6
Viola, Bill 29
visor effects 109–10
visuality 139
von Hantelmann, Dorothea 134, 135

Wall, Jeff 29
war: horrors of 53; and performance art 3–7; and US Civil War battle reenactments 7–11
War of 1812 23
War on Terror 171, 173
Warhol, Andy 28
Western theatre history 224n28
What Happened (Stein) 113
"What Have We Learned, If Anything?" (Judt) 24
Whitman, Walt 86

William, Raymond 96
Wilson, Robert 63, 76
Wilson, Woodrow 11
Winter Soldier: Iraq and Afghanistan 184–5
witnessing 9–10, 25, 33, 51–2
WLM Demo Remix (Kelly) 176–7
"Woman on Painting" (Cuenca) 3
Women and Performance (Mussmann) 73
Wood, Catherine 134–5
Woodhead, Chuck 33, 37, 39–41, 42, 45, 198n28
Woodward, Kathleen 35
Woolf, Virginia 78
Woolfork, Lisa 13
Wooster Group 13, 16, **16**, 111–23, **117**, **120**, 124, 136, 137, 138, 182
words 87; afterlife of 88
"The Work of Art in the Age of its Technical Reproducibility" (Walter) 17
Worthen, W. B. 88, 95, 125, 149
writing 107
Wyspianski, Stanislaw 112–13, 116–21, 127, 130, 216n15

Yates, Frances 213n60
You Can Live History 25
Young, Elizabeth 55
Young, Harvey 215n83, 229n77

Zdroj, John 200n64
Zinn, Howard 169, 179–86
Žižek, Slavoj 198n38